MANAGING DERIVATIVE RISKS

WILEY FRONTIERS IN FINANCE

MANAGING DERIVATIVE RISKS

The Use and Abuse of Leverage

Lillian Chew

John Wiley & Sons
Chichester • New York • Brisbane • Toronto • Singapore

Published 1996 by John Wiley & Sons Ltd
           Baffins Lane, Chichester,
           West Sussex PO19 1UD, England

                 National 01243 779777
                 International (+44) 1243 779777

Library of Congress Cataloging-in-Publication Data

Chew, Lillian.
    Managing derivative risks : the use and abuse of leverage / Lillian Chew.
        p.   cm.
    Includes bibliographical references and index.
    ISBN 0-471-95622-8
        1. Derivative securities.   2. Financial leverage.   I. Title.
    HG6024.A3C4854   1996
    332.6 — dc20   95–37963
                                                       CIP

British Library Cataloguing in Publication Data

A catalogue record for this book is available from the British Library

ISBN 0-471-95622-8

Typeset in 10/12pt Times from author's disks by Laser Words, Madras, India
Printed and bound in Great Britain by Biddles Ltd, Guildford and King's Lynn
This book is printed on acid-free paper responsibly manufactured from sustainable forestation,
for which at least two trees are planted for each one used for paper production.

Dedication

For Kenneth and Justin, whose support
and endurance of various degrees of neglect
made this book possible.

Contents

Foreword

Looked at from the perspective of physiology rather than pathology, financial innovation is the force driving the global financial system toward its goal of greater economic efficiency. In particular, innovations involving derivative securities can improve efficiency by expanding opportunities for risk sharing, lowering transaction costs, and reducing information and agency costs. Some see the extraordinary growth in the use of derivative securities over the past five years as just a fad. However, a more likely explanation is the vast savings in transaction costs, which for some institutions can be a tenth to a twentieth of the cost of using the underlying cash-market securities. These costs will be further reduced by improving technology and the growing breadth and experience in the application of derivatives as both users and producers of derivatives move down the learning curve. With such prospective cost savings, derivatives are a permanent part of the mainstream global financial system.

Derivative securities have provided effective instruments for controlling systematic risk exposures to interest rates, currencies, commodities, and equity markets. Financial engineering employing derivatives has helped to link individual national financial systems into a global system for capital and risk transfers. These efficient 'adapters' allow both corporations and sovereigns to tap global capital markets for financing by providing a smooth transition across currencies and across often widely different regulations, tax rules, and institutional practices in those national systems.

A consequence of all this is the need for greater understanding of risk management by users, producers, and regulators of derivatives. Moreover, improvements in efficiency from derivative products cannot be effectively realized without concurrent changes in financial 'infrastructure' — that is, the institutional interfaces between intermediaries and financial markets, regulatory practices, organization of trading, clearing, back-office facilities, and management-information systems. When treated atomistically, innovations in derivative products can be implemented unilaterally and rather quickly. In contrast, changes in financial infrastructure must be co-ordinated and, therefore, will take longer to implement. Thus, for example, it is not surprising that revisions in accounting standards used in external risk monitoring and implementation of regulations often do not keep pace with derivative-product innovations.

Imbalances between derivative-product innovation and the evolution of the infrastructure to support it are inevitable, and could at the extreme, become large enough to jeopardize the very functioning of the system. Hence, the need for government policy to protect against such breakdown, even if the likelihood of such a systemic event is quite small. But a single-minded policy focused exclusively on systemic-risk concerns could derail the engine of innovation and bring to a halt the financial system's trip to greater efficiency. Successful public policy depends as much on recognizing the limits of what government can do to improve efficiency including when government inaction is the best policy.

Much has been written by government agencies and supervisory bodies for financial institutions about the essential role of risk management and control by both producers and users of derivatives. That is, of course, the subject of this book, and therefore requires no further discussion here. Instead, I touch briefly on a few issues surrounding public policy that support those private-sector risk-management activities.

Prime among them is development of effective means for measuring risk exposures that are created or reduced by the use of derivatives. In particular, measurement of the systemic risk exposure of derivatives must be evaluated relative to the risk exposure of the alternative financial structure that they replace and not in some abstract, absolute terms as if there was no systemic risk exposure prior to their introduction.

Financial accounting must undergo fundamental revisions to facilitate risk measurement. Current practices are focused on valuation, which is inherently a static measure of financial condition. Because derivatives can significantly alter the risk characteristics of a firm's liabilities and assets, the accounting system must expand to report exposures to changes in the levels and volatilities of interest rates, currencies, commodity and equity prices. This new risk-accounting approach with its focus on exposures to changes is inherently a dynamic measure of financial condition because it indicates how the individual balance-sheet values are likely to change in response to changes in the financial and economic environment. Effective risk management, especially for derivatives, is only possible with a risk-accounting system.

The increasing flexibility and global mobility of financial institutions, together with an expanding derivatives technology for creating custom financial services at low cost have far-reaching implications for future regulation of financial services and national stabilization policies. Effective regulation will have to shift from an

institutional framework to a functional one in which economically equivalent transactions are treated the same. Implementation of such comprehensive regulations
will be a major challenge. The recent proposal for global capital requirements on
marketable securities put forth by the Basle Committee on Banking Supervision,
which Lillian Chew covers in the chapter on Value at Risk, is an encouraging step.

Policymakers are essentially speculating against a trend of declining transactions
costs if they assume that 'traditional' frictions within individual financial systems
will permit the pursuit of national monetary and related financial policies with the
same degree of control as in the past. Central-bank and public-finance policymakers
are likely to find it increasingly necessary to understand risk management and
financial engineering with derivatives. This expertise is not just to permit informed
supervision of private-sector financial activities but also to perform central-bank
stabilization functions more effectively.

In the pages to follow, Lillian Chew provides a non-technical introductory treatment of the inherently technical subject of managing derivative risks. She teaches
the basic risk-management calculations of exposures for derivatives in the context
of examples drawn from actual and well-publicized derivative cases. This approach
puts much in plain view for both private-sector practitioner and public policy-
maker. Too often the debate on derivatives has been polarized between those who
emphasize the benefits and ignore the risks; and those who only see the risks and
not the advantages. Lillian Chew tries to bridge the gap but focuses heavily on
the pathology of derivatives misuse with relatively fewer cases on the benefits of
effective derivatives use. Perhaps this is an appropriate weighting to underscore
the oversight issues so germane to the management of derivative risks.

Robert C. Merton
Harvard University

Preface

Books grow, change. I had initially intended to write a non-technical primer about derivatives. The reason for this is simple; I have written about these instruments for the past eight years and found it to be an area in which quantitative minds thrived. I myself have an antipathy to differential equations, so in the course of my work have had difficulty grasping some of the concepts which are at the very root of option risks in particular. But I felt sure that there were many people like me who wanted to understand derivatives but were put off by the mathematics that seemed to permeate this arcane world.

I therefore decided to keep mathematical formulae to a minimum. Where possible, I have tried to relate technical and mathematical concepts to familiar things and to give an intuitive feel for the Greek letters that so dominate derivatives. That was the only way I myself could come to terms with these concepts. Some of these analogies might seem forced, but I make no apologies for taking this route. Too often I have found derivative professionals retreating behind 'Geek-speak' when explaining the structure of a new product. The mathematically illiterate person walks away no wiser — although he may think he is. There are many people who can define a lookback option, a liquid yield option note or a differential swap, but how many can explain the relationship between increased uncertainty and the value of a simple option?

I modified my plans for the book because of the events of 1994. That was an *annus horribilis* for the derivative industry in terms of media exposure. Barely a month went by without yet another firm announcing losses because it had dabbled in 'complex' derivatives. There is no denying that these are powerful but dangerous tools. Yet the excesses owe more to management failure than to the incomprehensibility of derivatives. I wanted to draw some conclusions from those failures.

This is not a textbook. It does not go into the mechanics of option or swap pricing: those have already been covered by many excellent books. Nor does it teach a firm how to use derivatives to manage its currency or interest-rate risk: that also has been explored in many other books, not to mention derivative providers' marketing presentations. Instead, it attempts to explain the risks of derivatives.

Derivatives are sold as risk-management tools, which they are, but they also have risks of their own. This point seems to have been missed by some end-users, blinded as they are by the brilliance of a structure that promises them something for nothing. At the other end of the spectrum are those potential users who are so terrorized by derivatives' dangers that they fail to see their benefits. The following pages seek to move both groups to a middle ground: to help them to understand the risks and rewards of instruments that will shape finance in the 21st century.

This book, more than most books, is not the sole effort of the author. It owes its final form and content to the following people:

Lieng-Seng Wee of Bankers Trust; Peter Udale of Cambridge Financial Products; Leslie Rahl of Capital Market Risk Advisers; Christopher Goekjian and Alistair Ross of Credit Suisse Financial Products; Richard Cookson of the Economist newspaper; Michael Allen, Robert Gumerlock, and Christopher Matten of SBC Warburg; Raymond Iwanowski of Salomon Brothers; David Creed of Tate & Lyle; TJ Lim of Union Bank of Switzerland and Denis Mirlesse of University of Lausanne.

Their knowledge of derivatives and insight into the industry enabled me to understand the subject matter well beyond the immediate brief of the book. Without their help, this book would not have seen the light of day.

For their invaluable input, I am deeply grateful.

Lillian Chew

PART ONE
SETTING THE SCENE

INTRODUCTION

Derivatives — contracts such as options, swaps and forwards, whose values are derived from other assets — can have an enormous impact on a firm's financial well-being. This can be either positive or negative.

This makes managing derivative risks partly a function of self-knowledge and honesty. If an end-user is clear about why he is using derivatives — hedging, position-taking or both — he can manage efficiently the trade-off between risk and return. If not, disaster may lie around the next corner.

This is the topic discussed in the three chapters that follow. In particular, we examine why derivatives are used and how they can affect shareholder value. Chapters 1 and 2, 'Derivatives — the beauty' and 'Derivatives — the beast' show how the same instruments can be put to good or inappropriate use. Chapter 2 also shows that companies' motives for using derivatives are often mixed and can change halfway through a transaction, to disastrous effect.

Finally, Chapter 3, 'Beauty v the beast', examines the gap between perception and reality — between what a company's board thought they were doing and their actual position; between what shareholders are told and what they should be told. All too often, it suits companies themselves not to disclose what they are up to. How, we ask, do you tell the beauty from the beast?

1
Derivatives — The Beauty

Financial markets have grown more volatile since exchange rates were freed in 1973. Interest rates and exchange rates now fluctuate more rapidly than at any time since the Crash of 1929. At the same time, companies' profit margins have been squeezed by the lowering of trade barriers and increased international competition. The result is that companies worldwide have been forced to come to terms with their financial risks. No longer can managers stick their heads in the sand and pretend that because their firms make cars, or sell soap powders, they need only worry about this year's convertible or whether their new formula washes whiter than Brand X. As many have found to their cost, ignoring interest-rate, currency or commodity risks can hurt a company just as badly as the failure of a new product.

Derivatives offer companies the chance to reduce their financial risks — chiefly by transferring them to someone (usually a bank) who is willing to assume and manage them. As they realize this, more and more companies are using derivatives to hedge their exposures. America's General Accounting Office reported that between 1989 and 1992 derivative volumes grew 145% to $12.1 trillion (in terms of the notional amount represented). This does not include about $5.5 trillion of foreign-exchange forwards. Interest-rate risk was the main risk hedged — at the end of 1992, interest-rate contracts accounted for 62% of total notionals, compared with 37% for foreign exchange.

In the US companies can now be sued for *not* hedging their exposures. In 1992, the Indiana Court of Appeal held that the directors of a grain elevator co-operative had breached their fiduciary duty by failing to sell forward the co-op's grain to hedge against a drop in prices. Since 90% of the co-operative's operating income came from grain sales, its shareholders argued that it was only prudent for the directors to have protected the co-op from the huge losses it suffered (*Brane v Roth*, Indiana Court of Appeal). In another case, shareholders sued Compaq

Computers for violating securities laws by failing to disclose that it lacked adequate mechanisms to hedge foreign-exchange risks.

Hedging does not necessarily remove all of a company's financial risk. When a firm hedges a financial exposure, it is protecting itself against adverse market moves. If the markets move in what would normally be the company's favour, the hedger could find itself in a position that combined the worst of both hedged and unhedged worlds. For many firms, though, this is a worthwhile price to pay for ensuring stability or certainty for some of their cashflows. To illustrate this point, let's review the basic derivative instruments. Those familiar with these building blocks can skip straight to the section 'Mixing and matching'.

THE BUILDING BLOCKS

Forwards/Futures

A *forward* contract enables its buyer to lock in today the future price of an asset, be it a currency, an interest rate, an equity or a commodity. The buyer has to pay this pre-agreed price on the settlement date whether or not the asset has moved in his favour; equally, the seller has to deliver the asset on the settlement date irregardless of the price in the spot market.

There is no up-front fee payable on a forward and no money changes hands until the contract matures. Some contracts are cash-settled: there is no delivery of the underlying asset but one party has to pay the other the difference between the contractual value of the forward and the spot price of the asset.

A *futures* contract is simply a forward contract traded on an exchange. Unlike forwards, which are traded over-the-counter and can be customized to suit buyers' needs, futures have standard terms. Anyone buying futures must make an up-front payment, and often further payments to reflect the changing value of the contract. These are known as margin payments.

FUTURES MARGINS

There are three types of margins on futures contracts — initial, variation and maintenance. All exchanges require a customer to deposit an *initial margin* with their clearing house before he is allowed to trade on the exchange. This margin can be in the form of government securities, cash or bank guarantees. It is set at a level high enough to cover the likely one-day change in the price of the contract that is to be traded.

Every day the clearing house marks to market the value of all open positions. If the value of the contract has fallen below a *maintenance-margin* level — the minimum level that must be maintained, usually

Continued on page 7

[margin note: marks to market / market]

Continued from page 6

very slightly below that of the initial margin level — the customer must deposit more money to bring his account up to the initial-margin level. These margin calls are known as *variation margins*. The customer is required to meet these margin calls immediately or the exchange has the right to close out his contracts. If the value of the contract increases, however, the customer can withdraw the surplus in his margin account.

Margins are not static — when markets are volatile, exchanges tend to increase them. And the margins on different contracts vary, depending on the volatility of the underlying asset. Equities for example, demand larger margins than government securities.

Both forwards and futures protect against adverse price moves. But since users are locked into the transactions, they cannot profit when prices move in their favour. This was painfully driven home to Japanese companies such as Showa Shell, Kashima Oil and Japan Airlines, all of which bought dollars forward during the mid-1980s because they had large requirements for dollars. Japan Airlines, for example, spends more than $1 billion every year on fuel and aircraft. Because they bought their dollars in advance, the three companies knew for certain what the yen cost of their oil or aircraft would be; but they paid a heavy price for this certainty. Japan Airlines started selling yen forward in 1985, contracting to buy dollars at a rate of ¥165.97/$1. At the end of 1994, the yen/dollar exchange rate was ¥99.4/$1 and in April 1995 the yen rose to an all-time high of ¥80/$1. In 1994 Japan Airlines reported unrealized losses of ¥176 billion ($1.8 billion, based on a rate of ¥99.4/$1). Showa Shell reported unrealized losses of ¥166 billion ($1.7 billion), and Kashima Oil ¥153 billion ($1.5 billion).

Swaps

A swap is an agreement between two parties to exchange cashflows throughout the life of the contract — in effect, a series of forwards. As with a forward, the contract is binding on both parties: they are both obliged to exchange the cashflows whether or not the contract is to their advantage.

The most common form of *interest-rate swap* is the fixed-floating swap, where one party pays a fixed interest rate on a notional sum (known as the *notional principal*) and the other pays a floating rate on the same sum. There is no exchange of principal.

In a *currency swap* the parties exchange principal amounts denominated in different currencies both at the start and at the end of the transaction. The exchange rate for the two currencies is decided at the start of the transaction, so both sides lock in a future exchange rate. At intervals throughout the life of the swap the parties exchange interest-rate payments (either fixed or floating) denominated in the relevant currencies.

No up-front fees are payable in either kind of swap. This is due to the way swaps are priced. At the start of a swap, the expected *net present value* (NPV) is zero for both parties: for a fixed-floating swap, for example, the floating leg is theoretically worth the same as the fixed-rate leg. That's why swaps are a zero-sum game at origination: neither party is better off than the other — which is why they are both willing to execute the trade.

At the start of a swap, if the NPVs of both legs are not exactly equal, one party has to compensate the other by paying a higher rate. Take a simple interest-rate swap in which a corporate treasurer pays fixed (because he wants to lock in his cost of funding) and receives floating. If the NPV of the floating leg was higher than the present value of the fixed leg (at inception), the corporate treasurer has to pay the other party the difference between the two legs.

This adjustment is made through the swap spread — the basis-point spread over the Treasury rate which equates the NPVs of the fixed and floating-rate payment streams. Although the NPV of the floating-rate payments is uncertain, since the floating payments themselves are uncertain, swap dealers will use the implied forward rates obtained from the yield curve for other cash instruments. Next, a fixed rate is found (by iteration) such that the NPV of the fixed payments equals the NPV of the floating payments.

Once interest rates move, the NPV of the swap changes from zero to a positive or negative value. If interest rates rise, the cashflows on the floating leg increase, as does its NPV. The swap has a positive value for the treasurer who is paying fixed, since he will now find the present value of his floating-rate inflows higher than the present value of the fixed-rate outflows. At this point, the two parties to the swap transaction are no longer indifferent to whether they are paying fixed or floating cash-flows. Now the party with the positive net present value, i.e the treasurer paying fixed, shows a profit on the swap, and the counterparty a loss.

Interest-rate and currency swaps, Figures 1.1 and 1.2, make up the bulk of the over-the-counter derivatives market. But the technology for swapping interest-rate and currency cashflows has now been applied to other asset classes. *Equity swaps* involve one party exchanging floating interest-rate payments for the total return

Figure 1.1   Interest Rate Swap — Plain Vanilla.

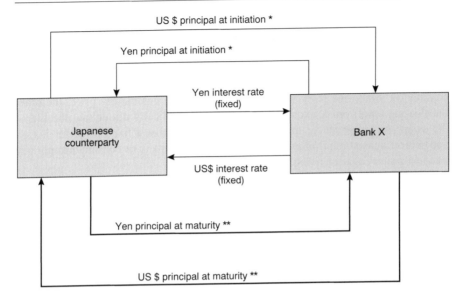

* at spot rate
** at exchange rate agreed at the start of the swap

Figure 1.2 Currency Swap — Plain Vanilla.

or price return of an equity index, or a basket of stocks, or a single stock. (*Bond swaps* work along similar lines.) Sometimes parties exchange cashflows based on equity indices from two different countries.

Equity swaps can be used either as investment tools or to hedge existing portfolios. If an investment manager wants to hedge an equity portfolio, for example, he might pay the return on that portfolio and receive a floating interest rate. This is similar to selling his shares and investing the cash, with the intention of switching back later. The same reasoning applies to equity swaps involving two equity indices. Such structures allow an investment manager to hedge an equity exposure without the transaction costs of selling his physical portfolio. In addition, the manager does not have to deal with operational, custodial and tax issues.

For managers who are not allowed to use exchange-traded futures, equity swaps are a convenient and often more suitable surrogate. Since equity swaps are over-the-counter instruments — unlike futures — they can be customized to the investment manager's requirements. If his portfolio consists of 60 out of the 100 stocks that make up the S&P 100 index, for example, he could pay the return on only those stocks in an equity swap. The closest futures contract is based on the whole of the S&P 100, which might not mirror the performance of his 60 stocks, and hence not provide a perfect hedge.

If a fund manager wants to create or increase equity exposure via an equity swap, he would pay a floating interest rate and receive an equity-linked return.

Commodity swaps involve the exchange of cashflows where at least one leg of the swap is based on a commodity price. Unlike foreign-exchange, interest-rate, bond or equity swaps, whose notional principals are expressed in cash terms (perhaps dollars for an interest-rate swap), a commodity swap is specified in terms of the usual unit of the commodity (for example, barrels for an oil swap). For a commodity swap, one party will agree to pay a fixed commodity price, the other the floating (spot) price, exchanging cashflows periodically throughout the life of the swap. An oil producer might use a swap to receive a fixed price for his oil and protect against a fall in prices, while a utility company or consumer might pay fixed to protect against rising oil prices.

Commodity swaps are usually based on natural gas, metals, some agricultural products like wheat, or, above all, oil. Like equity swaps, they can be customized to match the user's exposure. A company limited to using futures, by contrast, has only a limited range of hedging instruments to chose from. A firm wanting to hedge naphtha prices, for example, might have to use futures on West Texas Intermediate crude oil. This mismatch between an exposure and its hedge is known as *basis risk*.

Options

There are two main types of options. A *call* option gives the buyer the right to buy an asset (interest rates, equities, currencies, commodities, precious metals) at a predetermined price, known as the *strike*. A *put* option gives the buyer the right to sell the asset at the strike. Both puts and calls can further be described as either *European* or *American*. These terms have nothing to do with geography: a European option allows the buyer to exercise his option only on maturity, while an American option allows exercise any time during the option's life. This is what distinguishes an option from a forward or a swap — the buyer of an option is not obliged to engage in a deal. The buyer of a call option, for example, will walk away if asset prices move lower than his strike price, since he can buy the asset more cheaply on the open market.

For the privilege of being allowed to walk away from the deal or exercising the option, the buyer has to pay a *premium* to the seller of the option. This premium can be seen as the cost of buying insurance against financial risk. It is money wasted if the option is not exercised, but it also represents the maximum loss the option buyer will suffer from the transaction. On the other hand, the buyer has all the potential upside if the market moves in his favour.

The value of being able to walk away from a contract is clearly illustrated in the case of the Japanese companies described on page 7. All three wanted currency protection. If they had bought call options on the dollar, they would have had protection if the dollar did indeed strengthen against the yen, since they could exercise their dollar calls at their strike rates. Since the dollar weakened against the yen, these options would have expired worthless — but the companies would have been able to profit from the appreciating yen.

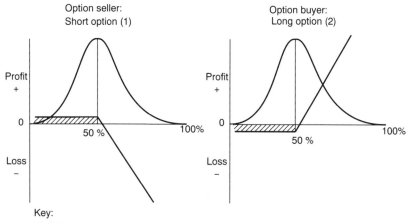

Key:
(1) ▨▨ Premium of option
(2) At 50%, the option is said to be at-the-money, i.e.
     the option's strike price is at the same level as the forward price of the underlying asset

Figure 1.3 Position of Option Buyers and Sellers.

The position of an option seller is completely opposite from that of a buyer. His upside is limited to the upfront premium, but his downside is open-ended (see Figure 1.3). He is exposed totally to changes in the price of the asset on which he has sold an option, and his losses can be huge if the market rises sharply (if he has sold a call) or falls (if he has sold a put).

Option buyers and sellers view risk differently, then. An option buyer is prepared to sacrifice premium (i.e. accepts small losses) for protection against a large loss. The option seller, on the other hand, believes that over time premium income can more than offset losses from extreme price movements.

Three common terms need to be understood when discussing options: *out-of-the-money*, *in-the-money* and *at-the-money*. They describe the relationship between an option's strike and the forward price of the underlying asset. As expected, an option whose strike is at the same price level as the forward value of the underlying asset is at-the-money, one whose strike is less than the forward price of the underlying market is in-the-money, while one whose strike is greater is out-of-the-money.

Three other terms that crop up frequently when discussing options are cap, floor and collar. A *cap* can be looked upon as a series of call options. A company with large borrowings might buy an interest-rate cap to limit its exposure to increases in LIBOR. If interest rates rise above the cap's strike price, the seller will pay the buyer the difference between the floating rate and the strike rate. The payments will be based on a notional principal amount (as with a swap) and will typically be made every three or six months.

Like a swap, a cap provides a ceiling to a buyer's costs. However, while a swap locks a company into a fixed rate straightaway, a cap allows it to continue paying

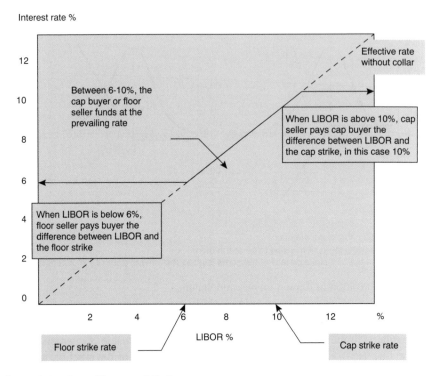

Interest rate %

Figure 1.4 Caps, Floors and Collars.

market rates if they are lower than the cap's strike. The cap buyer has to pay a premium for this flexibility, which increases the effective cost of whatever it is hedging until rates reach the strike price. *Break-even* comes when market prices reach the cap strike plus the premium (see Figure 1.4).

To reduce its effective borrowing rate, a cap buyer can sell a *floor*, which can be seen as a series of interest-rate options. The buyer will usually be an asset manager who wants to guarantee a minimum rate for his floating-rate assets. If interest rates fall below the floor's strike, the seller will pay the buyer the difference.

Buying/selling a cap and selling/buying a floor creates a *collar*. In a *zero-cost collar* the premium earned from selling the floor/cap offsets the premium that has to be paid to buy the cap/floor.

It is clear that there is an asymmetry of risks between buyers and sellers of options, while a symmetry exists for buyers and sellers of forwards and swaps. Options are one-sided — the seller has unlimited risks and limited profit (premium earned) while the buyer knows his maximum potential loss (premium cost) from the start, but not his upside. In a forward-based transaction, both parties are exposed to the possibility of prices moving against them or in their favour. They are both exposed to unlimited price risks resulting from movements in the underlying asset.

Table 1.1   Notional/Contract Amounts of Derivatives held ($ billion).

Product type	1989	1990	1991	1992	% of 1992	% increase from 1989 to 1992
Forwards	3034	4437	6061	7515	42	148
Futures	1259	1540	2254	3154	18	151
Options	953	1305	1841	2263	13	137
Swaps	1952	2890	3872	4711	27	141
Total	7198	10172	14028	17643	100	145

Note: forwards comprise foreign exchange, equity and commodity forwards, plus forward rate agreements.
Reproduced with permission from Bank for International Settlements, International Swaps and Derivatives Association, Federal Reserve Bank of New York, Swaps Monitor Publications, Derivatives Strategy and Tactics, various annual reports, and GAO analysis.

Table 1.1, contained in the May 1994 GAO report on financial derivatives, shows that forwards continue to be the most popular derivative instrument. Whether increased uncertainty will encourage greater usage of options will be one of the trends to look out for as derivatives come of age.

MIXING AND MATCHING

The main building blocks — forwards, swaps and options — can be used separately to reduce the financial risks facing a firm; or they can be combined to form structures that meet a customer's precise needs. Let us take the case of a British fund manager with a portfolio of US equities. Every time the manager buys IBM shares, say, he exposes himself to three risks: prices in the US equity market generally, the price of IBM stock specifically, and the dollar/sterling exchange rate. Derivatives allow him to separate these three risks and neutralize those he does not want. If, for example, he is bearish about the dollar's medium-term prospects and the overall US stock market, he can use the forward market to hedge the currency risk, sell S&P 500 futures to neutralize the overall market risk, and be left only with exposure to IBM's share price. Without derivatives, he would have had only two choices: buy IBM stock and accept currency and market risk, or keep his money in the bank.

What if the fund manager is not allowed to use exchange-traded futures, or is unwilling to execute three transactions (buy IBM stock, sell S&P futures, sell dollars forward) to produce the desired risk profile? A derivative provider could spare him all this trouble by packaging the three transactions into one product — an equity swap denominated in sterling. The fund manager would receive the price performance of IBM shares in sterling terms and pay sterling LIBOR (see Figure 1.5). This would again give him exposure to IBM's share price, without the currency or overall market risks.

And what if the fund manager suddenly becomes nervous about IBM's short-term prospects? What if the stock looks cheap but there are rumours of an imminent corporate restructuring? In such a situation, the manager could buy an option to

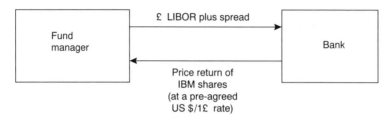

Figure 1.5 Quanto Equity Swap.

enter into an equity swap with the terms described above. He would have to pay a premium for the option, but that might be a reasonable price for the flexibility of entering into the swap at a later date, or walking away if the restructuring plans do not pass muster.

This is a simple example of how the basic building blocks can be assembled to produce a product that meets individual needs. The derivative providers — in effect, the banks — have created many complex structures. Options can be combined with swaps, or options with options, or swaps with swaps. The long list of new terms — *differential swaps, index-amortizing swaps, accrual notes, Lyons, guaranteed-return notes, straddles, strangles, butterflies* and *condors*, to name but a few, show how far the banks have combined and repackaged the basic building blocks to allow consumers to unbundle their financial risks and to neutralize exposures they do not want.

THE ADVANTAGES OF LEVERAGE

That's not the only advantage of derivatives, however. Robert Merton, a leading academic at Harvard Business School, put it most clearly in 1994 when he said:

> Some see the extraordinary growth in derivative securities over the past five years as only a fad — an electronic Ponzi [pyramid] scheme. However, a more likely explanation for the enormous increase in volume is the vast savings in transaction costs from their use. The costs of implementing financial strategies for institutions using derivatives can be a tenth to a twentieth the cost of using the underlying cash-market securities. ... With such cost savings, we are not going back: derivatives are a permanent part of the mainstream global financial system.

(For a fuller discussion of finance innovations in the last decade, see Appendix 1.)

These cost-savings are not negligible where hedging is the goal, but they are particularly important when it comes to making investments. Derivatives are in many cases the most efficient investment devices available. Why are they so efficient? Because of their built-in *leverage*.

The concept of leverage is not new; every time a company borrows more money than its cash in hand, or what its assets are worth, it is gearing itself up. Similarly, every time a fund manager borrows money to invest, he is leveraging the fund and increasing its sensitivity to changes in market conditions (see box on hedge funds). The point about derivatives is that they hugely increase the leverage that can be achieved.

Leveraging with Futures

Derivatives make it possible to start large positions with small amounts of money. Suppose, for example, an investor believes interest rates are going to fall, which will give him capital gains on any fixed-income securities he owns. If he buys bonds in the spot market, he will have to borrow a dollar for every dollar he stakes: if he wants to buy $1 million-worth of Treasury bonds, he will have to find $1 million. If he uses futures, however, he can gain the same exposure for just $15 000. That is because he needs to pay only 1.5% up-front to buy Treasury futures. This payment is known as the initial margin, and is seldom more than a small fraction of the cost of the underlying securities, although it does vary from contract to contract. Futures on the S&P 500, for example, require initial margins of 5 to 10%, while Nikkei 225 futures on Singapore's derivatives exchange require 10 to 15%.

The same investor could spend his whole $1 million on margin payments and gain an exposure dozens of times larger than the $1 million. Suppose, for example, he spends only $500 000 in initial margin, keeping the rest in reserve in case bond prices fall, which would make it necessary for him to make further margin payments. This $500 000 will still give him exposure to more than $33 million of Treasuries. He would have to be very sure of his views, however. Treasury prices only have to drop by 3% to wipe out his $1 million.

The same investor could have leveraged his bets by borrowing money and buying Treasuries in the spot market. But the level of leverage here is limited to the amount of money he can borrow — nowhere does it come close to the leverage offered by futures.

It was precisely this sort of leverage (compounded by the absence of adequate controls) that sank Barings, the United Kingdom's oldest merchant bank. Barings' top futures trader in Singapore, Nick Leeson, used futures to build up a position representing $7 billion of Japanese equities (via Nikkei 225 futures) and $20 billion of yen bonds (via Japanese government bond futures and Euroyen futures), even though the bank's capital base was only £375 million ($615 million). Leeson did not need much money to set up the positions, but he needed huge infusions of cash to keep them going when prices moved against him. The Tokyo stock market did, and Barings is now history.

The investor could also make his money work harder just by taking advantage of the cost-effectiveness of futures, without taking on any more price risk than if he had bought $1 million of Treasuries. To do so, he would pay the $15 000 initial margin, set aside a cushion to meet margin calls, and place the rest of the $1 million on deposit to earn interest. The extra performance comes from the interest earned by the money on deposit. Is this a true leveraged trade? Not if leveraging means magnifying your exposure so that your portfolio is more sensitive to changes in market conditions, this portfolio is no more sensitive than a cash portfolio; neither is it more risky. But if leverage means getting more 'bang for your bucks', then it is: our investor would still have the opportunity of gaining an equivalent profit, at the risk of a capital sum considerably smaller than the actual purchase and sale of the asset itself. The bang, albeit a small one, comes from the interest earned on the spare cash.

Leveraging with Options

Options can be bought either out-of-the-money, at-the-money or in-the-money. If the Nikkei 225 stood at 15 000, for example, a call option would be out-of-the-money if the strike was at 16 000 (the buyer would lose money if he exercised the option), at-the-money if the strike was at 15 000, and in-the-money if the strike was at 14 000 (the buyer would make money if he exercised the option).

Futures, forwards and physical instruments, by contrast, are always at-the-money. This makes the leverage afforded by options more subtle than that of futures. Because an out-of-the-money option is always cheaper than one that is near or at-the-money (everything else being equal), the premium payable is smaller. Thus, the further the option is out-of-the-money, the larger the exposure than can be gained for the same amount of money.

The 'moneyness' of an option also casts a different complexion on the trade described above. There is no difference in price risk between buying Treasury futures worth $1 million and buying $1 million of the underlying securities, but the same does not hold true for a leveraged trade using options. Unless the investor buys a call option that is at-the-money, he will need Treasury prices to move up to the option's strike level before he is on par with an investor with a cash position. If the market does not make that move, he will have wasted all his option premium. (In fact, he does not make any money until the option has moved far enough into the money to have paid for his option premium.) This trade has more price risks even though the nominal exposure is the same, because the out-of-the-money option needs a larger price change before the investor breaks-even. An investor buying an out-of-the-money option must therefore be more bullish than one buying futures or the underlying securities.

Leveraging with Over-the-Counter Derivatives

Forwards are over-the-counter (OTC) futures, and if an investor has a credit line with a bank, they offer better leverage than futures. In most cases, he does not need to pay any margin and will rarely have to provide collateral up-front. Money changes hands only when the contract matures. The customer can gain his desired exposure as long as it is within the bank's credit tolerance. And if the market moves in the investor's favour, he can sell the forward contract before maturity, making a profit without having to pay any money at all. Swaps offer the same kind of leverage as forwards, since a swap is just a series of forwards, but if a swap is not unwound (cancelled in return for a payment reflecting its value) before the first interest payment date, the exchange of cashflows can be viewed as a margin payment.

With exchange-traded contracts, the amount of leverage is constrained by the margin requirements. With OTC derivatives, most of which are not margined or collateralized, leverage, both obvious and obscured, is present in every transaction and the amount can be as big as the investor wants (or what the bank counter-party is willing to grant). This is unlike conventional leverage, which was always constrained by the size of the balance sheet or the amount of collateral the investor could pledge. This leverage is what makes derivatives such powerful tools (and also extremely dangerous).

Synthetic Leverage

The leverage described above is fairly explicit. But derivatives, or investment technology, have given birth to a new dimension of leverage. Leverage can now be incorporated into almost all instruments, bonds and swaps are the most obvious examples, so that their notional values no longer give an accurate view of an investor's price exposure.

A good example is the *inverse floating-rate notes* bought by California's Orange County before the disasters of 1994. The three-times leverage embedded into their payout formula meant that every one *basis point* (0.01 percentage point) move in interest rates was magnified three times. As a result, when Orange County bought an inverse floater with a notional amount of $100 million, it had an exposure equal to non-leveraged inverse floaters worth $300 million. This type of 'synthetic' leverage allows an investor to execute leveraged plays with cash instruments, and without having to borrow funds.

ORANGE COUNTY: TRADITIONAL LEVERAGE MEETS SYNTHETIC

The financial collapse of California's Orange County in 1994 made Robert Citron the best-known user of *repurchase agreements*. But Orange County's treasurer was not alone in appreciating their ability to create leverage.

Repos (as they are commonly referred to) are acknowledged as a cheap and easy way of borrowing money. The full process should be described as a sale and repurchase agreement. When an investor executes a repo, he sells a security to another party but simultaneously agrees to buy it back at a later day. The price at which he sells and buys

Continued on page 18

Continued from page 17

back is agreed ahead of time. A reverse repo is simply the other side of the transaction.

Both buyers and sellers find repos advantageous. A bond buyer finds the repo market a cheaper source of financing than borrowing money from a bank. This is because he posts the bond he buys from the securities dealer as collateral for the loan he took out from the dealer to buy the bond in the first place. The dealer is happy to lend him the money at a cheaper rate because the loan is collateralized by the bond. Thus banks with spare cash to lend short-term find the repo markets a safe and easy way to extend credit. The yield they receive is less than an interbank deposit, because the money is collateralized, but more than a comparable government security, because there is credit risk involved (as houses which conducted reverse repos with Orange County learnt to their cost).

Investors like repos because they provide an inexpensive way of financing their long positions. If they are short, they find it convenient to be able to borrow bonds from dealers to meet their delivery obligations in the spot market. Most repos have overnight maturities, but can be and are constantly rolled over.

Participants who use the repo market to finance a *long position* in bonds can often make money just from the net cost of carry. This is because they can often borrow short-term money from the repo market at a rate lower than the interest rate they earn on their bond purchases. This is called positive carry and tends to happen when a positive (upward-sloping) yield curve exists. When the yield curve is negative (downward-sloping), the short-term borrowing rate is higher than the yield on the bond, so there is negative carry. It is this *cost of carry* that is reflected in the sale and buyback price agreed to at the start of a repo — nothing else. Whether the value of the bond in question will change during the repo period is immaterial to the agreed buyback price.

The investor who borrows money from the dealer to buy $10 million bonds is not loaned the full $10 million. Dealers want a protective cushion because they know the value of the bonds will fluctuate, so they demand a haircut, which is similar to a margin payment on a futures contract. And, like a margin, the percentage of face value required depends on the volatility of the bond posted as collateral. The dealer is allowed to trade the bonds that are held as collateral, but it is the investor who bears the price risks of the bonds.

Borrowing money via the repo markets is in many ways like borrowing money to buy a house. A bank or building society will usually be willing to lend most of the value of the house because it holds the deeds as

Continued on page 19

Continued from page 18

collateral. Let's assume a housebuyer doesn't buy houses to live in them: he trades them. If he manages to persuade a few banks to lend him 98% of the value of the house (posting the deeds to the houses as collateral), he could make a tidy profit (and a very high return of the small sum of money he really has), should house prices continue to rise. But house prices don't go just one way, and neither do bonds.

That was the undoing of Citron. When US interest rates started to rise in February 1994, the bonds posted as collateral fell in value, so the dealers who lent him money under the reverse-repo agreements asked him for more collateral or cash to make up the shortfall. Citron had difficulty meeting some of these collateral calls throughout 1994. The proceeds of a $600 million bond issued in July 1994 were earmarked for bolstering Orange County's cash resources (a euphemism for meeting its collateral calls?).

When Orange County issued a statement about its paper losses of $1.5 billion (7% of its total investment portfolio) on 1 December 1994, some of its lenders refused to roll over some of the reverse-repo agreements. CS First Boston, for example, refused to roll over $1.25 billion. By 6 December 1994, Citron had run out of cash and was unable to meet the margin requirements imposed by the repo dealers. The county quickly filed for bankruptcy under Chapter 9 of the US Bankruptcy Code (the public sector's equivalent of Chapter 11) to prevent repo dealers from selling their collateral. It was too late — lenders dumped about $10 billion bonds, and two weeks after the storm broke Orange County itself decided to liquidate its portfolio, capping losses at about $2 billion.

Orange County's collateral calls were exactly like the margin calls Metallgesellschaft's US subsidiary faced on its energy contracts (see Chapter 5) or Barings on its Nikkei 225 and Japanese interest-rate contracts (Chapter 10). The property speculator is luckier — banks don't *mark to market* the value of the houses on which they have lent money, and they do not collect extra deposits if the house is worth less than the loans extended.

Citron managed to borrow $12.9 billion through the repo markets. This enabled him to accumulate $20 billion securities even though the fund he managed only had $7.7 billion invested in it. This was the first level of his leveraged investment strategy.

The second is to be found in some of the securities he bought. Orange County bought inverse floating-rate notes: securities whose floating coupon payments decline when interest rates rise, as opposed to conventional floaters, whose payments increase. The bulk of these

Continued on page 20

Continued from page 19

inverse floaters had embedded leverage: the payout formulas that determined the coupon payments had a multiplier which magnified the effects of any changes in interest rates.

Leveraged inverse floaters, totalling $8 billion, have been singled out as the largest category of leveraged investments in Orange County's portfolio. This means that Citron's leveraged bet on interest rates falling was larger than the total cash invested in the fund ($7.7 billion). What is more, the $8 billion was just a notional value — with leveraged investments, it is the true exposure that is important. If the leveraged floaters had an average multiplier of three, then, in effect Citron had an exposure equal to $24 billion of unleveraged inverse floaters.

Because Citron's leveraged bets were on rates falling, he did very well until February 1994. His leveraged strategy made him one of America's top municipal fund managers, and his fund returned an annual average of 10.1% for 15 years — way above the mean of similar funds. But when US interest rates started to rise in February 1994 (the US Federal Reserve raised interest rates by 2.5% in that year alone), Orange County's portfolio started to tumble in value. And because some of the instruments had leveraged payouts, they fell faster in value. Instead of a one-for-one fall (as in an unleveraged structure), they fell on the multiple of the leverage. A presentation given by Merrill Lynch to Citron's office in February 1994 indicated that for each one percentage point rise in interest rates, the market value of the structured securities portfolio — i.e. the leveraged inverse floaters — would drop by about $270 million. In the final analysis, it was leverage — through the repo markets, coupled with the synthetic leverage of inverse floaters — and not complex, exotic derivatives that sank Citron.

It has always been theoretically possible to leverage the payout formula of a bond. A bank which structured a bond for an issuer could have declared that the bond would pay three times the yield of a five-year Treasury note, for example. But this synthetic leverage was not used before the widespread use of derivatives, because lead managers were not able to break the structured security down into the basic derivative building blocks and from there hedge its risks. Without the knowledge and liquidity needed to hedge such risks, no bank would dare offer such payout formulas.

By 1990–93, however, this was being done, and many structured notes put together over this period did have a multiplier embedded in the payout formula. This multiplier often enabled the bank which structured the note to tailor the terms of the note to meet the precise objectives, constraints and market views of the buyer.

Bond investors often make their decisions against the *forward curve*; that is, the changes in the yield-curve shape that are discounted in the current interest-rate environment (see Figure 1.6). But sometimes the forward curve is distorted by a temporary blip in supply and demand which affects the spot market.

For example, a perceived change in Bundesbank monetary policy might cause a stampede out of two- and three-year German government bonds, causing that sector to be offered artificially. That distorts the forward curve, so an investor who wants to buy bonds will have to choose carefully the part of the forward curve in which to invest.

Many fixed-income investors like their portfolio to have an average *duration* of seven. In other words, the average weighted life of the present values of the cashflows should be seven years. (For more on duration, see Chapter 4.) To achieve this target duration, they normally buy ten-year securities. But if the forward curve is temporarily distorted, the ten-year sector may not be the best area to invest. It may not perform as well as a sector that is artificially well-offered, in this case the two-year sector.

Buying a two-year bond, based on the two-year forward rate, would give the investor a duration of, say, 1.8. That is far below his target duration of seven. To achieve seven or thereabouts, the two-year rate is multiplied by four. The structured note now meets the objectives and market views of the buyer — he gets the price action of a ten-year bond based on the best possible part of the forward curve — the two-year sector which allows him to make most of his expectations versus the implied forward rate.

Synthetic leverage comes in many forms, and defining it is not easy. This is brought home by the Federal Reserve Bank of New York's definition of what constitutes a leveraged derivative transaction. It defines a leveraged trade as one

> where (i) a market move of two standard deviations in the first month would lead to a reduction in value to the counterparty of the lower of 15% of the notional amount or $10 million and (ii) for notes or transactions with a final exchange of principal where counterparty principal (rather than coupon) is at risk at maturity, and (iii) for coupon swaps, where the coupon can drop to zero (or below) or exceed twice the market rate for that market and maturity, and (iv) for spread trades that include an explicit leverage factor, where a spread is defined as the difference in the yield between two asset classes.

In attempting to make the definition of synthetic leverage as wide as possible, the Federal Reserve Bank has distilled leverage to mean what an investor could ultimately lose. This is the essence of items (i) and (ii). For any bond with a notional principal above $67 million, a leveraged trade is one which causes the investor to lose more than 15% in the first month. (The lower of $10 million or 15% makes a notional amount of $67 million the cut-off point.) But the potential losses of any investment instrument come firstly from the volatility of the underlying asset and secondly from the leverage (or multiplier). For example, a bond linked to Mexican or Brazilian equity indices carries the risk of far greater losses than a bond linked to five-year Treasury rates, because the former is indexed to a more

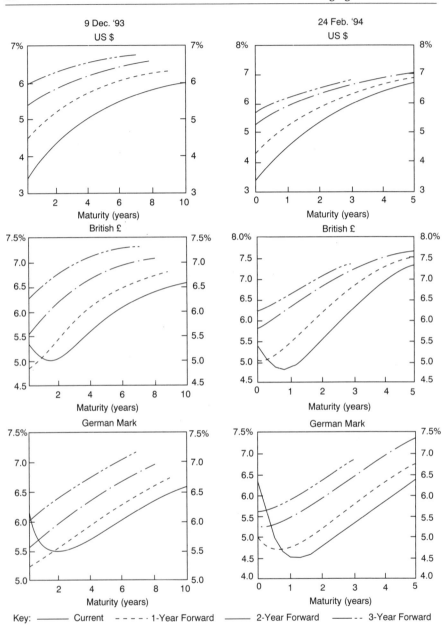

Figure 1.6 Sample Forward Curves as at 9 Dec 1993 and 24 Feb 1994. Reproduced by permission from Salomon Brothers.

volatile asset. A bond linked to Mexico's IPC index with no multiplier, whose notional principal could drop by 15% or more in one month, could be considered a leveraged transaction under the Federal Reserve Board's definition because the underlying asset is so volatile, while a bond linked to constant-maturity Treasuries (CMTs) with a multiplier of two would not, because CMT rates are a lot more stable, and one-month market moves would not result in the CMT-linked bond losing more than 15% of its notional value. The Federal Reserve Board's definition of a leveraged trade thus means that for very volatile assets there needs to be no multiplier while the multiplier for unvolatile assets can be much higher than the multiplier for semi-volatile assets.

Table 1.2 shows historical volatilities for a range of assets — the table shows that government bonds are the least volatile of assets and the stock indices of the less developed countries almost on par with commodities in terms of volatility. An investor buying a bond linked to the performance of a volatile underlying asset will make (or lose) more money than an investor who buys a bond linked to an underlying asset which exhibits great stability. Thus for very volatile assets, there is no need for a multiplier in the payout formula for the bond to qualify as a leveraged transaction under the Federal Reserve's definition of leveraged transactions. A two standard deviation, one-month move in ten-year gilts would have resulted in a 7% profit/loss in the bond. (To arrive at a figure for a two standard deviation,

Table 1.2 Historic Volatilities[1] (% annual).

Country	Stock indices	Bonds (7–10 years)
US	8.9	5.9
Japan	16.9	6.4
Germany	14.9	4.9
Italy	20.5	9.8
UK	11.5	8.6
Hong Kong	26.4	
Singapore	13.9	
Brazil	62.1	19.7[2]
Malaysia	20.3	
Mexico	28.7	17.1[2]
Currencies		
Dollar/Sterling	8.2	
Dollar/Deutschmark	9.6	
Dollar/Yen	10.5	
Dollar/Italian lira	10.0	
Dollar/Mexican peso	29.6	
Commodities		
West Texas Intermediate crude oil	22.6	
Heating oil	21.7	

Notes: 1. January 1993 to March 1995.
       2. Brady Bond index.
Reproduced with permission from Salomon Brothers, JP Morgan.

one-month move: divide the annual volatility of the asset by the square root of time, in this case the square root of 12 because there are 12 months in a year [this is a standard statistical technique]. Because it is a two standard deviation move, multiply the answer by two.) The same move would have caused a 15% profit/loss in the bond linked to the Hang Seng index, which means that a bond linked to Hong Kong's equity index does not need an embedded multiplier to qualify as a leveraged transaction. Thus the dividing line between structures which can have embedded multipliers of more than one and none at all are those whose underlying assets which have annual volatilities of less than 26%. That is the magic volatility number that turns Cinderella's carriage into a pumpkin, or vice versa, (depending on your views of leverage).

Items (iii) and (iv) are relatively straightforward. In an interest-rate swap, leverage could result in one counterparty receiving no interest at all (but still paying interest, remember that a swap counterparty simultaneously pays and receives interest), or paying a coupon that is twice as high as that of a comparable plain vanilla swap. The spread-trade description is the only one that explicitly stipulates a multiplier of more than one.

Synthetic leverage is another example of how technological innovation has opened up a whole new vista in finance. Derivatives themselves are a product of this technological innovation. Their inherent leverage and the ability to mix and match various types of derivatives, plus the ease with which multipliers can be incorporated into payout formulas, make them powerful tools. They offer legitimate and efficient solutions to the problems of investors and corporate end-users. What is more, these solutions need no longer be compromises. This is what ensures the place of derivatives in the financial landscape of the future — end-users have learnt to demand and expect customized products to meet their specific requirements. They have savoured the delights of stripping out the exposures they want and discarding those not to their taste. There is no turning back.

WHAT IS A HEDGE FUND?

Extract from the Bank of England's Quarterly Bulletin, May 1994

There is no precise definition of a hedge fund; the term is used loosely to refer to an investment fund structured so as to be exempt from investor-protection requirements and thus able to follow a flexible investment strategy. The funds' trading strategies typically involve taking both long and short positions, as well as leveraging those positions. Positions are often not hedged; 'leveraged fund' is therefore a more accurate term. Leverage (or gearing) can be achieved by borrowing (either unsecured or against a fund's existing assets, perhaps using sale-and-repurchase

Continued on page 25

Continued from page 24

agreements) and investing the proceeds, as well as by trading derivative products. By leveraging in this way, the return on funds' positions becomes more sensitive to marginal movements in the prices of the assets concerned.

SIZE AND STRUCTURE

Information on leveraged funds as a whole is sketchy, and needs to be treated with care. Conservative estimates nevertheless indicate that there are around 800 leveraged funds worldwide, handling investment funds of at least $45 billion. The funds vary enormously in size; a handful of the largest (and most well known) account for perhaps half of the total. Although the majority of leveraged funds are still aimed towards US markets and investors, leveraged-fund activity is growing in Europe and may continue to do so. As in the United States, growth in Europe is likely to be based offshore, because of restrictions on investments for onshore funds. The typical investors in leveraged funds still largely appear to be rich individuals but the funds' active asset-management style is likely to prove increasingly attractive to institutional investors.

Typically, a leveraged fund is established by a trader, or a small group of traders, with a proven track record at a well-known institution or on the floor of an exchange. Traders are attracted to setting up their own funds by the independence it brings and by the prospect of high performance fees (typically at least 15–20% of profits). As the size of the fund grows, the number of traders may increase, but investment decisions usually remain in the hands of a few key individuals. Traders' reputations are crucial, both in gaining capital for the fund and in providing justification for their performance fees.

TRADING STRATEGIES

Leveraged funds, unlike most other asset managers, tend to aim for a total rate of return rather than gauging their performance against a benchmark. Their trading strategies differ enormously, from a market-neutral approach (typically based on quantitative methods and arbitrage techniques) to investing according to long-term fundamentals which may involve significant position-taking. The smaller funds appear to be largely quantitatively-based; they may leverage by up to 40 times or more — generally through the use of exchange-traded futures contracts — and probably have relatively short-term investment horizons.

Continued on page 26

— Continued from page 25 —

Larger leveraged funds tend to take a longer-term view (some larger funds require investors to commit their capital for three years or more). In taking these long-term positions, larger funds also seem to resort to less leverage. They may obtain leverage through a combination of secured and unsecured borrowing, sale-and-repurchase agreements and margin-based derivative transactions. The possible leverage available to a fund will therefore depend, among other factors, on the collateral and margin requirements imposed by its counterparties.

Leveraged funds are active in financial markets across the globe, and funds' activities may involve complex cross-product and cross-currency trades. Few other investors — apart from the proprietary-trading desks of their counterparties — undertake such broad cross-market and multi-instrument trades. Larger funds, however, tend to concentrate their trading in the more liquid markets so as to be able to take (and liquidate) major positions. The size of individual transactions undertaken by the larger leveraged funds can sometimes be very large indeed — up to several billion dollars. During 1993, total turnover in European bond markets — in particular repo business — increased rapidly and this may well have been due in part to the long positions taken by leveraged funds.

SUMMARY

This chapter assumes the reader accepts that hedging financial risks adds value for the shareholders of a company and that derivatives are one of the most flexible and efficient means of eliminating unwanted financial risks. An end-user can neutralize interest rate, foreign exchange, equity and commodity risks with the various types of derivative instruments — forwards, swaps or options — either separately or combined together; the exact configuration being dictated by the user. This flexibility to mould a derivative structure into any risk profile is one of the main benefits of derivatives.

Forwards are just a contractual agreement to buy/sell an asset at a predetermined price sometime in the future. Swaps are a series of forwards. Futures are exchange-traded forwards. Both parties in a forward, a swap or a future — grouped together under the generic title of forward-based instruments — are committed to the agreement when settlement time comes along, regardless of what the price of the underlying asset is at that point in time. Since both parties are obliged to go through with the transaction, both are equally exposed to the vagaries of fluctuating market conditions. In a forward hedge, the end-user gives upside potential to protect himself against downside risk.

The buyer of an option can, but is not obliged to buy/sell an asset on which the option is written. He is free to walk away if the underlying asset price does not favour him. There is an asymmetry of risks between the two parties of an option transaction — the buyer limits his loss to the premium paid, but enjoys unlimited upside potential. The seller on the other hand suffers unlimited downside risk (depending on future price levels of the underlying asset) but limited profit (restricted to the premium). If the option is bought to cover a position in the underlying asset (i.e. an option hedge), the buyer insures himself against unfavourable price movements (because he can exercise his option) but is still able to participate in any upside potential if prices move in his favour (by choosing not to exercise his option). He pays a premium for this luxury of choice.

The flexibility and cost efficiency of derivatives makes them ideal investment or speculative vehicles. Because only a small amount of money is needed to gain access to a large exposure, investors have used this leverage to make their funds more sensitive to changes in market conditions. The leverage of exchange-traded derivatives is constrained by the need to pay margins whilst that of the over-the-counter is determined by the derivative provider's credit line for the buyer.

2

Derivatives — The Beast

The use of derivatives falls into two main categories: to hedge financial exposures and to take positions. Reducing or fixing a firm's cost of funding falls into the former and increasing the total rate of return or yield of a portfolio, by taking on acceptable levels of risk, falls into the latter. How derivatives can be misused (either through ignorance, misunderstanding or wilful intent) and thus significantly increase, rather than decrease the risks for the end-user will be discussed in the context of these two main uses. The beauty of derivatives, as described in the previous chapter, is twofold: they can be moulded into any structure desired by the customer and they offer boundless leverage. But this beauty can be abused, both by providers and end-users. The structures can be made so complex and synthetic leverage so cleverly embedded, that it obscures the extra risks taken on. It allows market participants to hide these additional risks from their bosses and shareholders (in the case of end-users) and customers (in the case of derivative providers). The beauty can become the beast.

REDUCING FUNDING COSTS

Plain vanilla interest rate swaps have carved themselves a place in modern finance because they are extremely efficient at reducing or locking-in funding costs. Locking-in here does not just mean fixed interest rates, it can also mean floating interest rates. However when a company uses a swap to lock-in its floating costs, it always does it in relation to a floating interest rate benchmark such as *LIBOR* or US commercial paper rates. This is because most large companies can access short-term money at LIBOR or commercial paper (CP) rates by issuing either *floating rate notes* (FRNs) or commercial paper. Therefore, they will execute a swap only if the floating funding they achieve is cheaper than that achieved by issuing FRNs or commercial paper, i.e. they want to pay a spread below LIBOR or CP. The larger the spread under the floating benchmark, the happier the corporate treasurer because he is generating more cost savings (and thus seen to be doing a better job).

This desire to generate cost savings (and improve yields) gains greater urgency in companies where treasury departments are regarded as profit centres. Prior to the late 1980s, treasuries were considered a support function, managing the finances of the company by stabilizing earnings/cashflows of the company's core business (hedging financial exposures came into this scope). The late 1980s trend of turning them into revenue generators has caused treasurers who work in such 'profit centres' to take risks actively to generate profits from their treasury operations.

Treasurers who work in companies where the treasury is not considered a profit centre may still engage in aggressive treasury activities because they think they will be rewarded, either professionally or financially, for generating revenues for the firm. This pressure to perform may also be due to the greater prominence the treasurer has achieved in the last ten years. He is now visible at Board level. The treasurer may think that one of the ways he can demonstrate his performance is to show sub-LIBOR funding costs.

Therein lies the paradox — to achieve funding at five *basis points* below LIBOR, using simple interest rate swaps is still possible, depending on market conditions. On the other hand, achieving wider spreads below LIBOR often requires the treasurer to take on some other types of risk (some of which are not readily apparent to those who are not mathematically-inclined because the new risks can be cleverly camouflaged). This is due to the fact that a wider spread below LIBOR immediately implies an off-market rate. To achieve this while adhering to the principle that the net present value for both legs of the swap must be zero at swap inception means that one party must be compensated, somehow, for agreeing to receive a floating rate well below what he can achieve in the market. That compensation can be upfront, amortized over the life of the transaction or at maturity and it can come in all guises. In other words 'there is no free lunch', so if one party is obtaining a better-than-market rate, he must be paying for it somehow, somewhere.

By agreeing to take on some other risks, the treasurer must by definition have a view on the future direction of the underlying markets, since he hopes that future market moves will neutralize the new risks he has taken on. He is no longer adhering to a passive hedging strategy; he has moved to an aggressive one. In effect, he has slipped into the role of an investor who takes on risks to generate extra returns (in the treasurer's case to generate more cost savings). There is nothing wrong with such a strategy but end-users who embark on it must acknowledge what they are doing and manage such derivative activities separately and differently from those derivative activities which are pure hedging.

It is clear that management either never perceived or lost sight of this distinction in some of the more infamous cases of derivative losses. Many swaps were executed under the hedging banner, but if the treasurer (and maybe finance director and senior management of the firm) were intellectually honest with themselves, they would have to admit that executing swaps with embedded options and leverage is stretching too far the meaning of the word 'hedging'.

In this charade, they have been aided by the layman's commonly-held notion that swaps equals hedging. For most end-users, their first introduction to swaps is as a hedging tool. But they are just as useful as view-expression vehicles, because as will be explained in Chapter 3, the economic impact of receiving fixed and paying floating in a swap is the same as being long a fixed rate bond and short a floating rate note. If a treasurer thinks interest rates are heading downwards, he can engage in a swap transaction to pay floating and receive fixed even if he has no offsetting liabilities; he can leverage up his views by asking for the payout formula to magnify changes in interest rates in the same way as he can leverage a cash bond position through the repo market. Indeed, because swaps are over-the-counter transactions and not collateralized in most cases, the leverage afforded by a swap is much higher than through the repo market.

Leveraging a Simple Interest Rate Swap

To illustrate this point, let's use a plain vanilla interest rate swap where company X pays a floating rate equal to six-month LIBOR and receives fixed in return. If it felt that interest rates were to drop during the life of the swap, its treasurer might press for a high leverage on the floating leg because first, that would mean the fixed interest rate it would receive would be substantially higher than prevailing fixed rate investments of the same maturity (remember the two legs of a swap at inception must have a net present value of zero); and second, the leverage on the floating leg would mean that as interest rates fell, the floating payments of company X would drop on a magnified basis while it continued to enjoy a high fixed rate. Table 2.1 below illustrates the difference in floating payments for a plain LIBOR, LIBOR X2, LIBOR X3 and $LIBOR^2$ leg (of an interest rate swap). The fifth column of $LIBOR^2/6$ was included because that was the leverage formula of Gibson Greetings first leveraged swap, called the ratio swap.

The table shows how fast LIBOR payments drop in a leveraged swap — every time LIBOR falls by 100 bp, it falls by 200 bp in a LIBOR X2 swap, while the drop in a $LIBOR^2$ swap is 700 basis points. But if LIBOR were to rise, the pain would be as great since the multiplier works in the same way up and down.

Table 2.1 Scenario 1: Interest Rates Fall (All numbers in percentages. Assume LIBOR is at 4%).

6M LIBOR	LIBOR X2	LIBOR X3	$LIBOR^2$	$LIBOR^2/6$
4.0	8.0	12.0	16.0	2.67
3.0	6.0	9.0	9.0	1.50
2.0	4.0	6.0	4.0	0.67
1.0	2.0	3.0	1.0	0.16

Table 2.2   Scenario 2: Interest Rates Rise. (All numbers in percentages).

6M LIBOR	LIBOR X2	LIBOR X3	LIBOR^2	LIBOR^2/6
4.0	8.0	12.0	16.0	2.7
5.0	10.0	15.0	25.0	4.2
6.0	12.0	18.0	36.0	6.0
7.0	14.0	21.0	49.0	8.1
8.0	16.0	24.0	64.0	10.6

Payments on the LIBOR^2 swap are so horrendously large that few treasurers would ever contemplate such a risk unless they were 100% sure that rates would not rise during the life of the swap.

All swap payments are based on a notional amount — in a simple interest rate swap, a floating leg of 6% means payments of 6/100 X notional amount of swap. If the swap had a notional of $100 million, interest payments would be $6 million annually. If LIBOR was at 6% in a LIBOR squared swap, the floating payments will be 36/100 × 100 million, or $36 million annually. The floating payments in the second scenario are equivalent to company X having executed another five swaps each with a notional amount of $100 million, bringing the total notional value of its swap transactions to $600 million. In a LIBOR X2 swap, company X can be thought of as having executed one more swap with a notional amount of $100 million, and paying coupon costs of $12 million annually. But if LIBOR was to fall to 2%, that would be equivalent to the company halving the number of swaps it had executed, with its interest costs dropping to $3 million annually.

If leveraged swaps are conceptualized this way, then it is hard to view them as pure hedging instruments because it is difficult to see how any company's funding needs and corporate cashflows can increase so dramatically (and so geometrically) when interest rates rise, and decrease in a similar manner when rates fall. It is generally accepted that leveraged swaps were a vehicle used by some corporate treasurers to capitalize on their views that interest rates would remain low. Most of these swaps, executed between 1991–93, enabled them to enjoy comparatively high fixed yields and pay low floating costs, which could go even lower as rates fell.

But leverage works both ways as the tables above show. Since it magnifies a firm's portfolio sensitivity to changes in market conditions, it will multiply a firm's losses as much as it does its gains. In the rampant bull market atmosphere of the early 1990s, investors and corporate treasurers seemed to forget that it was a double-edged sword. They got greedy. They remembered only the beauty of leverage, consequently multipliers went up from 3/4/5 to ridiculous 50s. There have even been reported instances of 1500 and 19 000; admittedly the notional amounts in these cases was miniscule and their leverage effects must be placed in perspective, by looking at the size of the investors' total portfolio. But they do show the excesses, even stupidity, of the early 1990s. (For example in bond terms, a 50-multiplier is equivalent to the investor buying a 50-year zero coupon bond.

Such a bond does not exist because it is too difficult, and thus too dangerous to try to predict yields that far into the future.)

Procter Gambles

Procter and Gamble's (P&G) reason for entering into its leveraged swap with Bankers Trust (BT) was to achieve lower funding costs. It wanted floating rate funding at 40 basis points (bp) under the rate available on US commercial paper (CP) because they had achieved this target with a swap that was maturing. Bankers Trust's *rocket scientists* were happy to oblige P&G's demands, but in so doing piled on risks, some of which were obvious and others obscured.

Although P&G had stated that it wanted funding at 40 bp below CP, BT offered it funding at 75 bp below CP. The terms of the $200 million five-year swap executed on November 2, 1994 were: BT paid P&G a fixed rate throughout the life of the five-year swap and in return, P&G paid BT a floating interest rate 75 bp below CP for the first six months of the swap. For the remaining $4\frac{1}{2}$ years of the swap, P&G would pay BT 75 bp below CP plus a spread (see Figure 2.1). This spread was to be set at the end of the six months. i.e. 2 May 1994. The formula on this spread was:

Spread = (98.5* [five-year CMT yield]/5.78% − 30 year Treasury Price)/100

where CMT stands for *Constant Maturity Treasury*.

But there was a floor of zero bp to this spread, so even if the formula returned a negative spread, P&G would not pay BT CP minus 75 bp *minus* spread. Table 2.3 shows different spread levels, depending on five-year CMT yields and 30-year Treasury prices. If interest rates did not move during the six month period (i.e. five-year CMT yields remained at 4.95% and 30-year Treasury prices at 103.02%), the spread would be negative 1830 bp, come spread-setting day in May 1994. But P&G would never have enjoyed paying no interest to BT. If rates had gone up by 40 basis points during that six-month period, resulting in a negative spread of 644 bp, P&G was still committed to paying CP minus 75, not CP minus 75 bp

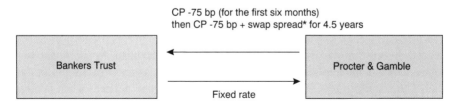

CP -75 bp (for the first six months)
then CP -75 bp + swap spread* for 4.5 years

Bankers Trust

Procter & Gamble

Fixed rate

Figure 2.1   Procter and Gamble's Leveraged Swap.

Where swap spread (set in six months time) = (98.5 [5 year CMT yield/5.78%]-30 year treasury price)/100

Table 2.3 Procter and Gamble's Leveraged Swap: Extra Dollar Payments Due Solely to Spread Coming into Operation. (Assume that both five-year CMT yields and 30-year Treasury yields increase by the same amount, i.e. parallel shifts of the yield curve)[1].

Five-yr CMT yields(%)	30-yr Treasury price (%)	Spread (bp)	Leverage[2]	Net spread (bp)	$equiv[3] (per year)
4.95	103.02	−1905		−1830	$1.5M
5.35 (+40 bp)	97.61	−644	31	−569	$1.5M
5.55 (+60 bp)	95.07	−49	31	−124	$1.5M
5.65 (+70 bp)	93.85	+243	31	+168	−$3.36M
5.75 (+80 bp)	92.64	+535	31	+460	−$9.20M
5.95 (+100 bp)	90.30	+1110	30	+1035	−$20.70M
6.45 (+150 bp)	84.86	+2505	29	+2430	−$48.60M

Notes to table:
1. Calculations are based on Treasury yields and prices provided by Bloomberg.
2. The leverage is obtained by dividing the spread derived from the formula and the increase in five-year CMT yields.
3. This dollar amount is not the net coupon payment per year on the swap. Such a dollar amount would have to take into account the fixed rate BT pays P&G as well as the existing CP rate. The fixed rate is constant throughout the life of the swap. P&G would pay the existing CP rate whatever it was, so the only variable dollar amount was that due to the 5/30 spread. The dollar equivalent here shows the annual interest cost resulting solely from the spread.

minus 644 bp. P&G's cheapest cost of funding under this swap was CP minus 75 bp because BT had incorporated a floor of 0 bp in the payout formula.

But as Table 2.3 shows, if rates rose by 70 basis points or more during those vital six months, then P&G's floating costs would increase significantly. For example a 100 bp increase resulted in a net spread of 1035 bp (1110−75) being added to the CP rate. It is clear therefore that P&G faced significant interest rate exposure if interest rates rose between November 1993 and May 1994.

Because this spread formula was ostensibly a play on 5 and 30 year Treasury yields, this swap came to be known as the 5/30 swap. Yet the predominant risk of this structure came not from whether the spread between 5 and 30 year yields narrowed or widened, but from a general rise in US interest rates due to the embedded leverage in the payout formula. The spread play between 5 and 30 year Treasuries was secondary to the payoff profile and risks of the swap.

The leveraged play in this transaction came from two fronts. First, any change in five-year CMT rates was magnified 17 times (derived from dividing 98.5 by 5.78). Second, because it was the 30-year Treasury *price* rather than the yield that was subtracted from the five-year CMT yield, there was extra leverage coming from this side of the equation too. Why? Because the price of a bond declines when interest rates (yields) rise and advances when rates (yields) fall, so the spread in this formula could only increase with every upward move in US Treasury yields since there was the simultaneous effect of five-year CMT yields rising and 30-year Treasury prices dropping. (The only way the spread could have decreased in the wake of US rates rising is for 30-year Treasuries to react inversely to a rate hike, i.e. their yields fall (and prices rise) when interest rates increase, which goes against all fundamentals of fixed income investments.) The flip side this statement was, if interest rates had fallen, then the spread could only decrease but that was immaterial to P&G because its minimum cost of funding under this swap was floored at 75 basis points below CP. Financially, P&G would not have been any better off. Its maximum benefit from this leveraged swap was $1.5 million per year for five years (derived from multiplying $200 million by 0.0075 [the maximum spread under CP]).

It is also no coincidence that the spread involved a 30-year Treasury — in the US Treasury family, these long-dated instruments have the highest duration and are therefore the most sensitive to changes in interest rates. At the time the swap was executed, 30-year US Treasuries had a duration of about 11.

Table 2.3 shows the risks to which P&G were exposed. The five-year CMT rate at the beginning of November 1993 was around 4.95% and the on-the-run 30-year Treasury had a price of about 103.02%. The table shows the spread calculations for various levels of five-year CMT rates.

It shows very clearly that P&G could only afford a 70 bp rise in five-year CMT yields before it got blown out of the water. The leverage made the spread formula hypersensitive to changes in US interest rates since each basis point move was magnified up to 31 times.

Why did Bankers Trust incorporate this spread into the swap cashflows? Why was P&G prepared to take on such risks? Because there is no free lunch. P&G could not achieve its funding target by executing a *plain vanilla* interest rate swap. To achieve such off-market rates, it had to assume some risks. It did so by selling a put option on 30-year US Treasuries whose payoff profile was repackaged into the spread formula. The premium it earned for selling this option was 75 basis points per year for five years which option specialists say was inadequate compensation for such an option. If rates stayed low within that six-month period, P&G would pocket the full premium and enjoy cheap funding. The maximum gain of $7.5 million for the term of the swap compared with unknown interest rate costs if US rates rose shows the risks run by option sellers who do not hedge their positions.

P&G knew the huge risks. It knew it had breathing space of only 70 bp because the option was so hyper-leveraged. But it also knew that the premium it earned from selling this highly-leveraged option was 75 bp compared with its funding target of 40 bp below CP. This was the base-line premium it needed to earn. P&G was in a conundrum: it could sell the six-month option, pocket the premium and take it on the chin if interest rates rose between November and May. On the other hand, it could try to manage the risks of this option by 'locking-in' early — i.e. cancelling the option sale so that BT could not exercise it — if market conditions became less rosy. (Remember the outlook for US interest rates in the fourth quarter of 1993 was still bullish, that is why all the large trading houses suffered such huge trading losses in 1994; they were all long bonds which turned out to be terribly wrong.)

There were two ways P&G could cancel this option sale — buy it back from BT or buy an offsetting put option (with roughly identical features) from another investment bank, which may have been tricky given that liquidity in customized products is limited. But for the transaction to make any economic sense in the first place, P&G had to satisfy itself that it could buy back the option at a cost of no more than 35 bp premium per year (so it could still meet its sub-CP funding target of 40 bp). For this event to materialize, a few basic conditions had to be satisfied. The only way the six-month put option could decline in value was for US interest rates to fall so that the option went further out-of-the-money, or for volatility and interest rates to remain stable so that the *time decay* on the option eroded its value. The faster this time decay, the earlier P&G could buy back the option and 'lock-in' its funding costs. P&G thus needed an option whose time decay was front-loaded. It finally sold BT an option that was so out-of-the-money on a forward basis that, when the deal was executed, the option had no *intrinsic value* and only time value. (The strike price of an option is often compared to the implied forward rate of the underlying asset, as opposed to the spot rate, because both buyers and sellers are more concerned about rate levels near or at the option's expiry date rather than rates prevailing at the start of the deal.) Consequently, 80% of the option's time decay was concentrated in the first three months of its life.

However if rates and volatility did not remain stable, then P&G had no hope of buying back at a cheaper price the option it had sold to BT, or buying another put option from the street at a price less than what it earned for selling the original option. Because the option was so hyper-leveraged, interest rates did not have to move much before the option zoomed into-the-money; dashing all hopes of buying it back cheaper, or 'locking-in.'

It is still not clear why P&G chose to sell a six-month option for 75 bp and then 'lock-in'. Why did it not just make life simpler for itself and sell a shorter maturity option for 40 bp premium? That would have enabled it to achieve its sub-CP funding target. Or did P&G want its cake and eat it ... did it like the idea of possibly earning 75 bp premium but locking in when it wanted to?

P&G insisted it did not have any prior information on how this lock-in price was calculated. Its court filings (P&G is suing BT) say,

> P&G entered the [5/30 swap] because, in response to P&G's repeated questions, Bankers Trust falsely assured P&G it would be protected against significant losses from rising interest rates because P&G could safely lock in its rates if interest rates began to rise. When rates did rise, Bankers Trust changed the rules, imposing on P&G a lock-in interest rate calculated under a secret, proprietary, complex, multi-variable pricing model with Bankers Trust would not share and to this day has not shared with P&G.

If locking-in just meant P&G buying back the option which it had sold too cheaply in the first place, then it is no wonder that BT could not price the lock-in in advance since that meant quoting a fixed option price, which was impossible given that option values fluctuate with changing market conditions. Even if BT had given P&G indicative prices they would be useless because these prices would not be valid as soon as there were changes in the variables that went into the pricing of this option.

If the company did not understand the mechanics of this lock-in mechanism — knowledge vital to how it managed the almost open-ended exposure of this transaction — then it took on risks it did not fully appreciate when it executed the swap. Like Faust when he pledged his soul to Mephistopheles, it was blinded to dark side of the deal; like Faust who yearned for all knowledge and experience, P&G had the very laudable aim of reducing its funding costs.

Gibson's Bleak Message

Even the toughest, meanest Wall Street trader who has never bought a greeting card in his life knows the name Gibson Greetings. The story of how this Cincinnati, Ohio greetings card manufacturer got entangled in arcane swaps and options vividly illustrates how derivatives, not properly understood and controlled, can turn into a nightmare. If it had not sued Bankers Trust, and both parties had not reached an out-of-court settlement in November 1994, Gibson's losses from derivative transactions over a period of two years would have cost the company $27 million. For a company whose net income was less than $50 million for the last five years (1989–1993), this was not an insubstantial amount. (Gibson sued Bankers Trust in September 1994 seeking to recover paper losses of $23 million, along with punitive damages of $50 million. Under the out-of-court settlement, Bankers Trust effectively released Gibson from $14 million the company owed under two swap agreements. In return, Gibson agreed to pay Bankers Trust $6.2 million which represented the balance of losses Gibson faced on those two contracts.)

The losses are all the more incredible since they resulted from a swap that had a notional amount of $30 million. But Gibson's later transactions were hyper-leveraged so that the behavioural returns on the swap bore no relation to the notional amount.

The Gibson case makes a fascinating story on how a company, with poor management controls, can be sucked into taking a riskier and riskier position; and in the process lose sight of its original aims. The company maintained it would not have done so had Bankers Trust made it cognizant of all the risks. Gibson did indeed end up with a raft of price risks, leveraged to the sky, and option risks.

Bankers Trust insists it did make Gibson aware of all the risks. But the fact remains that Gibson was never made aware of the true losses on these transactions because between October 1992 and March 1994, Bankers Trust representatives misled Gibson about their true value. There were differences of up to 61% between the negative value quoted to Gibson and Bankers Trust's internal book value. (See Appendix 3 Commodity Futures Trading Commission report on the case for details of Bankers Trust's misrepresentation, which significantly understated the magnitude of Gibson's losses.) While there will always be differences between a bank's in-house valuation of a product and the mark-to-market prices it gives to clients for their valuation, such a wide differential cannot be attributed to adjustments to reflect market risk, model risk, operations costs, as well as general credit reserves. (The value of Bankers Trust's derivatives portfolio, as reflected on BTNY's 1992 financial statements, was adjusted by general reserves intended to reflect market risk, model risk, operations cost as well as other valuation considerations, and general credit reserves. These reserves did not reflect any differential between values quotes to Gibson and the computer model value of Gibson's positions.

On BTNY's 1993 financial statements, the value of Bankers Trust's derivatives portfolio was adjusted by general reserves and by specific reserves intended to reflect the differential between the 'quoted values' of positions and the computer model values. With respect to Gibson, the specific reserve reflected 25% of the differential between the computer model value and the 'quoted value' of Gibson's position at the end of November 1993.)

Had Gibson known the true extent of its losses, would it have continued to roll its ever-increasing losses into more complex and higher-leveraged transactions? The negative values first reported by Bankers Trust might well have been within Gibson's stop-loss limits. (Gibson in its court filings always claimed that it told Bankers Trust representatives that it could not tolerate a loss greater than $2 to $3 million — it is not clear whether this was an official stop-loss limit or just a figure plucked from the air. It is, however, significant that when Gibson asked Bankers Trust representatives for a valuation of its derivative transactions as at 31 December 1993, Bankers Trust provided a negative 'mark-to-market' value of $2.9 million versus a Bankers Trust book value $7.47 million.)

The following description of the Gibson/BT trades its technical. Readers who are not mathematically-inclined or familiar with complex derivatives might wish to skip the section starting with 'ratio swap' and ending with 'swap transaction 10044'. However, the reader does not need to understand the mechanics of every Gibson/BT transaction to appreciate the fact that derivatives can be misused, both intentionally and unintentionally. The Gibson team did not understand the hidden or obvious risks embedded in their complex deals. Yet they took them on because they wanted to recoup the losses on earlier positions.

Their actions had all the hallmarks of a desperate player at the roulette wheel in Las Vegas, placing all his chips on only one number. Between November 1991 and March 1994, Gibson entered into approximately 29 derivative transactions, including amendments to existing transactions. Some deals were amended within weeks of execution. All had significant option risks (because Gibson sold *exotic options* like knock-outs and *digitals*) and most had embedded leverage in the payout formula. These transactions generated revenues of about $13 million for Bankers Trust.

The aim of Gibson's first foray into derivatives was also to reduce funding costs. In May 1991, Gibson issued a $50 million security with a fixed rate coupon of 9.33%. The notes had serial maturities from 1995 to 2001 and could not be prepaid earlier than maturity. This proved to be a thorn in Gibson's side as interest

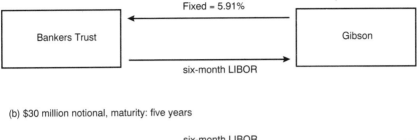

Figure 2.2   Two Plain Vanilla Swaps between Bankers Trust and Gibson.

rates fell, so the company looked at various ways of reducing its cost of fixed rate debt.

In November 1991, Gibson executed two plain vanilla interest rate swaps with Bankers Trust. Both had notional amounts of $30 million, one had a maturity of two years while the second had a life of five years. The two-year swap had Bankers paying Gibson six-month LIBOR while Gibson paid Bankers a fixed rate of 5.91%. The five-year swap had Bankers paying Gibson a fixed rate of 7.12% and receiving six-month LIBOR payments (see Figure 2.2). In effect, the two LIBOR payments cancel each other out, so that Gibson effectively earned the difference between 7.12% and 5.91% for two years. This interest rate revenue of 1.21% effectively reduced its interest rate cost on its $50 million bond issue. However, in mid-July 1992 both parties cancelled both swaps with Gibson making a profit of $260 000.

Why Gibson cancelled these cost-reduction swaps is not clear — it had reduced its cost of borrowing for one year, and the $260 000 realized profit on the two swaps, amortized over the life of the $50 million security, would further reduce its effective coupon costs. If these reduced costs were sufficient for the company, why did it then execute a ratio swap within three months of the first two swaps being cancelled?

Ratio Swap

The synthetic leverage contained in the ratio swap increased as LIBOR went higher. This was because Gibson paid a floating rate of LIBOR squared, divided by six, in return for receiving a fixed payment of 5.5% from Bankers Trust. (The larger the number, the greater the effect of squaring since the number is being multiplied by itself.) The five-year swap was for a notional $30 million and interest payments were to be exchanged every six months (see Figure 2.3). Gibson's first two LIBOR payments were set at 1.581% and 1.893% respectively, so in the first year of the swap, Gibson was a net receiver of funds. Yet, less than 90 days after it entered into the ratio swap, Gibson was told that the swap had a negative value of $975 000.

That the ratio swap had a negative value of about $1 million even though Gibson was then in the enviable position of paying 1.581% on the floating leg versus receiving 5.50% from Bankers Trust is due to the way swaps are valued. They are not valued on spot interest rates but on the forward curves — the markets' joint expectations of the changes in the shape of the current yield curve given today's rate environment. The forward curves for LIBOR for April 1994 to October 1997 (see Figure 2.4) showed that the markets were definitely expecting rates to go up; the $LIBOR^2/6$ (synthetic leverage) formula magnified these projected interest rates so that the swap ended up with negative value. (Whether the forward curves did indeed move up so dramatically within those 90 days to move the value of the swap from positive to negative $1 million is questionable.)

As can be seen from Table 2.1, the synthetic leverage of the ratio swap was not huge. But with the forward curves predicting a sharp rise in rates, especially towards the latter part of the swap's tenor, it is not surprising that the swap was

$30 million notional, maturity : five years

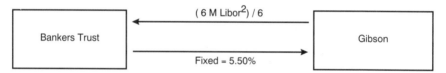

Figure 2.3 Ratio Swap between Bankers Trust and Gibson.

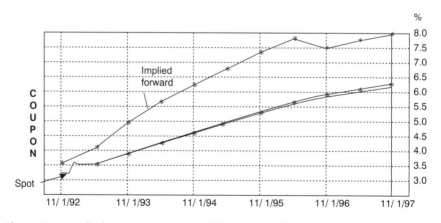

Figure 2.4 Implied Forward Curve of US$ 6-month Libor, as at 1 November 1992. Reproduced with permission from Bloomberg.

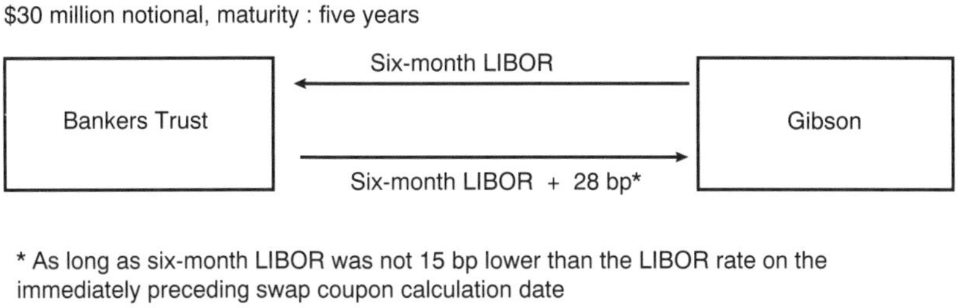

$30 million notional, maturity : five years

* As long as six-month LIBOR was not 15 bp lower than the LIBOR rate on the immediately preceding swap coupon calculation date

Figure 2.5 Periodic Floor.

amended three times (within a space of ten days), each time to shorten the maturity. It was finally cancelled on 21 April 1993, just six months after both parties had entered into the ratio swap.

Periodic Floor

Running concurrently with the ratio swap were two other derivative deals — the periodic floor and Treasury spread lock. In the periodic floor, BT paid Gibson six-month LIBOR plus 28 basis points, while Gibson paid BT six-month LIBOR flat; as long as the six-month LIBOR rate was not more than 15 basis points lower than the LIBOR rate on the immediately preceding swap coupon calculation date (see Figure 2.5). The floor had a notional value of $30 million and was due to run for five years. Gibson also 'lost' money on the periodic floor — as at 31 December 1992, BT informed Gibson that both the ratio swap and periodic floor had a negative mark-to-market value of $1 025 000. (On BT's books they had a negative value of $2 129 209.) The periodic floor was cancelled nine months after its initiation and its monetary obligations rolled into a time swap and amended knock-out call, which are discussed later on.

Spread Lock 1

On 11 January 1993 the two parties entered a $30 million five-year spread lock swap. Under this swap, Bankers would pay Gibson a coupon which was the sum of the 'mid-market swap spread' and the 'on-the-run Treasury rate' while Gibson paid Bankers a coupon equal to the sum of 'the spread lock' and the 'off-the run Treasury rate'. This spread lock was initially set at 38 basis points (see Figure 2.6). The first payments on the swap however did not start till $2\frac{1}{2}$ years after the two parties had signed the agreement, so in essence Gibson was taking a two-year view on swap spreads and Treasury yields.

This swap was amended nine times before it was finally cancelled a year after it was entered into and before any payments were exchanged. The first amendment, on 16 April 1993 changed the 'off-the-run Treasury rate' to the ten-year Treasury rate. The next three amendments, all taking place within a space of three weeks,

$30 million notional, maturity : $6\frac{1}{2}$ years

*Spread lock initially set at 38 bp, which was later
amended to 36 bp, 51 bp + 56 bp

Figure 2.6   Spread Lock Swap.

changed the spread lock from 38 bp to 36 bp, to 51 bp and to 56 bp. On 22
September 1993, Bankers Trust and Gibson amended the spread lock 1 swap (and
another spread lock 2) in exchange for linking an option, wedding band 3, to the
two spread lock structures.

Treasury-Linked Swap

Gibson entered into this transaction in return for BT shortening the maturity on the
ratio swap from five to four years. But by entering into this short-dated swap of
eight months, Gibson was actually crystallizing losses of $2.1 million on its ratio
swap because they were built into the Treasury-linked structure.

On the face of it, the Treasury-linked swap looked good for Gibson. It was to
pay BT LIBOR and receive LIBOR plus 200 bp in return. But principal repayment
at maturity was determined by a highly-leveraged formula which magnified by
21 times interest rate changes in the two-year Treasury yield (see Figure 2.7). In
addition, there was also a bet on 30-year Treasury prices. The principal exchange
terms required Gibson to pay Bankers Trust $30 million while Bankers would pay
the lesser of $30.6 million or an amount determined by the following formula:

$$\$30\,000\,000 \times \frac{1 - \dfrac{103 \times \text{two-year Treasury yield}}{4.88\%} - \text{30-year Treasury price}}{100}$$

This formula looks pretty similar to the one that determined the spread of
P&G's swap.

What happens to the Treasury-linked swap is continued under the knock-out call.

Spread Lock 2

Spread lock 2 was entered on 6 May 1993, but the first interest payments would
only be exchanged two years hence. The structure was similar to spread lock 1,
which both parties had entered only four months ago. The only difference was the
size of the spread which was set at 31.5 bp.

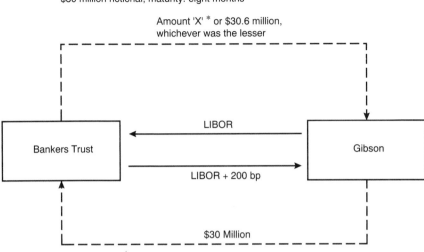

Key: principal flows at maturity - - - ->
* Amount determined by formula explained in text

Figure 2.7 Treasury-linked Swap.

This swap agreement was amended eight times before it was finally cancelled nine months after the two had entered into the swap. Most of the amendments were to change the size of the spread lock. But the main amendment on 22 September 1993, also involved spread lock 1 which as recounted earlier, was to incorporate an option, wedding band 3, into the structure.

Wedding Band 3

Wedding band 3 changed the payout obligations on spread lock 1 and 2. Under this structure the spread-lock payout was 48 bp plus a spread. But whether the spread came into operation depended on the level of six-month LIBOR on each London business day from and including 24 September 1993 to 24 September 1994. If LIBOR was between 3–5%, the spread was zero, so the minimum spread-lock of 48 bp came into effect. If LIBOR was outside that band, the spread in the spread-lock was determined by the following formula: $(LIBOR - 3.75\%) \times 0.85$, where LIBOR was the LIBOR rate on 24 September, 1994 (see Figure 2.8).

This agreement was amended once a month for its four-month existence; it was cancelled on 14 January 1994 and both parties entered into a time swap.

At the heart of the wedding band structure is the barrier option, which is a path-dependent option that is either cancelled or activated if the underlying instrument

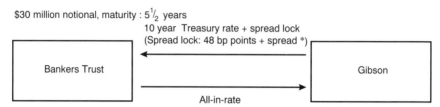

$30 million notional, maturity : $5\frac{1}{2}$ years

10 year Treasury rate + spread lock
(Spread lock: 48 bp points + spread *)

Bankers Trust

Gibson

All-in-rate

* Spread depends on the level of LIBOR as explained in text

Figure 2.8 Wedding Band 3.

reaches a set level. There are knock-outs (up-and-out, down-and-out) and knock-ins (up-and-in, down-and-in).

The wedding band contained a knock-in option, which was activated every time LIBOR traded outside its reference range of 3–5%. With this structure, Gibson was betting that six-month LIBOR would be outside the band for most of the reference period.

Knock-Out Call Option

On 10 June 1993, Gibson bought a knock-out call option to help it reduce its exposure on the Treasury-linked swap because it realized that it would be paying out far more principal than it would be receiving under the latter structure. With the knock-out call option, Bankers was required to pay Gibson on settlement date an amount calculated as follows: (6.876%- yield to maturity of 30-year Treasury security) × 12.5 × $25 000 000.

The payout of this option leveraged by 12.5 times, any changes in the difference between 6.876% and the yield of a 30-year Treasury so that if interest rates did decline, Gibson would be paid off handsomely by Bankers Trust. The trouble was that the call had a knock-out strike of 6.48%; once 30-year Treasury yields dropped below that, the option extinguished; but it was only at levels below 6.48% that the option was really valuable. Also, unless 30-year Treasury yields remained stable, Gibson's chances of exercising the option before it was knocked out were slim because it was only exercisable on maturity (see Figure 2.9).

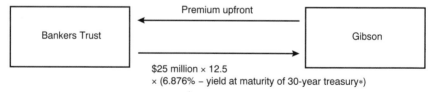

Premium upfront

Bankers Trust

Gibson

$25 million × 12.5
× (6.876% – yield at maturity of 30-year treasury*)

* If 30-year treasury yields dropped below 6.48%, option extinguishes

Figure 2.9 Knock-out Call Option.

The Time Swap

Two months after Gibson bought the knock-out call, it entered into a three-year $30 million time swap to amend the knock-out call and to rollover the obligations of the periodic floor. The three amendments to the knock-out call cost Gibson $3 million. In comparison, the maximum possible payout on the knock-out never exceeded $2.3 million. The time swap itself was amended six times during its five-month life. Again the notional amount on the swap was $30 million.

In the time swap, Bankers Trust paid Gibson six-month LIBOR plus 100 bp, while Gibson's floating payments to Bankers depended on LIBOR's level during the swap (see Figure 2.10). The formula for Gibson's floating obligations was as follows: six-month LIBOR $+ (N \times 0.5)$, where N is the number of days in a calculation period that the six-month LIBOR rate fell outside the designated range. The pre-agreed calculation periods and designated ranges were as follows:

6 August 1993–6 February 1994	3.1875%–4.3125%
6 February 1994–6 August 1994	3.2500%–4.5000%
6 August 1994–6 February 1995	3.3750%–5.1250%
6 February 1995–6 August 1995	3.5000%–5.2500%

Underpinning the time swap structure is the digital or binary option. Unlike conventional options, whose payoff depends on the in-the-moneyness of the option, the digital option's payoff is a step function. It is either zero or the payoff amount. So Gibson's floating payments could be either LIBOR flat or a fat spread over LIBOR, depending on whether LIBOR stayed within the pre-agreed bands. The time swap is also known as the *corridor swap*. Under the terms of this swap, Gibson was betting on interest rate stability — that six-month LIBOR would stay within narrow bands of less than 1% for the first two years, and larger bands thereafter. If this scenario materialized, Gibson's floating-rate obligations would be equal to six-month LIBOR. If interest rates were volatile (they did not need to be trending upwards or downwards), and spiked below or above the upper and lower bands, Gibson would have to pay a spread above LIBOR every time the bands were breached. The first two amendments, occurring on 12 August and 25 August 1993 (the swap was only entered into on 4 August 1993) increased the multiplier from 0.5 to 0.65, and from 0.65

$34 million notional, maturity: three years

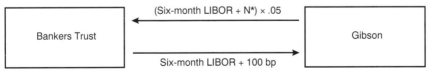

* Where N is the number of days six-month LIBOR fell outside a pre-agreed range as described in text

Figure 2.10   Time Swap.

to 0.92 (the leverage was increased in return for BT amending the knock-out call). Then the bands were changed on 10 September 1993 and 26 October 1993 causing the termination dates to be changed too. The first change was to end the swap on 6 February 1995 and the second on 6 August 1994. The swap was finally terminated on 14 January 1994, in a transaction that included terminating the spread locks and amending wedding band 3 in exchange for entering into a LIBOR-linked swap and wedding band 6. By agreeing to the following two transactions, Gibson immediately incurred an additional unrealized loss of approximately $4 954 000.

LIBOR-Linked Payout and Wedding Band 6

The notional amount on this swap was $25 million. The payoff was dependent on the trading range of LIBOR between 14 January 1994 and 15 August 1994. If LIBOR was less than 5.75%, BT would pay Gibson a payment based on the following terms: $25 000 000 \times ([\text{spread}/0.00335 + 0.125] - 1)$ where the spread was the difference between ten-year Treasury notes and six-month LIBOR.

If LIBOR was more than or equal to 5.75%, BT would pay Gibson a payment based on the following terms: $25 000 000 \times ([\text{spread}/0.00335] - [\text{LIBOR}_2/4.25\%])$ where LIBOR_2 is six-month LIBOR on 15 August 1995 (see Figure 2.11). These payments were to made on the second business day following 15 August 1995.

Gibson's payment to BT was a function of LIBOR during the term of the transaction. If LIBOR_1 for any day during that term was outside the band of 3–5% and LIBOR_2 was greater than 3.75%, then Gibson would pay BT the product of $119 700

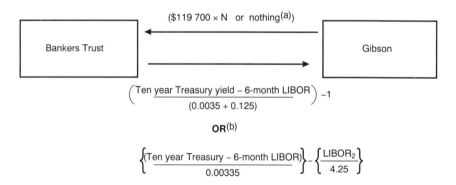

Figure 2.11   LIBOR-linked Payout and Wedding Band 6.

Maturity: 1 year 3 months

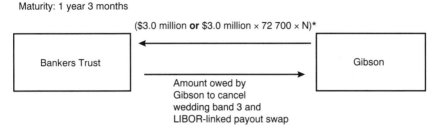

Key: *Depending on the level of six-month LIBOR on 7 June 1995.
        If it is ≤ 3.90%, then $3.0 million
        If it is ≥ 3.90%, then $3.0 × million 72 00 × N where N =
        LIBOR RATE – 3.90% and no more than 200 bp.

Figure 2.12   Swap Transaction S10044.

and the number of basis points by which $LIBOR_2$ exceeded 3.75%. $LIBOR_2$ was the six-month LIBOR rate on the termination date of the agreement; i.e. 24 September 1994. If $LIBOR_1$ was within the 3–5% band, and $LIBOR_2$ was less than 3.75%, then Gibson owed nothing (see Figure 2.11). The swap agreement was amended on 7 February 1994 to change one of the multipliers from $119 700 to $79 800.

These transactions went under water once the Federal Reserve Board raised interest rates on 4 February 1994. Gibson claimed that it was first made aware of the magnitude of its losses — negative $8.1 million — on 24 February 1994. (Bankers Trust's books actually showed the true figure at $15.45 million.) Wedding band 5 and LIBOR-linked swaps were cancelled on 4 March and Gibson entered into its final swap transaction with BT.

Swap Transaction S10044

This swap, entered into on 4 March 1994, aimed to cap Gibson's losses at $27.5 million. (Gibson claimed BT issued it an ultimatum — either to agree to swap transaction S10044 or to pay $17.5 million immediately.) If LIBOR on 7 June 1995 was less than or equal to 3.90%, Gibson would pay BT $3 million. If it was greater, then Gibson would pay BT $3 million × $72 700 × the number of basis points (this is the leverage or multiplier in this deal) by which LIBOR on 7 June 1994 exceeded 3.90% (see Figure 2.12). The multiplier would have been open-ended had BT not capped it at 200 basis points. BT agreed to pay Gibson an amount equal to the total amount owed by Gibson to BT as combined consideration for the cancellation of wedding band 3 and the LIBOR-linked payout swap.

Hyper-Leverage

A key point emerging out of the Gibson and P&G stories is synthetic leverage's flexibility and size. Notice how the leverage could be changed so quickly and easily in Gibson's case; many of the amendments just involved increasing the multiplier. There also appears to be little constraint on the size of leverage embedded in payout formulas other than both counterparties' appetite for it. Procter and Gamble's swap with Bankers Trust for example was leveraged up to 31 times. The swap had a notional amount of $200 million and Bankers Trust is said to have had hedges worth at least $3 billion to neutralize its exposure.

The same New York bank allowed the Gibson treasurer to spin the roulette wheel 29 times before it closed him down. BT's credit department must have become increasingly nervous as Gibson's leveraged bets soured because the bank's credit risk (emanating from Gibson's transactions) was becoming larger and larger. The credit department knew that if interest rates retained their upward course, BT would be forced to unwind its positions with Gibson because the latter had reached its credit limit. This was probably why Gibson was told that its positions had deteriorated by about $11 million in just two months; in stark contrast to having been told that its losses over the previous fourteen months were less than $3 million.

On 31 December 1994 Gibson was told that it was negative $2.9 million. The figure went to negative $8.1 million on 23 February 1994 and increased to a negative $13.8 million two days later. On 3 March 1994 Gibson was told that its positions had deteriorated a further $3.5 million (when on Bankers Trust's books it had only increased by about $1 million), with a warning that its liability was potentially unlimited. No wonder Gibson's management went into a state of catatonic shock and accepted Bankers Trust's proposal to cap it losses at $27.5 million rather than pay out $17.5 million immediately. In their minds, their positions had deteriorated by approximately $15 million in just two months.

Table 2.4 below illustrates how Bankers Trust tried to close the gap between what Gibson thought it was losing and its actual losses all in a short space of two months but mostly in the last week of February 1994.

BT's credit department was keen on closing out the deals when Gibson's losses hit $17 million (probably the credit limit with which BT was comfortable) but the bank offered to cap losses at $27 million because that was probably Gibson's uppermost credit limit. (Many banks have two unofficial credit tiers to deal with the dynamic nature of the credit risk of derivatives: they have a limit above which the customer cannot open a new trade because they want to leave free the difference between that and the upper limit to absorb passive changes in the existing exposure, and they have another limit where they start to get worried even about the passive exposure.)

Table 2.4 Closing the Gap between Stated and Actual Losses.

Date	Valuation given to Gibson (millions)	Bankers Trust internal valuation (millions)
31 December 1993	−$2.9	−$7.47
23 February 1994	−$8.1	−$15.45
25 February 1994	−$13.8	−$16.25
3 March 1994	−$17.3	−$17.3

Besides credit availability, the other factor that influences the leverage appetite of a derivative provider is its ability to hedge the deal. It is no coincidence that many leveraged deals involved plays on US interest rates — there are numerous hedging vehicles and deep liquidity in the some of them. The latter is very important. In contrast, leveraged plays involving say Italian lire government bonds (BTPs) or French government bonds (OATs) were less common because it is more difficult to hedge large exposures in these instruments. But the volatility of the underlying asset is also a key influencing factor — the more volatile the asset, the higher the potential exposure facing both parties. US interest rate-based instruments are less volatile than say Mexican bonds. The structures can be highly leveraged but still have the same exposure profile as a Mexican bond structure leveraged only 1.5 times (see Chapter 1).

If a bank is comfortable with the potential exposure of a leveraged deal, it is happy to offer leverage to any customer as long as the true exposure of the deal is within that customer's credit line. Why? To the bank it does not make any difference whether it does one simple interest rate swap leveraged twice or two simple swaps — both result in the same exposure which it has to hedge and both generate similar profit margins. If the swap is a complex structure, the bank makes even more money because complex structures have a wider profit margin per swap; so leverage just means multiplying the profit margin per complex swap by the leverage factor.

Some buyers have to provide collateral or an upfront margin for their over-the-counter trades. This acts as a cap on the leverage embedded in any payout formula since the collateral or margin will be set as a percentage of the full (true) exposure of the transaction rather than being set as a percentage of the notional amount. But collateral or margin-posting tends to be restricted to firms whose credit is not good enough to be given a blank-cheque credit line.

INCREASING INVESTMENT YIELDS

P&G's and Gibson's losses were sustained in corporate treasury activities. Other American companies like Atlantic Richfield and Dell Computers suffered their multi-million dollar derivative losses in their investment activity, when the principal value of some of the securities they had bought fell well below par. Britain's Glaxo admitted to losing £115 million on its investments because it had bought *structured notes* and mortgage-backed securities.

These companies joined a long list of professional money managers (Robert Citron of Orange County comes up again), which had to announce that their investment strategy for 1993 went badly astray. Many of them fingered complex derivative products as the culprit for the losses. Most members of this club are mutual funds, but even county councils and colleges in the mid-West, and the Shoshone Indian tribe seem to have found the charms of derivatives too hard to resist. Many of these professional money managers did not invest in derivatives *per se*; instead they bought structured notes/bonds (see box for list of main types of structured notes) and *collateralised mortgage obligations* because these bonds offered higher returns than conventional floating/fixed rate securities in a low interest rate environment. But when interest rates started to rise, these structures had features which responded even more negatively than conventional bonds to rate rises, thus depressing total returns and resulting in large portfolio losses.

MAIN TYPES OF STRUCTURED NOTES

In general, structured notes introduce significant market risk through features such as caps, frequency of coupon resets and the different indexes to which their coupons are tied. (These indexes do not always move in tandem with money market rates, thus introducing what Standard and Poor's calls index risk.)

1. Capped and collared floaters. In the former, LIBOR payments cannot exceed the capped rate. The issuer of a capped floater has effectively bought an interest rate cap from the investor. This cap sets a ceiling, say 8%, on his LIBOR payments throughout the life of the floater. The investor is thus in a short option position. As interest rates rise, the value of this cap (to the issuer) increases while the option seller (the investor) finds himself in an increasingly exposed situation.

Collared floaters have a cap and a floor. The investor here has bought a floor (guaranteeing a minimum interest rate, say 3%, on his investments) and sold a cap, 8%. With a collared floater, the investor enjoys full LIBOR payments between 3 and 8% — if LIBOR rises above 8%, he is capped out and will not earn anything above 8%; similarly if LIBOR fell below 3%, he will enjoy a guaranteed minimum coupon of 3%.

2. Inverse or reverse floating rate notes (shortened to inverse floaters or inverse FRNs). These instruments have coupons that increase as rates decline and decrease as rates rise. The standard formula is set by subtracting a floating rate index from an appropriate fixed rate which itself is doubled. So a typical payout formula is: 12% (2 × 6%) minus three or six-month LIBOR. If this formula involves a multiplier on both the fixed rate and floating rate (for e.g. 4 × 6% minus 3 × three-month LIBOR) then it is a leveraged inverse floater since the multipliers magnify changes in interest rates. (See Chapter 8 for a decomposition of an inverse/reverse FRN.)

3. Index-linked floaters. The coupon payable is tied to long-term interest rates such as the five or ten-year constant maturity Treasury (CMT) in the United States, or constant maturity swap in Europe. If the yield curve

Continued on page 51

Continued from page 50

changed shape with short-term rates rising faster than long-term, the value of the floater could fall well below par (100%) since it would then pay a below-market floating rate. Some floaters have coupon resets based on indices that materially lag short-term interest rates, such as 11th District Cost of Funds Index (COFI). They could also trade below par if short-term rates rose without the indexed rate increasing by the same amount. (The COFI index is a rate based off deposit rates offered by Californian thrift institutions.)

4. Deleveraged and leveraged floaters. So named because the formula determining the coupon contains a multiplier which tends to either down-play (in the case of deleveraged floater) and magnify (in the case of a leveraged floater) changes in interest rates. In a deleveraged floater, the coupon payments are a fraction of a specified index. Consequently, the coupon on the floater does not increase or decrease as rapidly as the index to which is it is pegged. The formula for a deleveraged floater, could be for example, 0.5 × CMT plus 150 basis points. This 150 bp spread is compensation for the coupon not increasing as rapidly as the index and results in the initial coupon being higher than that achieved on a conventional floating rate note. Indeed, this initial coupon could be made even higher by decreasing the deleverage factor to 0.4 or 0.3 — i.e. the investor is giving up more of his potential coupon increases for a higher upfront yield. Since an investor's coupon receipts will always lag overall moves in money market yields, the market value of this investment in a rising interest rate environment could be well below par.

In leveraged floaters, the multiplier is more than one so that changes in interest rates are magnified. The trouble is that this magnification works both ways — if interest rates fall, the investor's returns are greater than the change in interest rates, and if interest rates rise, so are his losses.

5. Dual index notes. The coupon payments are tied to the difference between two indices, typically the CMT and LIBOR. If interest rates increase but not the spread, the coupon remains unchanged so the coupon resets on this note will lag changes in money market rates. The situation worsens if the difference between the two indices narrows as interest rates rise — the note could well have a smaller coupon than it had originally and thus trade below par.

6. Range floaters. They are also known as _accrual floaters_. Such floaters pay an above-market fixed interest rate as long as the reference rate (often LIBOR) stays between an established range, say between 5–7%. For each day that LIBOR is outside the band, the floater earns no interest. (A range floater is decomposed in Chapter 8.)

Some of these losses would have been hidden if financial institutions still adopted accrual accounting. But technological progress has facilitated corporate accountability so that more and more corporates, fund managers and financial intermediaries have started to *mark-to-market* their portfolios; giving an accurate picture of their treasury activities and investment gains and losses.

Indeed, as an aside, the savings and loans (S&L) fiasco in the United States at the end of the 1980s could have been avoided or at least discovered much earlier if mark-to-market accounting was widespread. This is because at the end of the 1970s, S&L firms were in the position of selling 30-year fixed rate mortgages to customers and funding them with short-term (and lower interest rate) deposits. This strategy worked as long as long-term money yielded more than short-term, i.e. the yield curve was positively sloped. But when the US Federal Reserve Board under Paul Volcker started to raise interest rates to combat inflation, short-term rates rose faster than long-term, causing the yield curve to become inverted. As a result, short-term deposits cost more than 30-year fixed rate mortgages, so the S&Ls found themselves in the position of lending money cheaper than they could borrow. No one knew how much trouble they were in because they were not required to mark-to-market. It took the better part of a decade to quantify the disaster.

Structured Notes

There is no doubt that structured notes were the success story of 1993 — Standard and Poor's estimates $85 billion were issued in that year alone. They found welcoming arms in the increasing numbers of professional money managers who measure their performance against a floating-rate benchmark. These buyers were attracted by the comparatively high coupons of structured notes. But these notes only carried a higher coupon because they contained an embedded short position in interest rate options. In other words, often when an investor bought a structured note, he simultaneously sold an interest rate option. The premium earned from selling this options was amortized over the life of the note and converted into a higher coupon. If the investor did not subsequently hedge these embedded options, he was exposed to risks similar to those of an option seller (see Chapters 6 and 7). Consequently, his downside risks were higher than buyers of conventional fixed and floating securities.

The embedded leverage in some structured notes also enabled buyers to enjoy higher yields while markets moved in their favour. This type of synthetic leverage was no different from that taken on by Gibson in its swaps — it magnified price risks. If the buyer's hunch on the underlying markets proved correct he made more money; if he was wrong, he lost greater sums than in an unleveraged environment.

Make no mistake about the underlying rationale of buying structured notes in the early 1990s — the sophisticated investor was expressing his view that interest rates would remain low and was prepared first to sell embedded options to profit from that view, and second, leverage his views by asking (or accepting) multipliers in the payout formula. As in leveraged swaps, the notionals of leveraged structured notes gave no indication of the real exposure of the instrument.

There is no doubt that some less knowledgeable investors did not realize that by buying these securities, they were selling options or engaging in leveraged bets, because some of these features were quite cleverly concealed. They assumed that their principal losses would be limited if market sentiment changed because they had bought floating rate assets. Traditionally, 'floaters' always trade near par because their coupons are reset every three or six months; they thus offer yields which reflect prevailing market rates. This investment principle does not hold true for structured floaters. When US interest rates started to rise, their prices collapsed. This was due to the short option positions, which became more valuable to the buyer as rates went up, and the synthetic leverage which magnified the effects of the upward move in rates.

Yet even if these less knowledgeable investors could not deconstruct their purchases into the basic building blocks (see Chapter 8) and from there derive their value and the risks, they could still have worked out the payout profile of these instruments under different interest rate scenarios. Such an exercise would have shown them how much their coupon receipts would nosedive once interest rates rose.

The Older and Younger Generations

Not all structured notes should be tarred with the same risky/complex brush. A large majority and certainly the first generation of structured notes was made up of capped, collared and inverse floaters. There were no embedded multipliers in the payout formulas and the investor sold simple interest rate options. The second generation consisting of range (accrual) floaters, quantoes, constant maturity Treasury floaters and dual index floaters, to name a few, was more complex and risky. They contained embedded short positions in exotic options and large multipliers in the payout formulaes.

This second generation did not develop in a vacuum — they evolved because banks (or more accurately, their rocket scientists) responded to client demands. The early 1990s saw short-term rates worldwide plunging — six-month US LIBOR touched 3% (Figure 2.13). Professional fund managers, particularly those who manage funds which come under the US Securities and Exchange Commission Rule 2a-7 of the Investment Company Act 1940 which allows investments only in short-term instruments, clamoured for assets that could be classified as short-term, but would better the paltry returns of pure money-market investments. (The criteria that mutual funds must meet in order to conform with SEC Rule 2a-7 on money market funds are: a money market fund can only invest in securities with the highest credit rating [US government agencies and AA-rated corporate debt] and are determined by the fund's board of directors to present minimal credit risks. The maximum maturity of securities is 397 days, but the average maturity must be

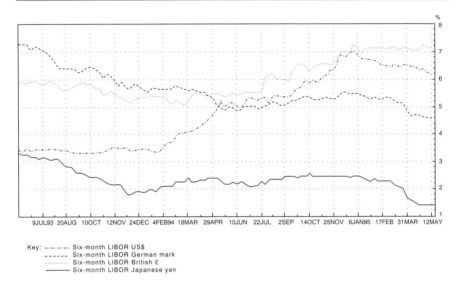

Key: ·—·—·—· Six-month LIBOR US$
        — — — — Six-month LIBOR German mark
        ············ Six-month LIBOR British £
        ———— Six-month LIBOR Japanese yen

Figure 2.13 Short-term Rates: US, Japan, Germany and UK. Reproduced with permission from Bloomberg.

90 days or less.) Banks responded and an array of structured notes slowly found their way into the portfolios of institutional investors, i.e. corporates like Arco and Glaxo and money managers like Piper Jaffray Companies of Minneapolis, and the fund management arms of Bank of America, PaineWebber and Kidder Peabody. Although the precise structure of these notes vary considerably, most of them were designed to perform well in stable or falling interest rate environments, and poorly when interest rates rose.

Structured notes are not the only bonds with embedded options. Neither are embedded options unique to wholesale capital markets. The American homeowner who takes out a fixed rate mortgage enjoys an embedded free option to prepay his mortgage at any time — this causes prepayment risk as shall be explained in Chapter 7, and which has spawned a raft of structures going under the generic title, mortgage-backed securities. *Convertible bonds*, which have been around as long as the Euromarkets and an accepted way of companies raising money, are actually bonds with an embedded equity option. In this case, the company issuing the convertible has sold the investors a call option on the company's stock. A bond whose principal is linked to the value of Japan's Nikkei 225 index or the price of gold (such structures were common in the 1980s) is a bond with an embedded call option on the Nikkei 225 or gold respectively. The difference between the old structures and the ones that appeared in the early 1990s is that in the former, the investor bought options. Consequently, the coupons on such structures were always less than comparable plain vanilla bonds — the option premium the investor had to pay for the option was amortized over the life of the bond and subtracted from the coupon.

In the new structures of the 1990s, the amortized option premium was added to the coupon because the investor had sold options. In this way, they were no different from callable bonds which allow the issuer to call the bond when interest rates decline. A callable bond investor has a fixed rate asset and a put option liability. The issuer would exercise his put option when interest rates fell. A callable bond thus protects an issuer from being stuck with a high coupon issue in a falling interest rate environment. The investor's compensation for this call risk was earning a higher coupon vis-à-vis a plain vanilla issue.

The risks of buying structured products was hammered home when a number of funds were forced to announce their losses. Bank of America's Pacific Horizon Prime money market fund — which used derivatives to increase its yield to 3.22% when the average fund-yield was 2.93% — paid the price because it was forced to plead for a cash bailout of $67.9 million from the parent bank itself. Fund manager Piper Jaffray was reported to have lost at least $700 million; the firm had shareholder equity of $168.9 million at the end of June 1994. PaineWebber had to inject $268 million into a short-term bond fund and subsequently relieved the president of its mutual fund business, Joyce Fensterstock, of her duties.

As of mid-October 1994, there were seven instances of bank holding companies in the United States taking action to support the $1.00 net asset value of proprietary funds advised by their subsidiary banks. Essentially, the holding companies absorbed the losses on their portfolios but in different ways. In four cases, the parent holding companies bought structured notes that were trading below par-value at par, resulting in nominal losses for the parent. In two cases, the holding companies made cash contributions to support the $1.00 net asset value level. In one case, the parent committed to buy from the proprietary fund the structured notes at par, even though the notes were trading way below face value. The parent company in this case also established a reserve to cover possible future losses.

In June 1994, Standard and Poor's, the US rating agency which rates money-market funds (amongst other things), also initiated a review of such funds. It publicly expressed concern that the net asset values of money market funds holding structured securities did not reflect an accurate market value of their underlying portfolios; the agency also warned that it was considering downgrading these funds. In an effort to keep their high ratings, some funds divested the bulk of their structured notes.

Regulators Step In

In the summer of 1994, the US's Securities and Exchange Commission (SEC) and the Office of the Comptroller of the Currency (OCC) issued cautionary memorandums on the risks, and more importantly, the advisability of buying structured notes. Initially, the SEC tried a softly-softly approach by drawing attention to Rule 2a-7 which restricted managers of money market funds to buying securities with less than 397 days remaining maturity. This rule was framed on the premise that the value of such short-dated securities would not fluctuate much from par (100%). But this same rule allowed money-market funds to measure the maturity of a floating rate note to the security's next coupon reset date. So many medium and long-dated structured notes issued by US federal agencies met this criteria because their coupons were reset at least twice a year — the hitch was that some of these coupon resets were based on complicated formulaes resulting in below-market yields. Consequently, the value of these notes fell well below par after the coupons were readjusted.

In December 1993, the SEC was forced to draw attention to an amendment of Rule 2a-7. The release made it clear that measuring a note's maturity by its next coupon reset date was all well and good, but that the board of directors, trustees or the adviser to a fund had to be reasonably satisfied that the note would retain its par value at any time until final maturity or until the principal was recovered through demand. In other words, the SEC wanted money-market fund managers to adhere not only to the letter but the spirit of Rule 2a-7 — that the investments they bought had to have stable net asset values (which investments under a year usually have.) Structured notes, with leveraged coupons or returns tied to the relationship between two indices, or indices that have a delayed reaction to moves in short-term rates, may not have stable net asset values.

In June 1994, the SEC took a tougher approach to structured notes. In a letter to the Investment Company Institute, it stated that money-market funds should divest themselves of five specific types of structured securities: inverse floaters, cost-of-funds index floaters, constant maturity Treasury floaters, dual-index floaters and range floaters. As a result, most investments in structured notes are now regarded as unsuitable for money-market funds.

The OCC which regulates 3300 national banks, which account for 60% of US commercial banks assets, believed that the difficulty of assessing the risks of some structured notes made them an inappropriate investment for most national banks. Its health warning was pretty stark. 'The OCC considers it an unsafe and unsound practice for a bank to purchase material amounts of structured notes, or any other bank asset, without a full appreciation of the risks involved'. If the banks it regu-lated still wanted to buy these instruments, then the OCC wanted them to have the capability of evaluating possible changes in market value resulting from adverse price moves; and the consequent impact on the bank's earnings and/or capital. The OCC warned its members that the most complex notes also suffered very poor liquidity, resulting in significant price discrepancies in the secondary market so that banks had to be diligent and obtain several quotes.

An Epitaph for a Structured Note

Against a background of regulatory pressure and high profile losses the primary market in second-generation notes died. On its tombstone should be inscribed

'Abused or abuser?' Were structured notes abused by their buyers or did they abuse those who bought them?

They were sold as bonds but their only resemblance with low-risk government securities, or conventional corporate bonds, was the principal amount/issuer packaging. Due to their embedded options and leverage, structured notes were much more sensitive to changes in market conditions than conventional bonds. When they plummeted in value in response to interest rates rising, they shocked investors more familiar with the relatively sedate price action of conventional bonds.

But since structured notes result from a bank's rocket scientists mixing and matching swaps and options together to meet precisely a buyer's demands, they could have been sold directly without the bond wrapping. So why were they packaged with a US government agency or supranational agency name? (Indeed the packaging made them more expensive because a public-listing costs money and the issuer needs his fair cut of the deal, or else why should it want to do the deal in the first place?)

The packaging was key to the success of structured notes. Many money managers are not allowed to buy over-the-counter derivatives, but they are allowed to buy publicly-listed bonds issued by US government agencies or similar credits. A structured note — with the payout profile of a portfolio of options and swaps, but having the facade of a bond, a respectable issuer and a public-listing — allowed money managers to overcome some of the restrictions imposed by their board of trustees.

And with embedded leverage, it allowed some investors to get around restrictions on maximum exposure, since most exposure guidelines are still based on notional amounts. Say a fund manager was only allowed to invest 5% of a $1 billion portfolio in securities other than US Treasuries. He buys $50 million structured notes issued by the World Bank. These notes have an embedded leverage of five. The portfolio, in effect, now has $250 million structured notes although it only has $50 million in notional terms. The fund manager is keeping to the letter, if not the spirit of the guidelines; he is, to all intents and purposes, telling the truth when he reports to the trustees or his investors that the portfolio has $50 million structured notes.

Structured notes are the epitome of how investment technology helped and continues to help money managers circumvent guidelines that were framed to protect the interests of small, unsophisticated investors (who place their spare cash with money market funds; not the big boys who give it to speculative hedge funds). Many of these guidelines have not kept pace with derivative developments and the real world. Nowhere is this better illustrated than in the case of Orange County versus Merrill Lynch. Orange County's main argument was that Robert Citron was bound by Section 27000 of the California Government Code which required him to keep safely all money belonging to the County. He was also bound by Codes 53601 and 53635 which refined the broad mandate of Section 27000 and allowed investments in securities issued by US government agencies. As Orange County says in its court filings,

At the time of the enactment of California Government Code 53601 and 53635, the types of structured debt securities involved in this case did not exist. The debt instruments available from agencies and government sponsored enterprises (GSEs) such as Sallie Mae, Fannie Mae and Freddie Mac involved simply the obligation by the enterprise to repay principal and interest at a fixed time and rate. When the California legislative authorised investments in the debt instruments of government agencies and government sponsored enterprises, it was authorising investment in the safest securities available to the investing public, and was simply refining and further limiting the broad mandate of Section 27000 that County funds be kept "safely".

In approximately 1986, the financial markets were presented with the first of what are now called structured debt securities issued by GSE's. Today's GSE's are increasingly offering these types of structured debt instruments. Because the instruments are frequently customised for the needs of a particular investor, no longer are they capable of being generally described [sic]. However, one thing is certain, in many instances the basic "structure" of the instruments converted the obligations of GSE's from being the safest and most conservative in America to instruments of pure speculation. The simple question of law is whether these structured, speculative investments were ever permitted under the state statute that required safety as the primary goal of every county investment decision. They were not.

Conclusion

Investors used structured notes to hide some of the risks they were assuming purposely to generate higher returns. The hitch was that some of these risks were so well camouflaged that the less sophisticated buyers ended up taking on more risks than they had intended. And because these structures had all the appearances of a bond (issuer with good credit quality, publicly-listed, principal repayment, regular coupons), the really naive investor was hoodwinked into buying structures he thought safe. Structured notes are safe, from a credit-risk perspective but the more complex, highly-leveraged ones have substantial market risks.

There is no doubt that the bull market of the early 1990s resulted in excesses committed both by derivative providers and their customers. These excesses, common to corporate treasury and investing activities, centred on the misuse of leverage and over-complex transactions which masked the true risks. In many of the publicized losses involving derivatives, both leverage and complexity were intertwined. Derivatives and investment technology have made it imperative that managers take a long hard look at their internal guidelines to see whether they have caught up with new financial developments. They must differentiate between credit risk and market risk. Relevant guidelines to address these two major types of risk must be framed. Guidelines based on notional exposures must also be updated; they must be set on the true exposures of transactions, rather than their notional values. The use of notional amounts to control the risks of a firm/fund manager is ineffective. Synthetic leverage, unbridled by good management controls, and encouraged by greed, can and has caused some firms to blow up.

SUMMARY

The pressure to perform can cause end-users to misuse derivatives. To achieve a cheaper cost of funding or a better rate of return than those offered by existing market rates, some end-users will agree to structures whose risks are not apparent to the mathematically-untrained eye, or to take on more excessive risks than they should. The extra risks often boil down to the end-user selling simple or complex options and leveraging his exposure to future market moves.

The embedding of both options and leverage (in the form of multipliers) into bonds and swaps has helped end-users and derivative providers alike to misuse derivatives. Because embedding camouflages the risks of options and leverage, it allows unscrupulous salesmen to hide such risks from unknowing customers, or end-users to hide them from their own bosses, or to circumvent outdated guidelines.

Leverage and selling options are not inherently bad, but they must be consistent with the objectives and risk profile of the firm. Procter and Gamble's 5/30 year swap was leveraged up to 31 times, hardly in line with the firm's risk/reward profile. Gibson Greetings lost sight of its original aims in some of its 29 transactions. The firm punted on US interest rates remaining low, and took on option risks it clearly did not understand.

Investors who enjoyed the comparatively higher yields of structured notes and collateralized mortgage obligations (CMOs) did so only because they sold options when they bought such notes. The premium they earned was amortized over the life of the note and added to the normal coupon they would have received had they not sold any options. Many of these options were puts on US interest rates — once American rates started rising in February 1994, these short option positions showed large losses for their sellers. But because the options were embedded into a bond structure, their losses were reflected in the price of the host bond. Consequently, such structured notes and CMOs fell in price much faster than plain vanilla issues. Some of these structures also had embedded multipliers which magnified the effect of interest rate rises on the price of the bond.

Moral of the chapter: there is no free lunch.

3
Beauty *v* The Beast

Given the number of companies that have racked up losses with derivatives — Orange County, Metallgesellschaft, Barings, Japan Airlines, Procter and Gamble, Gibson Greetings and numerous American colleges — it is not surprising that many people view derivatives as inherently risky. Some even believe that allowing corporate treasurers and fund managers to dabble in them is equivalent to letting a ten-year old drive a Formula 1 racing car through busy city streets. As a result, they think these instruments should be banned.

Such an extreme view will recede as memories fade and the media hype dies down. But behind the misinformation and rhetoric is the realization that derivatives can damage your financial health. Derivatives can be consumed sensibly or addictively abused. The choice is entirely at the discretion of the user.

Like motorcars, derivatives have characteristics that can make them dangerous. Two in particular should be singled out. The first is their inbuilt leverage. Called gearing by some, this simply means that buyers can buy control of an asset with only a small outlay. The second characteristic that makes some forms of derivatives potentially hazardous is their *curvature*, or curved payoff profile. This is similar to the acceleration, as opposed to the speed of a car, and will be explained fully in Chapter 6. But while car manufacturers are forced to say how their vehicles will perform, providers of derivatives, until early 1995, were not bound by such disclosure requirements.

But companies should not be thought of as innocent neophytes, hoodwinked by unscrupulous salesmen into buying inappropriate products. That providers have not been forced to disclose the riskiness of the things that they are flogging earlier is partly because it often suits companies themselves not to disclose the products they are buying. This theme will be further developed when, later in the chapter, we look at the annual reports of two companies, America's Gibson Greetings, a card manufacturer and Britain's Gestetner, an office and photographic equipment distributor.

In doing so, we attempt to answer the all-important question: how do you tell the beauty from the beast?

Lack of corporate impetus to lift the veil has been given a helping hand by outdated accounting practices. Derivative instruments are 'off-balance sheet', i.e. they do not appear on either the assets or liabilities side of a balance sheet. Anyone looking at a firm's balance sheet cannot see what derivatives a firm uses, how risky they are, nor indeed how their value has changed over time. Before the use of derivatives was widespread, financial statements, even if they did not give a complete and up-to-date picture of a firm's financial profile at least gave a useful sketch of it. Now they do not. A swap here, an option there, and a firm can tweak its financial exposures without an outsider knowing anything about it. And this can be done very rapidly and cheaply. (Which is, of course, why their use has grown so dramatically in recent years.) But coupled with minimal disclosure, the ability to transform their balance sheets rapidly can be, and has been, abused by firms anxious to shore up poor performance with quick profits from a punt on, say, interest rates. Yet firms' activities in derivatives are covered only with a few inadequate 'notes' in their annual reports.

Nowhere do companies take more advantage of this opacity than in their use of swaps. There are, of course, very good reasons why companies should want to use these. Take, for example, a company that thinks interest rates will rise, but has predominantly floating-rate liabilities. It might enter into a swap in which it would 'swap' its floating-rate payments for fixed rate ones, thus protecting itself against a rise in rates. It is for this reason that swaps have become synonymous with hedging. But swaps can also be used to take positions: there are no rules that say that a company must have an offsetting exposure before it can enter into a swap. The economic impact of a swap for both parties to the transaction is similar to owning (selling) a fixed-rate bond and selling (owning) a floating-rate bond. A firm which is paying floating and receiving fixed is in the same position as it would be if it is short floating-rate notes and long fixed-rate bonds, see Figure 3.1.

A company treasurer expects interest rates to decline. Without a clear brief of what he can or cannot do, he can use the above interest rate swap as a surrogate for a long fixed-rate bond position. He is using the swap to take on interest rate risk as he would do if he bought fixed-rate bonds. If rates fell, he could unwind the swap and record a profit in the same way as he would sell a fixed-rate bond and reap capital gains. Because it was a swap (i.e. a hedge in the eyes of senior management), few questions would be asked. The profit would be reported in the financial statements of the company and everyone would be happy. But what if rates rose rather than fell? The swap would then be loss-making, but, if it was not unwound, there would be no need to say anything about it in a British annual report and only the merest mention would be required in an American one. Better still, senior management or shareholders will ask few or no questions because they thought the swap was a hedge, not a speculative position gone sour.

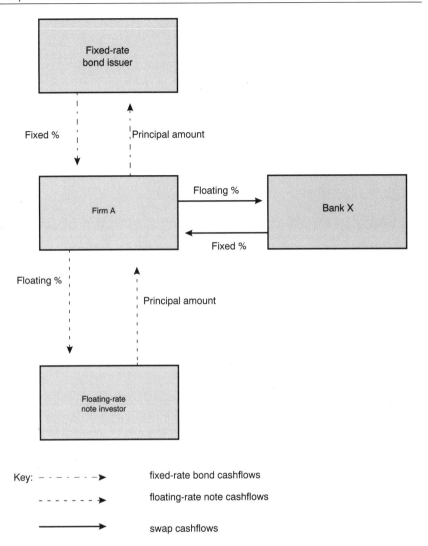

Figure 3.1   Economic Impact of a Fixed-Rate Swap.

Encouraged by falling interest rates in the early 1990s, many companies, mainly American, thought that easy money could be made by betting that rates would fall even further. They entered into various forms of interest-rate swaps. When rates started to rise at the beginning of 1994 (see Figure 3.2), many of these companies had their fingers severely burned. Because the swaps were off-balance sheet, these losses came as a nasty surprise to shareholders when the companies were forced to realize their losses. So whereas in the past, by looking at a company's financial statements over a period of years, you gained an appreciation of the risks, a feeling

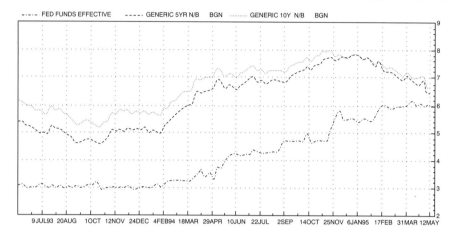

Figure 3.2   US Interest Rates — July 1993 to May 1995. Reproduced with permission from Bloomberg.

of its financial prudence by looking at how its costs and level of gearing changed over time, today that can be changed overnight because derivatives allow rapid transformation of a firm's financial risks.

A Cap on Leverage

Nowhere is this combination of opaqueness coupled with being off-balance sheet more deadly than in leverage. There is nothing unusual with leverage *per se*. Firms, like individuals, gear up when they have insufficient money to invest in things that they need, be it another factory, more equipment, shares, bonds or real estate. All gearing increases the risks run by the firm (or individual). But traditional ways in which firms leveraged themselves were always reflected in the balance sheet. Moreover, the balance sheet itself exercised a restraining influence on the amount that firms could borrow since the loans were based on either the company's assets or its free cashflow. No prudent lender for example would lend funds on which the interest costs were less than twice covered by the firm's earnings before interest and tax. The amount of debt tolerated for any length of time is generally no higher than 75% of a company's total assets. So traditional corporate leverage was both visible and constrained.

But, of course, firms' balance sheets can no longer perform that restraining function if the instruments that they use are not recorded on it. Now invisible leverage can be large enough to blow a company. Ask the unfortunate shareholders of Barings.

Because you only need to put up a small amount of money (margins in the case of futures, premiums in the case of options) to acquire a large position, you can gear up your exposure to a much higher level than you could with cash instruments. Think of it this way — imagine that a company wants to buy shares in American Telegraph and Telephone (AT&T). If it borrows money to buy them, both transactions are recorded on the balance sheet. But if the company buys an option on AT&T, the two transactions are distilled into a single number — the premium it pays, a small percentage of the notional value of the option.

This would be similar to a company borrowing money to build a factory, offsetting the factory against the loan, and only showing the net position on the balance sheet. Because the net number is so much smaller than the full amount of the loan, the company can then go out and borrow more money because it appears to be so under-geared. Thus options offer a lot more leverage than cash instruments; because they are not on the balance sheet, this leverage can be easily abused.

But bringing derivatives onto the balance sheet would not, of itself, do much good unless there is more disclosure on the precise nature of each transaction since the leverage in many of them is hidden. Take structured bonds which contain embedded options or have payout formulas which multiply the effect of interest rate changes. These securities are on-balance sheet items. Describing them in notional value terms is meaningless because the notional masks the amount of leveraged bets the firm is making.

The travails of Orange County, a Californian county council which went bankrupt in 1994, after racking losses of about $2 billion, provide a good example of this (See Chapter 1). True, it also leveraged a lot by borrowing heavily, posting bonds as collateral for its loans, but some of its losses were caused by instruments that go by the snappy title of leveraged inverse floating-rate notes, which magnified the ill-effects of rising short-term rates. Similarly, the British pharmaceuticals giant, Glaxo, lost £115 million (about $185 million) last year from investing in leveraged structured notes and collateralized mortgage obligations, which are bonds issued off a pool of underlying home mortgages. Although the firm was rich enough to shrug off these losses, shareholders might be forgiven for thinking that the firm was less than open about the risks that the company was running. In its 1993 annual report it notes, 'The market risk associated with financial instruments is controlled by means of trading limits and other monitoring systems. The issuers of these financial instruments comprise governments, corporations, major banks and financial institutions with the highest credit ratings.' There is no mention that about 10% of its portfolio was in high-risk structured notes and collateralized mortgage obligations whose returns were skewed to falling rates.

Profit and Loss Transparency

The transparency of derivatives has two dimensions: profit and loss and the risks posed by such instruments. Traditional accounting methods adequately address the profit and loss aspect of conventional instruments: valuing them at cost or at their present value, whichever is the lower, ensures that, for these instruments, bad news showed up in the accounts. But, other than in America, where the

Financial Accounting Standards Board (FASB) has issued directives on disclosing losses, there is precious little profit and loss transparency on a firm's derivative transactions.

Generally, only financial institutions (which mark their trading activities to liquidation value) bring derivative positions onto the balance sheet. For these, big losses cannot be deferred to later periods. Western corporates as a whole try to disguise or delay reporting derivative positions that have gone sour until the potential losses are large enough to materially impact future profit and loss statements or when the losses are realized. But they look like paragons of honesty compared with their Japanese counterparts. Many of these have dragged their feet for ten years and more before telling the world, and their shareholders, about losses that they have made on forward currency transactions. These came about because many Japanese companies bought dollars in the mid-1980s, thinking that it would strengthen against the yen. It did not and they racked up huge losses which they were able to disguise by 'rolling over' these contracts (forwards were off-balance sheet so their shareholders were none the wiser).

In April 1992 the Ministry of Finance banned companies from rolling over these losses and 'asked' them to realize their losses. Few did. Then, in March 1994, the Ministry of Finance told companies that they had to realize their losses by March 1995. That autumn huge currency losses started to crawl out of the woodwork of corporate Japan. According to a Japanese research institution, Tokyo Shoko Research, 211 Japanese companies reported combined currency losses of ¥99.6 billion (US$1 billion) for the year September 1993 to September 1994. Japan Airlines' losses for that same period accounted for half Tokyo Shoko's estimates. (JAL's total unrealized losses from forward transactions since the mid-1980s, including the ¥50 billion loss for September 1993 to 1994 was ¥176 billion ($1.77 billion). The US dollar equivalents are based on a yen/US dollar rate of 99.4).

JAL's story is not unique. Kashima Oil, a refiner of imported oil, suffered a similar embarrassment. As long ago as 1988, Kashima realized that it had huge unrealized currency losses. At the time, these amounted to some ¥100 billion (US$1 billion). As the yen rose they mounted. By April 1994, unable to stand the pain any longer (and, no doubt, with a few promptings from the Ministry of Finance) it declared losses of ¥153 billion ($1.53 billion). This came as a bit of a shock to shareholders who had been led by the company to expect pre-tax profits for that year of ¥12.5 billion ($0.12 billion).

International accounting bodies have made moves to close such loopholes and to improve the profit and loss transparency of derivatives. America's Financial Accounting Standards Board (FASB) has set the pace. In November 1994, it suggested an approach that would move derivatives onto the balance sheet. Hedge accounting would be replaced with *mark-to-market* accounting for all derivative transactions. All firms would be required to state whether a derivative contract was being used for trading or for hedging. Gains or losses from trading them would have to be taken into the income statement immediately but those from hedging transactions could be shown in a new adjustment to shareholders equity until the gains or losses are realized. There would also be no restrictions on the type of exposure that could be hedged nor a test of whether a derivative was an effective hedge.[1]

FASB's crusade in the P&L transparency area started with its Statement 105. This required companies to disclose information about 'the extent, nature, terms and credit risk of financial instruments with off-balance sheet risk of accounting loss and the concentrations of credit risk for all financial institutions.' Subsequently, Statement 107 required firms to disclose, either in the body of the financial statements, on in the accompanying notes, the fair value of financial instruments.

But because options purchased have no risk of accounting loss, they were not covered by both statements. In October 1994, FASB issued Statement 119, to address this shortcoming. Companies with assets of $150 million or more had to comply with Statement 119 in their 1994 year-end financial statements, and those with less in their 1995 year-end reports.

For options and other derivatives not covered by Statement 105, a firm must disclose either in the body of the financial statements or in the accompanying notes the following information:

1. The face, contract or notional amount.

2. The nature and terms, including, at a minimum, a discussion of (i) the credit and market risk of those instruments, (ii) the cash requirements of those instruments (iii) the related accounting policies.

Statement 119 also makes it clear that firms which use leveraged instruments must disclose the leverage features and their effects when they disclose the notional amounts of their derivative instruments. This disclosure requirement affects derivatives covered by Statements 105, 107 and 119, i.e. swaps, forwards, futures, interest rate caps and floors and options held.

American companies must also make a distinction between derivatives held for trading purposes and for purposes other than trading. For the former category, a firm must disclose the average fair value during the reporting period as well as the fair value at the end-of-the reporting period; and the net trading revenues. For the latter category, the firm must disclose its objectives for holding or issuing the derivatives, its strategies for achieving those objectives, their recognition and measurement policies and information about hedges of anticipated transactions.

As a result of the FASB's initiatives, American companies now, more than companies anywhere else in the world, provide information about their derivatives activity. Moreover, FASB has tackled the issue head on by issuing guidelines in the more contentious area of accounting standards (the numbers part of an annual report) as opposed to the more accommodating, descriptive first half. In the US this is known as the Management's Discussion and Analysis (MD&A) and in the United Kingdom as the Operating and Financial Review (OFR.)

In contrast, the UK's Accounting Standards Board (ASB) and the Association of Corporate Treasurers (ACT) have channelled their energies on improving derivative disclosure in the OFR. The ASB and the ACT recommend that directors provide the following details about their treasuries' activities:

1. The effect of exchange rates and inflation differentials on operating activity;
2. The capital structure, with details on the firm's borrowings broken into type, currency and maturity bands, relevant measures of interest cover and gearing, and what covenants the firm has in place. Information on funding activity should include the purpose and effect of major financing transactions and the effect of actual and potential interest costs on profits.
3. The objectives of interest rate and foreign exchange risk management including a policy statement on hedging and how derivatives are used and the way in which such activities are controlled.
4. Identifying liquidity needs, showing peak borrowing requirements and liquidity margins as well as the short- and medium-term facilities the firm has in place
5. Cash generation.

This sort of information can be very useful if the firm wants to disclose its derivative activities; bland if it does not because a firm can hide behind waffly platitudes while maintaining that it is trying to make its derivative activities more transparent.

Risk Transparency

FASB initiatives are important to promoting risk transparency because only if it does succeed in achieving P&L transparency is there any hope of getting companies to come clean about the riskiness of the derivatives they are using.

It is generally agreed that balance sheets have never really captured all the financial risks facing a firm, indeed that they were not designed for such purposes. The function of balance sheets, some accountants would say, is to account historically, i.e. to tell shareholders what the management of a company has done with their money. While inferences can be drawn, for example, that there is credit risk and interest rate risk in a loan portfolio; these risks cannot be quantified without further information on maturities, counterparties and the proportion of secured versus unsecured lending. Balance sheets are past certainty, risks are future uncertainty — the two are diametrically opposed.

Firms have always had off-balance sheet risks. Leasing is one good example, currency risks are another. If off-balance sheet risks are not new, why the fuss about derivatives? Simply, because the advent of derivatives has increased hugely the volume and complexity of off-balance sheet risks. Investors now have a far tougher time deciding what a company's off-balance sheet exposures are, and how they relate to its balance-sheet risks.

Investors also have to cope with the fact that off-balance sheet transactions can alter the nature of on-balance sheet risks. Hedging the price of jet fuel with crude oil futures contracts, for example, opens an airline company to a new, though lesser *basis* risk, i.e. that changes in the price of jet fuel are not always tracked, step by step, by changes in crude prices. To understand the ramifications of such new risks on a company, financial reports need far better disclosure of the risks that companies are running.

Once again FASB is leading the assault. Not only does it now require companies to give more information on how off-balance sheet items have affected their income (Statement 119), it also encourages them to be more open about the *market risks* of these activities and to provide detailed descriptions of their derivative policies, strategies and controls.

True, this is not mandatory. FASB was concerned that some firms would have difficulty gathering and calculating the necessary information for the 1994 year-end statements. But there is a more fundamental problem. There is no agreement about of the best method of quantifying market risks, nor the form in which this information should be presented. This is why FASB has suggested a variety of ways in which it can be presented. These include giving more details about current positions (including leverage factors if any), the hypothetical effects on the firm's annual income or equity resulting from several possible changes in market conditions and the money the firm might lose or gain due to changes in market conditions, over a given holding period and a specified *confidence interval* (so-called *value at risk*, see Chapter 9).

Analysis of Two Annual Reports

Greetings from Gibson

The story of Gibson Greeting Cards illustrates how poorly served investors are by annual reports, even after FASB's new guidelines. Gibson has been singled out not because it is any worse than other American companies, but because, having taken on some derivatives trades that back-fired, information about its derivative activity since 1992 is in the public domain. This allows a comparison between what was reported versus what is now known. (Gibson's losses from derivative transactions over a period of two years could have cost it $27 million; not an insignificant amount since its net income for the years 1989 to 1993 was less than $50 million per annum. It sued Bankers Trust, the counterparty to all its derivative transactions and reached an out-of-court settlement in November 1994.)

The 1992 annual report contains the following disclosures about its derivative activities:

> The Company periodically enters into interest rate swap agreements with the intent to manage the interest rate sensitivity of portions of its debt. At December 31, 1992,

the Company had four outstanding interest rate swap agreements with a total notional amount of $67 200 (000). Two of the agreements, with terms similar to the related bonds, effectively change the Company's interest rate on $3 600 (000) of industrial revenue bonds to 6.67% through February 1998. The other two agreements, the original terms of which were five years and four and one-half years, effectively change the Company's interest rate on $30 000 (000) of senior notes to 5.41% through April 1993 and 5.44% through October 1993 and thereafter to a floating rate obligation adjusted semi-annually through October 1997. The estimated cost to terminate the Company's swap portfolio would be $775 (000) at December 31, 1992.

From this, the company's derivative activities seemed fairly ordinary. They weren't. More information about the firm's derivative activities became available when Gibson sued Bankers Trust Company of New York, the bank with which Gibson had been dealing, and when the *Commodity Futures Trading Commission*, the regulator that oversees most of the derivatives industry, and the *Securities and Exchange Commission* fined Bankers Trust. A number of key points about Gibson's swap transactions were not included in the 1992 disclosure.

- Gibson originally entered into two plain vanilla interest rate swaps, each with a notional value of $30 million, kept them for eight months and then cashed them in for a profit of $260 000 in July 1992.

- For three months, the company made no attempt to enter into other swaps to bring down its interest cost on its fixed-rate bonds. Then, in October 1992, it entered into two new derivative transactions, each with a notional amount of $30 million. Had they been given in the 1992 notes, details of these transactions would have given Gibson shareholders a better appreciation of the financial risks the company was taking. With these structures, the Gibson treasury team was, essentially, taking a massive punt that US interest rates would continue to fall. (for an analysis of these structures see Chapter 2).

- After year-end, but before the annual report was published, Gibson had entered into two more derivative transactions, each again with a notional of $30 million. Again these swaps carried substantial risks if interest rates rose.

Why did Gibson enter into two complex swaps, three months after it took profits on plain vanilla ones? Did they reduce the costs of its debts more? One of them, the ratio swap, certainly appeared to be a good deal. For the first two payments (covering the first year of the swap), Gibson had to pay interest rates of only 1.581% and 1.893%. In return it received fixed payments of 5.5% from Bankers Trust. This yielded Gibson a guaranteed income of $600 000 in 1993. The flipside was that Gibson was left extremely vulnerable to interest rate increases from year two onwards. It found this out the hard way.

Why did Gibson take this risk? The clue lies in a letter that its chairman, Benjamin Sottile, sent to shareholders, in which he told them that Gibson's largest customer, Phar-Mor Inc had filed for bankruptcy protection under Chapter 11 in

August 1992. Gibson was forced to foot the costs of writing off all the long-term sales agreements related to Phar-Mor. This resulted in a third-quarter loss of $20.1 million.

It is not possible to compare Gibson's disclosure of its swap activities in the 1993 annual report with its 1992 annual report because the firm was forced to withdraw the former because it was inaccurate. This was due to one of Gibson's subsidiaries, Cleo, overstating its inventory which resulted in an approximate 20% overstatement of Gibson's consolidated net income as well as the accrual of an unrealized market value of $3.1 million on two derivative transactions, which did not qualify as hedges, partially offset by the recognition of a $2.0 million previously deferred gain from certain derivative transactions entered into and/terminated during 1993 which also did not qualify as hedges.

But in its mandatory annual report filing to the Securities and Exchange Commission, the 10-K/A, the firm amended its 1993 consolidated financial statements. A shareholder might be forgiven for thinking that he was reading about a different company, so complete is the apparent U-turn in Gibson's use of derivatives compared with what it claimed to be up to in its 1992 annual report.

This is an extract from item 7 of the amended management's discussion and analysis in Gibson's 10-K:

The Company periodically entered into interest rate swap or derivative transactions with a financial institution to manage the interest rate sensitivity of a portion of its debt. Certain of the derivative transactions executed during 1993 did not qualify as effective interest rate hedges and, accordingly, the proceeds realised from such transactions (approximately $2.0 million) have been recognised as a component of the loss on derivative transactions, net in the accompanying 1993 Consolidated Statement of Income. Additionally, the estimated current market value of two derivative transactions outstanding at December 31, 1993 which likewise did not qualify as effective interest rate hedges, was a loss of $3.1 million which was accrued in the accompanying 1993 consolidated financial statements. The market value of the derivative transactions at December 31, 1993 was determined by a financial institution's valuation based on the projected future value of the transactions at maturity.

On March 4, 1994, the Company announced that, based on trading of swap/derivative positions subsequent to year-end, the Company had entered into two new transactions with a financial institution which will result in a minimum loss of $3.0 million and a maximum potential loss of $27.575 million. These two transactions have caps on the Company's total exposure and replace previous uncapped positions. The new transactions, which mature in June and August 1995, may be liquidated at any time prior to maturity and had an estimated cost of termination of approximately $17.5 million at March 4, 1994. As these positions do not constitute effective hedges, they will be reported at their current fair market value until they mature or are closed out, and fluctuations in such value will affect earnings in future periods. The combined effect of these two transactions is that the Company's losses on these transactions will be between $3.0 million and $27.575 million. The Company's losses would be minimized at $3.0 million if the six-month LIBOR rate is at or below 3.9% on June 7, 1995 and the basis point spread for interest rate swaps (the swap spread) relative to the 10.75% US Treasury note maturing August 15, 2005 is at or above 33.5 basis points on August 15, 1995. On the other hand, its losses would be maximized at $27.575 million if the six-month LIBOR rate equals or exceeds 5.90% on June 7, 1995 and the swap spread is 20 basis points or less on August 15, 1995. The Company may elect to liquidate the transactions at any time prior to maturity based on market conditions prevailing at the time. As of June 30, 1994, the six-month LIBOR rate was 5.25% and the swap spread was 25.2 basis points. These transactions are still held by the Company and at June 30, 1994 had an estimated net cost of termination of approximately $23.0 million.

Gibson gave so much detail about its swap transactions because the potential losses it was forced to disclose were so vast in relation to the size of the company that they threatened its very survival (although the company went out of its way to try to stress that these losses of up to $27 million were accounting rather than real losses). The firm had a net income of about $20 million in 1993, $7 million in 1992 and $42 million in 1991.

These revelations were a trifle late. Shareholders would presumably have preferred to know about these exposures — and how much they might cost the company — before they nearly brought the company to its knees.

Gestetner's Incomplete Fax

Compared with other companies, the derivative losses suffered by Gestetner, a UK-based company specializing in office and photographic equipment distribution were trifling. The company declared in September 1994 that it had suffered exceptional losses of £6.1 million on two leveraged swaps. No other details were given with the one-line declaration, no explanation of why the company had entered into leveraged swaps, i.e. swaps whose cashflow payments magnify changes in interest rates. Shareholders had to be content with the explanation of Steven King, the finance director, in the financial review section of the 1993 annual report. 'Interest rate risk is managed to provide a measure of long term certainty whilst enabling advantage to be taken from favourable interest rate movements. Various financial instruments, such as swaps and *forward rate agreements*, are used to implement Group policy.'

It is unclear whether this vague policy statement allowed the use of leveraged swaps. Shareholders were left in the dark as to when the two leveraged swaps were first executed or how big they were. (Press reports suggested one swap was for $20 million and the other for £20 million. There was no mention of their maturities.) Small though the absolute loss amount was, it was a comparatively large figure for Gestetner since its profits before tax for the 14 months ending 31 December, 1994 were only £22.2 million.

Gestetner was equally unilluminating when it made big profits from its swaps transactions. Its 1993 annual report noted that it made £4.2 million in 1993 and £3.0 million in 1992. Profits from interest rate swaps therefore contributed 15% of its 1993 trading profit or 70% of its dividend. Despite their materiality, details of its swaps were delineated neither in the group's profit and loss accounts nor in the notes. There was no attempt to explain how Gestetner was managing to make more money through swaps than it was on the whole of its UK business, which only made £2.7 million. When the company announced its interim results in July 1994, there was no warning of any adverse impact that rising rates may have had on the swaps' market value. This, despite the fact that the board was aware of a small potential liability. Two months later, in September, Gestetner closed the swaps, announced its £6.1 million losses and saw its market capitalization drop by 15% in one day.

Gestetner's response to these losses was to appoint Price Waterhouse to advise on risk management, announce that it no longer entered into leveraged deals and that from henceforth, all swaps had to be approved at board level. There was no explanation about why it executed these transactions in its 1994 annual report. Chairman David Thompson's letter to the shareholders cast no light either. 'It was regrettable that we had to announce in September 1994 an expectional loss of £6.1 million arising from geared interest rate swap contracts. The improvements in management controls that were being implemented prior to this event are now sufficient to ensure no repetition of such a problem in the future.'

And this is probably the biggest difference between the UK and the US. In both countries, companies may serve up equally misleading platitudes about the risks they are running in their derivatives positions. But at least companies in America are forced to come clean when they do trip up. This, of course, is too late. So both annual reports beg a question. Does the absence of widely accepted and recognized accounting practices for off-balance sheet items (and the resultant lack of transparency) mean that firms are more willing to assume greater risks than if they had to disclose the risks that they were running?

Conclusion

Most regulators or trade bodies believe that treasury management has a direct impact on shareholder value. However few companies, other than financial institutions, would regard it as a driver of shareholder value. Most companies strive for competitive advantage in their core businesses via product innovation, lower costs, better service, etc. When a firm needs to use consistently treasury operations to make a reasonable group profit, something is clearly wrong. Corporate treasuries are a support function. To add value, they can use a whole range of instruments aggressively, but with the proviso that such actions do not increase the aggregate financial risks to which the company is exposed to by its core business.

Yet, at the moment, it is rare for a company report to give a clear picture of a company's derivative philosophy either in the balance sheet notes or in the management overview. Few make it clear, for example, whether their treasuries are allowed to sell options. Few state in black and white what discretion the treasury is given for hedging, and what risks may arise from such activities.

Only after it took a derivative write-off of $102 million on its 1994 third quarter earnings, did Procter and Gamble issue a statement clarifying its financing philosophy. The 1994 annual report notes:

Our philosophy about the use of financial instruments is to manage risk and cost. Our policy on derivatives is not to engage in speculative leveraged transactions.

The Company has taken steps to substantially increase the oversight of the Company's financial activities, including the formation of a Risk Management Council.

The Council's role is to insure that the policies and procedures approved by the Board of Directors are being followed within approved limits, that transactions are properly analysed prior to implementation, and that they are regularly monitored once implemented.

The Risk Management Council goes well beyond normal corporate operating controls. With these new procedures in place, the shareholders of the Corporation can be assured that the Company's management has taken the appropriate steps so that the situation which led to the Third Quarter write-off will not happen again. (The P&G case is discussed in Chapter 2.)

P&G has learnt its lesson the expensive way. So have many other companies. Others have escaped unscathed. But that does not mean their positions are any less dangerous; and shareholders should be informed of the kind of things that they are buying. The only way to do so is to have full and honest disclosure of their off-balance sheet risks.

SUMMARY

Derivatives can be properly or improperly used because they are off-balance sheet instruments. It is hard for an outsider to judge whether a firm is using them wisely or not because there is no onus on a company to enlighten its shareholders on the objectives and details of its derivative deals and the attendant risks. Extracts from Gibson Greetings' and Gestetner's annual reports show that some companies prefer to indulge in the policy of divulging less rather than more.

The Financial Accounting Standards Board of the United States has made the most headway in forcing companies to report more about their derivative activities; consequently American firms lead the world in corporate derivative disclosure. Statement 119 requires companies to disclose the objectives and full details of all their derivative transactions and to make a distinction between derivatives that are used for hedging and those that are held for trading purposes. Firms are required to inform shareholders of the average fair value during the reporting period and at the end of the reporting period for those derivatives used for trading. Companies with assets of more than $150 million had to comply with this Statement in their 1994 annual reports, and those with less in their 1995 reports.

REFERENCE

1. *Highlights of Financial Reporting Issues,* January (1995) Financial Accounting Standards Board, Connecticut, USA.

PART TWO
ANALYSING THE RISKS

INTRODUCTION

Derivatives were invented and remain popular largely because they mitigate financial risks by reducing uncertainty faced by firms. But these instruments themselves are manifestations of the different types of financial uncertainty, and their risks spring from these variations. This section examines these risks.

Chapter 4 deals with spot-market risks. The increasing trend of marking-to-market and the need to aggregate all risks into a single base currency has resulted in a situation where the volatility of asset prices — by themselves and relative to a base currency — from one marking period to another, is key to quantifying overall uncertainty. The ascendancy of marking-to-market means that these spot risks would have been apparent even without the arrival of derivatives; indeed spot risks are the most important risk of derivatives.

Derivatives are contracts whose performance require asset flows occurring at future dates. For those derivatives involving future asset flows whose date and amount are known, the uncertainty inherent in them can be reduced to computing the 'present' value of receiving or paying such assets at their future date. This is the job of the forward market. Factors affecting the spread between the current price of an asset and its forward price include considerations of financing charges, delivery nuances as well as supply and demand. Because the cost of funding is the main factor, it is appealing to reduce the study of forward risks to interest rate sensitivity, but the non-finance forward risks which nearly toppled Metallgesellschaft are a reminder that forward risks are more than just interest rate-related.

Chapters 6 and 7 introduce specific option risks. Options introduce a whole new dimension to the word 'uncertainty'. With spot risks, a firm is certain about how much of a given asset/liability it owns/owes, but is uncertain about its future value relative to its base currency. With forward risks, a firm is certain of the date on which it will pay/receive a certain amount of a given asset but is uncertain about how to 'present value' that future asset relative to its current spot price. With options nothing is certain — whether the asset flows happen at all, as well as how large and on what dates they will occur. (That is why mortgage-backed securities fit into a discussion on options better than they do in fixed-income bonds.)

Ordinary European options have fixed dates and amounts, not unlike forwards; the only additional uncertainty is whether the flows happen or not, which is at the discretion of the option buyer. American options introduce uncertainty about the date on which the asset flows will occur, if they happen, again at the discretion of the option buyer. Index options (and other 'contracts for differences products') display uncertainty about the amount of the asset flow, plus whether and when they will occur. 'Exotic' derivatives can bundle several of these uncertainties together. Simply valuing a contract with these additional levels of uncertainty is challenging enough, not to mention the task of attempting to quantify the sensitivity of the contract to those inherent risks.

This section analyses these three types of risk — spot, forward and option — from a qualitative standpoint. The discussion is not purely conceptual, as there are copious examples throughout. Consistent with the rest of the book, the assumption here is that a lay reader can grasp the essentials of risk types without drowning in stochastic calculus.

4

Spot Risks

Derivatives are a means to an end; they have flourished because they allow an individual or a firm a way of mitigating the effects of future price uncertainty. But in so doing, they serve another purpose — they transmit information about how market participants feel about the future. Seen from this perspective, derivatives are integral to the efficient functioning of economies and markets; in an informational sense they link the present with the future.

The spot market is the touchstone of any capital or commodity market, fulfilling the primary and essential function of assigning a current value to any security or commodity (currencies, wheat, oil, equities, World Bank bond, etc.) It is a precondition to the efficient functioning of any economy. But because this current value changes in response to fundamental and technical factors, it is crucial that a well-functioning spot market be open as continuously as possible. In this sense the currency markets are closest to operating on a 24-hour basis as major currency trading books are passed from the Far East to Europe to America and back to the Far East.

Keeping markets open all the time deals with only one aspect of price dynamism: the current value. In many markets, it is useful, even necessary, to supplement current spot prices with a mechanism that allows participants to anticipate the future, so that they can neutralize this future uncertainty. Enter the forward market, a conduit for market participants to determine today the expected value of assets at different points in time in the future. In its most primitive form, a forward market may contain a few prices for a few future dates; as the forward market deepens and becomes more liquid, it is possible to form a forward curve, where expected values can be projected for virtually every date between today and say, up to 30 years into the future. This knowledge of the 'best guesstimates' of future valuations as well as the ability to transact now, for the future, allows participants to inject more precision into their planning, and in so doing, lessen the debilitating effects of not knowing what is going to happen in the future.

Yet forward prices alone are not enough. Any forward price represents, in some way, the 'average' estimate of the future value of an asset; there could be a fair number of disparate views which make up that average. This dispersion of individual estimates reflects uncertainty about likely events that could affect the future value of these assets. Because the forward market distills the information it imparts about an asset on a given future date down to a single price, it is impossible for it to illustrate the uncertainty inherent in that 'average'. (For example, say we have two shares both trading at £5. One has been trading between £4.50–£5.50 for the past year while the other had been trading at between £3–£7 for the past year and only hit £5 yesterday due to takeover rumours. It is obvious that there is far more uncertainty in the latter case.)

Techniques that have been developed to measure price uncertainty include moving averages, trading ranges and historical volatilities, but all suffer from the disadvantage of looking backwards to historic prices. While it is true that the past has some bearing on the future, historical data can never adequately predict the future. This is where options come in. One way an economy or market can assess future uncertainty itself is by creating an option market to supplement a forward market. Because an option pays off in only one direction, its value is proportional not only to the 'average' forward price, but also to the amount of uncertainty surrounding that average forward price; the greater the uncertainty, the higher the option price. Options thus communicate how confident market participants are about their current projections of future prices. But it is not the option price that is the precise measure of this level of confidence; it is the volatility implicit in the current option price.

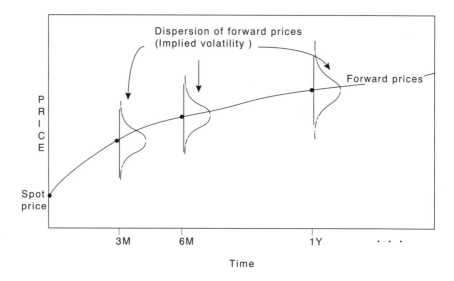

Figure 4.1   Relationship between Spot, Forward and Option Risks.

Figure 4.1 illustrates the relationship of spot, forward and option markets. It is clear that all three markets are manifestations of how market participants cope with the various dimensions of price dynamism; that the latter two allow the management of risks across time. But since forwards and options derive their value from spot prices, the starting point of managing derivative risk is to understand and manage the risks of the spot market.

SPOT RISK — SPOT INSTRUMENTS

The spot markets are the cash or physical markets of the various asset classes: equities, interest rates, currencies, precious and base metals and commodities. Anyone dealing in spot instruments knows that the main concern is price changes. So spot risk has become synonymous with price risk and whenever anyone talks about spot risk, he is referring to the directional risk that is associated with the spot price of an asset moving up or down.

A phrase that has become very fashionable is *market risk* but what exactly does it mean? Market risk is a blanket term that covers all the risks facing a portfolio manager arising from changes in market conditions. For a portfolio consisting of Intel and Merck shares, Treasury bonds and gold, movements in market conditions are almost exclusively reflected in the changing prices of those underlying assets. For this portfolio, market risk is almost equal to price risk, since adverse price changes can severely impact future profitability. The qualification 'almost' is used because the manager of the above portfolio must also worry about liquidity and credit risks. But if he bought only US Treasuries then his market risks can be distilled to only one thing: whether interest rates move up or down thus affecting the price of his US Treasury, i.e. price risk. (It is assumed of course that the US government will never go bankrupt (therefore no credit risk) and that there will always be a bid-offer price for US Treasury obligations (no liquidity risk), but if we do not assume that, then we might as well throw most of modern finance out of the window.)

But once this manager's portfolio consists of forwards, or options, or even just one US dollar-denominated bond with an embedded option, the market risk of that portfolio is more than just price risk. The portfolio is no longer exclusively sensitive to moves in interest rates or the price of Merck shares, but also to changing volatilities of US interest rates and Merck share prices, and even the passing of time. A fuller description of the components of market risk is given in Appendix 3, which is full text of the *G-30* working paper of the valuation and market risk management subcommittee.

So the generalization that a cash portfolio comprising spot market instruments such as bonds, shares and gold only has price risk is for the most part true. But it is a generalization that is slowly being eroded because more and more of these cash instruments have derivatives embedded in them which means they have more than price risks. Having said that, price risk is still the single largest risk facing all market participants; in their jargon it is a first-order risk.

If not managed properly, price risks can bring a financial entity to its knees. Indeed, as we saw in Chapter 1, forwards and options were created to help corporates, investors and financial intermediaries rid themselves of price risk. If an investor had a portfolio of German government bonds and was worried that its price would plummet in the short-term, but was confident of its long-term prospects, he did not need to sell them. He could protect himself against this temporary setback by selling German bond futures or buying a put option. (In doing so, he has laid off his spot risk but has taken on interest rate risk if he sold futures, or volatility risk if he bought an option.) But because the value of the future or the option was dependent on the price of the underlying German bond, they too had spot risk. The varying nuances of this spot risk in relation to forward-based and option-based instruments will be explained in detail later in this chapter.

Chapter 1 recounted the role of leverage in the $2.0 billion losses suffered by Orange County. But this rich opulent county south of Los Angeles was also a victim of price risk because its treasurer, Robert Citron, did not hedge the $21 billion portfolio against the ill-effects of rising interest rates. As a result, Citron had tremendous price risk — although he did have exposure to some option risks because there were embedded options in some of his bonds, the fact that he was totally exposed to the directional moves of interest rates was his undoing. Citron bet the ranch on rates remaining low or falling. And by leveraging the funds at his disposal, he magnified his price risk by the factor of his leverage.

Mark-to-Market

But the Orange County story illustrates another important point of the stories of financial losses that so dominated the press in 1994: the rise of mark-to-market accounting in the past ten years which has forced many financial entities to be more candid. Orange County did not mark-to-market its portfolio on a daily or weekly basis; if it did, it might have been able to avoid some of the large losses it suffered because Citron's superiors would have been able to see the hammering the portfolio was taking as interest rates climbed, and taken corrective action earlier. All major financial institutions and firms like Glaxo and Intel with large investment portfolios are marking-to-market because it is the only valuation technique that correctly reflects the current value of a portfolio. The G-30 survey, conducted in July 1993, found over half of the end-users polled marked-to-market their positions. The follow-up survey conducted in late 1994 showed that two-thirds of end-users marked-to-market, although only 21% did it on a daily basis while 31% did it monthly.

There are no longer any material impediments to firms not marking-to-market because the technological advances of the past decade have made it so easy and relatively cheap. The widespread use of computers, the relative cheapness of processing power and the ease of accessing market data have also facilitated more accountability since staff at corporate treasuries are now forced to give senior management an accurate picture of their treasury activities and investment gains and losses. This switch from accrual to mark-to-market accounting concentrates the mind on market risks wonderfully, since a manager can no longer hide losses in the morass of accrual accounting and wait for the bond to be redeemed at par on maturity, or the market to move in his favour. Marking-to-market may just be a paper loss, but it certainly exposes the weaknesses of the strategies pursued by anyone running a large trading portfolio.

Indeed one can even venture the proposition that price risks were not a widespread concern until the adoption of mark-to-market accounting, since if you did not mark-to-market, you did not have to quantify your price risks. The spot risk was always there — it was just hidden or deferred until the loss was actually taken.

So the losses that have been reported are not unique to these times — they have just been highlighted because for trading portfolios, the switch from accrual accounting to mark-to-market has resulted in higher swings in reported returns, therefore increasing the need for managers to focus on the volatility of the under-lying markets.

Marking-to-market has therefore introduced spot price uncertainty into a firm's valuations. In spite of the shortcomings of marking to original cost, there was at least the element of stability in a firm's valuation. Once a firm's valuations depends materially on dynamic market parameters, then any 'snapshot' valuation is incom-plete without some accompanying description of the stability of that number, i.e. the volatility of the asset concerned. Marking-to-market thus requires supplemen-tary information to quantify the amount of uncertainty (or risk) involved in the valuation.

But market valuations are ultimately presented in one base currency, normally the currency in which the equity of the firm is denominated. (The need to translate it into a base currency is to enable aggregation into a single number to take place.) So a firm with assets and liabilities in several currencies introduces another element of uncertainty into its valuations, other than that of the price volatility of the relevant asset/liability. Regardless of how carefully the valuation in local currency has been done, this currency translation means that firms must pay attention to the risks that arise from the imperative of bringing the valuation of various assets and liabilities into a single base currency. To arrive at the full mark-to-market picture, a shareholder or analyst must have information on the volatility of the base currency in relation to currencies in which the firms deal.

Volatility

The more volatile an asset's prices the more exaggerated the price risks. Although all assets go through bursts of volatility, it is an accepted fact that some asset classes are more volatile than others. Intuitively, you know that equities are more volatile than bonds and that commodities are more volatile than equities. But within each asset class there is a whole spectrum of volatilities. Mexican Brady bonds for example are more volatile than German bunds and Hong Kong shares move around a lot more than British shares.

Volatility must therefore be expressed in a standardized manner if it is to impart any objective information about the riskiness of an asset/instrument, precisely because market participants' impressions of volatility are clouded by their experience. An investor who specializes in emerging markets has very different views from a fund manager who only invests in OECD countries on what constitutes a volatile asset.

Measuring volatility, however, requires a statistical method or model to be imposed on an asset's prices. Modelling an asset's prices implies modelling the distribution of its prices, thus the volatility of the asset can be measured and expressed in statistical terms. Since asset prices are supposed to move randomly, they are assumed to have a form of cumulative distribution called lognormal distribution. (Lognormal distribution rather than *normal distribution* is used because commodity or financial asset prices can rise indefinitely but cannot fall below zero.)

Volatility is measured in terms of *standard deviations* of the asset's returns, and the norm is to express the volatility of an asset as a one standard deviation of the price change, in percent, over a one-year period. So if an asset has a volatility of 15%, that means that the asset's price would be expected to fluctuate within a range 15% higher or lower than the forward price. A one annualized standard deviation (68%), means this price range would be expected for two-thirds of the days in a year.

There are different types of volatilities and these are explained in detail in Chapter 7 under option risks. Volatility as a risk is unique to options because it affects the value of an option, but although it does not affect the spot market value of an asset, it is a factor that should be borne in mind when looking at the price risks of an instrument. The mark-to-market value of a portfolio consisting of Latin American debt will flail around a lot more than a European bond portfolio, but without knowing the volatilities of the constituent parts, how is one to interpret the mark-to-market numbers? In the same way, knowing the volatility of the underlying spot markets places a derivative contract in its context. An investor who bought two identical $100 000 options on Microsoft and Singapore Airlines shares will not know which has the higher potential exposure unless he knew which underlying stock was more volatile, because the option that is based on the more volatile stock will be more sensitive to changes in market conditions. And, as pointed out earlier, the volatility of a base currency in which all mark-to-market numbers are finally presented (to enable aggregation to take place) is also important information. The volatility of the asset being marked-to-market may not be high but the volatility of the, firm's base currency into which the asset's current mark-to-market has to be translated could be. The base currency volatility thus affects the ability of the firm to get a good handle on the potential exposure of the asset in question (see Table 1.2 on page 23 for a sample of historical volatilities).

DURATION AND CONVEXITY

For debt instruments, spot risk has a special name: *duration*, which is similar to but not identical to maturity because for bonds, duration is not equal to maturity. To be precise, there are two types of duration: Macaulay duration is defined as the weighted average life of the present values of all future cashflows from a bond, while modified duration refers to the percentage price sensitivity of a bond. Numerically, both durations are very close in value. (Since zero coupon bonds only have one cashflow at maturity; for them duration does equal maturity.)

Similar to modified duration is the price value of a basis point (PVBP) or dollar value of a 0.01% change in yield (*DV01*). This is simply the change in the present value for a bond/portfolio of bonds, given a one basis point change (upward or downward) in interest rates. It follows therefore that the higher (longer) the duration, the more sensitive the bond should be to changes in interest rates.

Bond managers were forced to turn to duration when they found that using a bond's time to maturity to gauge its price/yield response was inadequate. Just because a six-month Treasury bill is twice as responsive to changes in interest rates as a three-month Treasury does not mean that a nine-year bond is three times as sensitive as a three-year bond or that a 30-year bond is ten times more sensitive than a three-year bond.

Since duration provides a common measure of a security's sensitivity to changes in the overall level of interest rates, it can be used to compare directly the price sensitivity of different bonds. It has thus become the major tool for bond managers to measure the effect of interest rate changes on different components of their portfolio. Indeed many bond managers measure the 'riskiness' of their portfolios by referring to its duration.

Most fixed-income instruments have positive duration, i.e. their prices move in the opposite direction to interest rates. Their prices decrease when interest rates rise and increase when interest rates fall. Some instruments however show the opposite behaviour. The prices of Interest Onlys (a type of collateralized mortgage obligation, see Chapter 7 for explanation) increase when interest rates rise and decrease when interest rates fall. They are said to have negative duration because their sensitivity to interest rate changes is the inverse of other fixed-income instruments.

A portfolio's duration is the price weighted average of the durations of the all the individual bonds. When a portfolio manager expects rates to climb, he might try to mitigate some of the ill-effects by reducing the duration of his portfolio. He wants to make his portfolio less sensitive to

Continued on page 86

Continued from page 85

rate rises. He can achieve this by selling bonds (the spot instruments) or futures and options (derivatives) or even buying instruments with negative duration (Interest Onlys.) When he expects rates to fall, he does the reverse by extending the duration of his portfolio so that it is more responsive to every successive rate decline.

Duration is often used to estimate the price change in a bond resulting from interest rate changes. A duration of 12 means that the price of a bond will change by 12% for every 1% move in interest rates, or 6% for every 0.5% move in interest rates. This is a good rule of thumb to use if a fund manager wants approximations of how a bond would react to interest rate changes but it is only effective for interest rate changes of 1% or less. Table 4.1 provides some rough duration approximations for general classes of bonds.

If the portfolio manager wants 100% accuracy, then he cannot use duration alone because duration is not constant across the interest rate spectrum: it increases at lower yields and decreases at higher yields. The fact that the price-yield relationship of a straight, long-term fixed-rate bond is not represented by a straight line but a convex curve is the reason why using duration to estimate the price changes of a bond will

Table 4.1   US Treasury Benchmarks as at 31 March 1995.

Maturity	Coupon (%)	Yield (%)	Modified duration
02/08/1997(2 yrs)	6.875	6.78	1.76
02/05/1998(3 yrs)	7.250	6.90	2.54
02/29/2000(5 yrs)	7.125	7.09	4.07
02/15/2005(10 yrs)	7.500	7.20	6.87
02/15/2025(30 yrs)	7.625	7.43	11.78

Other OECD countries — sector benchmarks (all 7−10 years) as at 31 March 1995

Country	Average coupon (%)	Modified duration
Japan	4.5	7.13
Germany	5.91	7.05
France	5.88	7.31
UK	5.89	8.57
Italy	5.15	9.78

Source: Salomon Brothers.
Since duration is a function of both maturity and coupon, a 30-year Treasury with a coupon of 10% has a different duration from one with a coupon of 5%. As long as the maturity and coupon are roughly similar, the duration of bonds denominated in different currencies is similar.

Continued on page 87

Continued from page 86

result in larger and larger errors as yield changes increase. This shape, this degree of curvature is referred to as *convexity*. Technically, it is defined as the difference in the rate of the price change of a fixed-income instrument, from that implied by its duration, for a given move in interest rates. Intuitively, it measures how stable a portfolio's price sensitivity is during fast-moving markets.

Just as there is positive and negative duration, there is also positive and negative convexity. An instrument is positively convex when its price increases at a faster rate than it decreases than that suggested by its duration. This means the instrument is more sensitive to yield changes when interest rates are declining and less sensitive when rates are advancing. Fixed income bonds, and plain vanilla swaps (receiving fixed) exhibit positive convexity; a behaviour that all portfolio managers like because it gives them the best of both worlds — less sensitive when rates are working against them and more sensitive when rates are in their favour. Positive convexity means that the interest rate risk inherent in any fixed-income portfolio will be declining as interest rates rise. Negative convexity is the reverse — the instrument's price increases in price at a slower rate than it decreases. Mortgage-backed securities and index-amortizing swaps (receiving fixed) are negatively convex.

The usefulness of duration as a fixed income management tool is reduced by the fact that while all interest-rate instruments have convexity, duration itself is a linear measure. Another limitation of duration is that it gives no information about an instrument's sensitivity to changes in the shape of the yield curve, in other words it assumes parallel shifts of the yield curve, which does not always hold true.

SPOT RISK — FORWARD-BASED INSTRUMENTS

By definition derivatives must have spot risks since their value depends on an underlying asset or instrument. So when the price of the underlying asset changes, so does the price of the derivative. But the nature of this relationship depends on the type of derivative contract.

For a forward-based instrument such as a future, a forward or a swap, the change in the price of the derivative is roughly proportional to the change in the price of the underlying asset. Its price sensitivity, or *delta* can be plotted linearly (see Figure 4.2). Delta is the first of the Greek words to which you will be introduced in Part Two of this book.

Delta is often expressed in numbers (0.0 to ±1.0, or 0 to ±100% if expressed in percentage terms), but these figures are just a numerical expression of how sensitive

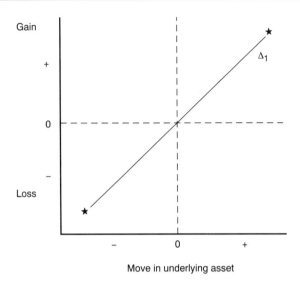

Figure 4.2   Payoff Profile of a Forward-Based Transaction.

is the price of a derivative to changes in the price of the underlying instrument, rather like the numbers in duration for debt instruments. (Indeed both duration and delta are similar concepts — the former measures the price sensitivity of a fixed income security while the latter that of a derivative.) The formula for delta is the change in the value of the derivative divided by the change in the value of underlying instrument/asset. If a $5 increase in the price of the underlying results in a $5 increase in the value of the forward-based derivative, then by virtue of its definition, the delta of all forward-based instruments is roughly 1 or 100%.

Price risk is the first risk any provider of derivatives must manage. It is easy to manage the price risk of forward-based transactions since their prices move in step with the prices of the underlying assets. Say a derivative provider is a fixed rate payer in an interest rate swap, which is equivalent to being short in a fixed rate instrument and long a floating rate note. To hedge the price risks of the swap, he could buy fixed rate bonds or US Treasuries with the same duration as the swap. These securities create a hedge against capital loss if long-term interest rates rise, and also generate fixed rate income which offsets some of the fixed payments on the swap. He could also hedge the price risk of the swap by buying futures. How much he buys is determined by the delta of the transaction, and once this hedge is in place, it is to all intents and purposes, *relatively* static. The fixed rate payer does not have to watch it constantly.

The qualification 'relatively' is used because the delta of some forward-based transactions (for example an interest rate swap) does change with the passing of time and the level of interest rates. This is due to positive convexity, which as explained in the box on duration, means that prices advance faster when interest rates fall than they decline when interest rates rise. But this convexity of swaps, while not unimportant, is not of equal rank with the convexity of options, which will be discussed in Chapter 6. The convexity of options is so great that it been given its own Greek letter, gamma, and has even acquired a special name, curvature. It is so large that for options, convexity can be as big a risk as the first-order risk of price risk.

SPOT RISK — OPTION-BASED INSTRUMENTS

Options and option-based derivatives are different from forwards because the relationship between their price sensitivies and that of the underlying asset is not linear but convex (see Figure 4.3). The degree of curvature depends on the price of the underlying asset relative to the strike price at that particular point in time, the volatility of the asset and time to expiry of the option.

The deltas of most options are either positive (0% to 100%) or negative (0% to −100%). A call option, i.e. an option that gives you the right to buy an underlying asset has positive delta because it moves in the same direction as the underlying. Because most options can never gain or lose value more quickly than their underlying asset, they have an upper bound of 100% and a lower bound of 0%. (Leveraged options and some knock-in options are an exception — they can lose or gain value more quickly than the underlying asset.) At its upper bound of 100% the option will move one-for-one with the underlying price. The lower bound of 0% is dictated by the fact that a call option cannot move in the opposite direction of its underlying asset. A put option, which gives the buyer the right to sell an underlying asset, has negative delta because the put position moves in the opposite direction to the underlying asset — when the underlying asset rises in price, the put option loses value; when the underlying asset price falls, the put gains value.

The delta of an option depends on whether it is in-the-money (there is a net financial benefit if the option is exercised immediately), at-the-money (the option's strike is at the same level as the underlying asset), or out-of-the-money (no financial benefit if the option is exercised immediately) because deltas reflect the moneyness of an option, or the chance of there being a net financial benefit if the option is exercised

Figure 4.3 Payoff Profile of an Option.

immediately. Generally at-the-money (forward) options have deltas of about 50%; those that are out-of-the-money have deltas less than 50%, and those in-the-money, more than 50%. An option that is very far out-of-the-money has a delta closer to 0% and one that is deep in-the-money has a delta approaching 100%. (Since most options are priced off the forward price of the underlying asset, it is assumed that the terms at-the-money, in-the-money, out-the-money describe the relationship between an option's strike and the forward price of the underlying asset.)

The delta of an option shows how a change in the underlying asset's price will affect the option's value. A high delta of say 80% means that the option's value is very sensitive to price moves in the underlying while a low delta of 5% means underlying price changes have negligible effects. In quantitative terms, the in-the-money option with a 80% delta changes its value at 80% the rate of the underlying, while the out-of-the-money option with a 5% delta at 5% the rate of the underlying. Once an option's delta reaches 100%, the option price will move one-for-one with price changes in the underlying asset. Its behaviour is exactly the same as that of the underlying asset. (Because put options give the buyer the right to sell an asset, their values move in the opposite direction of the underlying asset, so their deltas are expressed from 0 to −100%, but the same generalizations apply.)

The Delta Zone

Delta is a mathematical expression of the price sensitivity of a derivative to price movements in the underlying. But it can also be conceptualized as a measure of the certainty of asset flows inherent in the instrument. The upper (100%) and lower (0%) bounds of delta are certainty; thus an option with a delta of 100% or 0% has known asset flows just like a forward-based transaction or spot instrument that only have deltas of 100%.

These upper and lower bounds can be equated to day and night — night equals 0% and day equals 100%. Anything in between is twilight or uncertainty. For most of their lives options are in the twilight zone (because their deltas are between 1–99%), and are trying to resolve themselves into day or night. (The buyer of an option wants it to become day and the seller night.) Forward-based and spot instruments on the other hand are never in twilight zone — it is always day time for them. This makes their risk management easier because their asset flows are not as uncertain as those of options.

The twilight zone can be represented graphically. The delta of an option is usually represented by the S-shaped curve in Figure 4.4. This S-shaped curve is basically made up of three parts — a flat part at the bottom, a curvy part in the middle (basically between ±2 standard deviations,) and then another flat part near the top. The curvy part can be thought of as twilight, the bottom flat line as night and the top flat line as day.

The option's location in the twilight zone depends on the relationship between its strike and the underlying asset's price — its moneyness. At-the-money options

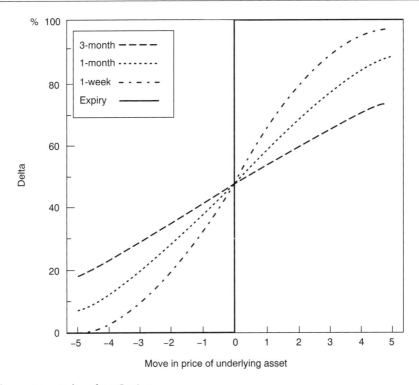

Figure 4.4 Delta of an Option.

with deltas of 50% sit in the middle of twilight, out-of-the-moneys with deltas less than 50% nearer night and in-the-moneys with deltas more than 50% nearer day.

A move in the price of the underlying asset will help an option resolve itself. It either becomes more in- or out, or even at-the-money. An at-the-money option either becomes in- or out-; it cannot maintain its status quo. So a change in the price of the underlying asset affects the location of an option in the twilight zone, it helps the option to resolve itself by moving it towards day or night. (Any move in the price of the underlying asset results in the option having a new delta, all else being equal.)

But an option's delta is also affected by two other variables — time and the volatility of the underlying asset. Both contribute to uncertainty — rising volatility and the lengthening of time to more uncertainty, declining volatility and the passage of time to less uncertainty. Both help an option to resolve itself without the underlying asset price having to budge at all.

In Figure 4.5 the S-shaped delta curve is mapped onto a bell-shaped curve. The graph shows that the S-shaped line is a stretched out version of the bell-shaped curve, which itself graphs normal distributions. The returns of financial prices are assumed to be normally distributed so the bell-shaped curve describes the price

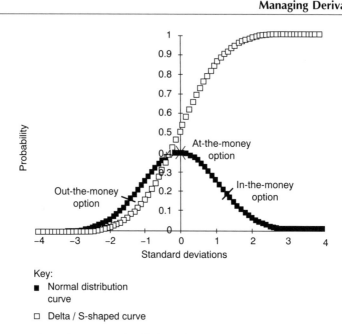

Figure 4.5   S-shaped Curve and Bell-shaped Curve.

distribution of assets on which options are written. Statisticians and mathematicians say that the delta curve is the cumulative of the bell curve or that the bell curve is the differential of the two points in the delta curve. Any generalizations derived from the changes in the shape of the bell-shaped curve can be applied to the S-shaped curve, and thus delta, because Figure 4.5 has established that the bell-shaped and the delta S-shaped curves are related.

Let us use as a starting point the shape of the bell curve in Figure 4.5. When prices of the underlying asset become more volatile they will be distributed further from the mean which will result in a widening of the width of the bell curve. Increased volatility equals increased uncertainty. So anything that increases uncertainty flattens the bell-shaped curve causing it to have gentler slopes. If this new bell-shaped curve was now stretched out into the S-shaped curve, the curvy part of the S-shaped curve will account for a larger proportion of the entire S-shaped curve than it did under the original bell-shaped curve. This shows there is more twilight. Increasing uncertainty brought about by more volatility or the lengthening of time (physically impossible!) spreads the twilight zone. The option will now take a longer time to resolve itself, to travel from day to night or vice versa.

Anything that reduces uncertainty will make the width of that bell curve narrower. This is because the expected distribution of prices of the underlying asset will be clustered nearer the middle. Consequently, the curvy part of the bell-shaped curve will be steeper and the tails on either end longer (i.e. the flat part of the distribution.) If these tails, which are equated to certainty (i.e. day and night) account for a greater proportion of the delta curve, twilight or uncertainty must by definition be shorter. The option will resolve itself faster. What reduces uncertainty? The passing of time and declining volatility.

Shaking the Bell Curves

The precise effect of increased and decreased uncertainty on an option's delta is shown in Figure 4.6 and summarized in Table 4.2. It is clear from both figures that their impact on an option's delta depends on whether the option is at-the-money, in-the-money and out-of-the-money.

These changes are not obvious and learning the table off-by-heart is not easy, so the bell-shaped curve of Figure 4.5 will be used to make things a little clearer.

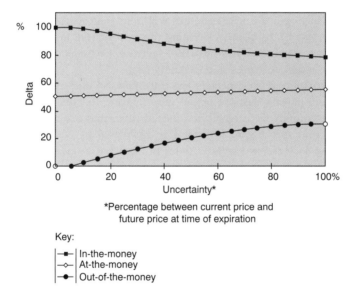

*Percentage between current price and future price at time of expiration

Key:
—■— In-the-money
—◇— At-the-money
—●— Out-of-the-money

Figure 4.6 The Effect of Uncertainty on an Option's Delta.

Table 4.2 The Effect of Uncertainty on an Option's Delta.

	Increasing uncertainty		Decreasing uncertainty	
Type of option	Increasing volatility	Lengthening of time	Decreasing volatility	Passing of time
Delta of:				
at-the-money	no change	no change	no change	no change
out-of-the-money	increases	increases	decreases	decreases
in-the-money	decreases	decreases	increases	increases

At-the-money options with a delta of 50% always sit on the peak of a bell-shaped curve because that is the middle of the curve. It can also be seen from Figure 4.4 that the peak coincides with the middle of the S-shaped curve where delta is 50%. Out-of-the-money options sit on the left-hand side of the slope (because anything on that side of the slope has a delta of less than 50%) and in-the-money options sit on the right-hand side (because anything on that side has a delta of more than 50%.)

Think of an option's delta as the chance (probability) of it ending in-the-money. Increasing uncertainty — brought about by more volatility and time lengthening — widens the width of the bell-shaped curve, making it a flatter bell. Imagine an out-of-the-money option sitting on the original curve and one sitting on the new bell with a lower peak (see Figure 4.7). If one were to shake both bell-shaped curves, which out-of-the-money option has more chance of being flipped to the other side of the bell, i.e. the in-the-money side of the curve? Answer — the option on the flatter bell because its peak is lower and its slopes gentler. So an out-of-the-money option's delta increases with rising uncertainty. What about the in-the-money option? Its chances of being flipped from the in-the-money side of the curve to the out-of-the-money side also increase. Consequently, the delta of an in-the-money option decreases as uncertainty rises.

Reduced volatility makes markets less uncertain. So does the passage of time since with each passing day, the option moves nearer to expiry date. Decreasing uncertainty transforms the original bell-shaped curve into one with steeper slopes and a higher peak (see Figure 4.8). Imagine again shaking two out-of-the-money options sitting on these two bells in order to flip them to the other side of their

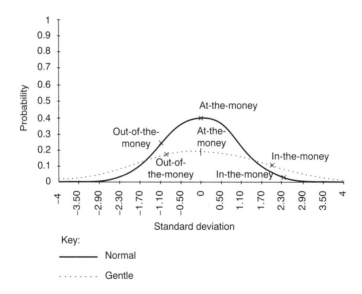

Figure 4.7   Gentle Bell-shaped Curve.

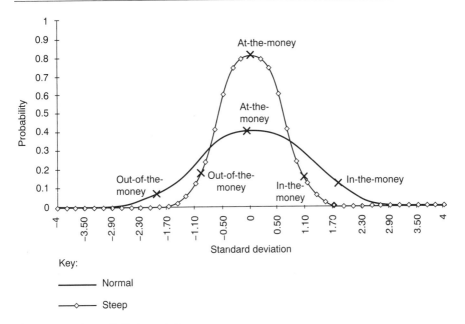

Figure 4.8 Steep Bell-shaped Curve.

respective bells. It will be harder to flip the out-of-the-money option sitting on the steep bell than it is the one on the original curve. If delta is thought of as the probability of the option being in-the-money, then it is clear that the delta of an out-of-the-money option decreases as uncertainty declines, since the chances of the out-of-the-money option going to the other side of the bell are reduced. The chances of the in-the-money option being flipped to the out-of-the-money side of the curve also lessen when the peak is high; consequently the delta of an in-the-money option increases since it is more likely to stay on the in-the-money side of the curve.

And what about the impact of increased and decreased uncertainty on the delta of an at-the-money option? The at-the money option which sits on the peak of all three bells has a 50-50 chance of being flipped onto either side of the curve whatever the shape of the bell. So the delta of at-the-money option remains the same whether uncertainty increases or decreases.

In reality there are often simultaneous fluctuations in prices and volatilities (not forgetting that time does not stand still) resulting in changes in the shape of the bell curve occurring together with a location shift. You could have a situation where the influences of all the variables reinforced each other, or where they cancelled each other out, so it is hard to generalize which influence emerges strongest. An out-of-the-money call will change its position very quickly in the twilight zone if prices and volatility rose. But if prices declined and so did volatility, the net result could be the option sitting still. During the Crash of 1987, some call options went up in price even though the underlying S&P index tumbled by 500 points. This was because the sharp increase in volatility more than offset the underlying asset's price effect on the option.

The Hedge Ratio

A bank which has sold an option does not sit still once it has done the transaction, it must neutralize or hedge the exposure resulting from the deal. The largest risk is price risk. To hedge its price risk, the bank takes an equivalent position (opposite in the case of a put) in the underlying market. The amount of the underlying it buys (in the case of a call) or sells (in the case of a put), is dictated by the delta of the option.

Say the bank has sold a call option on 10 000 IBM shares. The call option had a delta of 40% which means the bank must buy $40/100 \times 10\,000$ IBM shares in the cash market to hedge its position. This is where the terms hedge ratio or delta neutral come in — by buying the required number of contracts in the underlying market dictated by the hedge ratio (i.e. the delta of the option), an option seller is said to be delta neutral. At that point, he has hedged what he knows to be the certain asset flows emanating from the option sale (i.e. the resolved portion of the option's irresolution). Instead of just using the cash market, the option seller can hedge these risks by taking equivalent positions in the futures or forwards markets or a combination of all three. The choice really depends on which alternative is the cheapest to transact and the most liquid.

Delta-Hedging

The trouble with options is that their 'resolved' asset flows keep changing because their delta changes. So an option seller who delta-hedges his options must continuously adjust his cash or futures positions, or both, to match the option's known asset flow commitments at that point in time. This is why *delta-hedging* is also called dynamic hedging. Let's go back to the sale of the call option on IBM shares. With a hedge ratio of 40, the option seller buys 4000 IBM shares. That position is correctly hedged but only at the outset. This is because delta represents an equivalent underlying position only under a very tight band of market conditions, and changes with different price levels of the underlying asset, the passage of time and volatility. Because delta changes, so must the amount of the underlying asset that the option seller has to buy or sell if he wants to remain hedged.

This need for continuous adjustment can be also be explained by remembering the payoff profile of an option versus the underlying asset (or a forward). Options have convex (curved) profiles while cash and forward instruments have linear profiles. Hedging the former with the latter can be likened to fitting tangent lines to a convex line — the more tangent lines you draw to the convex line, the better the fit since you are smoothing out the facets that the tangent lines make with the curved line, but the fit can never be perfect because it is like fitting a square peg into a round hole. In that sense, delta-hedging an option suffers from the general problem of trying to replicate something that has curves with something that is straight. It is a lot of hard work and there are many compromises to be made. See Figure 4.9.

The fine-tuning of the cash/futures hedge is not without costs. And even if costs were negligible, it is easier said than done as shall be explained later. Every time an option seller adjusts a hedge by buying or selling in the cash or forward markets, it pays away the *bid/ask spread* which can add up to a costly sum when the adjustments are frequent, which is normal if markets jump around a lot. (The bid/ask spread comes from buying at offered prices and selling at bid prices.) What complicates matters is that in volatile markets, the bid/ask spread tends to get even wider and thus makes delta-hedging even more expensive. So the cost of dynamic hedging could be greater than originally calculated because the actual volatility of the underlying asset turned out to be higher than expected volatility. You could end up with a situation where the total *transaction costs* on the hedge was higher than the premium earned from selling the option.

To reduce transaction costs, option sellers have to make qualitative assessments on how often these hedge ratios should be adjusted. But they then come up against

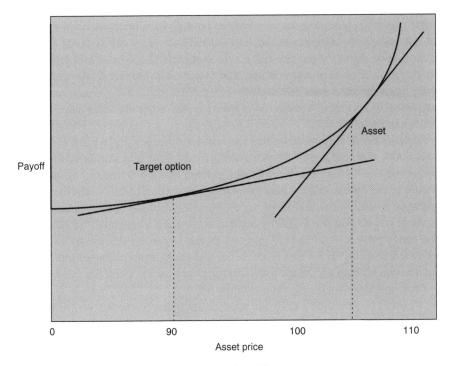

Figure 4.9 Fitting Tangent Lines to a Curved Profile.

another problem: the fear of missing significant market moves between adjustments. Once there is a large market move between two adjustments, the option seller will find his hedge in tatters. The financial performance of the hedge will be inferior to that of the option itself. If the market has rallied, he will be significantly underhedged and if it has crashed, he will be overhedged. He has a new hedge ratio on his option position but by the time he goes out and covers that shortfall, the market would have moved again. He is like a dog chasing his own tail.

The more infrequently a hedge ratio is adjusted, the greater the chance of missing a significant market move and finding oneself exposed. So an option seller seeking to hedge his option sale faces an uncomfortable dilemma: does he adjust frequently and incur large transaction costs, or does he adjust infreqeuntly and risk missing a large market move?

Even if he chose to adjust frequently, he has to contend with the problem of asset prices moving in both directions — they can go up, up and then down and up again; or worse up, down, up, down, up, down. Let us return to the IBM example to see why this makes life more difficult for the delta-hedger. If IBM shares rallied after the option seller had written the call, that would change the delta of the option. The option seller is then forced to buy more shares since the original hedge ratio is insufficient. A few days later, rumours circulate in the market that IBM is about to make a shocking earnings announcement and the price of IBM falls. The option seller now finds himself in an over-hedged position because the delta of the option has decreased. To compensate, he sells some IBM shares but in doing so suffers a 'double-whammy' — first he has had to buy extra IBM shares at a higher price when the share price initially rallied, and then he has had to sell them at a lower price when the IBM price fell. Delta-hedging often requires the hedger to buy high and sell low because the hedger is required to buy when the asset price rises and sell when the price falls.

Delta-hedging also presumes that the calculated hedge ratio is right. However, it may not be, because one of the main components of the equation from which delta is derived is volatility. But the volatility number that is fed into the option pricing model is the option seller's best estimate of how volatile the underlying asset is going to be during the life of the option. Precisely because it is an estimate, there is no guarantee that this volatility number is right. Consequently, the chances that the hedge ratio is right is only as good as the option seller's ability to estimate expected volatility in the first place. If the underlying prices turn out more volatile than assumed, then the hedge ratio is wrong, and the option seller must fine-tune his position more frequently than anticipated.

Changes in an option's delta are much faster when the option is near or at-the-money and is close to expiry; and when market moves are large. The rate at which an option's delta changes is known as *gamma* (see Chapter 6 for further details). Because the price changes of an option are not linear, its delta must be changing, which is why options have a curvature so great that it makes option-hedging much trickier than swap or forward-hedging. Curvature is the reason for many option sellers preferring to hedge their option positions with other options.

Despite its limitations, delta-hedging is a cornerstone of modern financial risk management. Practitioners have learnt to appreciate its limitations through painful experience (the Crash of 1987 and the European currency crisis of 1992 are the two most obvious examples). Still the concept is firmly entrenched as a risk management technique. Why? First of all, its limitations pertain only to options so that a participant with only forward-based instruments in his portfolio will find that hedging his position with equivalent positions in the underlying is fine. The second reason for the widespread use of delta-hedging lies in its very ability to relate derivatives to their roots — the underlying on which they are based. Because the delta of any derivative can be interpreted as the equivalent position in the underlying, it allows risk managers to distil the price risks of all derivatives to a base number of the family to which they belong. There is something very convenient and comforting in being able to describe an option in terms of 4000 IBM shares, especially if the option seller has underlying cash positions in those same shares in other parts of his portfolio. Not only is delta a great simplifying mechanism; it also facilitates aggregation across all instruments (be they derivatives or cash) because delta expresses them in units of their underlying. Market participants can thus manage their price risks on a residual exposure basis since all the derivative and cash positions can be netted off each other, to arrive at a final number.

Dynamic Replication

But delta-hedging is more than a risk management device, it can also be seen as a way of articulating one's views about future market direction in the same way as buying an option. If an option can be hedged by taking its delta equivalent in the underlying, then by the same token so can its payoff profile be synthesized via the underlying markets. That is why delta-hedging is also known as *dynamic replication* — rather than buy an option, the market participant replicates its payoff profile by buying and selling continuously (dynamically) the requisite amounts of cash and futures positions.

Theoretically, the transaction costs of dynamic replication (i.e. the profit and losses on the complete set of hedging trades over the life of the option) should equal the premium of the option. So anyone who is offered a choice between buying an option at fair value and dynamic replication will opt for the former because it saves him the trouble of trying to predict volatility, having to monitor the markets continuously so that he will not miss a large market move, predicting rollover costs at the start of the programme, etc. A market participant will therefore only dynamically replicate if he felt than an option was seriously mispriced, if he could not find an option that met his specifications, or a mirror option to offset his option risks.

Dynamic replication's most famous proponent is Hayne Leland, the inventor of *portfolio insurance*. He first came up with the concept of insuring one's equity portfolio against a chosen (and livable) loss in 1976 when he was a professor of finance at the University of California, Berkeley. He realized that limiting the losses on a portfolio was similar to buying a put option on the entire portfolio. However at that time there were no over-the-counter or exchange-traded contracts offering options on equities or equity indexes. Leland realized, however, that he could synthesize a put option by replicating its payoff using the cash and futures markets. But earnest marketing of the idea did not begin till 1979, when he set up shop with two other now well-known personalities — Mark Rubinstein and John O'Brien. The company they set up, Leland O'Brien Rubinstein, landed its first portfolio insurance client in 1980. Portfolio insurance continued to grow despite the introduction of exchanged-traded S&P 100 options and index futures in 1983. LOR was so successful at marketing its concept that between $75 billion and $100 billion of portfolio insurance programmes were in force in the summer of 1987.

The rest is history. Portfolio insurance worked well enough till the stock markets nosedived the 19 October 1987. While the jury is still out on whether portfolio insurance was the culprit of the Crash, it is not debatable that the strategy did not work when it was most needed. Fund managers who thought they were protected found out that their losses were not limited because the insurance programmes could not sell stock or futures fast enough to keep up with the plummeting market. Also as the market plunged, buyers disappeared. The strategy broke down because portfolio insurance, like delta-hedging, presumes orderly and liquid markets and that there would always be buyers of the constituent stocks of the S&P 100/500, or futures buyers for the index. As the market plunged, there were none. Even those who were initially brave enough to stick up their heads above the parapet were swept away by the torrent of sell orders that were automatically required by the portfolio insurance programmes.

Dynamic replicaters must remember one crucial point: when markets fall, a put option seller has no choice but to fulfil his obligations if the option is exercised — that is why he is paid a premium; the same is not true for the cash or futures markets since the traders there are under no obligation to quote a bid price, or more accurately a realistic bid price for the specified amount. So a fund manager who is dynamically replicating a put option cannot expect other investors to buy shares or futures contracts while the market is falling because they have made no advance commitment to do so, as portfolio insurers found out to their cost in 1987. The dynamic replicater cannot expect other investors or traders to play the role of the put option seller who is obliged to buy back the shares. The lack of buyers tends to coincide with large market moves and liquidity drying up so that the limitations of dynamic replication have more to do with curvature risks rather than spot risks.

And if it is large market moves that show up curvature risks, (see Chapter 6) one can conclude that it is curvature rather than price risk that causes the financial performance of dynamic replication to be inferior to that of buying the option. By implication therefore, in normal markets, dynamic replication (and delta-hedging) should work.

SYSTEMIC RISK

Some regulators have expressed fears that the combined weight of delta-hedging activities of the world's leading derivative players could lead to widespread difficulties in all market segments of the financial system (systemic risk.) How could that happen? Two traders sell the same type of option, say a two-year call option on the ten-year German bunds and hedge it dynamically in the spot market. It can easily happen that they both attempt to adjust their hedge at the same time. If there is sufficient liquidity in the underlying spot or in the companion futures markets, then both can execute their delta-hedges. But if there is insufficient liquidity in the cash or futures markets, then the two traders competing for German bunds will find themselves caught in a situation that resembles a short squeeze. This competition could have a dangerous feedback loop: as their competing bids push up the cash prices further, the delta of the two option positions would grow bigger, thus necessitating both traders to increase the amounts they must buy in the cash market just to keep themselves delta neutral. This requires them to make even larger bids which push market prices further up. This feedback loop is the fundamental difference between managing a short option position and managing a long option position. With a short option position every adjustment in the spot market requires a trade in the same direction as the market is moving, i.e. selling when market prices are falling and buying when prices are rising. With a long position, the adjustment in the spot market requires a trade in the opposite direction of the market; i.e. selling when the market is rising and buying when the market is falling, which serves to mitigate rather than exacerbate the market direction. The key question in trying to determine whether the combined hedging activities of option sellers can cause a 'financial nuclear meltdown' is to assess whether the liquidity needs of those who have chosen to manage their short option positions will overwhelm natural market liquidity.

LIQUIDITY RISK

Market *liquidity risk* arises when a large transaction in a particular instrument has a significant effect on its price, making it difficult for a market participant to hedge or lay off its positions. An institution could therefore find that it cannot easily unwind or offset a position without moving prices against itself, thus increasing the cost of hedging. In illiquid markets, bid/ask spreads are likely to be larger, further increasing that cost. (The size of the bid/ask spread of an instrument generally gives a good indication of the liquidity of a market — the narrower the spread, the deeper the depth.)

The spectre of illiquidity, especially for non-standard products, haunts derivative providers and end-users alike but it is more material for the latter. The former say they are less worried about specific product liquidity because their risk management techniques have moved beyond that of individual issues. The trend among derivative providers is to break down complex products into their fundamental elements and from there manage the risks. For example, an index amortizing rate swap need not (and seldom is) hedged by another IAR swap. Instead it can be hedged by a combination of other swaps, futures, forward rate agreements and interest rate options, or even Treasury notes. In other words, complex derivative instruments are unbundled into the *basic building blocks* of spot, forward and options and into their general risk classes of interest rates, foreign currencies and equities. As a result, derivative providers' worries about liquidity risks centre on whether there is sufficient liquidity in a general class of instrument, say all deutschemark-denominated instruments, which are all sensitive to German interest rates, to allow them to lay off their German-related risks, rather than a specific instrument.

However, end-users are right to worry about individual issue liquidity, particularly for esoteric or customized products. They are not in a position to manage liquidity risks by unbundling. They need a reasonable bid/ask spread and the more complex a product, the less the likelihood of them getting a reasonable bid/ask price from any house other than the bank from which they bought it, even in normal markets. Under abnormal market conditions, their chances are nil — this inability to unwind a transaction when they need to should be a key consideration when end-users buy complex or customized derivatives.

That liquidity for popular but not particularly complex products can evaporate overnight was proved when the secondary market for collateralized mortgage obligations collapsed in March 1994. As soon as market conditions turned sour in February 1994, two-way prices for simple structures such as inverse floating rate notes or Principal Only bonds were not to be found. There were only offers in the market.

Mortgage derivatives are however a special case (for details on this sector, please see *prepayment risks* in Chapter 7). Because they are not synthetic securities (unlike most complex products which are packaged together from unrelated underlying instruments), they cannot be repackaged again, since to do so the investment bank must find the necessary pieces from a specific tranche. But since structured products are synthetic, there should, theoretically, always be a bid/offer price since the investment bank which bundled them together in the first place can unbundle them to arrive at a price that reflects the basic components of the structured note.

Since end-users need individual product liquidity to unwind a position, they have to address the liquidity risk issue by making worst case assumptions about close-out costs. Before buying such instruments they have to consider what potential bid/ask spreads could be when markets are distressed, and the effect such high close-out costs could have on the financial performance of the instrument. They have also to ask themselves if there was no bid/ask spread whether they will be prepared to hold the instrument to maturity. The disappearance of realistic prices for complex products when markets are under stress does place a question mark on a firm's reliance on marking-to-market for an accurate reflection of the current worth of its portfolio. At such times, the gospel of marking-to-market takes a severe knock since the market is not there. Even if an end-user was able to find a price, it may not reflect the true value of the instrument. (The valuation of complex products is discussed further in Chapter 8.)

Market Shocks

A distinction between disruptions in market liquidity affecting a few products/instruments and a breakdown which is all encompassing such as that of the stock market crash of 1987 is important, because it has different implications on how to manage liquidity risk. If disruption is confined to a few instruments, then the issue is one of valuation; if it results from a market shock whose waves affect a whole class of risk instruments (for example all spot, forward and option instruments affected by a plunge in the Dow Jones index), then liquidity risk should be a risk control issue.

This is all the more pertinent for derivative providers since they argue that individual issue liquidity (including the questionable liquidity of esoteric instruments even in normal market conditions) is immaterial to them since they manage everything on their fundamental elements. This unbundling distils any non-standard product into spot, forward and options components, so one has still to think about liquidity in all three markets. However illiquidity resulting from a market shock affects all three at the same time, so if there was no liquidity in the spot market, there would be none in the forward or options markets because the latter two are generally not as deep or as mature as the spot market. (The exceptions to this statement are the S&P 500 index futures and the US Treasury futures markets where liquidity can be deeper than that prevailing in the underlying spot markets.) Under this scenario, liquidity risk should be addressed by asking how long it would take for liquidity to return to the relevant market so that a position can be closed out at an acceptable cost; and setting position limits using this time horizon. The shorter this *holding period*, the more liquid we assume the markets to be, and therefore the less conservative the risk limits. The longer the time interval, the more the likelihood of a large price change and thus the more conservative the risk limits. Adopting a long time interval protects against the problem of an unforeseen lengthening of the holding period resulting from a sudden contraction in liquidity. The trouble is it is anyone's guess as to when liquidity returns after a market shock event. Is one week sufficient or is one month a better measure?

It is also true that liquidity returns at different speeds to different markets; returning to the spot markets first and options probably last. Should risk limits then be based on the time horizon assumed for traders to cover their positions in the spot markets since the liquidity of this market underpins the other two and because all forward and option positions can ultimately be reduced to their respective deltas? Because if unbundling was taken to its purest form, it is to the spot markets that a derivative provider will turn to hedge its forward and option risks making it ultimately dependent on spot liquidity. If one does use the time horizon for spot liquidity to return, one must remember that for options in particular, delta-hedging is not a good surrogate especially in stressed markets.

Only market liquidity risk has been discussed here. The other type of liquidity risk faced by all participants is funding risk: the inability to meet investment and funding requirements at an acceptable price as they become due. Metallgesellschaft, a large German company, suffered serious funding problems in its exchange-traded futures activity and needed a consortium of German banks to bail it out. Barings' inability to meet its margin calls was the immediate cause for its demise. The lessons to be learnt from their experiences are discussed in Chapters 5 and 10.

SUMMARY

All financial instruments are exposed to the risk of markets moving against them (market risk). For spot or cash instruments, this market risk can be reduced to the chance of prices of the underlying assets moving in an unfavourable direction. So for spot or cash instruments, market risk is equal to price volatility. Increased use of mark-to-market accounting has highlighted the price risks of spot instruments.

Derivatives derive their value from the spot markets and so have significant price risk which is a first-order risk that must be managed. Derivative providers can hedge their price risks by buying or selling the requisite amount of spot instruments. This is relatively easy to do if the derivative is a forward-like instrument since the change in the price of a forward, future or swap is roughly proportional to the change in the price of the underlying asset. So once the hedge is established, it is relatively static since the forward-based instrument's price sensitivity is always about 1. Also there is little uncertainty about future asset flows under a forward-based contract — if a bank has sold dollars forward against yen, it knows it has an outstanding dollar/yen obligation.

Hedging the price risks of an option-based derivative is more complex. There is no certainty about the future asset flows of an option since the option will be only be exercised if the buyer finds it financially advantageous. An option can be viewed as an instrument which spends its entire life trying to resolve itself into something worthwhile or worthless, so the instrument is affected by anything that increases or decreases uncertainty. More uncertainty, brought about by increased volatility (or time lengthening — but that is impossible), makes it harder for the option to resolve itself. Less uncertainty, resulting from decreased volatility or the passage of time, makes it easier for the option to resolve itself.

Yet despite the uncertain asset flows inherent in any option, an option seller must hedge whatever flows are known or expected at a particular point in time. The expected flows can be measured by an option's delta. But delta, which is defined as an option's price sensitivity to changes in prices of the underlying asset, is not constant. To hedge an option by selling the requisite amount of physical assets (or futures contracts) dictated by its delta thus requires continuous adjustment. The relationship between the delta of an option and price changes in the underlying asset is complex and is known in the industry as 'curvature'. Curvature depends on the price of the underlying asset relative to the strike price of the option at that point in time, the volatility of the asset, and time to expiry of the option.

Delta-hedging is fine in theory but fraught with difficulties in practice. End-users who want to replicate the payoff profile of an option by taking its delta equivalent in the underlying markets must bear this in mind.

5

Forward Risks

Under this umbrella come the risks associated with forward-based instruments such as swaps, forward rate agreements, forwards and futures. Their risks are not too dissimilar to those encountered in the spot market because a 'forward' (the word is used here generically) is just agreeing to buy or sell an asset in the future. The price of a forward is thus the future value of an asset in today's terms. To arrive at such a value requires the 'present valuing' of future asset flows, which in turn demands that assumptions be made about future interest rates. This immediately brings into orbit the issue of uncertainty about future interest rates.

The price of a forward is a function of the current asset price plus the cost of carry. For financial assets, the latter is just the funding cost. But because most financial assets offer their investors some sort of interest compensation, the funding cost which is used in calculating a forward price is the net cost of carry. For example the pricing of a forward-based derivative on a fixed-income security uses the net number resulting from the difference between the short-term funding rate and the yield on the underlying instrument. For equities, it is the difference between the stock's dividend and the short-term rate. For foreign exchange (forex) forwards, the cost of carry is the differential between the two interest rates of the currencies involved in the transaction; indeed forex forwards are solely influenced by interest rate differentials and do not reflect anticipated movements in spot rates.

But non-financial assets such as energy-related and agricultural commodities and non-precious metals have more than just funding costs in their cost of carry. For such assets, the cost of storage, transportation and insurance have to be included in the cost of carry. But even for these, the risk of the cost of carry is mainly interest rate-related.

So uncertainty about interest rates is the extra dimension of risk of forward-based transactions, over and above price risk, which forwards have in common with spot instruments. This uncertainty about future interest rates has different manifestations. There is absolute, or outright rate risk, i.e. rates rising or falling; spread risk arising from the changing yield differences between a corporate bond and a government security of similar maturity; and curve risk which occurs because long-term and short-term rates seldom move in tandem.

The precondition for spread and curve risks is the existence of a pair, and unless both parties in a pair are perfectly identical, risks will spring from the fact that they are different. Spread risk arises between two types of instruments — say a bond and a swap; or between the same instruments which carry different credit ratings, for example between government and corporate bonds, or supranational and corporate issuers. That there are yield differences between these instruments is not a problem, the risk arises because the spreads between the two are not static. Curve risk springs only from a difference in maturity. And it would not be a big issue if short-term and long-term rates had similar responses to rate hikes and cuts by central banks. Rarely do they and when they do it is termed a parallel shift in the yield curve. Moreoften, they do not, with short-term responding more than long-term rates or vice versa, and that condition is described as the shape of the yield curve changing.

Non-interest rate spread and curve risk has a special name — basis risk, which arises whenever the exposure being neutralized and the hedge instrument are not identical, so there is a chance that both parties in the pair react differently to changing market conditions. Viewed this way, curve risk and spread risk can both be seen as subsets of basis risk. Spread and curve risks apply only to interest rate instruments while basis risks covers a whole gamut of asset classes. If an airline hedges its jet fuel costs by buying crude oil futures contracts, it will suffer basis risk because the two types of oil may not react identically to a crude oil price hike.

Credit risk has been placed in this chapter because it is a manifestation of interest rate risk. It is true that all instruments and markets bear the risks of a counterparty defaulting on future payments but when the layers have been peeled off what is the base line of credit risk? How is one party compensated for taking on a lesser credit? By earning an extra spread over government bonds or prime rate. Indeed yield spreads arise mainly from the differing credit qualities of various issuers, so spread risk is a different dimension of credit risk.

INTEREST RATE RISK

OUTRIGHT

Generally speaking, if interest rates increase, so does the cost of funding, and so accordingly should the price of a forward-based transaction, assuming of course that the price of the asset concerned does not change, since funding costs are a secondary component of forward pricing. A seller of a forward would profit if interest rates decrease while a buyer would lose since the forward contract would decrease in value. (Similarly, if interest rates increase, the buyer would profit and the seller lose.) While this interest rate risk inherent in any forward-based transaction is a secondary concern, (the primary concern is still the price performance of the underlying asset); it is important and can affect the financial performance of a hedge.

Say an investor sells FT-SE 100 futures to hedge his UK equity portfolio. The stock market goes into a bearish decline. Yet the forward contract may not mirror the actual decline of the constituent FT-SE 100 stocks because the Bank of England has jacked up interest rates in the meantime. Interest rate risk thus impacts the effectiveness of the forward-based hedge; the degree depends on the price volatility of the asset being hedged. If the former is very volatile, then the risks posed by interest rate moves is swamped by the asset's primary price risk.

In general, a forward transaction with a longer maturity is more sensitive to movements in interest rates than one with a shorter maturity, since the cost of carry has a bigger impact of the final forward price. But a dealer pricing a long-term forward contract does not necessarily use the long-term rate as his cost of carry — many fund from the short-term markets especially if the yield curve is sloping upwards. The fact that short-term rates are more volatile than long term can thus affect the pricing of forward contracts.

Short-term rates are heavily influenced by overnight rates, which in turn can be manipulated by central banks controlling the tightness of money supply to help prop up weak currencies under pressure, or dampen demand for strong ones. So governments contribute to the volatility of short-term rates because their intervention in the short-term markets are often dictated by political and currency exigencies rather than sound economic policies.

Overnight Lessons from the ERM Crisis

The importance of not assuming stable overnight rates was painfully brought home to many forward and option traders during the 1992 European Exchange Rate Mechanism (ERM) crisis. To stem the run on the weaker currencies (Italian lire, Swedish krona, Irish punt for example), the relevant central banks raised their lending rates to 'squeeze' short sellers. The idea was to inflict as much pain as possible on speculators who had expressed their bearish views by selling the currency forward. To cover their short sales, they had to borrow short-term funds from the domestic money markets, typically the overnight market. By making these short sellers pay ruinous overnight rates, the central banks hoped to stem the run on their currencies. The manipulation of overnight rates during the September crisis led to Europunt rates hitting an incredible 48 000% and sterling peaking at 160%.

Sweden was a textbook example of the limits of an aggressive interest rate defense under conditions of a large fiscal deficit and significant financial fragility. The three-month siege of the krona began on August 21 with a sequence of increases that moved the Riksbank's marginal lending rate from 13% to 500% on September 16. The pass-through to other interest rates was rapid. For example, the ask rates for interbank one-month funds

jumped from 16% to 70% between September 7 and September 17 .... The price at
which they would buy (bid for) funds was 50%.[1]

A speculator against the Swedish krona could borrow krona from a bank and
buy a bank deposit denominated in deutschmark.

The one-month interbank rate (ask) quoted for banks selling deutschmark in the retail
market was 9.25%, and the price at which they would buy funds was 9.15%. ... A
speculator that borrowed Swedish krona and acquired a deutschmark interbank deposit
paid 70% on the Swedish krona loan and received 9.15% on the deutschmark deposit,
therefore facing an interest rate spread of 60.85%. Before the speculator could make a
profit, the krona would have to depreciate by 60.85% on an annualized basis. Over a one-
month period, the speculator's break-even rate of depreciation would have been 5.07%.[1]

(See Figures 5.1, 5.2, and 5.3 for overnight rates during the ERM crisis.)

While the target for all this overnight rate manipulation were the short sellers,
the pain it inflicted rippled through both the forward-based and options markets.
Those who had sold any sterling or Swedish krona-denominated short-term forward
contracts found that they had assumed too low funding rates so their short contracts
went well under water. The same applied to option traders.

Most option models assume relatively stable interest rates, but the jump in overnight
rates from 24% to 500% in Swedish krona, for example, would be way beyond the scope
of even those models that attempt to take into account shifting interest rates. [Delta-
hedgers tend to use overnight funding too because the constant rebalancing means they
do not know how much they have to fund each day.] The shorter the option, the greater
the impact on profit and loss. The expense of funds, coupled with the inability to delta
hedge, would have led to substantial losses for some players.[2]

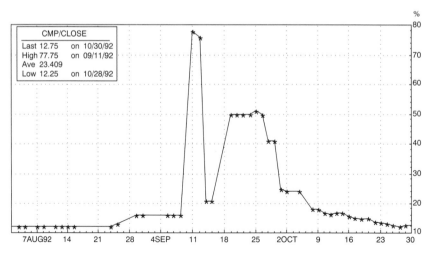

Figure 5.1 Swedish Krona Overnight Rates. Reproduced with permission from
Bloomberg.

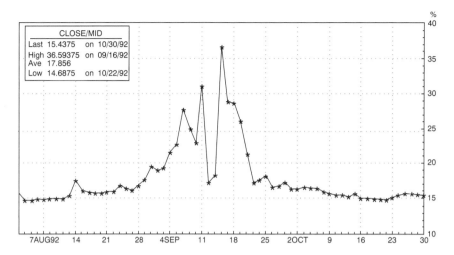

Figure 5.2 Italian Lira Overnight Rates. Reproduced with permission from Bloomberg.

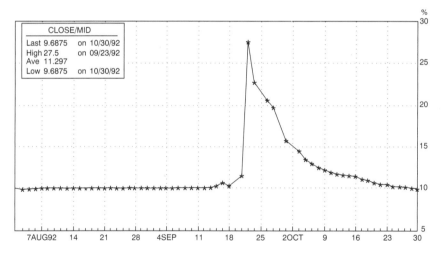

Figure 5.3 French Franc Overnight Rates. Reproduced with permission from Bloomberg.

SPREAD

In an ideal world, dealers hedge their swaps with other swaps, preferably mirror images of their open positions to eliminate any risk. In the real world, dealers are forced to hedge their swaps with government bonds or short-term interest rate futures contracts. In both instances, swap dealers are exposed to spread risk, the risk that arises from changing yield differentials between a swap and its comparable government bond.

The fixed rate leg of a swap trades at a spread over a government bond of the same maturity because the former represents both the current level of interest rates and credit concerns, while yields of the latter reflect only the general level of interest rates (since government bonds are regarded as credit risk-free securities). Consequently, swap rates are always quoted at a spread over government bonds, for example the five-year fixed swap rate could be five-year US Treasury yield plus 100 bp. This extra 100 bp is the corporate credit spread embedded in swap rates.

Spread risk arises because the differences in the yield of a swap and its comparable government bond, or for that matter between a corporate and government bond are not static. Indeed the spreads move around a fair bit. They change due to *arbitrage* factors, but primarily because of demand and supply. If there are a lot of end-users who want to pay fixed in a swap, they will drive down the spread between swaps and Treasuries and if there is a lot of demand to receive fixed, the spread will widen. In general, spread risk cannot be hedged. Dealers have to wary of spreads moving against them because it affects the profitability of a swap. With margins on plain vanilla swaps being so thin, even a two basis point shift in spreads can make all the difference between being in the black and in the red. Say a swap dealer quotes a price of 9.0% paying, 9.05% receiving on a five-year US dollar interest rate as swap. Five-year US Treasury notes are trading at 8%, so the swap spread on the pay side here is 100 bp and 105 bp on the receive side. The dealer enters into a swap with a customer where the dealer pays 9% fixed. After executing the first deal, the dealer finds that the swap spread has narrowed to 95 bp, so that the same swap is being quoted as 8.95% pay (8.00 + 95), 9.0% receive (8.00 + 100). If the dealer hedges his original transaction by executing a mirror swap now, he will make no money. Indeed if the swap spread had narrowed by more than 5 bp, he would lose money on the transaction since he would be receiving less than 9% on one swap and paying 9% on the original swap.

Since it is not always easy to hedge a swap with a mirror transaction, many dealers hedge their fixed rate exposure on a swap by selling or buying comparable government bonds. In the example above, the swap dealer would buy US Treasuries since he is paying fixed in the swap (i.e. he wants to be long a fixed-rate instrument to offset the short fixed-rate position resulting from him paying fixed in a swap.) If interest rates decline, the profit he makes on US Treasuries should offset the loss on the swap and vice versa. Say interest rates decline by 0.5%, so the dealer records a profit on the US Treasury position because 5-year US Treasuries now yield 7.50%. His swap shows a loss because he is paying a 9% fixed rate compared with the 8.30% fixed rate now available on five year swaps because the swap spread has narrowed to 80 bp from 100 bp. The loss the dealer suffers on the swap is greater than the profit made on US Treasuries — he loses 20 bp on the notional principal of the swap at each payment date.

The yield differential between Treasury bill and Eurodollar futures contracts of the same maturity is known as the TED spread. Swap dealers are exposed to TED-spread risk when they hedge shorter maturity swaps (under two years) with US Treasuries. If the price of Eurodollar futures change, it will cause swap spreads to change even if Treasury prices remain the same, because short-term swaps are priced off the Eurodollar futures contract. (This is because most dealers hedge their short-term swaps by executing Eurodollar futures contracts on the Chicago and London exchanges.)

End-users also face spread risk. If they enter into a swap, only to find swap spreads narrowing two days later, they will find themselves paying more than they had to. But they can also turn this spread volatility to their advantage. Say the five-year swap spread is historically tight at 50 bp over US Treasuries. The end-user has no real need for a swap where he pays fixed. But he could enter into such a swap simply because he believes that swap spreads will widen. If the latter does widen to 80 bp, the end-user's swap will move into the money even if the underlying US Treasury shows no yield movement at all.

CURVE

For financial assets the cost of carry is often a net number. Arriving at the net number is simple enough, but because interest rate instruments of different maturities can respond differently to rate movements, curve risk is a major risk inherent in any portfolio consisting of a large number of interest rate related instruments. (See Figure 5.4 for parallel and non-parallel shifts of yield curves.) These non-parallel shifts in the yield curve, which cause the curve to sometimes assume the most contorted of shapes, affect even the most basic of swaps.

A dealer paying fixed and receiving floating in a plain vanilla swap (denominated in US dollars) is in the same economic position as another dealer who is short a fixed-rate bond and long a floating-rate note. The fixed-rate bond is a long-term liability while the floating rate note is a short-term asset. The swap dealer in this instance has the price sensitivities of a long-term liability and a short-term asset.

Say the Federal Reserve Board lowers the federal funds rate by 0.5%. The yield curve from three months to 30 years had responded uniformly with a 0.5% downward shift to the last three rate hikes. But this time a non-parallel shift occurs. Only short-term rates respond by dropping 0.5%. Long-term rates do not budge at all. The dealer is left in a position where his floating interest receipts have declined but his fixed costs remain the same. He had hedged his fixed rate payments on the swap by selling long-term US Treasuries so that the gains he makes on the hedge offset the loss on his swap. Unfortunately this does not materialize — since long-term rates did not react to the Federal Reserve rate cut, no capital gains are made on the long-term Treasury. Yet he suffers a loss on the swap because short-term rates have declined.

But if short-term rates had not reacted and long-term rates declined, the dealer would have made more money than he anticipated. He would profit from two fronts — the gains on his long-term Treasury position and the profit on his swap.

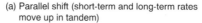

(a) Parallel shift (short-term and long-term rates
move up in tandem)

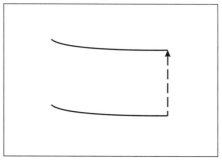

(b) Non-parallel shift (short-term rates increase
with no movement in long-term rates)

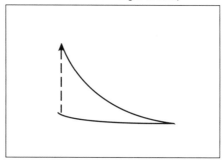

(c) Non-parallel shift (long-term rates without
a concurrent shift in short-term rates)

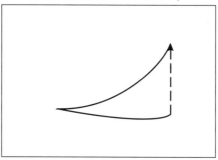

Figure 5.4   Parallel and Non-parallel Shifts of Yield Curves.

Because yield curves change shape financial institutions have developed a whole range of products which allow end-users to speculate on parts of the curve they think will be most responsive to movements in interest rates. Spread swaps, where one party pays the fixed two year rate and the other the fixed five year rate, are just one example. In such structures the two parties are betting that spreads between different maturities will narrow or widen. So curve risk can be actively sought or a passive by-product of any interest rate transaction that involves different maturities. P&G's 5/30 year swap (see Chapter 2) is an example of an end-user taking on curve risk (and outright rate risk) to bring down its cost of funding.

Curve risk need not involve a derivative on one side, it can arise between two physical assets, one of which is used to hedge the price action of the other. During the bond market crash of early 1994, many large trading houses sustained substantial losses on their bond positions. Two American houses, Goldman Sachs and Merrill Lynch were reported to have been badly hit while trading Japanese government bonds. Both firms were forced to buy back billions of yen-worth of 20-year Japanese government bonds from non-Japanese institutional clients. These trades took place while the Tokyo markets were closed. Rather than running the outright price risk of leaving these purchases totally unhedged, the two firms immediately hedged their positions by selling short ten-year Japanese government bonds. The trouble was that the yield curve steepened and 20-year bonds (which the firms now held) dropped much further in price than the ten-year bonds they sold as a hedge. The firms lost money as a result of curve risk.[3]

The curve risks taken here were probably not intentional but were forced upon the traders as the cost of covering the absolute price risk they took on when they honoured the buy-back pledges their firms had given institutional clients. Because market conditions were then very volatile, taking on this second-order curve risk, was preferable to leaving the positions completely unhedged and exposing the firms to what would have been even more costly first-order price risk.

Time Buckets

Curve risk forces trading firms to adopt a two-pronged approach to managing their interest rate book — they calculate their price risk to uniform (parallel) shifts in the yield curve and then supplement it with a detailed decomposition. Normally this is achieved through the time bucket, or maturity band system. This allows them to pinpoint the location of their interest rate risk; information vital to coping with non-parallel shifts of the yield curve. By breaking up the interest rate risk of an institution into time buckets, the firm can simulate the sensitivities of the each time bucket flow to interest rate changes and the impact that has on the overall interest rate risk of the firm.

The fact that there are mismatches or gaps in the maturity structure of most trading firms' interest rate books makes this detailed composition very important. It is pretty risky to have net inflows/outflows that are bunched up with large gaps in between; yet a single net number will not give you this vital mismatch information.

Thus part of interest rate risk management is a well thought out set of time buckets — their design is not cast in stone and differs from institution to institution. How granular should a firm's time buckets be? If they are too narrow or too comprehensive then asset flows which should be aggregated (since they have similar sensitivities to interest rate moves) are not, and the firm wastes time simulating separate sensitivities for each bucket because it does not glean any more information than if it had added them together. But if the bands or buckets are too wide then divergence in the sensitivities of asset flows will not be caught because they are grouped together. For example, some institutions scoop interest rate flows after ten years into one bucket and treat them as one number, assuming little curve risks in that one net number. But as the Japanese government bond experiences of Goldman and Merrill show, that may be too wide a time bucket. Under such a scheme, both the long and short Japanese government bond positions in question would have been placed in the same time bucket, resulting in a low risk number for that time bucket. Indeed, the traders concerned might have satisfied themselves that the ten-year instruments were good enough surrogate hedges for the 20-year bonds until market events proved them wrong. (Market conditions at that time were extreme though.)

Some large US financial institutions have time buckets of 15-day periods for the first three months, with the remainder grouped monthly. The Bank for International Settlements proposed 13 time buckets in its April 1993 and April 1995 proposals for market risk capital — up to 1 month, 1 to 3 months, 3 to 6 months, 6 to 12 months, 1 to 2 years, 2 to 3 years, 3 to 4 years, 4 to 5 years, 5 to 7 years, 7 to 10 years, 10 to 15 years, 15 to 20 years, and over 20 years. For instruments with less than 3% coupons, the BIS suggested 15 time buckets. The bank made it clear in its April 1995 proposal that a minimum of six time buckets was needed for any material interest rate positions. Fixed rate instruments are slotted into the relevant bucket based on the remaining time to maturity and floating rate instruments according to the next coupon *reset* date. When the market risk proposals are implemented at the end of December 1997, the BIS scheme of time buckets could be the template for the world's banks. (The BIS is looked upon as the world's central bank.)

Interest rate risk is managed by ensuring that the net inflows and outflows are balanced across time (reducing the curve risk to manageable proportions) as well as being totally balanced in the portfolio as a whole (keeping price risk to a parallel shift of rates at an acceptable level.) Limits can be placed on the total price risk as well as the risk in any one time bucket.

The time bucket system helps firms quantify the curve risks inherent in any interest rate book. The net inflows and outflows in each time bucket, to a certain extent, should be offset against each other — different segments of the yield curve may react differently to interest rate changes but they do not react so independently that a net inflow and outflow in two adjacent time buckets should not be regarded as hedges for each other.

The problem is deciding on an accurate offsetting method. Because adjacent time buckets tend to move together, the offsets between them must be greater than between two buckets that are light years apart, where there should be no offsets at all. (If there were, the whole *raison d'être* for the bucket system is gone because the system will acknowledge the curve risk but not manage it.)

No firm will disclose how they offset these buckets, but the BIS proposals suggest a methodology. The BIS proposed that there should be two rounds of partial 'horizontal' offsets, first between the net positions in each of the three zones (zero to one year, one year to four years and over four years), and subsequently between the net positions in different zones. At each stage, the offsetting of positions is subject to a scale of disallowances expressed as a fraction of the matched positions, as set out in Table 5.1. These disallowances acknowledge the hedging effects of offsets between time buckets that are near each other and the lack of hedging effects between maturity bands that are far apart.

Although each time bucket has only one net number the instruments within each bucket are not homogeneous. If the buckets are as comprehensive as they are in the BIS proposal, then maturity differences are infinitesimal. But there will still be credit differences within each bucket, giving rise to spread risk. US Treasuries yields for example reflect only the general interest rate level, LIBOR rates or swap rates reflect the combined value of general interest rate levels and the credit spread. Some trading firms manage this aspect of interest rate risk by imposing spread limits.

Table 5.1 Horizontal Offsetting.

Zone	Within the zone %	Between adjacent zones %	Between zones 1 and 3 %
Zone 1 (0−12 months, four buckets)	40		
		40	
Zone 2 (1−4 years, three buckets)	30		100
		40	
Zone 3 (over 4 years, six buckets)	30		

Partial offsetting would be permitted between weighted long and short positions in each zone, subject to the matched portion attracting a disallowance factor that is part of the capital charge. The disallowance proposed within zone 1 is 40%, applied to one side of the matched amount. Within zones 2 and 3, the disallowance would be 30%.

The remaining net position in each zone may be carried over and offset against opposite positions in other zones, subject to a second set of disallowance factors. The disallowance factor between adjacent zones is 40%. The disallowance between non-adjacent zones is 100%.

Reproduced by permission from: 'The Supervisory Treatment of Market Risks, April 1993,' and 'Planned Supplement to the Capital Accord to Incorporate Market Risks, April 1995,' Bank Consultative proposals by the Basle Committee on Banking Supervision; Bank for International Settlements, Basle, Switzerland.

BASIS RISK

When basis is used in the same breath as forwards/futures, it is often defined as the price difference between the forward and spot price, so under such a definition basis includes the cost of carry. But a more restrictive definition is needed when discussing basis risk — in this instance it is the potential for loss resulting from the asset being hedged and the hedge vehicle not being identical. A perfectly matched hedge is selling one-year US Treasury futures to hedge $100 million of one-year US Treasury notes. A mismatched hedge is to sell the same futures contract as above to hedge a holding of $100 million of General Motors bonds with a remaining life of one year. The mismatch arises because Treasuries are credit risk-free securities while General Motors bonds are not. In this case, the basis risk springs from the credit spread between a US government obligation (supposedly the best credit in the world and generally looked upon as the benchmark of credit risk-free yields) and that of an A-rated US motor car manufacturer. If market factors force credit spreads to increase, the change in the value of the Treasury hedge will not fully offset the change in the value of the General Motors bond. Such a mismatch is small; there are circumstances where the mismatch is large, for example an airline which uses a crude oil futures contract (West Texas Intermediate or Brent Crude are the most popular) to hedge the price of jet fuel. The larger the mismatch, the larger the basis risk because changes in the value of one position may not be matched by identical price changes in the other position.

Both spread and curve risks are subsets of basis risk. Spread risk however is specific only to interest rates, unlike curve risk. The long-term forward price of an asset may react differently, to a market-moving event, from spot prices or near-term forwards. The case of Metallgesellschaft, which is discussed a few paragraphs below, vividly illustrates the dangers of curve risks in other markets. The existence of curve risks in interest rates and commodities require end-users to think carefully about whether it is effective to hedge their exposures with related instruments of different maturities.

Basis risk — under this definition — is also known as correlation risk. Correlation, like covariance, describes the relationship between two variables: the stronger the relationship, the higher the correlation. If the relationship is inverse, it is described as negatively correlated as opposed to positively correlated which is what happens when the two variables move in the same direction. Correlation is normally expressed as a number between 0 and +1 (for positive correlation) and 0 and −1 (for negative correlation.) The stronger the correlation, i.e. the closer it is to +1 or −1, the less the basis risk even if there was huge disparity between the two variables. (But strength also needs to be supplemented by stability — there can be potential for sizeable basis risk losses if the relationship is strong but very volatile.)

For end-users, the best way to erase basis risk is to ask for bespoke hedges. Say you are a natural gas producer who knows how much you will be producing in the next few years as well as the cost of this production in Canadian dollars. Current oil prices and the C$/US$ exchange rate mean that you can sell your gas at a small profit. You think gas prices might ease and you want to lock-in your profits to ensure the survival of your company. You could sell this natural gas forward, at regular intervals, at a fixed price in Canadian dollars. Such a hedge gets rid of both your oil price risk, currency risk and curve risk. Such customization comes at a price though since the provider wants to be compensated for taking on your basis risk.

Metallgesellschaft — Mismanagement of Basis Risk?

The jury is still out on who was ultimately responsible for the $1.3 billion hedging losses suffered by Metallgesellschaft in late 1993. The experiences in the energy market of this German industrial company illustrate the dangers of mismatched hedges and curve risks since Metallgesellschaft was hedging a long-term exposure with short-term contracts.

In 1992, Metallgesellschaft's US subsidiary, MG Refining and Marketing agreed to sell diesel fuel and fuel products to its customers at fixed prices for delivery every month, for up to ten years, from the date these contracts were originally agreed. These prices, fixed in 1992, were set slightly higher than the prevailing spot price.

MGRM customers were also given the option to terminate their contracts early if the price of the front-month New York Mercantile Exchange (NYMEX) contract exceeded the fixed-price at which MGRM was selling the oil or oil product. If the customer exercised the option, MGRM would pay in cash 50% of the price difference between the futures and fixed delivery price times the total volume remaining on the contract. But MGRM also amended some contracts allowing it to end fixed-price delivery if the front month futures price rose above an exit price. So the customers, in both cases, were only allowed to sell back their contracts when they were already in-the-money.

MGRM knew it had substantial price risks — to lock-in its profit, and to prevent itself from ending up in a situation where it had to buy oil more expensively than it had sold, it initiated a hedging programme. It bought futures contracts based on regular unleaded gasoline oil, New York harbour no. 2 heating oil, and the West Texas Intermediate grade light, sweet crude oil on NYMEX. But since there are no futures contracts extending out to ten years, and liquidity was a prime concern of MGRM, it concentrated its purchases in liquid short-term contracts. (By September 1993 MGRM had sold forward the equivalent of over 180 million barrels of oil which is equivalent to 85 days of Kuwait's oil output, so it needed to use the most liquid contract.) The most liquid futures contracts are near-term, one to three months. This maturity mismatch — one/three-monthly contracts to hedge exposures which had up to ten-year lives — gave rise to basis risk; a risk on which MGRM successfully capitalized when the strategy was first implemented.

This German industrial giant was not in the position to take physical delivery when the hedge contracts matured as it would then have had to hold the fuel until

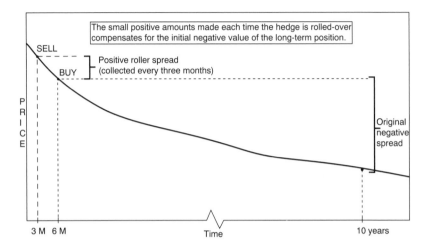

Figure 5.5   Metallgesellschaft's Hedging Strategy in a Backwardation Market.

the long-dated forward contracts became due. Instead it was forced to close the position by selling the near-term contracts and simultaneously reinstating the entire position by buying new ones. This pair of trades is known in the industry as rolling a long futures position to the next settlement date.

When MGRM first established these positions, the markets for crude oil and its distillates were in *backwardation*, i.e. the spot price and prices of near-term futures contracts on NYMEX were higher than the longer-term forward price, including the five to ten-year commitments MGRM had made to its customers. Buying highly priced near-term contracts and selling lower-priced forward contracts sounds like a recipe for disaster but not if the market is in backwardation. When short-term prices are higher than long-term, money is made every time a futures contract is rolled over. How? Because the expiring contract is sold at a higher price than the new contract being bought simultaneously. The accumulation of all these small rollover profits, particularly if there is a steep backwardation curve, can offset the initial negative price difference between the long-term customer trade and the short-term futures trade, (see Figure 5.5).

BACKWARDATION AND CONTANGO

Intuitively, the forward price of an asset should always be higher than the spot price since the forward price is made up of the spot price plus the cost of carry. Because carry costs are usually dominated by financing costs, which are never negative, the forward price should theoretically

Continued on page 121

Continued from page 120

be higher than the spot. An asset is said to be in contango when forward prices are higher than spot. *Contango* markets are also called 'carrying charge' markets, because the difference between the forward and spot price is completely explained by the difference between the yield of an asset and the cost of funding that asset. When assets can be easily borrowed or lent (to do that you need a liquid and well-developed repurchase agreement market, see Chapter 1), it is easy for speculators to arbitrage the price of a forward if it strays too far from the carry-cost basis. If the forward price is higher than the carry-cost basis, then a trader buys the spot (financing it by lending it out) and sells forward, ultimately capturing the mispricing increment on the settlement date of the forward, if not before. Conversely, if the forward price is lower than the carrying-charge basis, then the trader sells short in the spot market (by borrowing the asset in the repo market to satisfy the short sale delivery) and buys forward. Most currency, equity and precious metal markets are carrying charge markets.

Counter-intuitive as it may appear, there are times when the forward price is lower than the spot price. Such a condition is known as back-wardation and it tends to happen in markets where it is not easy to arbitrage the price difference between the forward and the spot, because that difference includes more than a carrying charge cost. Agricultural and energy-related commodities are good examples of assets which have inconvenient delivery or storage terms which make it difficult to arbi-trage the carrying charge difference away. For example if crude oil spot prices are higher than forward (as they were at the start of the MG saga), it is possible in theory to arbitrage the prices by short selling the rela-tively high-priced spot contract and buying the lower-priced forward obligation. Such a transaction would however require borrowing crude oil to satisfy delivery on the short sale in the spot market. If crude oil is not conveniently available in the ports designated for spot delivery, due to seasonal factors or because producers are keeping it aboard tankers outside the port, then such borrowing is impossible. Without the ability to borrow, the arbitrage necessary to bring forward prices into the academically-pleasing carrying charge relationship with spot prices cannot take place. Consequently, in such markets, backwardation can exist for a long time because they are essentially one-way markets. The forward contracts can get never get expensive relative to cash because if they did, market participants will just buy the physical asset and sell the future. But they can get extremely cheap relative to cash because in such a situation you cannot short the physical and buy the future.

Continued on page 122

Continued from page 121

The short-end of the oil curve moves largely in response to supply and demand factors so it is more volatile than the long-end which is

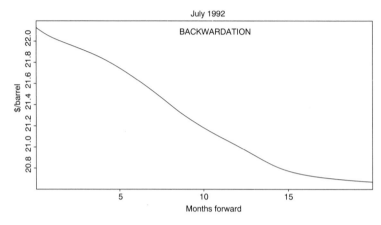

Figure 5.6   Backwardation.

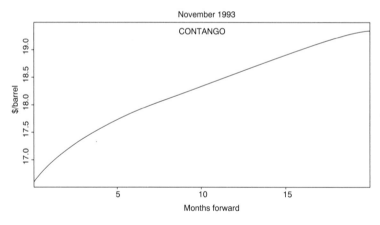

Figure 5.7   Contango.

mainly influenced by economic fundamentals. Price movements in the short-end are thus more pronounced than in the long-end; this effect is described as the 'horizontal tornado'.

Generally, the terms backwardation and contango tend to be associated with commodities rather than financial assets (see Figures 5.6 and 5.7 showing backwardation and contango).

Two events occurred which compromised the MGRM position. Other NYMEX floor traders could not help but notice its rollover positions, which became so large that MGRM required special exemption from the normal NYMEX position limits. (MGRM's hedging activities also resulted in open interest in the relevant contracts some two to three times larger than historical data.) These traders, true to their profession, began pricing the rolling of the futures contract in a predatory way — MGRM received less for the near-term contract and paid more for the mid-term contract than it had initially projected. That other traders began to take advantage of MGRM's rollovers is reflected in the West Texas Intermediates (WTI) forward curves shown in Figure 5.8[4] In June 1992, the WTI curve was still in backwardation. One year later, the curve has not become truly contango — more interesting though is the kink in it — it was very gently upward sloping up to three months, and then levelled off. So even before the forward curve became truly contango, MGRM was losing some of its ability to roll at a profit because other floor traders were betting against the company.

The second event was the sudden fall in the prices of spot oil and near-term futures in the second half of 1993. The failure of the Organization of Petroleum Exporting Countries (OPEC) to agree production cuts in November 1993 only exacerbated the short-term glut. The plunge in near-term oil prices was far greater than the drop in long-term prices, causing the forward curve for oil to change shape. The curve flipped from backwardation to contango. This meant that on each rollover date, MGRM had to sell its old (near-term) contracts at a price lower than what it paid for its new contracts, resulting in losses.

The success of the entire MGRM strategy hinged on energy markets remaining in backwardation for the bulk of the life of the hedging programme.

Cash Squeeze

As soon as spot and near-term oil prices fell, the long positions MGRM had on NYMEX lost their value which prompted margin calls from the exchange. MGRM had to pay these margin calls immediately or face the exchange closing down its positions. These margin calls were substantial because MGRM had such a large open position on the exchange. In 1993, it was forced to pay a total of $900 million in margin calls on its oil hedges. It is no wonder that a liquidity crisis began to engulf the German giant's US subsidiary. Rumours that MGRM was in a cash bind prompted NYMEX to double the company's margin requirements, exacerbating its cashflow problems. (Because MGRM's long-term delivery contracts were over-the-counter, it also suffered from a negative cashflow problem — it had to pay margin on its hedges because they were exchange-traded contracts but collected no upfront cash from its OTC clients.) MGRM was forced to turn to the parent company for financial support. The parent company, MG AG responded not with cash, but by taking control of its US subsidiary and instructing its new management to sell the futures contracts. This forced liquidation was partly due to MG's German creditor

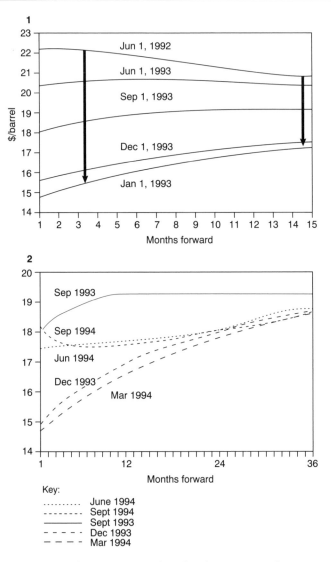

Figure 5.8   WTI Forward Curves. Reproduced with permission from *RISK Magazine*.

banks refusing to lend more money to the group just to allow it to meet its margin calls. The entire hedging debacle cost MG $1.3 billion. In January 1994, MG AG was saved from collapse only because its main lenders agreed to lend it $2.1 billion.

Nobel price winner, Merton Miller and another academic, Christopher Culp, argue that by panicking, MG's management and creditor banks turned paper losses into real losses. Because they did not extend credit, MGRM was not allowed to rollover its positions until the long-term contracts had expired. If MGRM's hedging programme had been allowed to run its course, it, would have resulted in profits rather than losses. Miller and Culp write,

> By the time MRGM began to unwind its positions in mid-December, the price of oil had fallen to roughly $14 per barrel. The precipitous liquidation of MGRM's futures hedge thus turned 'paper losses' on that leg into realised losses and left MGRM exposed to rising spot prices on its still-outstanding flow delivery contracts. And indeed, as noted earlier, when the new management awakened to its naked price exposure following the liquidation, it began negotiating unwinds of its flow contracts without demanding *any* compensation for its positive expected future cashflows.[5]

When Miller and Culp released their draft-paper in September 1994, spot oil prices had rebounded by $4 per barrel since December 1993.

Curve Risks

MG executives retorted that the company was forced to liquidate the positions because the rollover costs were too high. These rollover losses, stemming from a contango curve, amounted to $20 to $30 million a month and would have reached $50 million in December 1993, if the company had not begun unwinding its exchange-traded positions. (If the curve was in backwardation, the rollovers would have resulted in profits.) Therein lies the Achilles heel of Miller and Culp. Perhaps MG executives did panic in ordering the futures liquidation since with 20/20 hindsight spot oil prices did rise, but the thrust of Miller and Culp's argument rests on the assumption that the forward curve for oil would have gone back into backwardation and remained that way for the better part of the ten years of the hedge programme.

But in the six months leading up to December 1993, the oil curve was in contango — its shape flipped from backwardation in 1992 to contango in the second half of 1993 and 1994 and back to backwardation in October 1994. Such flips show that whenever an exposure is hedged with an instrument which is not identical, there will be basis risk.

This risk can work in your favour. When MGRM first put on the trade, the curve was in backwardation and it made money. When the curve was in contango, the basis risk worked against it because it was long the short-term futures contract. (If it had been short the short-term futures contract, a contango situation would have worked in MGRM's favour.)

MRGM had also to keep rolling its futures contracts because they were so short-dated. Even if the curves do not flip mid-way through a hedge programme, rollover costs can still make your trade less profitable. Since no one can predict rollover costs at the start of a transaction, it is a risk that has to be taken into account in any hedging strategy which requires constant rollovers. For example, if the backwardation curve becomes less steep, rollover costs eat into the positive price differential between the near-term and mid-term contracts.

Funding Risk

Any player who rolls positions in the futures market needs to consider the funding risk. This is especially relevant when the size of the position is large as it was with MGRM. Before embarking on such a strategy, MGRM had to consider whether it had sufficient liquidity to meet margin calls, and the cost of ensuring such liquidity. For many firms, meeting $20 to $30 million monthly margin calls is haemorrhage, and in this instance, it was a flow which had no definite staunch date.

In their paper[5], Miller and Culp suggest one upfront way of managing the substantial infusions of cash necessary to meet margin calls. They write,

> Firms hoping to initiate potentially cash-intensive combined delivery/hedging programmes like MGRM's might be well-advised therefore to do an unsecured borrowing upfront (in presumably calmer waters) equal to the initial face value of its total futures position — a so-called 'pure synthetic' strategy. Rather than depositing only the required minimum initial margin with the futures exchange clearinghouse, such firms could give this *total amount* to the clearinghouse in T-bills thus ensuring that no further cash outlays would be required over the life of the hedge, regardless of price movements.

Conclusion

The Metallgesellschaft story illustrates the dangers of basis risk, and how under certain conditions, one can lose a lot of money even though one has hedged the price risk. MGRM sought to eliminate its price exposure by purchasing near-term heating oil and gasoline futures, and it is accurate to say that had a uniform downward shift of all spot and forward energy prices occurred, MGRM would have been fine. But because energy prices do not respond uniformly across the curve, basis risk, in this case curve risks, proved to be MGRM's undoing. The story also illustrates how one can construct a position which has little absolute price risk but a lot of curve risk.

Miller and Culp are correct when they lambast the senior management of MG for liquidating the futures contracts without making alternative hedging arrangements. They rightly point out that MG's management actions exposed the company to the potentially more crippling risk of rising oil prices because the fixed-price contracts were still in place. The new management eventually realized its naked price exposure and offered to buy back contracts, at financially attractive terms, from some of its customers.

CREDIT RISK

Derivatives, just like traditional assets such as loans and bonds, carry *credit risk* — the fear that a counterparty will fail to live up to its financial obligations. The methods of reducing the credit losses of both on-balance sheet and off-balance sheet instruments are also similar, so once the peculiar credit risk characteristics of derivatives are understood and solved, they can be integrated into a firm's existing credit risk management procedures. Since the probability of a counterparty defaulting on what it owes from a derivative transaction is no different from that of a conventional loan, the default ratios published by Moody's or S&P can be applied to the credit risk amounts of derivatives, as they are applied to conventional loans, to arrive at the expected credit loss for such transactions. And collateral arrangements, letters of credit and third party guarantees are just as pertinent to reducing derivative credit risk as they are for on-balance sheet items.

The key differentiating feature between the credit risk of derivatives and conventional on-balance sheet items is the dynamic exposure of derivatives versus the static exposure of conventional loans. When a firm lends money or buys a security, it knows exactly what is at stake — the principal value of the loan/bond less any principal repayments that may have taken place since the funds were disbursed, plus any failed coupon payments.

Derivatives, must by definition have dynamic exposure since their value is derived from something else that moves. Their contract sizes are really 'notionals' in the true sense of the word — no money changes hands on the size of the notional contract (currency swaps are an exception); instead the notional amount is simply a reference point to calculate how much is payable or receivable in the future, which in turn depends on price movements of the underlying asset. So at any one time, the amount for which a counterparty is liable consists of two elements: the current replacement value of the transaction and the potential changes in this value because the underlying market will move during the life of the transaction.

The current replacement value of a derivative is its mark-to-market or its liquidation value (equal to the net present value of future expected cash flows.) This can either be negative or positive (since markets can move either way from the time the transaction was undertaken) but it is only the positive replacement value that represents a credit risk for the non-defaulting party. (A negative replacement value is not a problem for the non-defaulting party if the counterparty goes bust.)

Swaps and all forward-based derivatives have symmetrical credit risk; both parties to the transaction have a firm commitment to deliver to each other. The credit risk of options is asymmetrical — the seller of an option is obliged to deliver if the option is exercised while the buyer can walk away if the option is worthless. Consequently, the buyer of an option has credit exposure while the seller has none. The credit risk of swaps or bonds with embedded options is a bit more complicated. From a market risk standpoint, embedded options give their host bonds or swaps the characteristics of options; from a credit risk standpoint, options are swallowed into their host swaps/bonds so that the credit risk of such hybrids takes on the credit risk characteristics of their host instruments. This is because the payoff profile of the option is embedded into the cashflows of the bond/swap structure.

Replacement Values versus Notionals

There is little dispute over the notion that the current replacement value of a derivative contract is its mark-to-market. This is the 'loan-equivalent credit risk' of derivatives. Federal Reserve Bank data on US banks over the last few years showed that the replacement value of derivative contracts is only a fraction of their notional amounts; the precise number depends on the type of underlying asset and time to maturity, the two most important parameters in computing replacement values. The more volatile the underlying asset and the longer the time to maturity of the contract, the higher the average replacement value. But there are two aspects to replacement value: gross and net. If an end-user or bank only has one swap outstanding, the gross equals net replacement value. But once they have many transactions with a single counterparty, some of which offset each other, then it is the net replacement value that represents the true credit risk of an institution (provided the two parties have valid, legally enforceable netting agreements in place). Since gross or net replacement value is meant to measure the credit risk of a derivative contract, only the positive replacement values counts; i.e. when the transaction is in-the-money and the counterparty owes you money. When you owe the counterparty money, it is his credit risk not yours.

While the replacement value of a derivative contract fluctuates over time it does so within a narrow band. Federal Reserve data for US banks over recent years showed that for interest rate derivatives, gross replacement value as a percentage of notional value fluctuated between 0.6% and 2.4%; for foreign exchange between 1.1% and 3.8%. The average for interest rate derivatives was 1.5% and 2.5% for currency derivatives. The latter will always have a higher value because currencies are more volatile than interest rates. However because interest rate contracts tend to have longer lives than currency, the gap between the two is not as wide as it could be if volatility was the only influence. (The average original maturity of interest rate products is slightly above three years and for foreign exchange contracts under one year.)

Estimating Potential Exposure

There may be disagreement over how one marks-to-market (for example the model used to calculate replacement cost) but it is a smaller issue when compared with the more substantive problem of estimating potential exposure. That's where discussions become heated because such estimations are at heart, subjective. Estimating the possible changes in replacement value of a derivative contract over its remaining life is primarily a function of the time remaining to maturity (which is given) and the expected volatility and price of the underlying asset (subjective.) The G-30 report on credit risk, released in July 1993 and reprinted in Appendix 5, gives a clear non-technical description of the measurement of potential exposure, both expected and maximum. Generally though, potential exposure can be assessed using Monte Carlo or historical simulation studies, option valuation models and other statistical techniques. But these methods require extensive computer simulation and are more suitable for banks with large derivative portfolios which need to capture in detail the effects of various market moves.

Add-on Factors

End-users will not want to expend their resources this way because there are general rules of thumb which give an end-user adequate information. To capture changes in potential exposure, they can use an *add-on* factor, itself dependent on the type of instrument and remaining life of the contract. The add-on amount is arrived at multiplying the notional amount of the contract by the add-on factor, which itself is just a percentage number. The Bank for International Settlements promulgated a set of add-on factors under the 1988 Capital Convergence Accord which banks must use when calculating capital for credit risks. It released updated tables in July 1994 and April 1995 (see Table 5.2 for both add-on matrices). The add-on method requires the user to calculate the current replacement value first; this number is then added to the add-on amount to arrive at the credit exposure of a derivative contract. This method requires frequent re-computation of the current replacement value which can be obtained from the bank which sold the product. It also requires data on the maturity profile of the portfolio, which should always be available internally but not always to an outsider.

Table 5.2 BIS and S&P Product-specific Risk and Add-on Factors.

	Interest rates	Currencies	Equities
	All in percentage terms		
BIS risk factors (original maturity — 1988 Accord)			
<1 year	0.5	2.0	
1−2 yr	1.0	5.0	
2−3 yr	2.0	8.0	
3−4 yr	3.0	11.0	
BIS risk factors (original maturity — 1994 amendment)			
< 1 year	0.5	2.0	
1−2 yrs	1.0	5.0	
for each additional year	1.0	3.0	
BIS add-on (1988 Accord)			
<1 yr	0.0	1.0	
>1 yr	0.5	5.0	
BIS add-on (July 1994 and April 1995 amendment) (remaining maturity)			
<1 yr	0.0	1.0	6.0
1−5 yr	0.5	5.0	8.0
>5 yr	1.5	7.5	10.0
S&P risk factors			
futures and forwards	0.3	3.0	no differentiation -
options	2.0	4.0	all 15.0
swaps	2.5	10.0	

'Original Maturity/Exposure Method'

Another way of arriving at credit exposure is to multiply the notional amount by a BIS product-specific risk factor. Some industry practitioners say this method is too blunt to capture accurately both the current and potential exposure of a portfolio of derivatives. Their main criticism of the original maturity or exposure method (OEM) is that it generally overestimates the credit exposure of derivatives. The attraction of this method is that it requires only data on the original time to maturity and is thus very easy to use. It also does not require frequent re-computation. Since it attempts to substitute for both the replacement value and the add-on, risk factors are in general larger than add-on factors. The risk factor method has fallen out of favour because it cannot be used for netted contracts.

The 1988 Basle Capital Convergence Accord's risk factors for interest rate and currency contracts were broken down into maturity bands. The BIS amended these risk factors in April 1995 (see Table 5.2). These same risk factors can be used by non-banks to work out their derivative credit exposure — although they do not provide pinpoint accuracy, they give end-users a feel for the credit exposure on different types of instruments. For example, a $100 million three-year interest rate swap has a credit exposure of approximately $2 million ($100 million × 0.02) while a $100 million currency swap of the same maturity has a credit exposure of $8 million ($100 million × 0.08). This original maturity method is simpler to use than the add-on method which is two-stepped. Under the latter method, the end-user obtains the replacement value of the contract. Let's assume it is $1.5 million for the $100 million interest rate swap above. The add-on factor for this swap with a remaining life of three years is $0.5 million ($100 million × 0.005). The credit exposure on the swap is the sum of the replacement value and the add-on factor ($1.5 + $0.5 million = $2.0 million.)

In 1992, S&P, the US rating agency, released a set of risk factors which it computed from the empirical data of US banks. These factors were derived from taking the peak portfolio values over a relatively short period of time. Like the BIS, S&P has risk factors for different asset classes but has broken them into product

Table 5.3 Risk Percentages of the Swiss Federal Banking Commission.

Assessment	Fixed credit/debit rates (Risk factors %)		Market estimate (Add-ons %)	
	<1 yr	>1 yr	<1 yr	>1 yr
Interest rate contracts	5	10	0.2	1
Currency contracts	15	30	3	10
Equity index contracts	30	60	4	10
Equity contracts	40	60	6	10
Precious metal contracts	30	60	4	10
Non-ferrous metal contracts	40	60	6	10
Energy-linked contracts	50	75	10	20
Other commodity contracts	100	100	20	40

type. The S&P risk factors, like the BIS product-specific risk factors, can also be applied directly to the original notional amounts of the derivative contract.

Although the S&P factors are differentiated by product, they are also a decomposition by maturity. (This can be seen if the BIS and S&P factors were mapped together.) Futures and forwards have the shortest maturities while swaps have the longest maturities. The percentage factors suggested by both institutions increase with the assessed riskiness or volatility of products; thus equities have a much higher risk factor than interest rates because they are much more volatile.

These risk factors must be used with care though, the data is derived from large, balanced portfolios which have average distributions of products and maturities. End-user portfolios are not like that. Neither is a bank's exposure to a single counterparty because such a collection of engagements may be highly correlated and the potential exposure more dynamic than that of an aggregated portfolio. So the BIS add-ons, while being useful surrogates for calculating the future exposure of the whole portfolio cannot be useful for a single counterparty's engagements because they are too small. For single counterparty exposure, a set of higher add-ons and risk factors are needed. The only regulator that has come up with a set of risk factors and add-ons for large exposures is the Federal Banking Commission in Switzerland which released the following numbers in 1993.[6]

Because the Swiss Banking Commission's risk classes are more extensive than the original BIS add-ons, a comparison can only be made for the two common categories — interest rates and curries. The single counterparty percentages are two to three times larger than those for aggregated portfolios. Whether banks' empirical data supports these larger percentages is difficult to know because the Federal Reserve only requires aggregate data from each bank; it does not require the data to be split per counterparty.

Credit Lines

End-users need to know the credit exposure on their derivative transactions because they want to have a rough idea of how much is owed to them and how much they owe. Derivative providers, however, need their information to be more accurate because the credit lines they extend to their customers are based on replacement values, not notional values. There is no special credit line for derivatives — the replacement value of derivatives is just part of a large pool of credit to be extended to a customer which includes loans (notional amount) and foreign exchange transactions (also notionals). But while the latter amounts are relatively static and easy to monitor, the credit exposure on derivatives is changeable and much more difficult to monitor. Because the exposure to a single counterparty is much more dynamic than for the whole portfolio, it is even more important to make sure that the credit line is not breached when the replacement value of the contract has changed more than predicted. This is the main problem facing derivative providers — what level of comfort do they incorporate when drawing out the credit lines for customers?

Do they use the maximum possible exposure and extend a higher credit line; or an expected average number and a lower line? The cushion for potential exposure must also take into account the type of transaction — leveraged swaps need a higher cushion than plain vanilla interest rate swaps, exotic deals involving two volatile assets and digital options will have a lot more potential exposure than an inverse floater. Many players build in a margin for error by preventing any new transactions from being concluded if the sum of current and potential exposure reaches a predetermined percentage of the available credit line. Most active players also think in terms of two levels of credit lines (even though they may not formalize it) — a prudent level for exposures resulting from normal market events and a level which incorporates extreme conditions.

The need to get the potential exposure number right is all the more important because banks extend most of their customers a blank credit line for their over-the-counter transactions. Synthetic leverage makes these blank credit lines more dangerous because the potential exposure is even more dynamic. (From a credit perspective, it is interesting to note that the credit a bank is extending to a customer for his derivative transaction is incidental to the trade, whereas in a loan it is extending credit for credit sake.)

Credit Risk Reduction

There are a number of ways to reduce credit risk: the most common being pledging some form of collateral. This collateral — in the form of liquid assets — may be pledged upfront; triggered once the mark-to-market threshold of all transactions has been crossed; pledged real-time as a percentage of the mark-to-market value of the deals (similar to margining system on an exchange), or when the counterparty is downgraded. The first three require constant marking-to-market of positions, and monitoring in real-time the value of the collateral held and collecting (and returning) collateral if the need arises. Using collateral as a means of reducing risk thus requires the development of monitoring, valuation and reporting systems — and not all institutions have back-offices that are as efficient as those of the exchanges.

Although collateralization is in a philosophical sense much safer than a blank credit line, it is sometimes easier to obtain a blank credit line than it is a collateral line because the institution concerned just does not have the capacity to cope with the demands of real-time collateral management. The fact remains that credit risk in the OTC derivatives market is tackled very much in the 'yes/no' vein. This is reflected in the fact that for most houses that sell derivatives, less than 5% of their gross credit exposure to counterparties is collateralized; similarly less than 5% of their counterparties' gross exposure to these houses is collateralized.[7] For a weaker credit-counterparty, this state of affairs is simply wonderful because collateral costs money and imposes a ceiling on the amount of exposure you can have. A G-30 follow-up survey released in December 1994 (entitled *Derivatives: Practices and Principles, Follow-up Surveys of Industry Practices*) reported that only half of the firms that sell derivatives had established procedures to ensure that the collateral was adequate on a mark-to-market basis. The same survey showed that only half of them had written provisions to collect collateral once the exposure limits had been exceeded. (A quarter collect collateral upfront for the life of the transaction.)

Another way of reducing credit risk is to settle up periodically in cash. Here the party with the negative mark-to-market sends cash to the party with the positive replacement value. The terms of the transaction are then reset to try to maintain its value near or at zero. Corporate counterparties do not like this method of credit risk mitigation because if the transaction was really hedging an asset or a liability, they would be cashing out and realizing the losses or gains on the hedge while being unable to do the same on the underlying asset or liability.

Default Losses

As at the end of 1994, the default losses on derivatives was small. The International Swaps and Derivatives Association (ISDA) survey of default experience suggested that cumulative ten-year losses from derivatives totalled about $358 million, half of this was due to legal risk more than a counterparty being financially unable to pay. The ISDA survey covered a group which represented over 70% of the $4.34 trillion volume (measured by notional principal amount) of swaps, caps, collars and floors as reported by the year end 1991 ISDA market survey. In 1991, the UK House of Lords ruled that a local authority, Hammersmith and Fulham, was not empowered to deal in swaps and other derivative transactions. This ruling rendered void agreements between 75 banks and over 130 British local authorities.

The bankruptcy of names like Olympia and York of Canada, Development Finance Corporation of New Zealand, Drexel Burnham Lambert and Bank of New England of the US and British and Commonwealth Merchant Bank of the UK did little to dent the derivative industry's almost spotless record on containing default losses. This record however, if not showing cracks, is certainly being scratched. When it announced its 1994 results, Bankers Trust announced that it was setting aside $423 million on a 'cash-loan' basis, to cover potentially non-performing derivatives transactions. (This $423 million is the replacement value of the transactions at the end of 1994 — in the first half of 1995 US interest rates continued to move upwards so one can assume that their new replacement value was even higher given that some of the transactions involved leveraged plays on declining US interest rates.) The 'cash-loan' basis meant that Bankers Trust did not expect some of its customers to pay some or all of the money that they owed the bank. These 'credit losses' stemmed from leveraged derivatives — some of which are or have been under legal dispute. For example the costs of cancelling disputed contracts with Gibson Greetings and another American company, Federated Paper, were about $33 million. At least one-third of the amount set aside was to cover amounts due to Bankers Trust under transactions it had with Procter and Gamble. So in one fell swoop, one bank — Bankers Trust — identified in one year, potential default losses that were about $70 million more than what the bulk of the industry had suffered over ten years. Chase Manhattan Bank also announced (under the same 1994 results auspices) that it had lost $20 million from counterparties not fulfilling their financial obligations on derivatives transactions.

Bankers Trust's and Chase Manhattan's expected credit losses stem from the clients' unwillingness, rather than inability to pay. Unhappy end-users seem to be turning to the law courts to uphold their decisions not to pay. Such actions bring a new dimension to credit risk, which has always been managed on the assumption that a client would only fail to fulfil its financial obligations because it was financially incapable of doing so. Gibson argued that Bankers Trust had a fiduciary duty as an adviser, Procter and Gamble that Bankers Trust failed to disclose information when it sold two swaps tied to the five and 30-year Treasury rates and German interest rates respectively. Lehman Brothers and Credit Suisse Financial Products have been sued on the grounds that the traders who undertook the deals did not have any authority to carry out such transactions. The former was sued by two Chinese companies, the China International United Petroleum Chemicals Co. and MinmeLais International Nonferrous Metals Trading Company and the latter by Malaysia's industrial conglomerate, Berjaya Industrial, whose wholly-owned Cayman Islands subsidiary, Berjaya Corporation lost $14 million on an interest rate swap.

These defaults were tied up more with legal risks than with credit risks. Traditional ways of managing legal risk — like making sure that comprehensive master agreements had been signed — were inadequate responses. In all the above instances, master agreements were signed. For these cases, the default losses stemmed from disagreements over sales practices rather than from whether proper documentation was in place.

NEW ADDITIONS IN A NETTED ENVIRONMENT

In 1995 banks entered a new phase of capital adequacy. Provided they met local legal requirements and had the necessary agreements in place, banks were allowed by the Bank for International Settlements to offset their claims against each other on a replacement cost basis, recognizing only the net amount. Netting, as this process is called, not only reduces credit risk, but also the capital that banks have to set aside to cover credit risks.

Netting reduced a bank's gross replacement value by 50% on average. A bank which conducted a lot of inter-bank dealing — covered by master netting agreements — found its replacement value reduced by 60%. A bank which had more customer business, where there are less netting

Continued on page 135

Continued from page 134

agreements in place, found its replacement value reduced by 40%. Consequently, netting reduced a bank's capital charges for credit risk by 25–40%.

But banks are required to set aside credit risk capital that covers both current mark-to-market values and changes in these replacement values. Add-on factors are meant to capture those potential changes. Bankers have argued that since netting reduces current and potential exposure, the 1988 add-on factors should be changed because they do not take into account the reduction effects of netting.

Banking regulators have heeded this call. In April 1995, the BIS released a new add-on formula that recognizes the risk reduction effects of netting. (See formula below.) But the regulators have chosen to incorporate a scaling factor of 0.6 into the formula to make sure that the cushion for the add-on for future exposure can never be zero, and to absorb any variability in the relationship between a bank's net and gross replacement values. They have also expanded the add-on matrix to include charges for commodities, precious metals, and refined the maturity bands. The BIS has also advised national supervisors to ensure that the 'add-ons are based on effective rather than apparent notional amounts. In the event that the stated notional amount is leveraged or enhanced by the structure of the transaction, banks must use the effective notional amount when determining potential future exposure.'

The BIS formula for add-ons released in July 1994 was:

$$\text{add-on} = (0.4 \times \text{notional} \times \text{BIS\%}) + (0.6 \times \text{notional} \times \text{BIS\%} \times \text{NGR})$$

where BIS% is the proposed percentage factor for the contract type and remaining maturity, and NGR is the current netted market value divided by the current grossed market value. The NGR will not fall below 0 or exceed 1.

The 1988 BIS formula was:

$$\text{Add-on} = \text{notional} \times \text{BIS\%}$$

Table 5.4 1995 BIS Add-on Percentages (1988 in brackets).

Remaining life	Interest rates	Foreign Exchange and Gold	Equity	Precious metals	Other commodities
< 1 yr	0.0 (0.0)	1.0 (1.0)	6.0 (none)	7.0 (none)	10.0 (none)
1–5 yrs	0.5 (0.5)	5.0 (5.0)	8.0 (none)	7.0 (none)	12.0 (none)
> 5 yrs	1.5 (0.5)	7.5 (5.0)	10.0 (none)	8.0 (none)	15.0 (none)

Continued on page 136

Continued from page 135

The new and old BIS add-on percentages and also the percentages applied under the original maturity method (see Tables 5.2 and 5.4) show that the capital banks have to set aside to cover the credit risk of derivatives increases linearly. Yet options have a curved payoff profile which should mean that their credit risk capital should not be linearly-grounded. The BIS has however addressed the curvature of options through its 1995 proposals on capital for market risk. (See Chapters 6 and 9.)

SUMMARY

A forward-based instrument is an agreement to buy or sell an asset in the future. Thus the additional risk of a forward (the word is used here generically), over and above price risk, is mostly interest-rate-related since the price of a forward is the future value of an asset in today's terms.

There are many facets to this interest-rate risk. Interest rates could change significantly so that the original cost of funding used to present-value the asset is totally inappropriate. The European Exchange Rate Mechanism crisis of September 1992 showed the pitfalls of assuming stable overnight rates. Spread risk arises because the yield differences between the same instruments of different quality, or between different instruments change, primarily influenced by demand and supply. The fact that the short-end of the yield curve seldom moves in tandem with the long-end gives rise to curve risk. End-users have to be aware of both risks when they hedge their exposures with instruments which are not identical.

Metallgesellschaft's $1.3 billion hedging loss illustrates the danger of curve risk in particular, or of basis risk in general. The latter is present in any hedge where the exposure being neutralized is not exactly matched by the hedge vehicle. (Curve and spread risk are basically interest-rate manifestations of basis risk.) It also highlights the need to analyse future margin and funding needs when end-users use exchange-traded contracts for their hedging programmes.

The dynamic nature of derivatives differentiates their credit risk from that of traditional instruments such as loans. The amount on which a counterparty may fail to perform consists of the current replacement value and potential exposure. Many professional houses use proprietary models to compute potential exposure, but end-users will find that risk factors contained in the Basle Capital Accord useful surrogates to estimate the credit exposure of their derivative portfolio.

REFERENCES

1. Morris Goldstein, M., Folkerts-Landau, D., Garber, P., Rojas-Suarez, L. and Spencer, M. (1993) International Capital Markets. Part 1 — Exchange Rate Management and International Capital Flows, International Monetary Fund, April.
2. Cookson, R. and Chew, L. 'Things fall apart', *RISK magazine*, October 1992, **5**, (9).
3. *The Economist*, finance section, 19 February, 1994.
4. Falloon, W. 'MG's trial by essay', *RISK magazine*, October 1994, **7**, (10).
5. Culp, C. and Miller, M. (1995) 'Metallgesellschaft and the economics of synthetic storage', *Journal of Applied Corporate Finance*, **7**, (4), Winter.
6. Gumerlock, R. (1993) 'Empirical measurement of swap credit risk', *The Journal of International Securities Markets*, **7**, spring/summer.
7. 'G-30 survey on dealer and user practices' (1993) Working Paper of the Credit Risk Measurement and Management Subcommittee, July.

6

Option Risks:
Curvature and Time Decay

The risks of options will be dealt with in two chapters: Chapter 6 will discuss curvature and time decay since both are directly but negatively related, while Chapter 7 will describe volatility. Also, as a broad generalization, the risks of curvature and time decay are more associated with short-dated options while volatility is viewed as a risk of long-dated options. Chapter 7 also includes a section on prepayment risk because appreciating this particular dimension of option risks is key to understanding the losses that have plagued investors of mortgage-backed securities.

The non-linear price profile of options is the first warning sign to users that they are venturing into unfamiliar territory. Initially, it appears familiar enough — options have directional and interest rate risks, which users have come across in spot and forward land. Indeed, even the curved profile (curvature) of an option may not be so strange either — bonds, swaps and forward-rate agreements also have some form of convexity. But the curvature of options is dynamic as opposed to the relatively stable convexity of bonds and some forward-based instruments.

The landscape becomes more alien with two risks that are unique to options, time decay and volatility. Both increase or decrease the uncertainty of asset flows inherent in all options and both affect the value of an option in such a way that the underlying asset's price need not change for the price of the option to change.

Because all options represent uncertain asset flows, spending much of their lives trying to resolve themselves into day or night, they must have a maturity. On expiry date, they are either day — worthwhile, or night — worthless (see Chapter 4). The expiry date of an option forces the resolution of an option's uncertainty. Consequently, all options have time value and so suffer from time decay. With each passing day, the buyer of an option has one less day for the underlying asset to move in the direction which enables his option to come into-the-money. The put option buyer who has bought insurance to protect his portfolio against price falls or the speculator who has bought a call to profit from price rises will find that their options will lose value even if the underlying asset price and volatility have not changed. This is due to the time decay of the option.

Anything with an embedded option also takes on the risks of options. Swaps with one leg squared or cubed also have the non-linear risk characteristics of options even though they are not options. However, they do not suffer the uncertainty of asset flows like options.

GAMMA (CONVEXITY) RISK

The previous chapters made it clear that delta (the change in the price of a derivative in relation to a move in the price of the underlying) is not constant and that it changes primarily as a result of the underlying asset price moving. The rate at which delta changes is known by another Greek letter: gamma. Some also call it convexity or curvature, and all three are used interchangeably.

Delta and gamma can be thought of as the two flavours of a derivative's price sensitivity just as speed and acceleration are two aspects of how a car moves. Delta is like speed, it describes how fast a car is going at a particular point in time. Gamma can be likened to acceleration because it describes the change in speed for a given change in time. Both speed and acceleration are functions of distance and time, but acceleration is derived from speed (a second-order effect). In the same way gamma is derived from delta and a second-order effect, but both are needed for a complete picture of an option's price behaviour.

Yet the two risks are discussed separately, with delta coming under spot risks and gamma under option risks. Why, you may ask, since gamma is essentially just a different manifestation of price risk? Indeed, as the description of gamma risks unfolds in this chapter, the fact that there is no definitive demarcation between the two becomes clear since the serious problems of hedging delta are due more to an option's gamma rather than its delta. (It is the gamma of an option that brings about the new delta.)

The reason why these two flavours of price risks have been separated is because only options have curvature whose magnitude is so great that managing them is critical to ensuring a firm's well-being. Forward-based instruments and even fixed income bonds have curvature but the risks posed from their curvature are dwarfed by that of options. Underlying assets have zero gamma because they change one-for-one with themselves. This is why gamma or curvature is regarded specifically as an option risk.

For the rest of this chapter, gamma will be discussed in the context of options because it causes an option's delta to change like a chameleon — when market moves are large — making it *almost* a first-order risk for options. The true first-order risk is price risk but that affects all derivatives and cash instruments, and there is an implicit assumption among all large derivative providers that this price risk is usually hedged. Against this background, gamma is often seen as the most important option risk to manage (and why many people view it as a risk unique to options).

Gamma is the buzzword in the world of derivatives because gamma, not properly managed, can cause a firm to lose significant amounts of money. And what is gamma risk? It is the risk that results from options having dynamic price sensitivities, i.e. deltas that not only change but change fluidly. That really is not the issue; what causes problems is the fact the price of an option changes in a non-linear (curved) way while the price of the underlying asset, on which the option is based, moves linearly. The risk arises from the fact that if an option seller uses the underlying asset and/or forward-based instruments (which display none or little of this curvature) to hedge changes in his option value, he will find himself seriously underhedged or overhedged if the price of the underlying asset fluctuated significantly. The greater the curvature of the option, the greater the risk of finding himself unhedged and losing money. That's why some people refer to gamma as curvature risk.

The curvature of an option is rooted in the asymmetry of the payoff potentials that characterize the instrument. In one direction of the price movement of the underlying asset, the option is 'in-the-money' and its payoff resembles the underlying itself (delta approaches 100%.) In the opposite direction, the option is 'out-of-the-money' and pays nothing (delta approaches 0%). The curvature of options versus the linearity of spot and forward-based instruments means that attempting to imitate the option curvature with these instruments necessarily requires continuing adjustment. (This is the delta-hedging process described in Chapter 4.)

The more pronounced the curvature, the higher the number of adjustments. It is exactly like fitting tangent lines to a curve (see Figure 4.12 on page 97). The greater the curvature, the harder it is to fit the tangent lines to iron out the facets. And if the price of the underlying moved quickly from 10 to 15, there will be many tangent lines needed to imitate that curvature — something that the delta-hedger does not have the luxury of doing because he finds himself in a vicious circle. By the time he has finished drawing the numerous tangent lines to fit one part of the curve, the option's price behaviour will be represented by a different part of the curve.

Gamma Generalizations

Gamma measures how the price sensitivity of an option will change given a change in the price of the underlying. Essentially, it shows how quickly an option becomes unhedged. Thus, an option with a small gamma will not becomes unhedged as quickly as one with a large gamma; it is not as sensitive to price changes in the underlying asset as the latter option. (Mathematically, gamma is expressed in deltas gained or lost per one point change in the underlying asset price.) It was pointed out in Chapter 4 that a far out-of-the-money option has a low delta (close to 0%) and a deep in-the-money option a high delta (100%). But both these options have very small or zero gammas (because their deltas do not change when the underlying asset price moves; for the out-of-the-money it is because it is very price insensitive and for the in-the-money option, because the option is already behaving like the underlying).

A near-the-money option has a high gamma because the option's delta responds increasingly to price moves in the underlying; a small move has a huge impact on the probability of exercise. An at-the-money option has an even higher gamma, since a small change in the price of the underlying can make all the difference between the option being exercised or expiring worthless.

But an option's maturity also has a significant influence on its gamma. A near-the-money option that is expiring soon has a higher gamma than one with a longer time to maturity because the further from maturity, the more insensitive is the option's delta to price changes in the underlying. The long time to expiry means that even if the underlying market does change substantially, there is every chance that it would move back again. For short-dated options, a similar move in the underlying market would have a significant impact on delta since chances are high that the underlying would still be at the new level when the option expires.

Thus an option that is at-the-money and expiring soon has the highest gamma of all options. Why? Because even the smallest price moves of the underlying asset have a huge impact on the option's value; what's more the speed with which the gamma changes is very fast.

To generalise, gamma is a risk associated mainly with short-dated options; the gamma number always being higher for a short-dated option than a long-dated option, all things being equal. A large gamma number indicates a high degree of risk because the delta of the option will change more quickly than one with a small gamma. Since delta is also the hedge ratio of the option, a high gamma means the option becomes unhedged easily.

At-the-money options near expiration, having the highest gamma, are the most difficult to manage. The following example illustrates this point. Let's say a call option with a strike of 6% has three more days to run. Libor (or the index against which the strike is set) is at 6%. If in the next three days Libor moves down by even 2 basis points (5.98%), the option is out-of-the-money and expires worthless while if Libor moved up by even 1 basis point (6.01%), the option is in-the- money. The rate of change of delta in this instance is dramatic; with gamma being so high, delta hedging these almost instantaneous changes in sensitivities is problematic to say the least. It can be made even more painful if Libor whips around 6% rather than maintaining a steady course upwards or downwards.

The Gamma Mountain

Chapter 4 introduced the concept of the twilight zone, in which an option spent most of its life trying to become day (delta = 100%) or night (delta = 0%). Delta and gamma are two dimensions of an option's price behaviour. If delta indicates how much the option has resolved itself, then gamma shows the option's drive to resolve itself. An option with a high gamma indicates that the option will resolve itself more quickly than one with a low gamma because the former's delta will change faster. Three factors influence this resolution: the underlying asset's price, and increasing or decreasing uncertainty. In option land, uncertainty is directly related to volatility and the passage of time. Rising volatility and the lengthening of time contribute to increased uncertainty, and declining volatility and the passing of time to decreased uncertainty. Since gamma and delta are two dimensions of the price sensitivity of an option, these three factors influence gamma as they do delta.

Their impact is best illustrated by extending some of the analogies used in Chapter 4. Think of the bell-shaped curve as a mountain, and gamma being visually represented by the steepness of a mountain slope (see Figure 6.1). A gentle slope means low or reducing gamma and a steep slope means high or advancing gamma.

Chapter 4 established that the passing of time caused uncertainty to decrease which narrows the width of the bell-shaped curve, i.e. it transforms the mountain into one with steeper slopes. As time passes, i.e. the life of the option shortens. This is equivalent to the mountain becoming steeper and steeper so that in the end it looks like a pinnacle (see Figure 4.8 on page 95). Any option that sits on this mountain, whether on the peak or on the slopes, will accumulate more and more gamma (since the mountain slopes get steeper.) It is easy to see why any option with a few days left to maturity has very high gamma (because the slopes are so steep) and why a large gamma indicates a quick resolution. One false step on that pinnacle and the option crashes down to 0% or 100%.

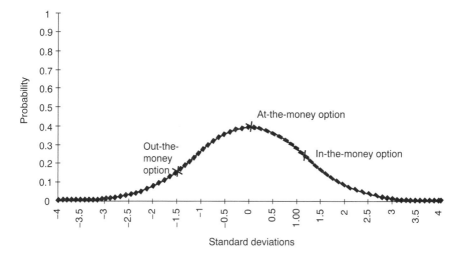

Figure 6.1 Original Mountain.

This same analogy can be used to explain why long-dated options have low gamma. If the passing of time decreases uncertainty then the extending of time increases uncertainty. This has the same effect on the shape of the mountain as increasing volatility — the mountain becomes a hillock with gentle slopes (see Figure 4.7 on page 94). Any option that sits on this hillock has a low gamma and will take a longer time to roll down to the bottom of the mountain.

Superimposing the hillock on the pinnacle, it is easy to see why at-the-money options expiring soon have the highest gamma. Chapter 4 established that at-the-money options always sit on the peak of the mountain because that represents the middle of the mountain, coinciding with a delta of 50%. The mountain becomes steeper with the passage of time so that on the last day the mountain is just a precipice. The at-the-money option perched on the top of this precipice is like Humpty Dumpty sitting on the wall — the only question is which side of the precipice is the option going to fall. Any vaguely decisive event, even a light breeze (i.e. small market move), could tilt this precariously perched option either way. That is why an at-the-money option, in its last days, has a gamma approaching infinity.

The same analogy can be used to explain why the gamma of an at-the-money option falls when volatility increases and rises when volatility decreases. When prices of the underlying asset become more volatile, they bring about greater uncertainty, which as was pointed out in Chapter 4 causes the mountain to become a hillock with gentle slopes. It is visually obvious from Figure 4.7 that the gamma of the at-the-money option sitting on this transformed mountain declines because gentle slopes mean descending gamma.

If market conditions then quietened down, it would lead to reduced volatility. When prices of the underlying asset become less volatile, they contribute to increased certainty. This makes the mountain a pinnacle again as in Figure 4.8 on page 95. A steep mountain means a high gamma. Figure 6.2 summarizes the impact of increased and decreased uncertainty on the gamma of out-, in- and at-the-money options.

Positive and Negative Gamma

Long call options have positive deltas while long put options have negative deltas. And if delta and gamma are two flavours of an option's price sensitivities, then by logical extension, call options should have positive gamma and put options negative gamma. Unfortunately, it does not work this way. Both long call and put options have positive gammas and this only becomes clear by using an example. Say a call option has a delta of 60 and a gamma of 5 and a put option a delta of −40 and a gamma of 5. If the underlying market rises, the call option has a new delta of 65 (60 + 5). The call goes deeper into-the-money and that is shown by its increasing delta. What about the put option — should its new delta be −45 or −35? If the delta of an option shows its moneyness, then the put option's delta should

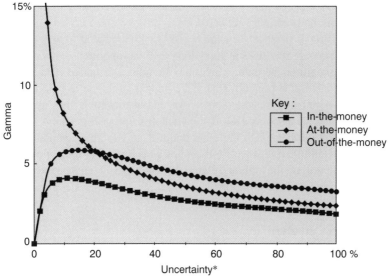

Figure 6.2   Effect of Uncertainty on Gamma.

now be −35 because the option is even further out-of-the-money, now that the underlying asset price has risen. Because negative numbers become less negative as they approach zero, (remember when a put option is really in-the-money it has a high negative delta and a low negative delta when it is out-of-the-money), the gamma of an option is always added to its old delta to arrive at the new delta when the underlying market price rises. Conversely, the gamma is always subtracted from the delta of an option, when the underlying asset price falls, regardless of whether it is a put or a call.

Unlike positive and negative delta, positive and negative gamma describe a market participant's option position. If he is long options, whether they are puts or calls, he has positive gamma. If he is short options, he has negative gamma.

Negative gamma comes from being short options in any form — from direct selling of naked options to buying structured notes or collateralized mortgage obligations which contain *embedded short options*. It is thus not surprising that negative gamma is also known as short gamma. The return characteristics of a negative gamma exposure are to make a little, make a little, make a little money most of the time, than to have an event occur which causes you to lose all those accumulated gains. Insurance companies selling household insurance policies (option sellers sell insurance against financial risks) face negative gamma risks — in most cases, they collect small premiums over many years and never have to pay out most of the time; but once in a while a natural disaster (earthquake, floods, tornadoes) strikes the area where most of the policy holders live, and they are forced to pay out sums much larger than the premiums collected.

From an end-user's perspective gamma risks can be reduced to negative (short) gamma risks. There are few risks in being long gamma (options) — an option buyer may waste the premiums he paid, which may be quite substantial if he bought at-the-money options and a princely sum if he bought in-the-money options, if the instruments then finished out-the-money. An end-user who is long gamma also suffers time decay, because as each day passes, his option loses some of its time value (see section on theta). On the other hand, if he was short gamma he would have potentially unlimited downside but his upside is limited to the option premium he earned from selling the option (Figure 1.3 on page 11 shows the difference between being long and short options).

Gamma versus Curvature

Negative gamma, not managed properly can seriously impact a firm's profitability, so it is vital that option sellers are able to forsee their gamma risks. But how do you do that? It is possible, for example, to have a position that has zero gamma but lots of curvature. This does appear a contradictory statement and part of the confusion seems to stem from the industry using the words gamma/curvature interchangeably. Although gamma and curvature of options are often regarded as the same thing, there is a subtle difference which has to be recognized when managing curvature risks.

Delta, it has been pointed out, changes with moves in the underlying asset price, volatility and the passing of time. Gamma measures that change in delta for one unit change in the underlying asset's price. If gamma is measured this way, then by definition gamma is a local measure, giving the option seller information about an option's price behaviour at that point in time and for small market moves around that point in time. Gamma can thus be seen as the localized curvature of an option, and indeed for small market moves may appear to be linear. (If there ever was a prize for a contradiction in terms this surely qualifies.)

The curvature of an option is a broader measure — it is that entire curved line showing how an option responds in a non-linear way to changes in the underlying prices; the larger the price moves, the greater the curvature. It is this broader picture of gamma that worries option sellers and should in turn, be a prime concern of those who manage them, and in turn those who regulate the managers.

An analogy for the subtle difference between gamma and curvature is whether the earth is flat or round. Seen from our window, the earth is flat because our perspective of the curvature of the earth is so small that we cannot see that it is round. That it is a globe can only be seen from outer space; similarly the full picture of the curvature of an option can only be appreciated from a distance.

Capturing Gamma Risks

The curvature of options, as opposed to their localized gamma, is another reason why anyone who deals in options cannot use the current delta of an option to extrapolate the future value of the option (and thus where its gamma risks lie). The following example taken from a paper written by Paul Kupiec and James O'Brien of the US Federal Reserve Board[1] illustrates this difficulty. Figure 6.3 below shows the value of put options on zero coupon bonds when interest rates are between 8 to 10%. The options are very far out-of-the-money when interest rates are at 8%; consequently their delta is small. When rates rise to 10%, the options are nearer-the-money. The dashed line shows the values of the options arrived by extrapolating their instantaneous delta. For relatively small increases in interest rates (e.g. up to 100 basis points), the delta approximation method gives a fairly accurate measure of the options' price changes. It is fair to say that when interest rates moved from 8 to 8.5%, or even 9%, the options had little curvature, i.e. their price sensitivities were pretty constant. But this generalization was completely wrong for large increases in interest rates. A move from 8 to 10% shows the full magnitude of the options' curvature; their deltas changed a lot when interest rates moved from 9 to 10%,

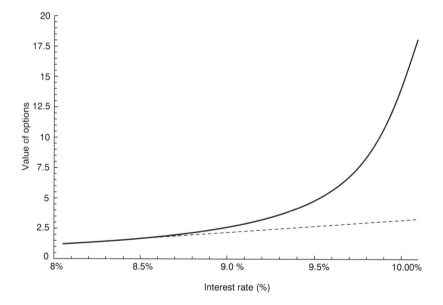

These put options are valued using the Black-Scholes option pricing formula. The "delta approximation" gives the change in the value of the options for a small change in the interest rate, evaluated at the initial interest rate. The dashed line shows the initial value of the option (at an 8% interest rate) plus the change in value obtained from the delta approximation multiplied by the change in the interest rate.

Figure 6.3   How Curvature of an Option Cannot be Captured by Delta Approximation. Reproduced by permission from US Federal Reserve Board.

so much so that their values increased from 2.75 to 19%. The instantaneous delta approximation method on the other hand shows the options' value increasing from 2.5 to 3.5%.

The Federal Reserve graph brings home the fact that option curvature is a risk management (or P&L) issue only if market moves are large. Curvature does not rear its ugly head when market moves are small. That is why having gamma limits based on current market sensitivities (the G-30 report recommends using a confidence interval of two standard deviations and a time horizon of one day to measure delta and gamma risks) represents only half of gamma risk management. Such gamma limits tend to take into account only at- or near-the-money options which already have high gammas and which do not need large market moves to make their gamma management tricky. But firms have learned to cope with this type of curvature-problem because they can forsee such gamma risks. It is thus not surprising that many firms keep such options, especially those near expiry, to a minimum.

But such limits do not capture potential gamma risks posed by out-of-the-money options. Neither are such risks thrown up by simulating at current or near-current market prices. The out-of-the-money options will remain out-of-the-money, their gammas will remain inconsequential and the option seller will be lulled into a false sense of comfort because his gamma camera did not have a lens with a wide enough angle to take the full picture. And because markets can move around a lot, a wide angle lens is compulsory.

The correct way to capture an option's curvature is to work out mathematically the valuation change over a number of price moves. That is why firms with large option books simulate various scenarios, assuming different degrees of market moves, to gain a full picture of all the potential gamma risks (though some say they do not do it on long-dated options because their gammas are small so it is a waste of resources to do so). Simulation enables the firm to have an inkling of what proportion of the portfolio could change from being just option positions to ones that to all intents and purposes act exactly like, and have the profit and loss characteristics of the underlying. The option seller is thus able to quantify the expected certainty of an option portfolio's uncertainty; to predict the amount, timing and type of future asset flows emanating from its option positions.

The simplest way of simulating large market moves is to use long time horizons because the longer the assumed holding period, the greater the assumed price changes. But how long a holding period? And should one look at ordinary events or extraordinary conditions? This is where the debate among derivatives professionals heats up and they are completely divided on the issue.

On one side of the divide are those who believe that short-time intervals and simulating ordinary events is adequate. For them using one-day or one-week and confidence intervals of two standard deviations as a base measure is fine. They accept that extrapolating the one-day risk measure into a longer time interval by multiplying by the square root of time is a crude approximation but that it gives enough information about a firm's potential gamma risks. (To scale up from a one day to a ten day measure, one cannot just multiply the one day number by ten. One has to use the square root of ten because time has a non-linear impact on option values. A two-month option does not cost twice as much as a one-month option. If a one-month option costs $5, then the two-month option costs 5 × square root of 2 = $7.07.) On the other side of the divide are those who insist that only by using long time intervals, say one year, can a firm capture extraordinary events. And a firm must simulate for extraordinary conditions because in financial markets, extraordinary events — such as the Crash of 1987, the Exchange Rate Mechanism crisis of 1992, the protracted bond market plunge of 1994 — happen more frequently than textbook statistics say they should. Only stress simulation allows a firm to identify its gamma black holes and the pain it will experience should those events materialize.

The Regulators Wade In

In April 1995, the Bank for International Settlements — through the Basle Committee on Banking Supervision — issued a supplement to the 1988 *Basle Capital Accord* which mandated banks to set aside capital to cover credit risks. The capital adequacy supplement proposes guidelines for the calculation of market risk capital. The potential impact of option curvature on a bank's financial health has so concerned the regulators that the Committee has concluded that banks' internal risk management systems must capture the non-linear price behaviour of options and so must the capital banks set aside to cover market risks. At the very minimum, banks must use a non-linear approximation approach to capture gamma. The Committee recommends that they should strive to use options risk management models (stress scenarios) to calculate all possible changes in option values resulting from moves in the underlying markets.

Because curvature will not show up with short (for e.g. one-day) holding periods, the Basle Committee has decided that banks must use two weeks (i.e. ten working days) as a minimum holding period when calculating capital for option positions. This two-week period also applies to positions that display option-like characteristics. Firms with significant option positions will not be allowed to scale up one day numbers. The Basle Committee's decision shows that a linear approach to regulatory capital (which underpinned the credit risk capital charges) is being discarded in favour of one that mirrors more accurately the market risks of options and option-like positions.

Gapping Markets

The curvature risks of options which come from large market moves is compounded when there are gaps in the prices of the underlying assets, i.e. markets opening way below or above where they closed. Unfortunately, the two seem to go hand in hand.

Witness the price discontinuities that plagued the Italian lire, the Spanish peseta and the British pound as they fell out of their Exchange Rate Mechanism bands in September 1992 or fixed income bonds as they plunged in February/March 1994 and the Mexican peso crisis in early 1995.

The markets crashed from one level to another with few transactions taking place. Prices were marked down drastically, like goods in a demolition or closing down clearance sale, even before transactions took place. Any option seller who attempted to hedge his delta/gamma risks could not rebalance fast enough because by the time he had hedged his option position, it would have become unhedged. In such conditions hedging the curvature of options through the cash/futures was well nigh impossible because this strategy assumes small market moves with ample liquidity. John Hull, co-author of the Hull-White model for interest rate options believes that during the ERM crisis, the price moves of the currencies under pressure (sterling, lira, peseta) were so large that rebalancing very hour would not have been enough[2]. Granted such conditions were extreme but it is precisely in such conditions that the position of option sellers becomes precarious.

The ERM crisis also highlighted another problem of hedging an option's two-dimensional price risk using cash and futures. Markets are assumed to be liquid, continuous and orderly. But during the crisis it was hard to get dealable quotes for large amounts — the markets were discontinuous and illiquid (in terms of dealable size and spreads), so even if a currency option seller knew how much of a currency he had to sell to hedge his put option, he could not find a dealer in the cash or futures markets willing to deal.

An International Monetary Fund report notes,

> According to most observers, the forex market — as well as domestic money markets in the ERM countries — generally worked well during the crisis. Given the huge volumes of securities and currencies traded during that period — as well as attempts to ration liquidity to those taking positions against existing parities — that outcome was hardly preordained. There were indeed strains. While forex spot markets operated continuously, spreads at times widened from five to ten times the norm in most of the ERM cross-rates. The size of trades also declined at times. For example, the normal size of a lira-deutsche mark trade is DM50 million, but this size was not available in mid-September (1992). Market makers in lira and sterling forwards and swaps stopped making two-sided quotes in mid-September, and on the eve of these currencies' withdrawal from the ERM, interbank activity had essentially come to a halt .... The forward sterling market recovered by the end of the week, but the lira market remained inactive for up to two weeks after the devaluation.[3]

Devaluation is a classic example of markets gapping and the ERM crisis showed how option sellers coped with curvature risks via the cash market. Sellers of out-of-the-money sterling put options initially had low price risk since these options had small deltas. If they had followed the rule-book, then they would have hedged the price risks of these options by selling the amount of sterling dictated by the options' deltas. But the prospect of devaluation cast a different complexion on the then current delta and gamma numbers.

The possibility of sterling being devalued was very real as 16 September 1992 approached and certainly after the Italian lira was devalued on 13 September 1992. Devaluation transformed overnight, these out-of-the-money put options to at-or in-the-money. Their deltas shot up instantaneously, they went from being night to day without spending any time in twilight. If the put sellers had just adhered to the deltas and gammas dictated by their option pricing model, they would have been significantly underhedged when devaluation took place. They could not find offsetting options at an acceptable price because by then everyone wanted put options. Their next best recourse was to par-hedge their positions[2], i.e. they hedged all 100% of it as opposed to the amount dictated by the delta. They believed that in such instances, the put options would go instantaneously from being out- or at-the money to being deeply in-the-money. Once they were deeply in-the-money, they had deltas of 100% and behaved like the underlying asset, so selling in advance the full amount of the to-be-devalued currency made sense.

Hedging Gamma

Gamma risks are best hedged by using instruments that have curvature, so it is obvious that options are the best hedge — buying other options if you are short and selling options if you are long. The safest way is to buy an option with roughly similar terms. The more closely matched they are, the less chance of some intervening event affecting one option and not the other. This is not always possible — the market in options for a particular asset may not be liquid enough for an option seller to find an offsetting position immediately.

Indeed, some option markets are one-way. For example, options on emerging market debt (i.e. Brazilian or Mexican bonds) or South East Asian equities were the rage in 1993. The trouble was there were lots of buyers but no natural sellers, so even if the sellers wanted to hedge with options, they could not find any. They were forced to delta-hedge their option positions in the underlying cash markets. (There are no futures markets for emerging market bonds nor are there any for South East Asian stocks, so this route of delta-hedging is also closed.)

Option-sellers can keep a delta-hedge in place until they identify a party willing to sell them offsetting options. Indeed, this combination course of action is very common for even the most developed of option markets — sell an option, delta-hedge the spot exposure and shop around for an option that meets your needs precisely. Or delta-hedge because the markets are expected to be quiet in the short-term (so it is relatively safe), and then switch to option cover once the markets become more volatile (when even the most continuous of adjustments may result in underperformance.) For all its limitations, delta-hedging affords the option seller the luxury of not scurrying around for option cover, and perhaps paying too much for it in the process, or buying an ill-fitting compromise.

Gamma-hedging is often achieved by a combination of options — mixed and matched so that the end result approximates the gamma requirements of the option(s) being hedged. In general, most over-the-counter options have maturities of more than one year, while the surrogate hedges for them are short-dated exchange-traded options. Because short-dated options have higher gamma than long-dated options, the hedger has to buy less short-dated options to hedge his gamma risks. But hedging gamma risks this way cannot be a static exercise — because the gammas of the options being used to hedge and the options being hedged change at different speeds, the firm with a large option book must continuously monitor and fine-tune the hedge. Gamma-hedging, unless it is done with mirror options, is a dynamic and time consuming exercise.

That is why end-users who sell options and have negative gamma risks should not consider gamma-hedging to neutralize their option risks. It is an exercise that only professional option sellers should undertake. If an end-user needs to gamma-hedge his option positions because they are naked and cannot live with their potential negative P&L impact, then he should not have sold them in the first place. It is unlimited downside for limited upside.

TIME DECAY (THETA) RISK

If an option's life is viewed as an exercise in resolving uncertainty, then it is impera-tive that all options have an expiry date. On maturity, the uncertainty regarding their asset flows is resolved. That is why the passage of time decreases uncertainty — as the option moves towards its expiry date, it knows it is going to resolve itself one way or another. (This is also the reason why there are no infinite options because that would mean open-ended uncertainty which would be impossible to manage.)

But the maturity of an option is also a component of its value; the other being intrinsic value. The latter is the financial benefit which the buyer enjoys if he exercised the instrument immediately; it is the in-the-money portion of an option's price. See Figure 6.4. The time value of an option represents the value to the buyer that during its life, the price of the underlying asset can move so as to make his position profitable. Consequently, long-dated options have more time value than short-dated options because the longer the period to expiration, the more time there is for the option to come into-the-money.

Because an option has time value, its total price will usually exceed its intrinsic value. For an in-the-money option, the intrinsic value is the difference between the current price of the underlying asset and the strike price of the option; anything above that is what the market places on the option's time value. It follows therefore that an out-of-the-money option has little intrinsic value and only time value since the difference between the strike and the underlying asset price is negative.

Since time runs in only one direction, the time value of an option can only erode. This is known as the theta or time decay of an option. It is a positive number regardless of whether the option is a put or a call and is expressed in

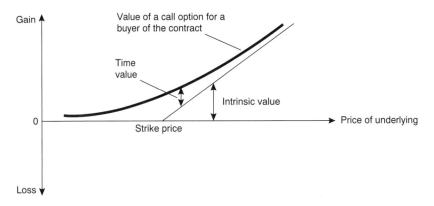

The value of an option contract (heavily shaded line) is composed of its 'intrinsic' value - the payoff on the option at expiration plus its 'time' value - the value attributable to the volatility in the underlying over the remaining life of the option. The 'hockey stick' profile shown by the other line reflects the intrinsic value of the option. The curved line represents the value of the option at some time prior to expiration.

Figure 6.4   Value of an Option. Reproduced by permission from the G-30 Report.

points lost per day. All other factors remaining equal, an option's price tends to decrease with time decay since there is less time for the underlying asset's price to move in a favourable way.

Theta risk refers to the risk that as an option matures, time value is lost without any increase in the value of other variables affecting the price of an option. But while long-dated options have more time value than short-dated options, theta is a risk more associated with short-dated options. Why? Because with long-dated options, each passing day means the option is losing only a tiny bit of its time value. With short-dated options, every passing day means that there is even less chance of the underlying asset price moving in your favour. The time decay is larger because the time value of the option is spread over less days so each passing day represents a sizeable chunk of its time value.

The Shape of Time Decay

The time values of options do not decay in the same way. In-the-money and out-of-the-money options lose their time value in a fairly linear fashion, more so than at-the-money options. Both exhaust their time value earlier in their lives than at-the-money options. Generally, in- and out-of-the-money options have no time value when they are on their last legs. This can be explained with the normal distribution graph that is used to describe the random price movements of financial assets (back to the bell-shaped curve of Chapter 4.). The at-the-money option sits on the peak again while the out-of-the-money and in-the-money options are situated on the slopes. It was pointed out earlier that the passage of time narrows the width of the bell-shaped curve. As the former narrows, the in-the-money and out-of-the money options are left high and dry since the tails are coming closer and closer. Consequently in the final part of their lives, out-and in-the-money options have no time decay because it is already fairly certain whether they would be exercised or not.

At-the-money options have the most time value and they display fairly non-linear time decay — initially, the time decay is constant and relatively linear. It then accelerates in the second half of the option's life and is at its most convex during the final days of an option's life (see Figure 6.5).

Each day is precious; the time value contributes substantially to the option's full value because the option could either move into or out-of-the-money. With each passing day, it suffers a large time decay because there is one less day for it to come into-the-money.

Since options lose their time value as they approach maturity they are at their cheapest then (all else being equal). End-users who buy such options and make a right call on the underlying market can make very high percentage returns on their small cash outlays. They have maximized the leverage offered by options — but

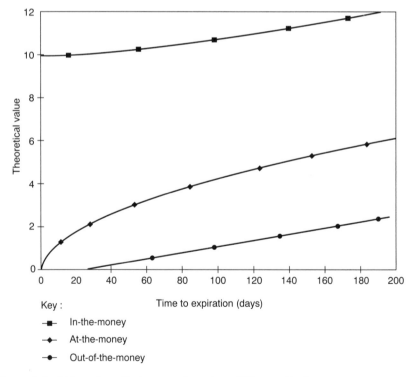

Figure 6.5   Value of an Option as a Function of Time to Expiry.

they are taking very high risks because the options have only a very small window in which to move into-the-money. If they do not, the premiums are wasted.

Hedging Theta

A long option position results in negative theta. This is because being long an option means losing time value every day. The corollary is a short option position has positive theta. But being long options also means having positive gamma while short options is negative gamma. So the gamma and theta of an option position have opposite signs — a short option position has negative gamma and positive theta and a long option position has positive gamma and negative theta. There is also a very strong relationship between their sizes. An at-the-money option near its expiry date has a large gamma, but it also has a large theta because an option's time decay is largest as it approaches maturity. (At maturity, an option's time value is zero and the option's value is equal to its intrinsic value.) Gamma and theta are often viewed as one risk because they are negatively related and their relative sizes are positively correlated. This is important from a risk management perspective because a hedge for gamma can be a hedge for theta.

Both risks are exhibited most by at-the-money options close to expiry. On a macro-level, theta is not as important an option risk as gamma or vega because being short those two risks can cause an option seller to lose a lot of money whereas the option buyer only loses premium. But on a micro level, it can be quite important in a market that is quiet in directional and volatility terms. Someone who is long options in such an environment will find his options losing value principally due to their time decay; this loss is greatest in the last few weeks of an option's life.

SUMMARY

The payoff profile of options is so non-linear that this curvature has been given its own Greek letter 'gamma'. An option has gamma risks because its sensitivity to price movements in the underlying assets (deltas) change fluidly. Gamma is a mathematical measure of how these price sensitivities change for given moves in the underlying and indicates how quickly an option becomes unhedged. Curvature in itself should not present risk management difficulties — the problem lies in trying to hedge the curvature of options with instruments that have linear profiles, a characteristic of spot and forward-based derivatives.

Anyone who sells options is short gamma, or has a negative gamma position. A person who buys options is long gamma. Gamma risk is most problematic when market moves are large or when markets gap; the person who is short gamma finds himself seriously under- or over-hedged and perhaps unable to rebalance his hedge quickly enough. Many professionals traders have lost money because they have found themselves short gamma, even though they thought they were gamma-neutral, because extreme market moves caused their out-of-the-money options to become at- or near-the-money. At- or near-the-money options have the highest gamma because they are extremely sensitive to price changes in the underlying asset.

The potential for losses is unlimited if a market participant is short gamma. On the other hand, a player who is long gamma faces the possibility of wasting his premium and the option losing value because of time decay. The best way to hedge gamma risk is to buy a similar offsetting option. End-users who sell options must evaluate whether they can withstand the profit/loss impact of being short gamma because hedging negative gamma by buying an offsetting option would probably mean paying away the premium earned from the original sale.

Options must have an expiry date because that forces their resolution. Thus all options have time value; with each passing day this value erodes because there is less opportunity for the underlying markets to move in the direction that enables the option to come in-to-the-money. The time decay of an option is known as theta risk.

Gamma and theta risk are often viewed as one risk because they are negatively related. A hedge for gamma is thus seen as a hedge for theta. Gamma risk although not unique to options is seen mainly as a risk of options while theta risk is unique to options.

REFERENCES

1. Kupiec, P. and O'Brien, J. (1995), 'The use of bank trading risk models for regulatory capital purposes,' *RISK magazine*, May, **8** (5).
2. Cookson, R. and Chew, L. (1992), 'Things fall apart,' *RISK magazine*, October, **5** (9).
3. Goldstein, M., Folkerts-Landau, M., Garber, P., Rojas-Suarez, L., and Spencer, M. (1993), 'International capital markets, Part 1. Exchange rate management and international capital flows,' International Monetary Fund, April.

7

Option Risks: Volatility and Prepayment

This chapter will discuss the various aspects of volatility that are pertinent to option users. In contrast to other instruments, option values are affected not just by price changes in the underlying assets but also by the volatility of those prices. This volatility is reflected in the amount of uncertainty surrounding the future price of an asset. The more volatile an asset, the more uncertain people are about its future price movements. And because it is future uncertainty that is the main worry; it is future not current or historical volatility that is a major preoccupation of option users.

The second part of this chapter will look at prepayment risk which is similar to the risks of having sold a call option. Unlike other topics covered under option risks — curvature, time decay or volatility, prepayment is not a subset of option risks. It has been included in this chapter because the prepayment risk inherent in all mortgage-backed securities has peculiar characteristics which warrants a section on its own. It was prepayment risk that caused many investors in 1994 — from cash-rich Glaxo (a British pharmaceutical giant) to small American colleges — to lose money. The former shrugged off its £105 million losses (its total investment portfolio was £2.2 billion). Odessa Junior College in Texas, one of the many American colleges, lost $22 million and had to borrow $12 million from local banks to cover running costs.

The final part of this chapter attempts to tie together the risks of derivatives — how risks are transferred and in the process transformed every time a derivative transaction is initiated. It will also point out how various risks can creep in easily at different stages in the risk transference process. Derivative providers are not magicians — they cannot pull bunny rabbits out of a hat, so anyone who obtains funding below the level of his credit rating, or investment yields above market rates, must be taking on other risks embedded in the structure.

VOLATILITY (VEGA) RISK

The more variable are the spot price movements of an asset, the more volatile the asset is said to be. But as a risk to be managed, volatility is unique to options, and is defined as the risk of an option position changing in value as a result of changes in the underlying asset's volatility.

Volatility is one of the key determinants of an option's price; but it is also the only input that is not decided at the discretion of the option buyer and seller or in some other market. The strike price and life of the option are decided by the buyer and seller or the standardized contracts of an exchange. The current price of the underlying is set in the cash market, while carrying costs are market-determined by the relevant yield curves. Volatility is the only variable that is decided by the option seller (or the option market).

Viewed in this way, it is clear that the market for an option on any underlying asset is in fact the market's price for the volatility on that underlying asset, quite separate from the price of underlying itself. That's why some traders quote the price of an option in terms of volatility rather than the premium one has to pay to buy an option, or receive on selling an option. And even if they don't quote option prices in volatility terms, the notion that volatility is a price itself is manifested in the way many traders work backwards from the price of an option to arrive at the volatility implied in the price. The most commonly used option pricing model is the Black-Scholes model. Five variables — the spot price of the underlying asset, the strike price of the option, discount rate, maturity of option and spot price volatility — are plugged into the model to obtain an option price. Reversing out the implied volatility means inputting an option price (as one of the variables) into the model to obtain the volatility. Intuitively, this implied volatility can be thought of as the *combined* but *current judgement* of the market about the *future uncertainty* of a given forward price — the higher the implied volatility the more uncertain they are about the forward price.

Types of Volatility

Implied volatility, as we have seen is the volatility number that is derived from looking at current option prices and solving standard option pricing models backwards, since all the other variables are known or given. Since implied volatility is the number that justifies an option price, an option buyer or seller can use that number to evaluate whether his or her option is cheap or expensive, by comparing it with the implied volatility of other options in the market. But since the number derived is dependent on the pricing model being used, different models can yield different results so these implied volatility numbers have to be used with care.

The option buyer can also compare the implied volatility with other measures of volatility — historical, future and forecast. Historical volatility measures the actual price movements of the asset over a period in the past. Two inputs go into historical volatility measurements. The first decision to be made is the time horizon over which the price volatility is observed i.e. should historical data go back as far as five years or two years or only the last year. Then the time intervals between the data points has to be chosen — having decided to use the past year's volatility data, does one use daily, or weekly or even ten-day volatility numbers? Both are specified by the user and should be consistent across all asset classes. The user also has to decide whether the data is equally weighted or whether more weighting should be given to recent data since the latter might be more representative of future volatility over the immediate and near-term. Since volatility is itself quite volatile, the fact that market participants have their own ideas of the historical time horizon of data they need gives rise to different volatility numbers for the same asset class. Since volatility is such a key input into option pricing and market risk measurement models, the discrepancies in volatility numbers can give rise to results which are significantly different. Although the past is no predictor of the future, historical volatilities give an option buyer an idea of an asset's range of volatilities, to help him judge whether current implied volatility, which is simply the market's forecast of volatility, is expensive by historical standards.

Future volatility is what everyone wants to know since if you knew the future volatility of an asset, you would be able to feed the correct number into the option pricing model and arrive at the right price. Forecast volatility is what traders think actual volatility will be in the future. Some people therefore argue, wrongly, that implied volatility can be used to predict future volatility although a number of academic papers have come to the conclusion that implied volatility is no better than historical volatility at predicting future volatility. This is because implied volatility is priced by traders who look at different segments of historical data and then decide subjectively which one is most appropriate for the option they are pricing. Implied volatility is also a function of demand and supply. If there was a lot of demand for put options on the US dollar, it would bid up the price of such options because there would be buyers but no sellers. Sellers would only reappear when the market quietened down or when implied volatilities are bid to such a point where it would tempt some brave souls to stick their necks out and start selling options. In times of market turmoil, implied volatility cannot be used to predict future volatility because it is so coloured by demand/supply considerations. For example during the ERM crisis of 1992, the implied volatility for currency options on sterling or the French franc was 25%. An International Monetary Fund report on the ERM crisis[1] noted that during the week ended 18 September, 1992, the OTC currency options market had disappeared.

This happened for a number of reasons. First, as the increased realignment risk meant that historical exchange rate volatility was no longer a reliable estimator for future volatility, option writers had to raise the implicit volatilities of their contracts, increasing their prices. Implied volatilities in the sterling/deutschemark options rose steadily from July onward from a low of 5%.

Second, option pricing models broke down during the crisis when their underlying assumptions were violated. For example interest rate volatility increased to approximately five times its post-1987 levels. Even those options pricing models designed to allow for discontinuities in interest rates could not cope with such volatility. Also options pricing became difficult, because the strike price is compared with the current forward exchange rate to determine how far in- or out-of-the-money the option is, and therefore to determine its price. Since banks were not quoting forward prices, it was impossible to price options. As a result, by 17 September, the interbank currency options market had dried up. Except for the dollar/deutschemark option, only very few customers were able to get quotes of currency options from their banks. Those quotes that were given carried large implicit volatilities, of about 25%, and bid-ask spreads had widened to 10%.

The potential rewards of getting future volatility right are so high that many derivative houses have devoted large sums of research money to model volatility. The most commonly used is the generalized autoregressive conditional heteroskedasticity (GARCH) model which economists have used for forecasting. It assumes that the market has a memory — that yesterday's volatility, the most recent change in the underlying market and the long-term average of volatility all have a bearing on today's volatility. In essence, these approaches try to formalize what a trader intuitively does when he tries to forecast volatility — using yesterday's and today's information to help him revise his estimate for the future. Central to all approaches — whether intuitive or mathematically driven is the observation that volatility will always revert to its long-term average. News of unexpected events will cause volatility to spike quickly; it will then take a long time to revert to its mean. The other characteristic of volatility is that it 'clusters'. High volatility is often followed by high volatility, and low volatility by low — until it becomes high again.

What does it mean when implied volatility (i.e. the market's estimate for future volatility) diverges significantly from forecast volatility (the quantitative analyst's view of future volatility)? Who is right if the traders are trading with implied volatilities of 15% and the quantitative analysts predicting 10%? Unfortunately, there is no way of knowing ex-ante. What it does mean however is that if the analysts are right, then it is better for an end-user not to buy an option at 15% implied volatility, but to replicate it synthetically by dynamic hedging, or for the option house to sell options and to hedge them dynamically. If both the traders and quantitative analysts are predicting the same level of future volatility then there should be no difference between buying the option and synthetic replication, since theoretically the time decay on that option should be equal to the plus and minuses of all the trades needed for dynamic replication.

How Volatility is Expressed

Measuring volatility requires a statistical method or model to be imposed on the asset's prices. Modelling an asset's prices implies modelling the distribution of its prices for the underlying asset. But to communicate this distribution in exact terms and to avoid the ambiguity of words (what exactly do you mean by 'very volatile' for instance) requires the quantification of volatility. Because asset prices are supposed to move randomly, their returns are assumed to have a form of cumulative distribution called lognormal distribution. (Lognormal distribution rather than normal distribution is used because commodity or financial asset prices can rise indefinitely but not fall below zero.) A lognormally distributed curve can be completely described by its mean and its standard deviation (i.e. how widely the observed asset prices are distributed around the mean). Once the standard deviation is known, it is easy, using mathematical models or probability tables to work out the likelihood of an event occurring. But with normal distributions, the following are fair generalizations:

- approximately two out of three outcomes (68%) will occur within one standard deviation of the mean;
- approximately 19 out of 20 outcomes (95%) will occur within two standard deviations of the mean;
- approximately 369 out of 370 outcomes (99.7%) will occur within three standard deviations of the mean.

Volatility is measured in terms of standard deviations, and the norm is to express the volatility of an asset as a one standard deviation price change, in percent, over a one-year period. So if an asset had a volatility of 15%, that meant that the asset's price would be expected to fluctuate within a range 15% higher or lower than the forward price. Because it is one annualized standard deviation, this price range would be observed two-thirds of the days in a year. The higher the volatility, the higher the expected price range and the more expensive the option (since the chances of the option becoming profitable are higher).

Volatility Skews and Smiles

The trouble with financial assets is that their probability distributions are not completely normal (the assumption of normality is used because normal distributions have statistical properties that make problem-solving very easy). The observed volatilities of financial assets tend to be clustered around the mean and have a wider dispersion of extreme events — called outliers — than normal distribution would predict. These outliers are also called 'fat tails' see Figure 7.1.

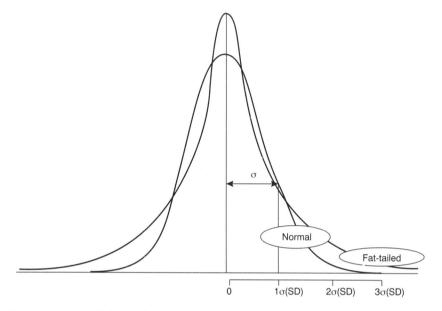

σ

Normal

Fat-tailed

0   1σ(SD)   2σ(SD)   3σ(SD)

Figure 7.1 Fat-tailed Distribution versus Normal Distribution.

The frequent occurrence of fat *tails* causes another condition called the volatility smile. All of these might sound pretty esoteric, which they are, but end-users will find it useful to remember the volatility smile when buying or selling options. Volatility smile refers to the situation where out-of-the-money options trade at a higher implied volatility than at-the-money options. The reason there is a smile is because option pricing models for the most part assume a normal distribution. But because this is not true, i.e. because option buyers and sellers realize that the possibility of more frequent extraordinary moves in the underlying asset is higher than that suggested by normal distribution, out-of-the-money options are far more valuable (maybe two to three times) than the theoretical prices dictated by the pricing model. For example, the US dollar can and has moved 10% in a week; yet it is a move not countenanced by normal distribution. But because market participants know that such a move could take place, they are prepared to pay more for an out-of-the-money (relative to the at-the-money option) to profit from such a price action.

But this volatility smile is not necessarily symmetrical which it would be if both out-of-the-money calls and puts traded at the same higher implied volatility. At times, out-of-the-money puts trade at a higher implied volatility than out-of-the-money calls, giving rise to the volatility skew. This phenomenon is largely the result of demand and supply.

This is easy to understand when the asset, say the Italian lira or the Japanese stock market, on which one is buying a put option is being thrashed downwards.

Demand for out-of-the money puts would definitely be higher than demand for out-of-the-money calls. So the implied volatilities for out-of-the-money puts would be higher than for out-of-the-money calls.

The situation is then reversed: the Italian lira is strengthening and the Nikkei 225 is on an upward streak. Demand for out-of-the-money calls (and thus their implied volatilities) should theoretically be higher than out-of-the money puts. Yet in reality this does not happen. The reason for this is that there is a larger and more natural demand for put options from end-users who buy them as a form of insurance. Take equities — most institutional investors are traditionally long in the underlying asset and are thus natural buyers of puts. The normal buyers of out-of-the-money calls are speculators whose needs are not as genuine as that of the put buyers. They are unlikely to be naturally short in the underlying asset for which they seek exposure.

In addition, empirical evidence has shown that markets are more volatile on the downside than on the upside. So the option-buying public are worried that the outlier event — the big market move — against which they are buying protection, will have more chance of occurring when markets are heading down rather than up. Both these factors contribute towards a greater demand for out-of-the-money puts and militate towards their higher implied volatilities.

Volatility smiles relate only to implied volatility since it is a phenomena that results from option pricing. The degree with which the out-of-the-moneys trade at a higher implied volatility than the at-the-moneys is reflected in the steepness of the smile — this shape can change from a broad grin to a grimace depending on market conditions.

The relationship between volatility and time is its term structure. Although this relationship can be constructed from historical volatility, the term structure of volatility normally refers to implied volatility. Consequently a six month at-the-money option has a different implied volatility than an identical one year at-the-money. The short-end of the volatility curve is always more volatile than the long end because it is more influenced by news events and incoming market information. Short-term implied volatility may be much higher or lower than long-term implied volatility — the curve can flip from positive upwards to negative downwards and stay that way for a long time because there is no way of arbitraging forward and spot volatility just as it is difficult to arbitrage energy-related commodities. (See Chapter 5, on backwardation and contango.)

Vega Generalizations

For someone who is long options, *vega* is always positive. When volatility of the underlying asset increases, so does the option price; when it decreases, the option price falls too, regardless of whether it is a put or a call. This relationship is almost linear (when compared with the relationship between gamma and theta and the price of an option), and independent of the price levels of the underlying

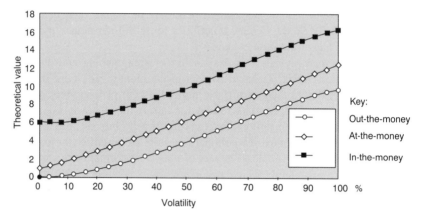

Figure 7.2   Value of an Option as a Function of Volatility.

asset. (See Figure 7.2). Volatility risk is more associated with longer-dated options because there is more time for the volatility of the underlying asset to work in the option buyer's favour. With each passing day, there is less time for the volatility to affect the value of the option, so the vega risk of all options declines as they approach expiration.

Volatility and time are closely-linked. Indeed in the Black-Scholes option pricing formula, volatility is always multiplied by the square root of time. Intuitively this makes sense — a buyer or a seller of an option only cares about the volatility of the underlying asset over the life of the option, yet it is this potential price variability that makes valuable the time value of an option. Previous chapters put forward the idea that changes in volatility and time both had the same effect on uncertainty. Declining volatility and the passing of time, i.e. less time, contributed to decreased uncertainty; and vice versa. Thus changes in both volatility and time have similar effects on an option's delta and gamma. (see Figures 4.6 on page 93 and 6.2 on page 145 for reference).

However, the graphs also show that the effect of increasing uncertainty (i.e. more volatility and time lengthening), or decreasing uncertainty, on an option's value, delta and gamma depends on whether the option is out-, in- or at-the-money. Options most sensitive to increasing volatility are those that are near- or at-the-money because at this point, greater variability in the price moves of the underlying heighten the chances of the option finishing in- or out-the-money. The longer the life of the option, the more this price variability can work for or against the option, so long-dated at or near-the-money options are the most sensitive, of all options, to volatility changes.

Correct volatility estimation is the holy grail of the options market. This is because a hedged option is seen as a claim on the volatility of an asset price rather than a claim on the asset itself, so that volatility risk can be interpreted as the price risk of a hedged option. It is for this reason that the Basle Committee on

Banking Supervision has stipulated that banks' risk measurement systems must treat the volatility of the underlying asset in the same way as they handle prices of those assets — as a market risk factor that affects the value of a bank's trading position. Banks with relatively large option portfolios are expected to break down their volatility risk factors by different maturities.

Correct volatility estimation also affects the management of the other risks of options — delta and gamma. The accuracy of an option seller's delta and gamma numbers depends on how right he was with his volatility estimation, because delta is derived from the option price (which is based on a formula in which one key variable is volatility) and gamma from delta. So if the option seller underestimated volatility and the price of the underlying varied more widely than expected, the delta-hedging strategy will prompt far more active trading, and thus higher transaction costs, than could be covered by the premium income earned from selling the option in the first place. This underestimation of volatility can prove very costly in turbulent markets when bid/ask spreads widen.

Hedging Volatility

Since volatility risk is associated only with options, it can only be safely hedged with other options. (If the underlying markets are used then that presumes that the option-seller is able to predict how volatile the underlying asset is going to be!) It is not always possible to find offsetting options so that an option seller must be prepared to hedge dynamically his book during that period. Even a few days maturity mismatch can expose an option seller to significant volatility time-gap risks. This is because there are certain dates for which implied volatility might be very high (perhaps these dates coincide with the release of monthly macro-economic data, or a US Federal Open Markets Committee or Bundesbank meetings), and other dates for which implied volatility is lower because there are no volatility-influencing events. An option seller is still short volatility if he hedged his short-option position with options that expire a few days before the sold options. He could manage this mismatch by dynamically hedging the position for those few days. But if those few days coincided with days of high volatility brought on by the release of unfavourable economic news or the collapse of a bank, then delta-hedging in this vital period would probably be ineffective and costly. Volatility time-gap risk thus occurs only when the long-option positions expire first and is costly if the market experiences extreme volatility during the mismatched period.

Assuming Volatility Risk

Anyone who is long options, whether it is to hedge an existing exposure or to speculate, takes on some volatility risk because it is inherent in all options. Buying options means you are going long volatility, as well as the underlying asset, in the case of a call option. This implies that the option buyer expects volatility to increase but is uncertain about the future price direction of the asset. He hopes the price of the asset will increase but he is unsure (because if he was certain it would rise, he would buy a future or a forward and not waste any money on paying premiums.) The buyer of a put option is effectively long volatility but short the underlying asset. He expects volatility to increase but is still uncertain about which way the underlying asset will move.

The seller of an option expresses the view that volatility will decrease. If he was an option dealer, he is indifferent to the future price direction of the asset since he will, at a very minimum hedge the price risk of the option by delta-hedging, the costs of which will fall if markets became less volatile. An end-user who sells options tends not to be indifferent to the future price direction of the underlying asset. They sell options to earn premium income and seldom delta-hedge the price risks. So the end-user who sells a call option is expressing the view that the underlying asset will fall in price while an end-user who sells a put thinks the opposite. When an end-user buys an option he is expressing two views on the underlying asset — price uncertainty but increased volatility. When he sells an option he is expressing directional views on both price and volatility. Suffice it to say that any option seller who assumes stable volatility for the life of the option — as Procter and Gamble in its lawsuit against Bankers Trust claims to have done — is taking on a huge risk because it is assuming that one of the main pricing variables remains constant.

If a trader or an end-user wants to express just a volatility view, he will have to hedge out the price risk of an option by delta-hedging. This is what volatility traders do since volatility is viewed as an asset class in itself and is traded in the same way bond traders buy and sell bonds. But the volatility risk of options can also be isolated (and thus traded) by a combination of option positions. There are a whole host of combinations which professional traders have constructured and continue to build. This is where the terms *straddles, strangles, butterflies* and *condors* enter the lexicon of derivatives. They are beyond the scope of this book and are covered in detail in other textbooks on options.

PREPAYMENT RISK

The option to prepay a security is similar to an issuer having bought an American option on the security. The following section on prepayment risk however concentrates on the special characteristics of the prepayment risk facing any buyer of mortgage-backed securities (MBS). This section has been included to help readers understand the special risks of such securities and why investors lost so much money in these instruments during the interest rate hikes of 1994.

Investors and traders in MBS have one common concern — the mortgage prepayment option that is given free to every American house buyer. This option allows the American homeowner to prepay at par, without any financial penalties, his fixed-rate mortgage at a time of his choosing. So any time this little man on the street prepays his fixed-rate mortgage he sets in motion a whole chain of events which affect the large institutional investors and the big boys on Wall Street who have invested in MBS. This is because these instruments are securities issued off or backed by pools of underlying fixed-rate mortgages. When the American home-owner prepays his mortgage, the pool shrinks. This causes the issuer of the MBS to call the security which then affects the large investor because his bond is called.

So prepayment risk is option risk. But unlike the call risk embedded in callable bonds where the investor knows in advance how much will be called and at what price, prepayment risk is plagued by uncertainty. The investor of MBS is uncertain about how much of his investments will be prepaid early, so the maturity and duration of his portfolio is uncertain. For an investor, owning MBS is like owning a fixed-income bond plus simultaneously selling call options — the only trouble is that he does not know what strikes or maturities these call options have. He can try predicting prepayment rates, like any other investor and trader in MBS, but realizes that he could be completely wrong-footed. Prepayment risk can thus be defined as the risk of unforeseen changes in the market's assumed prepayment rates, beyond those projected to occur with movements in interest rates.

Reading the Minds of Homeowners

Homeowners exercise their prepayment options inefficiently — they do not auto-matically pay off their more expensive mortgages when interest rates decline, and neither do they stop prepaying when interest rates rise. There is no doubt that lower interest rates are the main incentive for prepayment. But other factors — death, divorce, relocation to a new state and simply trading up, because the homeowner can afford a nicer house or needs a bigger home to house his growing family, are factors contributing to prepayment. This combination of factors makes accurate prediction of prepayment rates one of the most difficult tasks facing the army of quantitative analysts employed on Wall Street.

Salomon Brothers, one of the most quantitatively-driven houses on Wall Street was publicly wrong-footed trading MBS. The firm lost $660 million in 1994 compared with profits of $1575 million the previous year. Salomon did not disclose how much it had lost trading MBS (rumours have it at about $400 million.) But its chairman Deryck Maughan admits in its 1994 annual report that it suffered 'large losses in collateralized mortgage securities'. The chairman of the holding company, Salomon Inc, Robert Denham admits that their mortgage inventory was inadequately hedged. He writes in the 1994 annual report,

> Management of inventory and trading risks was weak in a few specific business units, contributing to significant losses in those units. Mortgages were particularly hard hit, as inventory that was too large and too old proved to be inadequately hedged for the sudden downdraft that began at the end of March [1994]. These weaknesses in management of inventory and trading risks, in mortgages and elsewhere, were identified and we began the necessary corrective action.

Although Salomon did not pinpoint why their mortgage inventory was inadequately hedged, there is no doubt that its in-house prepayment models had something to do with it. Like all other Wall Street models, they underestimated the rapid slowdown of prepayments, or the markets' joint decision to assume the worst-case prepayment scenarios, as soon as interest rates started to rise.

How fast a security prepays is very important because prepayment affects yield and total rate of return. If an MBS is bought at a discount, faster prepayment will result in a shorter average life and a higher yield; and if it was bought at a premium, it will result in a lower yield. An MBS priced at par has the same yield regardless of prepayments. This is not to say that its value is unaffected by prepayments. Regardless of price, the total rate of return from an investment in MBS is affected by the timing of principal repayments and market reinvestment rates.

It was pointed out earlier that owning an MBS was like owning a fixed income bond on which an investor had sold call options. But that only gives one side — the prepayment aspect — of the risk picture. This one-sided view is excusable given the prolonged bond market rally of the early 1990s, when prepayments reached historically high levels. But there is the other side of MBS' risks — that of extension risk which occurs when the MBS is paid off later than expected. (At any one time, the current market price of an MBS reflects the expected rate of prepayment for that particular pool of mortgages.) When mortgages are prepaid slower than the expected rate, the resulting MBS suffers from extension risk, which is equivalent to the investor having sold a series of put options on the bond. And if an MBS extends, the duration and maturity of the security lengthens just like it shortens when the MBS is prepaid. Therefore, owning an MBS is equivalent to owning a fixed income security plus selling a combination of put and call options, all of unknown strikes and maturities. The duration concerns of MBS investors are twofold. First they do not know the exact duration of their portfolio (duration is a key management tool for fixed income managers as explained in Chapter 4); to compound this uncertainty is the knowledge that the portfolio's duration would always be shortened when rates are falling and lengthened when rates are rising, i.e. at the worst possible times. No wonder investors — sophisticated and simple — have been so caught out by the peculiar characteristics of MBS. Understanding the driving forces of prepayment activity is easy; it is modelling how they react with each other that continues to be the outstanding analytical hurdle facing Wall Street.

A trading activities manual issued in March 1994 by the US Federal Reserve Board notes,

> Mortgage [MBS] valuations are highly subjective because of the unpredictable nature of mortgage prepayment rates. Despite the application of highly sophisticated interest rate simulation techniques, results from diverse proprietary prepayment models and assumptions about future interest rate volatility still drive valuations. The subjective nature of mortgage valuations makes marking to market difficult due to the dynamic nature of prepayment rates, especially as one moves further out along the price-risk continuum toward high-risk tranches. Historic price information for various CMO tranche types

is not widely available and, moreover, might have limited value given the generally different methodologies used in deriving mortgage valuation.

Collateralized Mortgage Obligations

And what are these high-risk tranches? They are collectively known as collateralized mortgage obligations (CMOs) or mortgage derivatives and their origins lie in buyers of MBS insisting on better insulation from prepayment risk. Traditionally, MBS were pass-through securities, i.e. the owner of the mortgage-backed bond had a pro rata share of the underlying mortgages and thus shared, proportionally, the prepayment risk. But as time passed, some investors wanted to be spared worrying about prepayment risk while others who were prepared to fret about it wanted to be compensated suitably. Since mortgage-backed securities are just a physical manifestation of the slicing up, in a number of ways, the principal and interest cashflows of the underlying pool of mortgages, Wall Street firms decided to ring together all the cashflows with prepayment uncertainty. CMOs thus redistribute the prepayment risk of an underlying pool of mortgages among different types of structures, with the one bearing the highest prepayment risk offering the highest yields.

CMO Structures — Planned Amortization Class and Companions

The most common CMO structures, and the ones that have caused substantial losses among corporates, fund managers and banks are principal only (POs), interest only (IOs), inverse floating rate notes and Z bonds. They are also known as companion bonds and always come hand in hand with the most dominant CMO structure — the Planned Amortization Class (PAC). The PAC behaves like a fixed-rate callable bond and will stick to a prepayment schedule as long as the prepayment rates of the underlying mortgage pool stay within predetermined bands. It is, to all intents and purposes, a surrogate for a corporate bond. But to give PAC buyers insulation from prepayment risk, the firms that repackage mortgages into bonds had to design accompanying structures that would absorb all the cashflow uncertainty inherent in the underlying pool of mortgages. Enter companion or support bonds. When prepayments are fast, companions support PACs by absorbing all the prepayments made in advance of the PAC schedule; and when prepayments are slow, companions do not amortize until the PAC pays down.

PAC and companion bonds have to be self-supporting, with the cashflows from the mortgage pool always being able to meet their cashflow requirements. Remember, the supporting pool of mortgages (a CMO's origin of being) receives a fixed interest rate. So whatever form the resulting CMO structures take (i.e. they can either be floating or fixed rate instruments), the end result must always be equal to the underlying pool of mortgages (in terms of total principal value and net coupon). This point is key because it is responsible for some of the features of the companion bonds described below.

Companion Structures — Floating Rate Notes and Inverse Floating Rate Notes (FRN)

A floating rate note backed by mortgages is like any other FRN — it pays a floating coupon normally based on a floating index, like LIBOR. But since it is issued off a fixed rate mortgage it must be capped, to ensure that the mortgage cash-flow will always be sufficient to pay the coupon interest. Unlike non-securitized FRNs, mortgage-backed FRNs have a schedule of principal prepayments before final maturity.

Capping the maximum coupon payable on the FRN does impact the price of the FRN if interest rates go above the cap strike. The FRN would trade below par in such circumstances because it would have a below-market coupon rate. Also slower prepayments would affect the price of the FRN. Without caps, the FRN would usually trade very close to par, and would be relatively unaffected by changes in prepayment assumptions. And if prepayments were very high, there would be very little principal balance to be affected by the rate caps, so the price would still be near par.

The principle of an inverse (reverse) FRN applies to both securitized and non-securitized structures. These securities have coupon rates that move inversely with the index factor. (see Chapter 8 for detailed explanation.) So an inverse floater could have a coupon of 12% − six-month LIBOR. If an inverse floater is issued in conjunction with a conventional floater, it must have a floor of 0% to balance out the cap on the conventional floater, so that the sum of the floating interest payments is always equal to that of the fixed coupon of the mortgage pool.

Both FRNs and inverse FRNs can be leveraged. As explained earlier, coupons on non-leveraged structures move on a one-to-one basis with the index (subject to caps and floors) while the coupon on a leveraged deal will move by more than a one-to-one basis. How much it increases or decreases is determined by the leverage or the multiplier. So a leveraged inverse could have a coupon of (36% − (3 × 6-month LIBOR)). The higher the leverage the more the likelihood of the floater paying 0% if interest rates rise.

Companion Structures — Principal- and Interest-only Strips

Mortgages can be stripped into Principal-Only (PO) and Interest-Only (IO) segments and sold separately to investors. A zero-coupon mortgage-backed security is referred to as a PO, and like zero-coupon bonds are sold at a deep discount to face value but redeemed at par. So its rate of return depends totally on when the issue is prepaid; the faster the better because the bond holder receives par on prepayment. POs are extremely sensitive to prepayment rates and if prepayment is delayed (as happened in 1994 when US interest rates were raised six times), they will plummet in value since there is no coupon income to cushion the effects of receiving par principal later than expected.

Interest Onlys (IOs) are securities representing the interest payments from an underlying pool of mortgages. They are also sold at a deep discount to their notional principal amount, although they have no face amount or par amount. The notional amount is the principal balance used to calculate the amount of interest due, so as it amortizes and is prepaid, the coupon income also decreases. Once the notional amount declines to zero, no further payments are made on the IO. So the faster the prepayments, the worse it is for the IO holder (unlike a PO holder who wants fast prepayments), because he might actually receive less cashflow over the life of the asset than what was initially invested. Like POs, they are very sensitive to prepayment rates but react in the opposite way, i.e. their value goes up as interest rates rise. This characteristic makes them unique among fixed-income instruments (most of which decrease in value as interest rates rise). This feature, called negative duration (see Chapter 4 on duration) makes them a suitable hedging instrument for other fixed income bonds.

The falling interest rate environment of the early 1990s was not kind to IO buyers. The Federal Reserve Trading manual reported that several financial institutions could have lost between $50 to $200 million on IO positions in 1992 and 1993 because prepayments were so high. On the other hand, one firm lost $300 to $400 million on POs in the spring of 1987 when prepayments slowed.

Companion Structures — Z Bonds

Z bonds are not zero-coupon bonds but securities that pay interest in the form of more bonds, which are added to the original principal amount. This process is known as accretion. They are usually issued with a face amount significantly lower than they would have had, had they been interest bearing instruments. They are usually the last bonds to be prepaid, and therefore have the longest average lives in a deal.

A Typical CMO Structuring Process

Let's start with an underlying pool of mortgages with a 10% fixed coupon. The bulk, maybe 75% of this pool will be securitized into PACs with a 10% coupon and limited prepayment risk. The remaining 25% will be repackaged into different sorts of support structures, all absorbing different degrees of prepayment risk. Say the face value of the companion bonds is $100 million, $50 million could be structured into floating-rate notes, paying LIBOR plus 50 basis points. If LIBOR was at 5%, the coupon on the floater would be 5.5%. But designers of these companion bonds have a 10% fixed coupon to redistribute — by only paying 5.5% on the floater, they are saving 4.50% on half of the face value of the companion bonds. They can pass these cost savings to another structure which they normally have to do to entice investors, because this final structure in the chain assumes the largest proportion of the prepayment risk of the underlying mortgage pool.

The remaining $50 million can be turned into an inverse floating rate note. The 4.50% cost savings on the conventional floater can be added to the 10% fixed coupon (the coupon of the underlying pool of mortgages) to give the investor a 14.50% coupon. But because CMO structuring is a zero sum game (the sum of the final parts must be equal to the starting point), LIBOR must be subtracted from the fixed 14.50% to get a net floating coupon. (Remember the other $50 million is a floater that pays LIBOR plus 50 basis points, so the two LIBORS must cancel each other out to get back to the 10% fixed coupon of the underlying pool of mortgages.)

Figure 7.3 shows the different permutations of a CMO structuring exercise. An investment bank starts off with an underlying pool of Federal National Mortgage Association mortgages, with an average fixed interest rate of 7.5%. It can carve this pool of mortgages into a variety of structures, depending on the outlook for US interest rates.

If the market expects interest rates and prepayments to be stable, the investment bank structuring the deal will opt for a simple sequential-pay structure (b), allocating principal payments sequentially to a series of bonds. All initial principal payments and prepayments from the underlying pool of mortgages are paid first to the tranche with the shortest maturity; only when it is fully retired does the second tranche start paying down.

If investors are worried about rates rising and prepayments slowing, then the structurer may opt for alternative (c) or (d). The Z bond receives interest in the form of more bonds. In this case, the new securities will accrete at 7.5%. This accretion process actually allows the issuer to redirect coupon flows (from the underlying pool of mortgages) which actually belong to the Z bond to the sequential pay-classes in the form of principal payments. The structurer may also create VDAM (very accurately defined maturity) bonds which derive all their cashflows from the interest accretions of the Z bonds. Because Z bonds are the last bonds to be prepaid. VDAMs offer the strongest protection against extension risk.

If the underlying pool of collateral receives a fixed interest rate higher than current fixed rates, then the bank structuring the deal can strip some interest cashflows before creating the rest of the classes. In alternative (e) a 50 bp Interest Only security is stripped and sold separately. The remaining collateral now has a 7% coupon and can be structured following alternatives (b), (c) and (d).

If the market expects prepayment volatility, then the structurer creates PAC/companion CMOs. Once the initial allocation of cashflows of PACs and companions has been decided (f), the structuring follows the same process as in box (c) — only this time PACs and companions are created (g) rather than sequential-pays and Z bonds. The PACs and companions can be divided further as shown by route (i) and (h). If an investor wants to buy a LIBOR-based floater with a relatively high spread and a five-year average life, the structurer can produce a five-year floater with a coupon equal to the Cost of Funds Index plus 65 basis points.

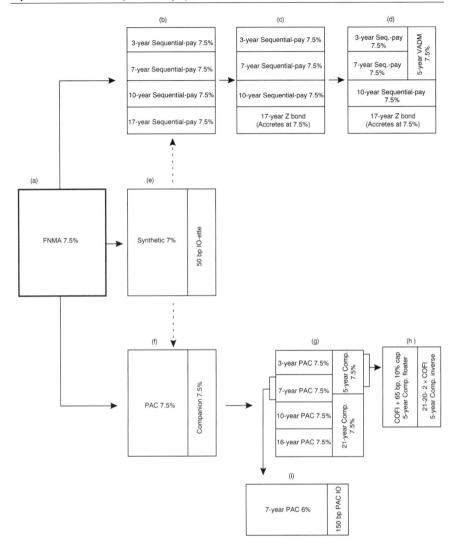

Figure 7.3 CMO Structuring Exercise. Reproduced with permission from Lehman Brothers.

At the same time, the structurer will look at the inverse floater market to determine yield and coupon (set by adjusting the multiplier) for the resulting LIBOR inverse floater. On the PAC side, there may be an investor who wants to buy a 6% coupon PAC as protection from the risk of high prepayments on premium-priced bonds. If so, the structurer can split the seven-year PAC into a 150 bp Interest Only security and a 6% PAC (i).

Leveraging CMOs

Leverage was introduced into the CMO sector for the same reason it was introduced in structured notes or derivatives — investors confident that the bull run in bonds would continue wanted to make a higher return per dollar. They leveraged their bets because they wanted to magnify any downward moves in interest rates. The faster-than-anticipated prepayments of 1990–93 was also a contributory factor. Investors, mindful of how early prepayments had affected their projected total rates of return, demanded even more compensation for taking on prepayment risk. But with US interest rates falling so low, the only way Wall Street rocket scientists could engineer attractive-enough yields was to build in leverage into the payout formulas.

It should be pointed out that leveraging a coupon is obvious leverage. More subtle is the implicit leveraged play on prepayment offered by POs and IOs. Leverage here does not mean a multiplier embedded into the structure — its use here is in the looser sense of the word. POs and IOs are said to be leveraged ways of betting on interest rates and prepayments because their returns on a yield table look like that of leveraged instruments rather than an ordinary Treasury bond of comparable maturity. It follows that the deeper the discount at which a PO is bought, the more the leveraged play on early prepayment. IOs are a leveraged play on delayed prepayment, since their total rate of return depends on how slowly the underlying pool of mortgages is prepaid. Indeed, because one can earn a negative yield on IOs, as in a very fast prepayment scenario, where cash received is less than cash invested, IOs can be looked upon as being an even more leveraged play on future prepayment behaviour than POs.

Hedging Prepayment (Extension) Risk

Prepayment risk is call risk and extension risk is put risk. Viewed in this light, both are manifestations of interest rate risk — if interest rates rise, people will not prepay or call their bonds; if interest rates fall, they will. For mortgage-backed securities, prepayment risk is also essentially interest rate risk since in a falling interest environment, refinancing will be the dominant factor in prepayments. But because homeowners' decisions to prepay are affected by other factors such as divorce, relocation and even sheer laziness, prepayment risk in MBS is not equal to interest rate risk. It is plagued by uncertainty because the American homeowner's decision to exercise his free option is unpredictable and can be economically irrational. The fact that this non-interest rate sensitive part accounts for a fair proportion of an MBS's prepayment risk is the main reason why MBS models fail to predict accurately prepayment rates.

This weakness is compounded by the fact that only in MBS can you have call (prepayment) risk changing overnight into put (extension) risk — this is exactly what happened on 4 February 1994 when the Federal Reserve Board raised American interest rates. No other security has such chameleon-like qualities; issuers of callable bonds may choose not to call their bonds against a background of rising interest rates but they are certainly not allowed to (put) extend the duration of the bond because it suits them.

Of course MBS buyers can deal with the extension risk issue by assuming worst case scenarios — that there will be no early prepayment on the underlying mortgages so that the MBS will have the maximum maturity possible. This is not really a viable course of action — an investor only buys an MBS if it offers him a suitable spread over US Treasuries, but to make that comparison he needs to make certain prepayment assumptions. Only in very rare instances are MBS priced using the part of the Treasury bond yield curve that coincides with the former's maximum possible maturity because then the MBS would be priced too cheaply and there would be no incentive for the whole securitization process.

The most logical way of hedging prepayment risk is to buy call options (to offset the short call option position embedded in the MBS). But here again, the investor has to make do with guesswork — how many options does he buy and at what strikes and maturities? In such hedging strategies, the size of the hedge is determined by a model that relates interest rate moves and shifts in the prepayment pattern. There will be slippage in the hedge if the presumed relationship between rate changes and prepayment patterns does not come to pass (as Salomon found out to its cost in 1994) — the investor would either have overhedged or underhedged his cash position. And what if the bonds suddenly extend on him; his call options would be useless because he would then find himself in the position of needing put options.

One could try using IOs since they react in the opposite way to POs and other CMOs to early prepayments. Such a construct brings with it basis risk because the two instruments are different and may not react identically to interest rate hikes or falls. (See Chapter 5 for curve risk brought about by non-parallel shifts of the yield curve.) Indeed it would be fair to say that there really is no way to hedge accurately prepayment risk. The various CMO structures are exercises in transferring the risk from one party to another, but in the end, someone has to accept it. Given the painful experiences of early 1994 (officials from Piper Jaffray, City Colleges of Chicago, Odessa Junior College can testify to that), the final party in the chain should demand what it regards as adequate compensation for accepting what can only be called an idiosyncratic option risk.

The Alternative Way

No wonder some investors (and Wall Street) have turned to instruments that offer similar yields to MBS but carry none of the attendant prepayment uncertainty.

Index amortizing rate swaps and *mortgage swaps* are just two alternatives. An index amortizing swap is an interest rate swap whose notional principal decreases (amortizes) as interest rates fall. How much it decreases depends on the schedule agreed at the start of the swap.

Table 7.1 A Snapshot: The relationship between Option Risks and The Underlying Markets.

Option position	Option risks	Underlying market/factor
If you are:	You have:	You want:
Long calls/short puts	Positive delta	The market to rise
Short calls/long puts	Negative delta	The market to fall
Long options	Positive gamma	The market to move fast
Short options	Negative gamma	The market to move slowly
Long options	Positive vega	The market to be volatile
Short options	Negative vega	The market to be stable
Long options	Negative theta	Time to standstill
Short options	Positive theta	Time to pass

IAR swaps are sold as a direct substitute to owning mortgage-backed securities. The investor (the receiver of fixed interest payments) earns a higher fixed coupon than in a plain vanilla swap because he has to be compensated for the risk that a proportion of the swap might be terminated early. This fixed coupon is similar to levels offered on a comparable MBS; but unlike a MBS where the investor does not know how much of his bond will be prepaid if interest rates fall, the investor in an IAR swap knows how much of his swap will be called since the amortization schedule is agreed at the outset. So an IAR swap provides the investor with mortgage-type bond yields and a similar risk profile but less prepayment uncertainty. It eliminates the non-interest rate sensitive portion of prepayment risk.

Mortgage swap agreements are interest rate swaps that replicate the economics of owning mortgage-backed bonds. Just like an IAR swap, the notional amount of the swap decreases as interest rates fall but not according to a schedule. Here the amortization follows the prepayment pattern of a reference set of mortgage pass-throughs that all have the same fixed coupon. So a fixed rate receiver in a mortage swap agreement is protected against pool-specific prepayment risk because the reference group of securities underlying the swap is a large set of agency pass throughs. A mortgage swap agreement thus provides some level of prepayment protection by diversification; it does not eliminate the idiosyncratic nature of MBS' prepayment risk in the same way as an IAR swap.

SUMMARY — RISK TRANSFORMATION

A simple interest rate swap can be used to illustrate the chain in risk transformation mentioned in the preface and the various types of derivative risks explained in Chapters 4 to 7. Company A wanted to lock-in its funding cost for five years, so it engaged in a swap where it paid fixed and received floating. (A swap's fixed rate is always set at a spread over comparable government bonds, while the floating leg tends to be indexed to six-month LIBOR.) Company A thus hedged its spot (price) risk against future interest rate increases by passing the risk to bank B which was the counterparty to the swap. Bank B was now committed to receiving fixed and paying floating. (For bank B, the economic impact of this swap is the same as being long a fixed-rate bond and short a floating rate note).

How did bank B protect itself against interest rates rising? If interest rates rose, it paid more than it received. To hedge against such a loss, it sold US Treasuries of the same maturity as the swap, so that the gains it made from such a sale offset the loss on the swap. (Bank B thus hedged its exposure to rate rises by shorting fixed income bonds (rates).) Such a hedge however protected bank B from the price risk of interest rates rising, but not against the risk of the spread between Treasuries and swap rates changing.

Say the spread was 50 basis points when the swap was initiated. When interest rates rose, it widened to 60 basis points, so the bank lost 10 basis points on the notional principal at each payment date just from spread risk. The spread between Treasuries and swap rates is a source of basis risk facing all swap dealers; the only way they can overcome this sort of risk is to find an offsetting swap but few dealers regard this as a realistic alternative.

If the swap was hedged by selling Eurodollar futures, there would still be basis risk. Swap dealers tend to use the Eurodollar futures contracts with the most liquidity and these are the near-term ones. They are priced off short-term rates and so are affected by moves in the short-end of the yield curve. A longer maturity swap of three years or more would be more influenced by moves in the medium to long-end of the yield curve. There would be no basis risk between the swap and the hedge if there was a parallel shift in the yield curve. But sometimes, the short-end moves up more than the long end or vice versa; or the short-end moves down while the long-end moves up and vice versa. When the yield curve changes shape in this way, there are non-parallel shifts in the yield curve which give rise to curve risk; yet another form of basis risk. Hedging a long-dated swap with the most liquid near-term Eurodollar futures contract makes the hedge vulnerable to non-parallel shifts and curve risks.

So the chain of risk transference and transformation is as follows. Company A lays off its interest rate risk to bank B. Bank B hedges this interest rate risk, but in so doing often takes on some form of basis risk (spread or curve being the most common.) This basis risk is unlikely to result in losses as large as those emanating from interest rates if rates did indeed rise and the bank was unhedged. Nevertheless, any hedger has to contend with possible losses from basis risk if the two instruments are not identical.

Company A could hedge its swap position against rates decreasing, by doing the opposite of bank B, but most end-users do not do so because they entered the swap to fix their cost of funding. To hedge it would be counter-productive. If rates fall, the company would record an 'opportunity loss' on the swap since it was paying a higher fixed rate than the prevalent market rate. But this 'loss' could be seen as the opportunity cost of having had the ability to fix its cost of funding; the 'price' the firm paid for reducing uncertainty in its cost of financing. If rates rose, then the company would have been able to record a 'profit' on the swap; representing the below-market rates of funding the company was now enjoying. The only time the company would record a real loss or profit was when it unwound the swap before maturity.

Paying fixed in an interest rate swap is similar to having a fixed-rate mortgage in the United Kingdom — when floating rates are lower than the fixed rate, the homeowner would moan and groan; when they are higher, he is all smiles. In both cases, he has not really suffered any realized loss or enjoyed any gain. But the fixed-rate mortgage does allow him a lot more certainty in his financial planning because he knows in advance his monthly mortgage costs.

Say company A has a fixed funding cost bogey which is $\frac{1}{2}\%$ less than the current five-year swap rate. It must achieve this fixed funding cost if the proposed project (for which the funds are designated) is to make any money. It knows it cannot achieve this targeted rate via a plain vanilla interest rate swap.

But it can achieve the target rate if it entered into a corridor swap. This is an interest rate swap where company A paid the current five-year swap rate minus 50 basis points and received floating interest payments. The floating payments were however reduced everytime six-month LIBOR traded outside a certain range, say between 3.5 to 5.0%. For every day that six-month LIBOR fell outside this corridor, the floating rate company A would receive would be reduced by two basis points. The treasurer of Company A was happy to execute this swap because he truly believed that six-month LIBOR would not rise above 5% over the life of the swap. And even if it did, it might still be worth his while because the upfront fixed costs savings outweighed the reduction in floating interest rate receipts towards the end of the swap (see Figure 7.4).

What company A really did was sell bank B some digital options. (A digital option has a payoff that is either zero or a predetermined amount once the strike has been triggered.) Whether he knew it or not, the treasurer of company A had packaged his interest rate views into an option. This repackaging of views is not

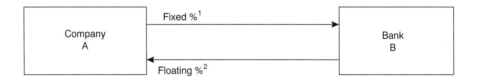

Note: 1. Fixed rate is 50 bp below market rate

        2. If six-month LIBOR is outside the 3.5 to 5.0% range,
        Then floating payments = six-month LIBOR – (N × 0.002)

Figure 7.4   Corridor Swap.

restricted to interest rates — it can be a view on currencies, equities or the spread between German floating and fixed rates (as in Procter and Gamble's second suit against Bankers Trust.) The option payoff is just built into the cashflow of the swap. And because company A is now in a short option position, it would be exposed to the main option risks of gamma and vega. These risks manifest themselves in different ways — the company could find itself paying out on the swap and not receiving any income in return or in the valuation it received from a dealer if it chose to unwind the swap before maturity. This example illustrates how company A hedged its obvious price risk — but in doing so took on other less obvious risks because it wanted to meet a funding target.

SUMMARY

Volatility is one of the key determinants of an option's price so its change will affect an option's value even if the underlying asset price risk is hedged. The more volatile an underlying asset, the higher its option price.

Pricing an option requires the seller to estimate how volatile an asset will be during the life of the option. Of the five factors that go into pricing an option, volatility is the only variable that is a matter of judgement, the other four are a matter of fact. Option writers use historical volatility to help them forecast future volatility. Implied volatility, which is the volatility number arrived at backing out the market price in an option pricing model, can also be seen as the combined judgement of a market about the future uncertainty of a given forward price. The higher the implied volatility, the more uncertain market participants feel about future prices. An option seller (or buyer) is only interested in the volatility of an asset over the life of the option, thus the volatility and time value of an option are inextricably linked. Indeed both are the only risks unique to options.

Volatility is measured in terms of the standard deviation of the returns of an asset, and common practice is to express it as a one standard deviation price change, in percent, over a one-year period. A volatility of 10% means the asset's price is expected to fluctuate within a range 10% higher or lower than the forward price. A one annualized standard deviation means the price range would be expected for two-thirds of the days in a year.

Volatility can be traded like any other asset. Buying or selling options is expressing a view not only on the underlying asset class but also on the volatility of that asset. Pure volatility traders neutralize the directional risk of options, either by delta-hedging or combining options into trading strategies such as straddles, strangles, etc. Volatility risk can only be hedged by going long or short similar options.

Investors of collateralized mortgage obligations have to contend with prepayment risk, which is similar to buying callable securities. Prepayment risk is however more idiosyncratic risk than call risk due to the origins of CMOs. American home-buyers are allowed to prepay their fixed-rate mortgages at any time without any penalty; their decision to do so is mainly, but not solely, influenced by whether they can refinance their mortgages at a cheaper rate. Unlike callable bond investors, CMO investors are uncertain about how much of their securities will be prepaid which is very important because prepayment affects yield and total rate of return. The prepayment risk of CMOs can change overnight to extension risk if the US Federal Reserve tightens monetary policy since the underlying mortgages will not be prepaid and the CMOs will have a longer than expected life.

REFERENCE

1. Chew, L. (1995) Backing Down, *RISK magazine*, January, **8** (1).

8
Unbundling Structures

This chapter is divided into two parts. The first attempts to guide the reader through some hybrid structures. They will be broken down into the basic building blocks — cash instruments, forwards, swaps, options — so that readers have a clearer appreciation of the risks of some of these complex structures. It is vital for corporate treasurers and fund managers to go through this process of reverse engineering since they are increasingly presented with structures that meet their financial objectives superficially but carry risks that are not apparent immediately.

Reverse engineering some of these structures at the very least forces them to face the question of whether they are being adequately compensated for the extra risks they are assuming. The old adage, 'there is no free lunch', is just as relevant in today's financial world as it was a 100 years ago — and if a fund manager is earning higher returns or a treasurer enjoying lower funding costs than those commonly available, then they are probably taking on risks in other dimensions. They should not be stopped but they must be responsible for their actions.

The following hybrid examples show that options (and therefore their special characteristics) are now embedded in instruments which have been traditionally classified as cash instruments or forwards. Examples of the former are accrual super-floating rate notes and of the latter index amortizing rate swaps. Once options are embedded in these basic structures, they display the optionality of an outright option position.

Yet as the example of the inverse floating rate note will show, heavy losses are not always related directly to complex products or instruments with embedded options. The treasurer of Orange County, Robert Citron bought inverse floating rate notes because he wanted to boost his fund's yields in a low-interest rate environment. Since he believed that rates would remain low or continue to fall, he leveraged up his bets. He bought an instrument which is easy to understand, whose payoff profile under different interest rate scenarios could have been worked out by high school students whose teachers the County had insufficient funds to pay once the bankruptcy was announced. Granted, the inverse floater had embedded options but the optionality in this instance was not important; nor did they make the instrument hard to understand or the risks difficult to see. The instrument illustrates the point that risks coming from relatively simple structures can cause as much damage as risks coming from complex ones since the inverse floater is not a complex derivative by any stretch of the imagination.

The second part of the chapter deals with the issue of sales practices — should the notion *caveat emptor* or buyer beware apply to derivatives as it does to everything else? How much information should be provided to the buyer and should the seller provide information which the buyer did not request? How transparent should the valuation be? And should the onus be placed on derivative providers to decide whether a proposed transaction is suited to a client?

REVERSE ENGINEERING

Hybrid 1 — Inverse (Reverse) Floating Rate Note

Conventional floating rate notes have coupons that increase with rising interest rates and decrease with falling rates. The coupons of inverse (reverse) floating rate notes behave in the opposite manner — the floating interest rate that the issuer pays the investor increases as rates decline, and decreases as rates advance.

The coupon on an inverse is typically:

$2 \times$ fixed rate (normally the prevailing swap rate of the relevant maturity)

$-$ floating rate (normally 3- or 6-month LIBOR)

So if the fixed rate was $6\% \times 2 = 12\%$ and LIBOR was at 3%, the floating coupon payable to the investor would be 9% for this payment period. If LIBOR went up to 4% in the next payment period, the coupon would be 8%, and if it went down to 2%, the coupon would be 10%.

A buyer of an inverse floater must therefore believe that rates are trending downwards, or remaining stable; if he did not think so he would be mad or irresponsible to buy such instruments. He might still buy inverses if he thought rates rises were on the cards but much further down the road than that implied by the forward curve. In such instances, the investor himself must judge whether the extra yield earned in the early stages of the transaction is enough compensation for forsaking future higher yields.

If he felt strongly that rates would decline, he could try to leverage his view by buying a leveraged inverse floater. In such a structure, the coupon formula would be:

$(3$ or 4 or $5 \times$ fixed rate$) - (2$ or 3 or $4 \times$ LIBOR$)$

Table 8.1 Coupon Payments on an Unleveraged and Leveraged Inverse
Floating Rate Note (all numbers in percentages).

Fixed coupon	Six-month LIBOR	Unleveraged inverse	Leveraged inverse (five times)
6	3	9	18
6	4	8	14
6	5	7	10
6	6	6	6
6	7	5	2
6	8	4	−2 (in reality 0%)

The multiplier magnifies any moves in interest rates and thus provides the investor with even greater exposure to fluctuations in interest rates. Without this multiplier (the leverage), the coupon moves on a one-to-one basis with changes in interest rates whereas in leveraged inverse floaters, the multiplier determines how much changes in interest rates are magnified.

The higher the multiplier, the faster the coupon payable on the inverse approaches zero, if rates rise. But the coupon can never be negative, i.e. the investor will never pay the issuer interest because embedded in the inverse floater is a 0% floor.

Short-term US rates rose by about 4% in 1994 — it is no wonder then that some of these leveraged inverses showed huge book losses since they traded at deep discounts to par rather than near par because the floating coupons they were paying were at zero or close to 0%. Their secondary market prices looked more similar to *zero coupon bonds* than those of conventional floating rate notes. (The latter tend to trade near par because their coupons always reflect prevailing short-term rates.) But if interest rates had declined, the coupons on such leveraged inverses would be very rich (way above market rates). The notes would subsequently have traded well over par and the investor would have shown large profits.

The payout profile of an inverse floater can be mimicked by a combination of interest rate swaps and a conventional floater. Its payout formula shows that there are three cashflows: two fixed interest rate and one LIBOR. The two fixed cashflows can be obtained by entering into two plain vanilla interest rate swaps where the investor received fixed. But that would also mean that the investor paid floating. If the investor also owned a floating rate note, the floating coupon he earned from that would offset one of the floating payment obligations on the swap. The investor is thus left in a cashflow position of two fixed coupons minus that of a floating, i.e. the same payout profile as that of an inverse. And if the inverse floater was leveraged, then the investor entered into as many swaps as that dictated by the multiplier on the fixed rate part of the formula (see Figure 8.1 for synthetic inverse).

It was pointed out earlier that inverse floaters have an embedded floor of 0% which the issuer has sold to the investor. This is to avert a situation where the

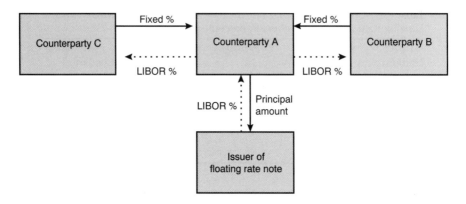

Figure 8.1 Synthetic Inverse Floater.

investor has to pay the issuer interest if LIBOR rose to such a point where the payout formula would result in negative coupons. But the investor has also sold the issuer an embedded cap with a strike equivalent to the fixed rate leg × the multiplier in the payout formula. This option places a ceiling on the issuer's maximum interest rate cost. In a leveraged deals, the number of caps and floors bought and sold depend on the multiplier on the deal.

Inverse floaters are thus constructed from the basic building blocks of swaps and options; but they are also a good example of how, sometimes, one of the building blocks has very little impact on the pricing of the structure. The optionality embedded here is minute; the options were so way out-of- the-money that they were not critical to the nature of the transaction and accounted for a very small component of the overall risk when the structures were put together.

Hybrid 2 — Accrual (Range) Super-Floating Rate Note

Compared to an inverse floater, this example is at the other end of the complex spectrum. Accrual super-floating rate notes are shown on balance sheets in terms of their notional amount which does not reflect the risks involved because the notional gives no indication of the leverage factor and the number and type of complex options embedded in the structure. This note subsequently appeared on the 'do not buy' list for some money managers who manage money market funds (see Chapter 2). It also carries the 'r' rating S&P has given to instruments with substantial market risks (see Appendix 8 for list of instruments). They were however very popular throughout 1993.

Accrual notes are short-maturity structured notes which accrue above-market interest only on days when a pre-agreed index rate (say three-month LIBOR) is below a pre-specified strike rate, or stays within an agreed range. If three-month LIBOR is above the strike or outside the range, the note pays no interest. Anyone who buys accrual notes is taking the view that rates will not rise as quickly as the forward rates imply since if they did, the buyer would earn no interest.

The linchpin of the accrual note is the digital option. A digital option is best explained by its other name: the all-or-nothing option. If the underlying asset is at or beyond the option's strike, the option buyer will enjoy a fixed and predetermined payout. If the asset is not, the option buyer receives nothing. Therefore the payoff of a digital option does not depend on the in-the-moneyness of the option (unlike a conventional option). Instead it is a step function (that is either zero or the payoff amount.) Once an investor buys an accrual note, he is selling a series of digital options — the premium earned is amortized over the life of the note and is reflected in the extra spread above existing market rates that the note pays, when it does pay.

A typical accrual super-range floater will have the following coupon structure. Say the range for the interest rate index, in this case one-month LIBOR, is set at 3.5 to 4.5%. If one-month LIBOR is less than 3.5%, then the note accrues interest at a rate equal to one-month LIBOR. If the latter is in the range, then the accrual rate is equal to $(3 \times$ one-month LIBOR$) - 7\%$. If one-month LIBOR is more than 4.5%, then the note accrues no interest. Assume this security has a maturity of one year (see Figure 8.2 for diagram showing payoff profile).

The fact that the coupon is leveraged by a factor of 3 when LIBOR is within the strike range is the reason why this is called an accrual super-range floater. Even without decomposing this note into its constituent blocks, one can see that

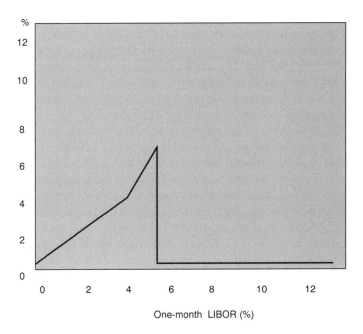

Figure 8.2 Payoff Profile of Accrual Super FRN.

this is a leveraged position which pays off well (anywhere between 68 to 250 basis points better than a conventional floater) if one-month LIBOR is stable and remains within the narrow range of 3.5 and 4.5%. Below 3.5%, the floater earns a coupon comparable to other conventional floaters. But once LIBOR breaks the upper strike range, the floater pays nothing. If that happens, the note will trade at a deep discount in the secondary market since it is to all intents and purposes a zero coupon bond.

To decompose this complex structure into its basic elements, we have to identify the ranges of one-month LIBOR where the nature of the payoffs change and to try to construct a portfolio which replicates the cash flows under any specification of one-month LIBOR. An investor who bought the above structure can be thought of as having bought: first, a floating rate note which pays a coupon equivalent to one-month LIBOR whenever LIBOR is less than 3.5% and second, caps with one year to maturity and a strike of 3.5%. When LIBOR is less than 3.5%, all the options are out-of-the money so the floater will only earn LIBOR. We know he is long caps because as soon as LIBOR touches 3.5%, the coupon kicks up quite dramatically — for that to happen, the investor must be long an instrument which pays him money once the trigger level of 3.5% is hit.

But the structure pays no interest once one-month LIBOR goes through 4.5%. How does that translate into an equivalent portfolio? Earning no interest is similar to the floater not being an asset of the investor — so we must effectively 'kill' it. We can do this by reducing the sensitivity of the payoffs to the level of one-month LIBOR once one-month LIBOR reaches 4.5%. On top of that, we must decrease the payoff to zero once that upper strike level of LIBOR is breached.

To achieve this payoff profile, we need to be short options. So at this point, the investor who owns this structure can be thought of as first, selling three monthly reset caps with one year to maturity and a strike of 4.5% to kill the sensitivity to one-month LIBOR which is implied by the long floater and cap position. Second, the investor can be thought of as selling 12 digital options, one expiring each month which pay either zero, if one-month LIBOR is less than or equal to 4.5% at expiration; or a pre-agreed payoff amount if one-month LIBOR is more than 4.5% at expiration. When one-month LIBOR is more than 4.5%, all these short option positions come into-the-money, so the coupon on the bond decreases to 0%.

It is very hard to do a total return analysis on an accrual note because its daily returns are totally dependent on the path of interest rates and future levels of one-month LIBOR. For example, if LIBOR were to bounce randomly above and below the strike range (4.5%), the final total return would be different from that experienced if LIBOR slightly exceeded the range and stayed there for the rest of the note's life.

A buyer of such a structure is extracting his incremental yield by increasing his exposure to movements in the underlying index through selling options. Although he has bought a cash instrument, his risk profile is similar to that of an option seller. He could try to hedge some of these risks by buying some offsetting digital options and caps. But if he did so, he would probably find that the incremental yield is eaten up by the premium costs of buying such options. If he had to hedge his positions this way, the trade would not make any financial sense.

So an investor who buys a complex structured note wants the position — he is articulating his strong views about the direction of interest rates by investing in a note that gives him a payoff profile to match his views. In the case of an accrual super-range floater, he is taking a speculative position against the possibility of one-month LIBOR rising above 4.5% during the life of the note. Even if he thought LIBOR might rise above 4.5%, but only towards the end of the life of the note, he could still find it advantageous to buy the note because he would accrue a significantly larger coupon than that of a conventional floater for most of the period.

Buyers of such instruments face liquidity risks — it not easy to sell these things back, and often one can only get a price from the financial institution which originally sold it to you. Indeed the illiquidity of such instruments especially in deteriorating market conditions is one of the few things about which investors can justifiably complain. It is hard to be too sympathetic to their complaints about the losses they have suffered. Many bought these instruments because they were seduced by the rich rewards of taking on such risks, totally ignoring the downside of these instruments. Having said that, many of these same investors also made a fair bundle in the bull years of 1990–93 when their speculative decisions paid off handsomely.

Hybrid 3 — Index Amortizing Rate (IAR) Swap

An index-amortizing rate swap is an interest rate swap, whose notional principal amortizes (decreases) at a predetermined rate, depending on the level of a specified short-term index. Often this short-term rate is LIBOR, which is why an IAR swap is also known as a LIBOR-indexed principal swap. The IAR swap made its first appearance in the second half of 1991, and became very popular in 1992 and the first half of 1993 when asset managers sought to increase current yields on their assets, and used them as an alternative to mortgage-backed securities.

Most asset managers executing an IAR swap are fixed-rate receivers and floating rate payers (from now on called the buyer.) (see Figure 8.3) Buyers receive a fixed interest rate higher than one they can earn on plain vanilla interest rate swaps because the net cashflows they receive over time will decrease as interest rates fall. This is because the interest rate payments (and thus the net amount) are based on a notional principal that decreases as interest rates decline. In other words, the buyer has sold the fixed-rate payer (the seller of the IAR swap) a call option which allows the latter to cancel part or all of the remaining swap if interest rates decline. The premium the former receives for selling this option is the reason why he earns an above-market fixed interest rate.

An IAR swap, from the buyer's viewpoint, is economically equivalent to owning mortgage-backed securities, since the latter also have an embedded call option

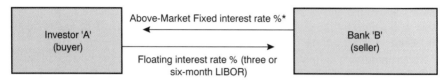

*The above-market fixed rate is fixed throughout the life of the swap but the notional amount of the swap, on which these coupon payments are based, decreases as interest rates fall.

Figure 8.3 Flowchart of an IAR Swap.

which allows the issuer to call the bond when interest rates fall. The fixed-rate payer in an IAR swap is like the MBS issuer — they both own call options which they bought from the fixed-rate receiver (investor in the case of an MBS.) The call option in an IAR swap is exercised according to a predetermined schedule whereas it is not always exercised in an MBS because its exercise depends on a combination of factors — the level of interest rates, relocation, death, divorce, etc. (See prepayment section in Chapter 7.) Indeed, the IAR swap was invented because prepayment options in MBS were exercised unpredictably; investors wanted a surrogate structure which paid similar yields but carried none of the idiosyncratic prepayment risk. (One point to note though — the embedded call option in an MBS is an option on long-term rates, while that in an IAR swap is tied to short-term rates.)

Most IAR swaps have a lock-out period during which the principal cannot amortize; but if interest rates have fallen sufficiently at the end of the lock-out period, the entire swap could amortize then. This is because IAR swaps are constructed with a minimum notional principal amount, or clean-up call; if rates drop so much that the swap's notional amount falls below the clean-up call then the swap terminates. If rates fall during the lock-out period but not enough to trigger the clean-up call, then the swap would amortize according to the pre-agreed schedule. If on the other hand interest rates rise, then the swap would amortize at a slower rate, ending up with a longer-than expected life or even its full maturity.

Few buyers of IAR swaps evaluate the swap using its final maturity; most use its expected maturity. And just like an MBS whose expected life can be shortened and lengthened, so can that of an IAR swap, depending on the existing level of LIBOR. An IAR swap can thus be thought of as a swap with an embedded straddle, i.e. the buyer of the IAR swap has sold put and call options, with the same strike and same expiry (just like a buyer of MBS.) As with any short straddle position, the buyer of the IAR swap benefits most when short-term rates move within a narrow range because if they climbed significantly, the put options would be exercised and if they declined drastically, the calls would be exercised. If rates stay within a narrow range, both sets of options are not exercised, allowing the option seller (IAR swap buyer) to enjoy the premium income.

It is hard to make a comparison of the returns of an IAR and plain vanilla swap without making assumptions about future LIBOR moves. This is because the payout profile of the IAR swap is totally dependent on the path of LIBOR since the options sold have strikes indexed to LIBOR. To determine the payout profile of the swap, one has to trace its exposure profile under different interest rate scenarios — not only just interest rates rising and falling across the yield curve (i.e. parallel shifts of short-term and long-term rates) but short-term rates increasing more than long-term rates (non-parallel shifts or changes in the shape of the yield curve) and vice versa.

But even if the IAR swap was not conceptualized as a swap with an embedded straddle position, its benefits vis-à-vis a plain vanilla swap under various interest rate scenarios can still be visualized. The buyer of an IAR swap will outperform a plain vanilla swap buyer if rates remain stable and underperform if rates are volatile. If rates remain stable, the swap would proceed along as projected and the buyer will earn rates above those of a comparable plain vanilla swap. If rates drop, the swap will amortize rapidly or even terminate after the lock-out period, and the buyer will be forced to reinvest his proceeds at lower fixed rates. If rates rise sharply, the swap amortizes slowly, lengthening the projected duration of the swap or even extending itself to its maximum life. Under such conditions the buyer will receive a below-market fixed rate for a longer period than he had planned.

But what if the yield curve changed shape? Say long-term rates rise, and short-term rates fall. Then it is like Christmas for the IAR buyer. This is because the swap will amortize according to schedule and release cash to the buyer who can then reinvest the proceeds at higher long-term rates. He can, for example, enter into a five-year plain vanilla swap and receive higher long-term fixed rates. But what if long-term rates fell, and short-term rates rise? Then it is still Christmas time for the buyer. The IAR swap will amortize more slowly than expected. The buyer is still happy because he would be earning an above-market fixed rate because long-term rates have fallen.

An asset manager (be it a bank, fund manager or insurance company) buys an IAR swap because he wants to enhance his yields. But he should not buy an IAR swap if he does not believe that rates will move within a narrow range during much of the life of the swap. He must expect a stable interest rate environment or else the options he has sold will be exercised and he will end up with a total rate of return less than that of a plain vanilla swap.

Since their invention, and up to February 1994, IAR swaps experienced falling interest rates. Many were terminated as soon as their lock-out periods were over. After February 1994, IAR swap buyers had to face extension risk because short-term rates rose. Since the swaps did not amortize the buyer found himself earning below-market fixed rates. In some cases, there was negative cashflow because the floating rate the buyer found himself paying was higher than the original fixed rate. Because liquidity in these instruments is limited, he could be forced to sit tight because he could not sell the swap at a reasonable bid/ask spread.

It is not easy for a buyer of an IAR swap to hedge the embedded option risks. The exact number and structure of interest rate options cannot be easily determined by looking at the amortization schedule since that depends totally on future paths of interest rates. He is unable to buy the correct number of offsetting options to hedge the cashflow risk because he does not know what the cashflows will be. To hedge the options sold, he needs a interest rate term structure model which will require him to make assumptions about volatility of rates, the future price path of rates and the correlation of short- and long-term rates, amongst other things.

The Federal Reserve Board's Trading Activities Manual released in March 1994 notes,

> Tracking the true profitability over time of an IAR swap can be difficult. Due to the IAR's path-dependent nature the instrument cannot be easily broken down into pieces that look exactly like other instruments whose prices are known. Hence, the product's valuation depends critically on pricing models. This dependence and the possibility of mispricing is known as 'model risk.'
>
> The set of possible interest rate paths over which an IAR's pricing and valuation is determined are usually generated using one or two factor interest rate models. One-factor interest rate models implicitly assume perfect correlation between short-term and long-term rates. On the other hand, two-factor interest rate models can simulate imperfectly correlated long-term and short-term rates. In this respect, two-factor models are better representations of the term structure than one-factor models. However, two factor models require their users to make explicit assumptions about the correlation between separately varying short-term and long-term rates. If inappropriate assumptions are made, then their results are less accurate.... Market participants have found that correlation is an especially difficult parameter to forecast reliably, and problems can arise because the models are particularly sensitive to the assumed degree of correlation.

Sellers of IAR swaps i.e. the banks, have not found it easy to hedge them either, despite their armies of quantitative analysts and state-of-the-art risk management systems. In December 1994, the New York Stock Exchange, censured and barred for two years a swaps trader, Neil Margolin for concealing losses he had sustained on trading and hedging IAR swaps in 1992. Margolin had tried to conceal losses worth $10 million while working at Kidder Peabody. (In March 1994, the Federal Reserve Board identified the top four dealers in IAR swaps as Merrill Lynch, Bankers Trust, Goldman Sachs and Kidder Peabody.)

Some market participants will regard the hybrids unbundled above as 'kindergarten material' when compared with some of the unpublicized over-the-counter structures done in 1992 and 1993. Some of the swap structures Gibson Greetings executed with Bankers Trust were complex but are only 'primary school level' in complexity, say observers. But as Gibson found to its cost, even reverse engineering some of these swaps was not easy. Certainly if a corporate or an investor did not have a professional Treasury department or employ a few quantitative analysts, unbundling these structures would have been too difficult. Yet any one who buys such instruments must go through the rigours of decomposing them into their basic building blocks so that they can clearly identify the risks. If they cannot do it themselves they have to ask the seller to do it for them. (The seller already has the information because the bank has to analyse the risks of the transaction and how they can be hedged before it is willing to sell the product.)

Without unbundled product information, the buyer cannot say honestly that he has evaluated the product in terms of whether it met his firm's funding or investment objectives, guidelines as well as his company's views on the future direction of the relevant markets.

BUYER BEWARE

While the onus should always be on the buyer to be responsible ultimately for what he buys, it should be qualified in the case of complex structures. There is some validity to derivative providers' arguments that it is up to the buyers to ask questions; but if the product is so complex how is the buyer to know what are the right questions. Or more importantly whether he has asked *all* the right questions. If *caveat emptor* is to remain the guiding principle, then new regulation on derivatives should make some effort towards protecting the consumer by making sellers disclose all the pertinent risks and assumptions inherent in any structured derivative product.

The plethora of law suits between derivative providers and their customers (many not publicized and settled out of court) has prompted some soul searching on the lack of transaction-specific disclosure, and marketing standards. The December 1994 written agreement between the Federal Reserve Bank of New York and Bankers Trust in which the New York bank agreed to a rigid set of policies and procedures for its leveraged derivative business focused minds even more on the issue of 'customer appropriateness'. The agreement required Bankers Trust to improve controls on how it assessed derivatives for its customers, how it marketed them, what information it provided on their value as underlying markets moved, and how it supervised the business.

The information that the Federal Reserve wanted Bankers Trust to provide, included at a minimum:

(1) New product identification and introduction

(2) disclosures to each customer of the nature, and material terms, conditions, and risks of leveraged derivatives transactions ('LDT') to be entered into with the customer; and

(3) distribution of (a) written term sheets and (b) sensitivity analyses designed to illustrate a broad range of outcomes and distribution of risks at maturity. Price sensitivity over the life of a transaction will be addressed by the periodic quotation of indicative prices and by the inclusion of appropriate disclosure language (to be agreed with the Reserve Bank) in term sheets, sensitivity analyses, and indicative price quote communications. A sensitivity analysis should be delivered (i) upon entering into an LDT, and (ii) upon receipt of a request from a customer for an update of such information. (Each term sheet and sensitivity analysis shall set out the definitions and assumptions used therein. Written communications to a customer after execution of an LDT shall include a notice to the customer that an updated sensitivity analysis is available upon request.)

The soul searching gained urgency when, in fining Bankers Trust $10 million in December 1994, the Securities and Exchange Commission deemed that some of the swaps Bankers Trust had sold Gibson were actually 'securities'. If this argument was extended to its logical conclusion then houses which sell swaps must provide the same extensive information on swaps as they do securities, and subject to the same anti-fraud conventions. No wonder then that derivative providers tried to preempt any formal regulatory moves with their voluntary codes of conduct which were released in March 1995.

The first code of conduct, entitled 'Framework for Voluntary Oversight' applied to SEC-registered broker-dealers and their unregulated affiliates. It was drawn up by the Derivatives Policy Group and comprised very senior officials from Goldman Sachs, Merrill Lynch, CS First Boston, Salomon Brothers, Morgan Stanley and Lehman Brothers. The second, entitled 'Principles and Practices for Wholesale Financial Market Transactions' resulted from the joint efforts of the Emerging Markets Traders Association, the Foreign Exchange Committee of the Federal Reserve Bank of New York, the International Swaps and Derivatives Association, the New York Clearinghouse Association, the Public Securities Association and the Securities Industry Association.

What are the Principal Risks?

Amongst other things, both codes attempt to deal with the issues of transaction disclosure and valuations. Both embody the basic principles espoused in the Fed-BT agreement, i.e the major risks of a transaction are explained and sensitivity and scenario analyses of complex transactions offered — unsolicited — to customers. Both stress that these analyses should be done as objectively as possible.

For example, the Derivatives Policy Group code recommends:

> If scenario or other analyses are prepared at a non-professional counterparty's request and the counterparty does not stipulate some or all of the assumptions to be used in making the calculations, the professional intermediary preparing the materials should effect the calculations on the basis of good faith assumptions and not with a view to presenting a misleading picture of the potential risks and benefits of the scenarios analysed.
>
> A professional intermediary that provides written materials to a non-professional counterparty that contain scenario or sensitivity analyses or other calculations should consider including legends with those materials that identify various assumptions underlying the analyses presented, describe market factors that may affect the analysis, and/or inform the party receiving the materials that a variety of assumptions and market factors may affect the analysis.

The push for more transaction details has rightly concentrated on non-technical information — consumers do not need to know the complex formulas that drive the payout formulas. What they need is a clear statement of each separate element of risk embodied in the transaction, assumptions about these risks (including the Greek letters) and their relationships with each other so that they can judge for themselves whether they agree with such assumptions, and which risks (transactional features) have the greatest impact on the value of the transaction. Such broad information together with sensitivity and scenario analyses information should give the consumer a clear appreciation of the profit and loss potential (market risk) of the transaction vis-à-vis his principal investment. The end-user must then ask himself whether his firm would be able to absorb easily the losses on a transaction if his market views turned out wrong. Most important of all, end-users must read the information they are given. This is painfully obvious, but some end-users have admitted to not reading about the downside of potential transactions during post mortems conducted in the wake of the 1994 losses. They ignored the downside analysis because they did not contemplate increases in US interest rates. End-users should also apply to their derivative buys a motto applicable to all other purchase decisions — they should insist that the dealer from whom they bought the transaction quote a two-way price (preferably a fixed bid/ask spread) and they must shop around for third-party quotes.

Valuations and Quotations

Valuation is a straightforward exercise if it is a plain vanilla swap — everyone can make you a price and they are all within a narrow range. Plain vanilla swaps are a commodity item and obtaining a secondary market price for them is similar to getting a second-hand quote on a Volkswagen Golf — they are common cars and there is an active second-hand car market in them. But try selling a Queen Anne bureau that has been a family heirloom since time immemorial, or better still a painting by Claude Monet on a subject that he seldom painted. The prices dealers will quote you will vary widely, in the case of the Monet sometimes as much as 100%.

The range of valuations for customized structures which have embedded swaps and options fall somewhere between the Queen Anne bureau and the Monet; and just like antiques and paintings they reflect, to a certain extent, the motivations, inventory and the customer base of the dealer. In derivative parlance, this is known as the trading axe. The more illiquid the market for the product, the greater the impact this trading axe has on valuations. If a dealer has a starting position that gives him a headstart over all others, he will be able to quote a more competitive price, or more accurately improve on the mid-market valuation price that the bank's internal model has churned out.

All derivative providers use internal models to produce valuations — so although the term is mark-to-market, mark-to-model would be more accurate. Most models return a mid-market valuation around which the trader or salesman has to fashion a reasonable bid/ask spread in order to make a real market. This real market price takes into account credit spread, cost of carry and use of capital, operational expenses, future handling charges and liquidity charges, to name a few. If a dealer has a trading axe, he could improve on the side of the bid/ask spread that capitalized on this favourable starting point.

But such a valuation assumes that the end-user wants to trade: he may not, all he may want is a valuation for book-keeping purposes. To avoid any misunderstanding about valuation, an end-user must tell the derivative provider whether he wants a close-out price or an indicative valuation. If the end-user has not made clear his intentions then the dealer should take it upon himself to clarify the nature of the quotation. A dealer who has sold a customer a transaction should be able to quote a close-out price that is better than any other dealers on the street — this reflects the trading axe again — he is familiar with the workings and hedges behind the deal. Closing it out will not only save transaction costs on the hedges but also time spent managing the risks of the transaction and managing the relationship with respect to the deal.

No number of precautionary safeguards will ever be exhaustive. Even if both the seller and buyer took what they thought were the necessary steps to ensure that the latter understood the nature of and risks inherent in a specific transaction, some areas could remain uncovered. But the point is to try. Among buyers, the responsibility for such transactions is a shared one — senior management has to frame broad policy guidelines while the staff who execute such transactions must have more specific lists of questions. Instilling the right mindset at all levels is key to avoiding large unexpected losses. The following checklist might be helpful.

THE TEN COMMANDMENTS

Before considering a derivative transaction:

1. *Forecast*   Have a view on the markets.

     Build a credible market scenario.

     Compare it with market consensus, for example implied forward curves.

2. *Analyse*   Work out your cashflows and your risks under various scenarios.

     Determine your target cashflows if you are right and how much you are willing to lose if you are wrong.

Reviewing the derivative transaction:

3. *Replicate*   Reverse engineer the transaction by decomposing it into its basic building blocks. De-leverage it if necessary.

     Understand its implied trading strategy.

     Understand which variables have the greatest impact on the value of the transaction.

4. *Simulate*   Compute the transaction's break-even and its evolution with the passage time and under different scenarios.

     Compute the leverage over time and under changing scenarios.

5. *Scale*   Determine the optimal size and leverage of the transaction.

6. *Commit*   Tie your dealer down to a maximum bid/ask spread, quote frequency and dealing size. What does his price represent — a dealing price or a theoretical mid-market valuation?
Check his pricing methodology, his credit standing and ... check prices with other market makers.

Approving the derivative transaction:

7. *Authorize*   Who can commit the firm to a transaction, what and how much can he commit to, and with whom.
Under what conditions can he commit the firm to a transaction, especially new structures with which the firm is not familiar.

8. *Limit*   Determine the acceptable overall risk profiles over time. For market risk, this includes risk limits for the 'Greeks' i.e. separate limits for delta, gamma, vega. For credit risk, there should be counterparty and concentration limits, collateral triggers and other sorts of credit enhancements in place.

9. *Establish*   Ensure that the appropriate systems, procedures, accounting, documentation and people are in place and able to keep abreast with the changing dynamics of a derivative transaction.

Entering into the derivative transaction:

10. *Monitor*   Set individual adjustment points in advance: for e.g. stop-loss limits or profit lock-ins which trigger an automatic close out of a transaction once they are breached. Establish procedures and the people who have authority to override these automatic close-out triggers.

Review and update the check-list; you have learned a lot going through it. And go back to point 1.

This checklist was developed with the help of the Finance Department of the University of Lausanne, Switzerland.

SUMMARY

The three hybrid examples illustrate how computer technology has changed the face of modern finance. Any payout profile can now be synthesized by crafting together the basic building blocks — cash instruments, swaps, forwards and options. The downside of such flexibility is that the risks of some of these hybrid structures are not always obvious. Reverse engineering any product, other than a plain vanilla bond, swap, forward or option, is essential if an end-user is to understand all of its embedded risks. The other disadvantage of customized products is their lack of liquidity; implying a greater dependence on the house that sold the product and its internal models for a mark-to-market valuation.

Derivative providers realize that they have an obligation to disclose the principal risks of the more complex structures and to provide objective sensitivity and scenario analyses. But the notion of *caveat emptor* still holds. Against such a backdrop, going through the ten commandments listed at the end of the chapter is a useful discipline for any one contemplating a derivative transaction.

PART THREE
MANAGING RISKS

INTRODUCTION

Practices and methods of managing derivative risks are still evolving. They reflect amongst other things, computer technology's state-of-the-art, the application of mathematical models both in designing and managing the risks of new products and the painful lessons inflicted by 'market shock' events in all major asset classes in the last decade.

But one thing has remained constant: strong corporate governance, which includes competent supervision by firms' boards of directors and senior management. This has, and always will be critical to managing derivative activities. First, top-level management must articulate its appetite for risk and then commit the firm to providing adequate resources to satisfy prudently this appetite. Trading operations vary significantly, so the amount of resources devoted to controlling the risk resulting from such activities differs but there are certain basic standards which have to be met regardless of size.

There should be sound management information and internal control systems in any firm that trades derivatives. A firm should not become involved in derivatives (or its different aspects/products) until senior management and all relevant personnel understand the products and are able to manage their risks and integrate them into the firm's risk measurement and control system. To do any less would be cavalier. Proper risk management processes should be seen as vital and integral to a firm's success; not as a non-revenue-generating millstone around an institution's neck. The collapse of Barings has shown that such an attitude can have disastrous consequences and that ultimately, the accountability for controlling derivative risks rests with the board of directors and senior managers, not with traders on the front line.

Bank ≡ hedge fund w/ 8% capital

{ set aside capital
for greatest risks

9

Just One Number

Dividing derivative risks into their various dimensions gives an appreciation of the characteristics of option-related versus forward-based structures and the differing relationship the two major types of derivatives have with the underlying spot (physical) markets. These risk dimensions are measured separately across the four major asset classes — foreign exchange, interest rates, equities and commodities. Risk managers at banks and securities houses that offer derivatives need such detailed information to do their jobs properly; the same is probably true for some active end-users. But presenting a whole series of numbers under Greek letter headings to profile a firm's currency or equity exposure is not terribly helpful to top management. What they want is a measure that sums up all these risks into one number which represents the firm's total potential market risk. This one-number summation of a firm's potential losses necessitates some simplifying assumptions which risk management purists may find naive, but if such simplications are required to present information that can be grasped intuitively by top management, they are a necessary evil. The need to distil market risks to one number has been made all the more urgent because banks will be required to set aside market risk capital from the end of 1997. The only way capital can be computed is off one base-market risk number.

Until recently, there was no agreement on the best way of measuring market risk. Each firm used its own method in the belief that theirs was the best; no one made any attempt to standardize the measurement or to share lessons learnt despite the fact that market risk had become the single most important concern for all large banks and institutional investors. This 'you go your way and I go mine' attitude would probably have continued had not banking regulators stepped in. They recognized the urgency of institutionalizing market risk capital — especially with some major banks being regarded as no more than 'hedge funds with 8% capital'; not mandating them to set aside capital for some of their greatest risks was like the

French building the Maginot line *knowing* that the Germans would go around it. (Government bonds, for example, carry no credit risk charge yet they often figure in the inventories of the proprietary trading arms of banks.)

In 1993, the Bank for International Settlements proposed a method by which market risk capital would be charged. The proposed methodology was so flawed that it galvanized the trading community into trying to find a common measurement standard to measure market risk. This is the *value at risk* concept which will now be the method going forward since the BIS, in April 1995, formally adopted it as the template for calculating market risk capital. It is ironic that had market risk capital been in force, Barings would not have been able to build such huge positions in Tokyo and Singapore because it did not have the resources to cover capital for market risks, demanded by the European Capital Adequacy Directive which is due to come into force in January 1996 or by the Bank for International Settlements at the end of 1997.

Regulatory

VALUE AT RISK

Value at risk (VAR) is the amount of money an institution could lose or make due to prices in the underlying markets changing. Since most firms are more worried about what they can possibly lose if the markets moved against them, VAR has become a potential loss rather than a potential gain measure. It is not a number derived from the forecasts of a few in-house gurus, but a statistical estimate based on historical data. It is immediately obvious that for such numbers to have any meaning, two more bits of vital information are needed. Is the VAR number what a firm could lose in one day or one week? And because it is a statistical estimate, what percentage of market price changes does it cover? So any interpretation of VAR numbers requires knowledge of the holding period (time horizon) and the proportion of price changes covered by the number (confidence interval).

potential loss

potential gain

Say we have two firms. Firm A has a daily VAR number of $10 million at 95% confidence interval while firm B has a weekly VAR number of $10 million at 95% confidence interval. Which firm has the more risky portfolio? The daily number means that firm A could lose up to $10 million on 19 out of 20 trading days. If one assumes that there are 20 trading days a month, then it could lose at least $10 million one day a month, or 12 times a year. The weekly number, on the other hand, means that in 19 one-weekly period out of 20 weeks, firm B could lose at least $10 million, and in one out of 20 weeks more than $10 million. Since there are 52 weeks a year, that works out to two to three (to be precise 2.5) one-weekly periods (times) a year.

But this does not mean that firm A with a daily VAR of $10 million has a portfolio about five times more risky than firm B with a weekly VAR of $10 million (12/2.5) This is because losing $2 million every day for a week is not the same as losing $10 million over a weekly period (five working days) because on some of those days in the weekly period, the firm might make money while on other days lose money. To make any meaningful comparisons, the two sets of VAR numbers have to be normalized to a common standard.

The choice of a common standard is subjective — but most senior managers (and shareholders) would probably like to know what their firms' annual losses, resulting from normal market moves, could be. But estimating such losses before the event requires some decisions — do senior managers want an annual number that estimates changes in value that result from 99% or 95% of normal market moves? Or are they happy with a predicted annual loss number that only covers 68% of normal market moves? Table 9.1 below shows that a daily, 95% $10 million VAR portfolio (firm A) could lose up to $224 million annually compared with $102 million for a weekly, 95% $10 million VAR portfolio (firm B), using 99% confidence interval. The figures drop to $159 million and $72 million if only 95% of market moves are taken into account. Firm B's portfolio with a weekly $10 million VAR is thus two times less risky than firm A's.

But what about firm C which has a daily VAR of $10 million and a higher confidence level of 99%? This means that firm C could lose up to $10 million 99 out of 100 days or at least $10 million one day out of 100. This works out to

Table 9.1 Whose Portfolio is Most Risky? At a Glance.

Parameters	VAR	Annual 1% loss[1] (99% confidence)	Annual 5% loss[2] (95% confidence)	Comparative riskiness
Daily, 95%	$10m	$224m	$159m	1(benchmark)
Daily, 99%	$10m	$159m	$112m	0.7 (2/3)
Weekly, 95%	$10m	$102m	$72m	0.5 (1/2)
Weekly, 99%	$10m	$72m	$51m	0.3 (1/3)
Fortnightly, 95%	$10m	$72m	$51m	0.3 (1/3)
Fortnightly, 99%	$10m	$51m	$36m	0.2 (1/5)

1(a) To convert a daily VAR into an annual figure, multiply $10 million by the square root of 252 (15.87), a weekly number by the square root of 52 (7.2), and a fortnightly number by the square root of 26 (5.1). (Assume that there are 252 trading days, 52 weeks and 26 fortnightly periods a year.)

The fact that the square root of time rather than time itself is the correct method of scaling up or down (i.e. using square root of 52 as opposed to using 52 outright when scaling up a weekly number into an annual number) is rooted in statistical theory and can be mathematically proven. In any process where events are random and independent of each other (for example, stock prices), it can be shown mathematically that the variance — i.e. the distance from the average — of the process increases proportionally with the number of events. This distance from the average is usually represented by the standard deviation which is obtained by square rooting variance. Since variance is proportional to time, it then follows mathematically that standard deviation is proportional to the square root of time.

(b) Since this column represents an annual 1% loss, VAR calculations based on 95% confidence have to be normalized upwards to 99% confidence. This is achieved by multiplying the annual 95% loss by 1.4. (1.4 is derived from dividing 2.33 by 1.65; 2.33 standard deviations is 99% confidence and 1.65 standard deviations is 95% confidence interval.)

2. Repeat 1(a) to obtain the annual VAR losses. Since this column represents 95% confidence, all VAR calculations based on 99% confidence have to be normalized downwards to 95% confidence. This is achieved by dividing the annual 99% loss by 1.4.

two to three times a year (because there are 252 trading days a year) compared with 12 times for the daily, 95% VAR portfolio. But a direct comparison of the two portfolios to see which one is more risky is not possible, even though both portfolios express their VARs in daily terms. This is because firm A uses 95% confidence level and firm C 99% confidence interval. Both portfolios must be placed on a level playing field, in terms of confidence intervals, before comparisons can be made. Normalizing both portfolios to an annual loss number — using 95% or 99% confidence level, i.e. either 1% or 5% loss — allows a meaningful comparison to be made. Table 9.1 shows that firm C's portfolio is about two-thirds as risky as firm A's because the former could lose up to $159 million a year (on 99% confidence) compared with the latter's $224 million.

The BIS's framework for market risk capital requires banks to calculate fortnightly-99% confidence VAR numbers. So a firm which has a $10 million two-weekly 99% confidence VAR could lose up to $10 million 99 out of 100 fortnightly periods or at least $10 million in one fortnight out of 100. Since there are 26 fortnightly-intervals in one year, this means that the bank could lose more than $10 million once in four years. This portfolio is about five times less risky than the portfolio of firm A (daily-95%) and three times less risky than the firm C (daily-99%) and two times less risky than firm B (weekly-95%). see Table 9.1

It is clear that information on the time period and the confidence interval are vital to how VAR numbers are interpreted and that the greater the security desired, the longer the time horizon and the higher the confidence interval specified. But it is also clear from Table 9.1 that deriving 'riskiness comparisons' of VAR numbers, which are based on different time horizons and confidence intervals, is not straightforward — the different numbers must be normalized to a common standard (both in terms of time horizon and confidence interval) before any meaningful conclusions can be made.

How Long a Holding Period?

Table 9.1 demonstrates the impact of time horizon and confidence interval on the interpretation of VAR numbers. But these two parameters are equally vital to how the VAR numbers are derived in the first place, and whether they reflect accurately a firm's potential losses. This question arises because implicit in the choice of holding period is the contentious issue of whether VAR numbers should reflect adverse price changes in normal markets or in extraordinary events.

The concept of value at risk incorporates two central elements of risk: the sensitivity of a portfolio to changes in underlying prices and the volatility of the underlying prices. The former reflects how well the portfolio is hedged (the better hedged it is the less sensitive it is to price changes) and the latter the likelihood of large price changes. But the issue of the size of the price change is inextricably linked with that of the holding period because the longer the holding period, the greater is the observed price change which leads to a higher potential for loss.

If the firm wants to know what it can lose in one day it is natural for it to use a one-day holding period but that means it also has to assume that the position can be hedged or closed out over a 24 hour period. This is a valid assumption for products where there is deep liquidity such as major currencies or US Treasuries; it may not be for products with poorer liquidity where it may take up to a week or even longer to neutralize the position. Unwinding a large position in Brady bonds or a basket of South East Asian stocks are cases in point. If a firm only has one position then it is easy to choose the appropriate time interval. But if it has a portfolio consisting of a diverse range of instruments, the choice of time interval is more complicated since each market operates on different liquidity assumptions. The G-30 report notes,

> Some dealers use a variable time horizon based on liquidity, but this practice makes sensible comparisons across businesses difficult. To aggregate risk and to assess aggregate risks in a meaningful way, risk measurements must be comparable across activities and products. This implies that consistent assumptions such as time horizon must be employed. One-day is recommended, corresponding to the recommendation for daily mark-to-market.

Even normally liquid markets can become illiquid when they experience extraordinary events such as the break-up of the Exchange Rate Mechanism in September 1992, the equity market crash of October 1987, and the bond market crash of 1994. At such times, it may be imprudent to assume that positions can be unwound within a day; but since it is anyone's guess how long it will take to cover those positions (i.e. for liquidity to return to the market), the choice of time interval is necessarily subjective. There is however no denying that assuming a longer time interval implies a more cautious attitude towards unwinding a firm's positions. A ten-working day assumption may be no more accurate than a one-day, but it is certainly more conservative because once you assume a longer time interval, the resulting number is automatically bigger than a daily number. The question of whether VAR numbers should reflect normal events or market shocks can thus be distilled to one of liquidity assumptions which in turn is reflected in the choice of the holding period.

Scaling Up

The one-day number can be modified to reflect a longer unwind period by multiplying the daily risk estimate by the square root of the number of business days thought necessary to unwind the position. (Under the BIS proposal, the square root of 10 will be used because there are 10 business days in a fortnight. The fact that the square root of time rather than time itself is the correct method of scaling up or down [i.e. using square root of 52 as opposed to using 52 outright when scaling up a weekly number into an annual number] is rooted in statistical theory and can be mathematically proven. In any process where events are random and independent of each other [for e.g. stock prices], it can be shown mathematically that the variance, i.e. the distance from the average, of the process increases proportionally with the number of events. This distance from the average is usually represented by the standard deviation which is obtained by square rooting variance. Since variance is proportional to time, it then follows mathematically that standard deviation is proportional to the square root of time.) Scaling up daily numbers is fine for linear products such as forwards and also generally for swaps (even though they have some convexity), but not good enough for options and option-like positions with pronounced curvature. Once a portfolio has substantial option positions (be they naked or embedded in swaps and bonds), it has gamma or curvature risks which will not be captured by extrapolating daily numbers.

Daily numbers capture the sensitivity of the portfolio to small market moves. With small market moves most instruments, even options, display fairly linear price behaviour. Other instruments continue to display this linear behaviour even with big market moves so that scaling up their instantaneous deltas captures their new price sensitivities. This delta-approximation method does not work for options whose non-linear price behaviour becomes more pronounced the larger the price moves (see Chapter 6 on gamma and curvature). The correct way of capturing this curvature is to completely revalue the whole option portfolio using longer holding periods because the latter assumes that the underlying assets will experience larger price moves. Multiplying the one-day measure by the square root of time obscures this curvature risk.

It is difficult to generalize whether this obscurity errs on underestimation or overestimation — indeed because no broad brush statements can be made, it makes life tougher for risk managers, their management and regulators. If the scaled-up number was always lower than a number produced by simulating the full time-horizon, then a 'safety cushion amount' can be incorporated in the delta-approximation methodology to give that extra degree of comfort.

This is not to be. The reason why no one can generalize can be traced to the very heart of the concept of value at risk. VAR measures how much a portfolio can lose over a specific time horizon and a given confidence interval. It is obvious that different portfolios have different VAR numbers and that these numbers change over time reflecting the make-up of the portfolio.

It is precisely because such numbers are portfolio specific that no broad generalizations can be made on whether scaled up numbers overestimate or underestimate curvature risk. To appreciate the full impact of options on a firm's portfolio, one must know the exact make-up of the option portfolio itself. For example, it is not possible to generalize that just because a portfolio has a fair proportion of options, the scaled up number underestimates curvature. Whether it does or not, depends on the specific combination of options since the curvature of an option portfolio as a whole is not the result of how many options the firm has, but how the risk profiles of the component options offset each other. If the option portfolio is hedged well enough to make it delta and gamma neutral even with large market moves, then scaling up would be fine. But if the options are not or inadequately hedged, then that portfolio would be very sensitive to large market moves and extrapolated daily VAR numbers will seriously underestimate/overestimate the amount at risk. Suffice it to say a firm with no options in its portfolio is spared all this soul-searching.

Despite the portfolio specificity of option curvature, some generalizations can be made about a simple option position in one underlying asset class. An option dealer who is long a call option has positive gamma. When the underlying market advances, the positive gamma works in his favour and any delta approximation results in the option dealer understating his gains. However, if the market declines, extrapolating instantaneous delta will result in the option dealer overstating his losses. The situation is then reversed — the option dealer is now short a call option. The market rises and the negative gamma works against him, resulting in him underestimating his losses. If the market falls, he will overestimate his gains.

Table 9.2 shows the magnitude of differences between numbers derived from delta-approximation and simulation. Two option positions in foreign exchange with starting values of $1 million each are examined. The delta-based numbers ($E[\delta TV]$) are derived from scaling up instantaneous deltas while the actual numbers (δTV) are obtained by revaluing the position at new shock prices. (TV is the theoretical value.)

For position 1, an upside move (assuming two-week, 99% confidence interval) in the market resulted in seven times overestimation of losses; for position 2, the

Table 9.2 Foreign Exchange Price Risk Sensitivities (all numbers in $).

Variable	Down shock (two-week, 99% confidence)	Starting position	Up shock (two-week, 99% confidence)
Position 1 (long options) Theoretical value (TV)			
TV (actual)	2 329 679	1 000 000	718 304
E[δTV] (delta-approximation)	1 864 777		−1 914 971
δTV (actual-revalued)	1 329 679		−281 696
Position 2[1] (Short options) Theoretical Value			
TV (actual)	−1 465 299	−1 000 000	−2 884 618
E[δTV] (delta-approximation)	452 264		−477 591
δTV (actual-revalued)	−465 299		−1 884 618

Reproduced with permission from Swiss Bank Corporation.
1. Although position 2 has been extracted from Michael Allen's article published in RISK magazine[1] this example has negative signs on the position (instead of positive signs) to show a short option position.

delta-approximation underestimated losses by four times. When the market went down (again assuming a two-week, 99% confidence interval market move), the delta-approximation method yielded an incorrect sign for position 2 — it returned a positive $452 264 number when the actual loss was negative $465 299. For position 1, it returned a number that was nearer the mark than all the other three delta-approximations — $1 864 777 compared with $1 329 679.

The BIS has thus decided that banks will not be allowed to scale up their daily VAR numbers for their option portfolios (which they will be allowed to do for their cash and forward-based portions.) To capture the non-linear price behaviour of options, banks must calculate changes in values based on two-week price movements in the underlying markets.

VAR Methodology ⟨ Value @ risk ⟩

There are three main approaches to calculating value-at-risk: the correlation method, also known as the variance/covariance matrix method; historical simulation and Monte Carlo simulation. All three methods require a statement of three basic parameters: holding period, confidence interval and the historical time horizon over which the asset prices are observed. Under the correlation method, the change in the value of the position is calculated by combining the sensitivity of each component to price changes in the underlying asset(s), with a variance/covariance matrix of the various components' volatilities and correlation. It is a deterministic approach.

The historical simulation approach calculates the change in the value of a position using the actual historical movements of the underlying asset(s), but starting from the current value of the asset. It does not need a variance/covariance matrix. The length of the historical period chosen does impact the results because if the period is too short, it may not capture the full variety of events and relationships between the various assets and within each asset class, and if it is too long, may be too stale to predict the future. The advantage of this method is that it does not require the user to make any explicit assumptions about correlations and the dynamics of the risk factors because the simulation follows every historical move. The Monte Carlo simulation method calculates the change in the value of a portfolio using a sample of randomly generated price scenarios. Here the user has to make certain assumptions about market structures, correlations between risk factors and the volatility of these factors. He is essentially imposing his views and experience as opposed to the naive approach of the historical simulation method.

At the heart of all three methods is the model. The closer the models fit economic reality, the more accurate the estimated VAR numbers and therefore the better they will be at predicting the true VAR of the firm. There is no guarantee that the numbers returned by each VAR method will be anywhere near each other as the following example in Table 9.3 clearly demonstrates.

The VAR numbers were based on the actual equity and foreign exchange derivatives portfolio of Swiss Bank Corporation. The confidence interval for both analyses was 99% and a two-week holding period was used.

Table 9.3 Value at Risk (all amounts in Swiss Franc Millions).

Methodology	Equity	Foreign exchange
Correlation	24.5	72.0
Historical simulation	41.1	42.8

One way of evaluating the accuracy of a firm's VAR methodology is to compare its estimated (ex-ante) VAR numbers produced by its internal model with its actual (ex-post) profits and losses. The BIS recognized that banks had to be given an incentive to ensure the predictive value of their VAR models, so the new capital adequacy rule directs that the closer the actual (ex-post) number is to the modelled (ex-ante) VAR, the lower the market risk capital requirement. The incentive is reflected in the multiplication factor which will be used to convert the VAR numbers generated by internal models into capital ratios. The more accurate the ex-ante VAR, the lower the multiplication factor. The April 1995 supplement proposed a minimum multiplication factor of 3. The Basle Committee decided that a multiplication factor was needed because it felt that internally-generated VAR numbers do not provide an adequate cushion against severe or prolonged adverse market movements or against specific risk.

Two major US money-centre banks, Bankers Trust and JP Morgan, disclosed information in their 1994 annual reports, which facilitated comparisons between their actual and predicted market risk numbers. Both however used different methods to show the accuracy of their ex-ante VAR numbers.

Bankers Trust disclosed its projected daily value at risk figures for the whole of 1994 — in January of that year, its VAR averaged about $70 million. This figure dropped to $30 million at the end of February 1994 and stayed in the $30–$40 million range for the rest of the year (see Figure 9.1). Bankers Trust's VAR — they call it the daily price volatility — is defined as the potential loss over a one-day holding period, using 99% confidence interval. Because this number measures only negative outcomes, it implies a one-tailed test since only the negative side of the normal distribution curve is needed. A one-tailed 99% confidence interval test means that the bank expects to exceed its projected VAR only on one-day out of 100 trading days, or 2–3 days in a year (assuming 252 trading days a year.)

Bankers Trust focuses on the loss potential of its portfolio because from a risk management perspective, they are more concerned about losses than with gains. So if the daily ex-ante VAR is $30 million and the ex-post loss is $10 million, the bank takes comfort from the fact that its realized losses are below its VAR estimate. Figure 9.2 plots the bank's daily actual profit and losses against its projected daily VAR for 1994. (All numbers in Figure 9.2 are on an absolute value basis.) The diagonal (45°) line through the middle of the graphs represent the point where the projected VAR is exactly equal to the realized profit or loss. Any observation below the diagonal line means the actual profit/loss is lower than the projected daily VAR

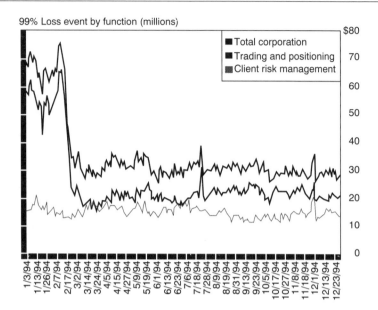

Figure 9.1 Bankers Trust's Daily Price Volatility 1994. Reproduced with permission from Bankers Trust 1994 Annual Report.

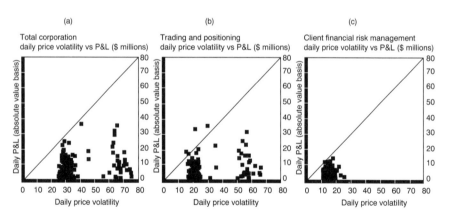

Figure 9.2 Bankers Trust's Daily Price Volatility against Daily Profit and Loss — broken into (a) Whole Bank (b) Trading and Positioning (c) Client Business. Reproduced with permission from Bankers Trust 1994 Annual Report.

for that day; and any observation above the diagonal line means that the actual profit/loss is greater than the ex-ante daily VAR. It can be seen from Figure 9.2(b) that on three days, the realized profit/loss was greater than the estimated daily VAR. This is in line with the statistical specification underlying the value at risk methodology — Bankers uses a one-day, 99% confidence interval one-tailed test;

which has to be translated into a 98% two-tailed test when looking at daily revenue figures. Since revenue numbers can be either profits or losses, both the positive and negative outcomes, i.e. both sides of the normal distribution curve, have to be taken into account. A 98% two-tailed test means that the actual profit/loss numbers are expected to exceed estimated VAR approximately five days a year, i.e. 2% of 252 trading days. (Figure 9.2(a) shows that for the bank as a whole, actual numbers never exceeded projected VAR, while Figure 9.2(b) shows that for the bank's trading and positioning activities, actual numbers exceeded estimated VAR three days in 1994, while on one day, the actual daily P&L was equal to the ex-ante VAR.)

The reader unschooled in statistics will find it harder to judge the accuracy of JP Morgan's VAR model, based on the information it released in its 1994 annual report. Morgan did not release its daily estimated VAR or its actual daily profit and losses; instead it disclosed its average daily revenue and its average ex-ante and ex-post VAR. So the only way to compare the ex-ante and ex-post numbers is to examine the clustering of both sets of numbers around the average daily revenues, i.e. the standard deviation over a given period. (When people speak of standard deviation, they are usually referring to one standard deviation, unless otherwise stated.)

Figure 9.3 shows that JP Morgan's trading activities in 1994 resulted in actual average daily revenues of $5.8 million. To relate the variation of the actual numbers to the predicted VAR requires some statistical manipulation.

According to its internal models, Morgan's lowest estimated daily VAR in 1994 was $10 million and its highest $26 million. Its projected daily VAR for

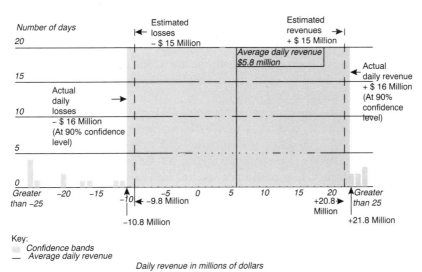

Figure 9.3 JP Morgan's Daily Revenue, 1994. Reproduced with permission from JP Morgan 1994 Annual Report.

1994 averaged $15 million. Morgan explains in its RiskMetrics documentation that its VAR calculations are based on a 1.65 standard deviation one-tailed test because 'since risk only measures a negative outcome, one side of the distribution is excluded'. A one-tailed 1.65 standard deviation test covers 95% of trading days. But as was pointed out earlier, daily revenue figures take into account both positive and negative outcomes or both tails of the normal distribution curve. The equivalent two-tailed test of a one-tailed 95% confidence interval test is a 90% confidence interval.

Morgan's disclosure that its projected daily VAR for 1994 averaged $15 million is thus equivalent to forecasting that on 90% of the trading days in the year, the daily revenue would be within $15 million of the actual average daily revenue. Since the actual daily average was $5.8 million and there are 252 trading days a year, that means that Morgan's internal models estimated that daily profits and losses for 228 days of the year would be within the range of +$20.8 million and −$9.2 million, (i.e. within $15 million of its average daily revenue.) This leaves the daily revenue for the remaining 10% of trading days, 24 days, falling outside this + or −$15 million of the average-daily-revenue-range. 10% of 252 trading days theoretically equals 25 trading days but that would result in 12.5 trading days for the loss tail (negative outcomes) and another 12.5 days for the gains tail (positive outcomes). Since there are no half trading days, it is assumed that 10% of trading days equals 24 with the 25th day counted as part of period covered by the 90% confidence interval. Since there is an even chance of losses and gains, the projected daily revenue on 50% of those days (i.e. 12 trading days) would be more than $20.8 million and on the other 12 trading days the projected losses would be greater than minus $9.2 million.

These were the daily ex-ante revenue estimations of the internal VAR models. What about reality?

The same starting point is used again, i.e. the actual average daily revenue of $5.8 million. The actual volatility of this daily revenue was $9.7 million, but this variation in daily revenues covers only 68% of probable events (one-standard deviation). One of the main parameters in Morgan's VAR model is the 95% confidence interval one-tailed test, equivalent to a 90% confidence interval two-tailed test. To compare both the modelled risk estimates with actual revenue variation, it is necessary to translate the one-standard deviation into the same 90% confidence level used in the VAR model. A confidence level of 90% is 1.65 standard deviations, which when applied to the volatility of actual daily revenue equals $16 million (9.7 × 1.65). This means that for 90% of the trading days, Morgan's actual daily revenue should have been within a range of +$21.8 million and −$10.2 million, i.e. $16 million above or below its daily mean. Of the remaining 10% of trading days, on half of those days, the actual daily revenue should have been above $21.8 million and on the other 12 trading days the actual losses should have been higher than minus $10.2 million. This is confirmed in Figure 9.3 which shows that for 92% of the trading days the daily revenue was within $16 million of the mean (the shaded area); it follows that for the remaining 8%, it fell outside the shaded area. The histogram shows that on 11 trading days in 1994 (compared with a predicted 12 days), Morgan suffered daily trading losses of more than $10.2 million and on approximately seven trading days (compared with a projected 12 days), enjoyed daily profits of more than $21.8 million.

Morgan's actual revenue variation for 1994 was $16 million (at the 90% confidence interval). Its VAR model produced projected numbers that averaged $15 million (at the same confidence level). Its actual (ex-post) daily revenue for 228 trading days ranged from −$10.2 million to +$21.8 million. Its estimated (ex-ante) VAR numbers suggested a range of −$9.2 million to +$20.8 million. The differences between the estimated and actual daily revenue numbers are thus very small (see Figure 9.3). Such comparability is reassuring, as it confirms that for Morgan, at least, the modelled VAR estimates are indeed useful ex-ante measures of true risk, if by risk one means daily revenue variation.

The advantage of the Bankers Trust method over that of JP Morgan's is that the former shows the size of the fat tails or outliers. Morgan's histogram just shows losses and revenues greater than + or −$25 million. The reader does not have any idea of how much greater than $25 million the actual losses were for those four outlier days in 1994 (compared with its largest estimated VAR of $26 million). The Bankers Trust approach shows the size of the outliers — an actual $33 million profit/loss against an estimated VAR of $22 million for one observation and a realized $35 million profit/loss against a projected VAR of $30 million for another observation.

Risk Factors

Whatever the model, good and comprehensive data is a prerequisite. To calculate the VAR number of a German firm with a single position in one-year US Treasury bills would require two sets of data: information on the yields and historical volatilities of one-year US Treasuries and the Deutschemark/US dollar rate. In risk management-speak, such market rates and prices that affect the value of a position are known as risk factors. In hierarchical terms, a market risk measurement system is first broken into the main asset (risk) classes — currencies, interest rates, equities and commodities. But within each asset class, there is a myriad of markets — for example there are at least 12 major equity markets or 15 currencies that are important to the portfolio of international firms. For any portfolio that spans a wide range of assets and maturities, the specification of a full set of risk factors that could affect the portfolio's value is an important step in the market risk measurement system.

Building such a matrix of risk factors is a tradeoff between the desire to specify a matrix that can capture all the risks inherent in portfolio versus a dataset that is manageable and quick to use. In general, the number of risk factors in each risk class and the level of detail involved in defining each risk factor should be greatest where the firm has large and/or complex positions because it needs to know as precisely as possible the market risks emanating from those positions. Another consideration to be borne in mind is the depth and liquidity of the markets underpinning each risk factor — for example, liquid markets with different types of securities of varying maturities will provide more comprehensive information on risk factor behaviour than less liquid, more thinly traded markets.

For interest rates, not only must there be risk factors for every currency in which the firm has interest-rate sensitive positions, there must be risk factors for various points on the government bond yield curve (to capture curve risk) as well as risk factors for non-government instruments such as swap rates (to capture spread risk). For significant interest rate positions, the BIS insists on a minimum of six maturity bands, each representing a separate risk factor. Equities, currencies and commodities are less complicated and just require risk factors for every market in which the firm has a position. The resulting risk factor matrix is pretty extensive and impossible to use without the aid of computers.

JP Morgan, which in 1994 released its in-house VAR methodology under the name RiskMetrics, believes that approximately 325 risk factors and consequently 53 000 correlations are needed to capture the profit and loss aspects of a globally diversified fixed income and equity portfolio. It believes that the following risk factors are needed to cover 15 markets:

1. up to ten points on the yield curve to describe each government bond market;
2. 12 points each to describe each money market and swap yield curve;
3. one foreign exchange volatility for each of the 15 markets except US$ (assuming that currency rates are quoted against the US dollar);
4. one equity market in each of the 15 markets except the European Currency Unit (because there is no ECU equity market).

Time Horizon of Data

Each of these risk factors is represented in terms of volatility. As we have seen, there are different types of volatility: historical, implied and forecast, and any can be used to work out the VAR number. Most firms use historical volatility — not because the past is a good predictor of how markets will move in the future, but because the other two are no better and suffer from disadvantages that do not beset historical volatility. Forecast volatility is by definition subjective while it is hard to get reliable implied volatility data for a wide range of risk factors — there is good data only for exchange-traded products.

But even using historical volatility to estimate future volatility requires certain subjective decisions — for example do you use historical volatilities calculated over the last five years, or the last year? And do you give equal weight to all the volatility observations for the chosen period or do you weight some? A firm which actively trades on short-term trends and volatility may want only volatility data of the last year because it wishes to assess its risk in terms of current market conditions. A firm which has a medium-term strategy will want to use data of a wider time horizon. The length of the observation period will result in different measures of exposure at any given point in time; also a firm which chooses a short horizon is not necessarily less conservative than one with a long horizon because a measure based on a short horizon will lead to a higher risk measure if recent volatility has been high. And because volatility itself is volatile, the time horizon of the risk factors has a material impact on the final VAR calculation. The BIS has decided that one year is the minimum historical observation period.

JP Morgan weights the data for its RiskMetrics calculations. The American bank argues that giving identical weight to all observations leads to volatility estimates that can decline abruptly once a large movement falls out of the sample. The RiskMetrics approach uses exponential moving averages to estimate future volatility because it believes the method responds rapidly to market shocks. Exponential averages assign the most weight to the most recent observation, with weights declining exponentially with time.

Aggregation and Correlation

A VAR number can be calculated for individual positions and a whole portfolio. If a firm has only one position the VAR number represents the potential loss of that instrument, for a specified time horizon and confidence interval. But once it has two instruments, it will have two VAR numbers. To arrive at one number for both positions, it is important to evaluate whether the positions offset or reinforce each other when markets move, and to what extent. These tendencies can be captured by the statistical measure of correlation which measures the degree to which changes in two variables are related. It is normally expressed as a coefficient between plus or minus one. A +1 correlation means that the variables move in the same direction to the same degree and −1 means that they move in opposite directions to the same degree.

The VAR number of one position also needs correlation data if it involves price data on more than one asset (say a US dollar-denominated Nikkei 225 equity swap) or more than one aspect within an asset class (a spread swap involving two and five year US Treasuries.) In all these cases, any VAR methodology has to take into account the positive or negative relationship of the two instruments or risk factors and the strength of the relationship.

Any VAR calculation for a large portfolio must take into account an intricate, complex web of relationships. The accuracy of the VAR number will be utterly dependent on how well these relationships are measured, and whether past correlation assumptions are valid for the future. In theory correlations should be stable, in reality they are not; being at their most unstable when markets are under stress. In short, correlations have a tendency to break down when you most need them.

So any producer of VAR numbers has to make certain decisions about correlation — does he use worst case, historical averages or weighted data? Or knowing that they are unstable does he disregard them all together, which will mean that he will have a high VAR number and thus err on the side of caution. But not using any correlation is not terribly realistic either, because in the real world risk factors do move together; sometimes, not all the time; and sometimes in opposite directions when they normally head in the same direction. Not using correlation or using correlation of +1 also distorts investment decisions because it gives the firm less incentives to diversify. The firm can plump for a compromise solution — it can use correlation offsets within a risk(asset) class and not between risk classes, i.e. it believes that is enough correlation evidence to support a case that bond positions in different markets can be offset but that there is insufficient data to do the same for equities and bonds.

This is the course of action for which the BIS has opted. Banks will have capital relief for offsetting positions in a risk class but not between. The VAR numbers for the various risk classes — interest rates, equities, currencies and commodities — must be added up to form the basis of a market risk capital calculation. This means that the BIS is assuming that the worst case outcomes for each asset class will happen simultaneously, i.e. that banks will experience the Crash of 1987 (equity), the ERM breakup of 1992 (currencies) and the bond markets plunge of 1994 (interest rates) at the same time.

The BIS justifies this decree on the grounds of conservatism. It wants banks to have market risk capital to support their positions in a doomsday situation, where the 'worst case' scenario hits all three asset classes simultaneously. In insisting on simple addition as the aggregation methodology, the BIS is not making any correlation assumptions between major asset classes. It is not assuming that there is no relationship between the various risk classes — if it did, it would have to aggregate the VAR numbers by squaring them first, and then to square root the sum of the squares. A square root-sum-of-squares aggregation technique will always result in a final VAR number that is smaller than one derived from simple addition.

VAR Numbers — Inherent Weaknesses

Setting aside the problems of correlation (and thus aggregation), one fundamental flaw of the VAR number is the assumption that prices of financial instruments follow a random walk. This is convenient because it allows their behaviour to be described in normal distribution terms. It is now accepted that the behaviour of financial assets cannot be adequately described by normal (lognormal) distribution because studies of the past few years have shown that:

- the price distribution of financial assets has fat tails, i.e. there is a wider dispersion of extreme events than that suggested by normal (lognormal) distribution. The mathematical term for fat tails is leptokurtosis. See Figure 7.1 on page 162 for reference.

- the peak around the mean is higher than that predicted by normal distribution.

- the distribution of the observations around the mean is not symmetrical because there are more observations in the left hand tail than the right hand tail. This is called a negative skew as opposed to a positive skew when there are more observations in the right hand tail.

The technical document that accompanied JP Morgan's release of RiskMetrics notes, 'Most of the distributions charted in our Data Analysis Sheets. . . show strong signs of kurtosis and leptokurtosis. Foreign exchange rates show distributions that are closest we have found to be normal. Money market returns deviate most from normality because of the discretionary nature of their underlying prices.' The latter is due to the fact that short-term rates in all countries is the result of action by central banks which can often leave short-term rates alone for a long time, then raise it or lower it in quick succession. Consequently, the price changes are not continuous and the shape of their distribution not normal.

The reason why quantitative analysts in finance stick with normal distribution assumptions is because normal distribution has lots of nice statistical properties that make problem solving easy. No other distribution makes life so easy, and the alternatives are not practical for processing large amounts of data. As long as financial statisticians bear in mind the fat tails and the skews, normal distribution assumptions will still yield usable results.

THE FAT TAILS OF FINANCIAL ASSET PRICE MOVEMENT

In statistical terms, the stock market crash of 1987 was a 20 standard deviation event. Over the past ten years, in any given year, there have been market moves of more than five standard deviations in every financial market. For any given year, there has been at least one market which has had a 10 standard deviation event. Under normal distributions such market moves would be considered extremely unlikely — both in terms of size and frequency. But perfectly normal distributions need their underlying variables to follow a continuous random walk. Financial instruments do not — their purely random price walks are forever being interrupted by the arrival of real news that affect their price movements, and therefore make their price distributions fat-tailed. There are two aspects of these sudden, extreme events or outliers which have ramifications on risk management: the higher than expected frequency, and size; both of which are clearly demonstrated in the accompanying graph and table.

Figure 9.4 of the daily returns of the Japanese yen/US dollar rate over the last five years shows the 'fat tails' and the higher than expected peak

Continued on page 218

Continued from page 217

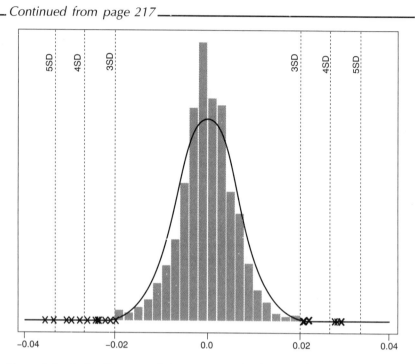

Figure 9.4 Daily Returns of Japanese Yen/US$ — to Show Frequency of Outliers. Reproduced with permission from Swiss Bank Corporation.

Table 9.4 Actual versus Expected Frequency of Extreme Moves (all figures in percentages).

	Actual moves			
Standard deviations	£	US$	DM	Random walk probability
3	2.3	2.8	1.5	0.3
4	0.6	0.4	0.2	0.006
5	0.2	0.4	0.0	0.0
6	0.2	0.1	0.0	0.0
Maximum SD move	6.4	7.6	4.1	

Reproduced by permission of Swiss Bank Corporation.

around the mean. The 'Xs' on the graph represent the outliers and the dotted lines 3,4,5 standard deviation levels of distribution. In the last five years, the yen/US dollar daily returns exceeded three standard deviations 18 times, four standard deviations seven times and five standard deviations twice.

Continued on page 219

_ Continued from page 218 _

The size of outliers in shown in the last row of the table below detailing the actual occurrences (in percentage terms) of the weekly returns of ten-year UK, US and German government bonds, exceeding three standard deviations and above. The maximum standard deviation move over the past five years for sterling government bonds was 6.4%, for US dollar Treasuries 7.6% and 4.1% for Deutschemark bunds. Table 9.4 also compares the normal distribution probability of these bonds exceeding 3,4,5 standard deviations (if they were normally distributed) against what actually happened — it is clear again that the frequency of these extreme moves is very high.

So How Useful Are VAR Numbers?

As a statement of frequency, VAR is a useful number because the problem is not so much with the distribution of events covered by the 95% (two standard deviations) or 99% (three standard deviations) confidence intervals but with what happens at the tails. A one-day 95% confidence $20 million VAR number gives a firm's management good information about its maximum losses on 19 out of 20 days. It however tells them nothing about what could happen on the remaining one day.

The managers of a firm cannot deduce that just because the firm cannot lose more than $20 million on 19 days that its losses for the 20th day would be between $25 and $35 million. They could, if the price movement of financial assets was normally distributed, since analysing the standard deviation can yield useful information about the size of the outliers. But the fat-tailed distribution that characterizes financial instruments means that these outliers can occur with maddening frequency and no amount of analysis of the standard deviation can help the firm predict the size of its possible losses on that one day a month (assuming 95% confidence interval) or one day in a 100 days (assuming 99% confidence interval.)

To predict the size of possible losses brought about by extreme market moves, a firm has to carry out stress simulations on extraordinary scenarios to determine its maximum losses. Stress simulations will enable it not only to determine the size of these outliers but also what events could lead to them. It puts the firm in a better position to anticipate outliers and to ask whether it wants that kind of exposure. For example, stress testing may show that one of the worst events for a firm is the US dollar depreciating significantly against Asian and European currencies. Having this kind of information will help the firm in its decision making, not make the decisions. Stress testing however is time consuming and expensive and not a viable course of action for many end-users, or even the smaller-resourced financial institutions. For the larger players though, stress simulation has become *de rigueur*, and many run a stress simulation system in tandem with a VAR system. The latter gives them information about what they can lose under normal market moves, the former supplements this information by trying to predict losses under abnormal market conditions.

A firm's trading-risk appetite can be inferred from its VAR since the latter measures the market risks of a firm. But the risk appetites of different firms cannot be compared by looking at their VARs alone. Each firm's VAR is not directly comparable with another because VAR methodologies/inputs differ from institution to institution. There are differences in the historical time horizon of the volatility data and correlation matrices used, and the degree to which correlation offsets between various risk factors within a risk class are allowed. Then there are firms which believe fundamentally that correlation between major risk classes (i.e. currencies, equities and interest rates) is too unstable to justify using correlation offsets to arrive at a final number and those who feel it is not realistic either to ignore correlation. Decisions about correlation determines the method of aggregation because the latter depends on the type of correlation assumptions. The most important difference however is how a firm integrates option curvature into its final VAR number.

That identical positions can produce a wide disparity of VAR results was brought home to the BIS when they asked 15 banks from major G-10 countries to produce VAR numbers (as well as individual values at risk for foreign exchange, interest rate and equity risk categories) for a sample portfolio of approximately 350 positions. The banks were asked to use a ten-day holding period and a 99% confidence interval, as of the same date; and to test four different variants of the portfolio: balanced and unbalanced; and each with and without options positions. The returned results were widely dispersed because each firm used different correlation assumptions, volatility data and treatment of options.

The BIS experience shows that it can be dangerous to try to draw conclusions about various firms' risk appetite just by looking at their VARs. But the concept does provide the ground rules for a common language which firms can use to communicate the level of their market risk to each other, analysts and shareholders. The VAR for JP Morgan and Chemical Bank are not directly comparable but neither is the return on equity for Volkswagen and General Motors because US and German accounting standards are different. But just because the latter is not directly comparable does not mean that motor industry analysts do not make return on equity comparisons — they do but with certain caveats. In the same way, the emergence of value at risk provides a common language to discuss market risks, but like any language where nuances and inflexions make impossible the precise definition of words, so too with VAR. The important thing is that a common language has been established.

Market Risk Capital

In framing market risk capital requirements for banks, regulators have to decide the type of events against which financial institutions should seek protection — normal or extraordinary events or somewhere in between. The ideal is a capital number that is prudent, practical, conservative but not crippling.

As the chairman of the US Federal Reserve, Alan Greenspan told a US Congressional subcommittee in May 1994,

> The temptation will be to embrace the notion that bank capital must be capable of withstanding every conceivable set of adverse circumstances. However, it is important for supervisors to recognise that bank shareholders must earn a competitive rate of return on the capital they place at risk and that capital requirements that are unnecessarily high will impede the functioning of the banking system.
>
> While the scenarios need to be sufficiently rigorous to provide prudential coverage in times of stress, we must recognise that, even in very adverse market circumstances, banks can take steps to reduce their risk and conserve capital. Finally, we must also recognise that when market forces threaten to build momentum and break loose of economic fundamentals, as they threatened to do in the stock market crash of 1987, sound public policy actions, and not just bank capital, are necessary to preserve financial stability.

The BIS's market risk capital requirements show that regulators are veering towards a number that will ensure financial institutions having enough resources to withstand shocks equivalent to the biggest market moves in every major asset class during the last decade. End-users are not directly affected by the BIS's pronouncements since they do not have to hold capital for market risk. Whether one agrees with the BIS depends on one's fundamental views on the role of regulators — should they ensure that venerable institutions in which small depositors hold money do not collapse because their trading activities have overstepped the mark, or should the Darwinian instincts of financial institutions be allowed to ensure that banks look after themselves? But end-users can glean useful management tips from the BIS proposal — they must have accurate information on their exposures and they must have adequate financial resources to support these positions if conditions deteriorated. Capital imposes a discipline, and information a tool to ensure that discipline is maintained.

SUMMARY

Value at risk (VAR) encapsulates a firm's total market risk into a single number. It is the amount of money an institution could lose or make due to price changes in the underlying market. From a risk management point of view, most firms are more worried about possible losses, so it has become synonymous with potential losses.

Interpreting a VAR number needs two accompanying bits of information — the holding period and confidence interval. A firm with a daily VAR of $10 million at 99% confidence interval means that the institution could lose up to $10 million on 99 out of 100 trading days and more than $10 million on the remaining one day while one with a weekly VAR of $10 million at 95% confidence interval means it could lose up to $10 million on 19 weeks out of 20. These two parameters are also vital to how these numbers are arrived in the first place. Table 9.1 shows that the less risky senior managers want their portfolios to be, the longer the time horizon and the higher the confidence interval they will specify.

In 1995, the Bank for International Settlements proposed that banks use a fort-nightly holding period and a 99% confidence interval when working out VAR numbers on which their market risk capital will be based. Banks are not allowed to scale up their daily numbers because extrapolating daily numbers by the square root of time obscures the curvature risks of options. The correct way of capturing option curvature is to completely revalue the option portfolio using longer holding periods because the latter assumes that the underlying assets will experience larger price moves.

To arrive at a single VAR summarizing the market risk of all positions requires an aggregation methodology. This is determined by the whether the firm believes there is a strong and stable relationship within and between asset classes because if there is, then the firm will want to offset positions within and across asset classes. For market risk capital, banks are allowed by the BIS to offset positions within an asset class but to simply add the VARs across all asset classes. The relatively long holding period for calculating VAR and the simple addition aggregation methodology shows that the BIS believes banks must set aside market risk capital to cover extraordinary market moves occurring simultaneously in equities, interest rates, currencies and commodities markets.

The main weakness of VAR is that it gives senior managers no idea of what the firm could lose on the days not covered by the VAR number. If a firm can lose more than $10 million on one day out of 20 trading days, senior managers want to know how much more. The answer to that question can only come from stress simulating the firm's portfolio.

REFERENCE

1. Allen, M. (1994) 'Building a role model', *RISK magazine*, **7**, (9), September.

FURTHER READING

1. The Basle Committee on Banking Supervision, Bank for International Settle-ments, 'Proposal to issue a supplement to the Basle Capital Accord to cover market risks,' (1995) April.
2. Chew, L. (1993) 'Good, bad and indifferent', *RISK magazine*, **6**, (6), June.
3. Chew, L. (1994) 'Market shock', *RISK magazine*, **7**, (9), September.
4. Gumerlock, R. (1993) 'Double trouble,' *RISK magazine*, **6**, (9), September.

10
Not Just One Man!

The chain of events which led to the collapse of Barings, Britain's oldest merchant bank, is a demonstration of how *not* to manage a derivatives operation. The control and risk management lessons to be learnt from the collapse of this 200 year-old institution apply as much to cash positions as they do to derivative ones, but the pure leverage of derivatives makes it imperative that proper controls are in place. Since only a small amount of money (called a margin) is needed to establish a position, a firm could find itself facing financial obligations way beyond its means. The leverage and liquidity offered by major futures contracts, such as the Nikkei 225, the S&P 500 or Eurodollars, means that these obligations, once in place, mount up very quickly; thus bringing down an institution with lightning speed. This is in stark contrast to bad loans or cash investments whose ill-effects takes years to ruin an institution as demonstrated by the cases of British and Commonwealth Bank or Bank of Credit and Commerce International (BCCI).

HOW LEESON BROKE BARINGS

The activities of Nick Leeson on the Japanese and Singapore futures exchanges which led to the downfall of his employer, Barings, are well-documented. The main points are recounted here to serve as a backdrop to the main topic of this chapter — the policies, procedures and systems necessary for the prudent management of derivative activities.

Barings collapsed because it could not meet the enormous trading obligations which Leeson established in the name of the bank. When it went into receivership on 27 February 1995, Barings, via Leeson, had outstanding notional futures positions on Japanese equities and interest rates of US$27 billion: US$7 billion on the Nikkei 225 equity contract and US$20 billion on Japanese government bond (JGB) and Euroyen contracts. Leeson also sold 70 892 Nikkei put and call options with a nominal value of $6.68 billion. The notional size of these positions is breathtaking; their enormity is all the more astounding when compared with the bank's reported capital of about $615 million (£375 million).

This comparison may be a trifle unfair because, as was pointed out in earlier chapters, notional amounts do not accurately reflect the true exposure of derivative contracts. The replacement value, or the mark-to-market of these contracts is a fairer measure. Using the rough rule of thumb method advocated in Chapter 5, for the S&P risk factors, the replacement value of these contracts was US$1.05 billion for the Nikkei 225 futures positions (0.15 × $7 billion) and US$60 million for the Japanese interest rate obligations (0.003 × $20 billion). Since the option contracts were split roughly equally between put and call options with the same strike prices and maturities, one can justifiably assume that only half of the options had positive replacement value with the other half worthless. On this assumption, the replacement value of the options was US$501 million (0.15 × $3.34 billion). Thus the estimated total replacement value of Leeson's positions at US$1 611 million was more than two and a half times larger than Barings' capital.

The size of the positions can also be underlined by the fact that in January and February 1995, Barings Tokyo and London transferred US$835 million to its Singapore office to enable the latter the meet its margin obligations on the Singapore International Monetary Exchange (SIMEX). (Exchanges ask for two types of margins — an initial sum of money, or collateral, to establish the position and top-up funds when the contract's value decreases. See box on margins in Chapter 2.)

Of the two futures activities, the Nikkei position attracted more attention even though its nominal size was one-third that of the interest rate contracts. This is because Japanese equities are at least three times more volatile than Japanese bonds; the Nikkei 225 has been known to drop 1000 points a day, and indeed the fact that it did, spurred Leeson to double up his bets. So the potential exposure (and losses) from the Nikkei contracts was the more dangerous of the two.

Reported Activities (Fantasy)

The build-up of the Nikkei positions took off after the Kobe earthquake of 17 January. This is reflected in Figure 10.1 — the chart shows that Leeson's positions went in the opposite direction to the Nikkei — as the Japanese stock market fell, Leeson's position increased. Before the Kobe earthquake, with the Nikkei trading in a range of 19 000 to 19 500, Leeson had long futures positions of approximately 3000 contracts on the Osaka Stock Exchange. (The equivalent number of contracts on the Singapore International Monetary Exchange is 6000 because SIMEX contracts are half the size of the OSE.) A few days after the earthquake Leeson started an aggressive buying programme which culminated in a high of 19 094 contracts reached about a month later on 17 February.

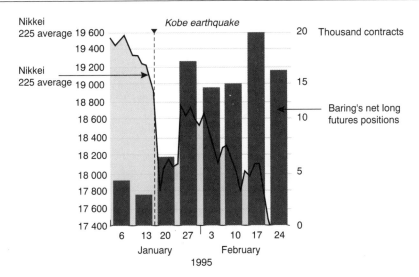

Figure 10.1 Barings' Long Positions against The Nikkei 225 Average. Source: Datastream and Osaka Securities Exchange.

But Leeson's Osaka position, which was public knowledge since the OSE publishes weekly data, reflected only half of his sanctioned trades. If Leeson was long on the OSE, he had to be short twice the number of contracts on SIMEX. Why? Because Leeson's official trading strategy was to take advantage of temporary price differences between the SIMEX and OSE Nikkei 225 contracts. This *arbitrage*, which Barings called 'switching', required Leeson to buy the cheaper contract and to sell simultaneously the more expensive one, reversing the trade when the price difference had narrowed or disappeared. This kind of arbitrage activity has little market risk because positions are always matched.

But Leeson was not short on SIMEX; in fact he was long approximately the number of contracts he was supposed to be short. These were unauthorized trades which he hid in an account named 'Error Account 88888'. He also used this account to execute all his unauthorized trades in Japanese Government Bond and Euroyen futures and Nikkei 225 options: together these trades were so large that they ultimately broke Barings. Table 10.1 gives a snapshot of Leeson's unauthorized trades versus the trades that he reported.

For the rest of the chapter, contracts will be discussed or converted into SIMEX contract sizes.

Unreported Positions (Fact)

The most striking point of Table 10.1 is the fact that Leeson sold 70 892 Nikkei 225 options worth about $7 billion without the knowledge of Barings London. His activity peaked in November and December 1994 when in those two months alone,

Table 10.1 Fantasy versus Fact: Leeson's Positions as at End February 1995.

	Number of contracts[1] nominal value in US$ amounts		Actual position in terms of open interest of relevant contract[2]
	Reported[3]	Actual[4]	
Futures			
Nikkei 225	30 112 $2809 million	long 61 039 $7000 million	49% of March 1995 contract and 24% of June 1995 contract.
JGB	15 940 $8980 million	short 28 034 $19 650 million	85% of March 1995 contract and 88% of June 1995 contract.
Euroyen	601 $26.5 million	short 6845 $350 million	5% of June 1995 contract, 1% of September 1995 contract and 1% of December 1995 contract.
Options			
Nikkei 225	Nil	37 925 calls $3580 million 32 967 puts $3100 million	

1. Expressed in terms of SIMEX contract sizes which are half the size of those of the OSE and the TSE. For Euroyen, SIMEX and TIFFE contracts are of similar size.
2. Open interest represents the number of futures contracts outstanding at a particular time. There are open interest figures for each contract month of each listed contract. For the Nikkei 225, JGB and Euroyen contracts, the contract months are March, June, September and December.
3. Leeson's reported futures positions were supposedly matched because they were part of Barings' switching activity, i.e. the number of contracts shown was offset by an equal number of contracts on either the Osaka Stock Exchange, the Singapore International Monetary Exchange or the Tokyo Stock Exchange.
4. The actual positions refer to those unauthorized trades held in error account '88888'.
Source: The Report of the Board of Banking Supervision Inquiry into the Circumstances of the Collapse of Barings, Ordered by the House of Commons, Her Majesty's Stationery Office, 1995

he sold 34 400 options. In industry parlance, Leeson sold straddles, i.e. he sold put and call options with the same strikes and maturities. Leeson earned premium income from selling well over 37 000 straddles over a 14-month period. Such trades are very profitable provided the Nikkei 225 is trading at the options' strike on expiry date since both the puts and calls would expire worthless. The seller then enjoys the full premium earned from selling the options. (See Figure 10.2 for a graphical presentation of the profit and loss profile of a straddle.) If the Nikkei is trading near the options' strike on expiry, it could still be profitable because the total earned premium more than offsets the small loss experienced on either the call (if the Tokyo market had risen) or the put (if the Nikkei had fallen).

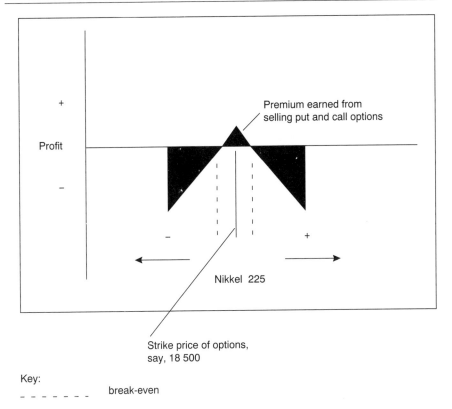

Figure 10.2 Payoff Profile of a Straddle.

The strike prices of most of Leeson's straddle positions ranged from 18 500 to 20 000. He thus needed the Nikkei 225 to continue to trade in its pre-Kobe earthquake range of 19 000–20 000 if he was to make money on his option trades. The Kobe earthquake shattered Leeson's options' strategy. On the day of the quake, 17 January, the Nikkei 225 was at 19 350. It ended that week slightly lower at 18 950 so Leeson's straddle positions were starting to look shaky. The call options Leeson had sold were beginning to look worthless but the put options would become very valuable to their buyers if the Nikkei continued to decline. Leeson's losses on these puts were unlimited and totally dependent on the level of the Nikkei at expiry, while the profits on the calls were limited to the premium earned.

This point is key to understanding Leeson's actions because prior to the Kobe earthquake, his unauthorized book, i.e. account '88888' showed a flat position in Nikkei 225 futures. Yet on Friday 20 January, three days after the earthquake, Leeson bought 10 814 March 1995 contracts. No one is sure whether he bought these contracts because he thought the market had over-reacted to the Kobe shock or because he wanted to shore up the Nikkei to protect the long position which arose from the option straddles. (Leeson did not hedge his option positions prior to the earthquake and his Nikkei 225 futures purchases after the quake cannot be construed as part of a belated hedging programme since he should have been selling rather than buying.)

When the Nikkei dropped 1000 points to 17 950 on Monday 23 January 1995, Leeson found himself showing losses on his two-day old long futures position and facing unlimited damage from selling put options. There was no turning back. Leeson, true to the image of traders as 'masters of the universe', tried single-handedly to reverse the negative post-Kobe sentiment that swamped the Japanese stock market. On 27 January, account '88888' showed a long position of 27 158 March 1995 contracts. Over the next three weeks, Leeson doubled this long position to reach a high on 22nd February of 55 206 March 1995 contracts and 5640 June 1995 contracts.

The large falls in Japanese equities, post-earthquake, also made the market more volatile. This did not help Leeson's short option position either — a seller of options wants volatility to decline so that the value of the options decrease (all other things remaining equal, see Chapter 7 for more details). With volatility on the rise, Leeson's short options would have shown losses even if the Tokyo stock market had not plunged.

Leeson engaged in unauthorized activities almost as soon as he started trading in Singapore in 1992. He took proprietary positions on SIMEX on both futures and options contracts. (His mandate from London allowed him to take positions only if they were part of 'switching' and to execute client orders. He was never allowed to sell options.) Leeson lost money from his unauthorized trades almost from day one. Yet he was allegedly perceived in London as the 'wonder boy' and turbo-arbitrageur who single-handedly contributed to half of Barings Singapore's 1993 profits and half of the entire firm's 1994 profits. The wide gap between fact and fantasy is illustrated in Table 10.2, which not only shows the magnitude of Leeson's recent losses but the fact that he always lost money. In 1994 alone, Leeson lost Barings £185 million (US$296 million); his bosses thought he made them £29 million (US$46 million), so they proposed paying him a bonus of £450 000 (US$720 000).

Table 10.2 Fact versus Fantasy: Profitability of Leeson's Trading Activities.

Period	Reported	Actual	Cumulative actual[1]
1 Jan 1993 to 31 Dec 1993	+ £8.83 million	− £21 million	− £23 million
1 Jan 1994 to 31 Dec 1994	+ £28.529 million	− £185 million	− £208 million
1 Jan 1995 to 27 Feb 1995	+ £18.567 million	− £619 million	− £827 million

1. The cumulative actual represents Leeson's cumulative losses carried forward.
Source: Report of the Board of Banking Supervision Inquiry into the Circumstances of the Collapse of Barings, Ordered by the House of Commons, Her Majesty's Stationery Office, 1995.

The Cross-trade

How was Leeson able to deceive everyone around him? How was he able to post profits on his 'switching' activity when he was actually losing? How was he able to show a flat book when he was taking huge long positions on the Nikkei and short positions on Japanese interest rates? The Board of Banking Supervision (BoBS) of the Bank of England which conducted an investigation into the collapse of Barings believes that 'the vehicle used to effect this deception was the cross trade'.[1] A cross-trade is a transaction executed on the floor of an Exchange by just one Member who is both buyer and seller. If a Member has matching buy and sell orders from two different customer accounts for the same contract and at the same price, he is allowed to cross the transaction (execute the deal) by matching both his client accounts. However he can only do this after he has declared the bid and offer price in the pit and no other member has taken it up. Under SIMEX rules, the Member must declare the prices three times. A cross-trade must be executed at market-price.

The BoBS inquiry notes,

> Barings Futures Singapore [Leeson was general manager of BFS] entered into a significant volume of cross transactions between account '88888' and account '92000' (Barings Securities Japan — Nikkei and JGB Arbitrage), account '98007' (Barings London — JGB Arbitrage) and account '98008' (Barings London — Euroyen Arbitrage)... . Many of the crosses transacted by BFS appear to have taken place in the 'post-settlement period', a period of three to five minutes after the official close where trading is allowed only at the official settlement price. It is likely that Leeson chose this period as being one where other market operators were least likely to wish to participate in the transaction, which they were entitled to do under the rules of SIMEX.
>
> It appears that after the conclusion of the trade, Leeson would instruct the settlements staff to break down the total number of contracts into several different trades, and to change the trade prices thereon to cause profits to be credited to the 'switching' accounts referred to above and losses to be charged to account '88888'. Thus while the cross-trades on the Exchange appeared on the face of it to be genuine and within the rules of the Exchange, the books and records of BFS, maintained in the Contac system, a settlement system used extensively by SIMEX members, reflected pairs of transactions adding up to the same number of lots at prices bearing no relation to those executed on the floor. Alternatively, Leeson would enter into cross-trades of smaller size than the above but when these were entered into the Contac system he would arrange for the price to be amended, again enabling profit to be credited to the 'switching' accounts and losses to be charged to account '88888'.

Table 10.3 is an example of how Leeson manipulated his books to show a profit on Baring's switching activity.

The BoBS report notes,

> In each instance, the entries in the Contac system reflected a number of spurious contract amounts at prices different to those transacted on the floor, reconciling to the total lot size originally traded. This had the effect of giving the impression from a review of the reported trades in account '92000' that these had taken place at different times during the day. This was necessary to deceive Barings Securities Japan into believing

Table 10.3   How Leeson Allegedly Conjured Profits on Barings' Switching Activity[1].

Date	No. of contracts in account '88888'[2]		Price per SIMEX	Average Price per CONTAC	Value per SIMEX ¥ millions	Value per CONTAC ¥ millions	Profit/(loss) to '92000' ¥ millions
	Buy	Sell					
20 January	6984		18 950	19 019	66 173	66 413	240
23 January	3000		17 810	18 815	26 715	28 223	1508
23 January		8082	17 810	18 147	(71 970)	(73 332)	(1362)
25 January	10 047		18 220	18 318	91 528	92 020	492
26 January	16 276		18 210	18 378	148 193	149 560	1367
							2245

1. This table is Figure 5.2 of Report of the Board of Banking Supervision Inquiry into the Circumstances of the Collapse of Barings, Ordered by the House of Commons, Her Majesty's Stationery Office, 1995.
2. This column represents the size of Nikkei 225 cross-trades traded on the floor of SIMEX for the dates shown, with the other side being in account '92000'.

the reported profitability in account '92000' was a result of authorized arbitrage activity. The effect of this manipulation was to inflate reported profits in account '92000' at the expense of account '88888', which was also incurring substantial losses from the unauthorized trading positions taken by Leeson. In addition to crossing trades on SIMEX between account '88888' and the switching accounts, Leeson also entered fictitious trades between these accounts which were never crossed on the floor of the Exchange. The effect of these [off-market trades, which were not permitted by SIMEX], was again to credit the 'switching' accounts with profits whilst charging account '88888' with losses.

The bottom line of all these cross-trades was that Barings was counterparty to many of its own trades. Leeson bought from one hand and sold to the other, and in so doing did not lay off any of the firm's market risk. Barings was thus not arbitraging between SIMEX and the Japanese exchanges but taking open (and very substantial) positions, which were buried in account '88888'. It was the profit and loss statement of this account which correctly represented the revenue earned (or not earned) by Leeson (see Table 10.2 for recap). Details of this account were never transmitted to the treasury or risk control offices in London, an omission which ultimately had catastrophic consequences for Barings shareholders and bond holders.

Figure 10.3, shows the number of cross-trades executed by Leeson. It is the difference between the solid line which represents all the Nikkei trades of account '92000' not crossed into account '88888' and the broken line which reflects the position Leeson reported to Barings management. The figure graphically illustrates the chasm between reported and actual positions. For example, Barings management thought the firm had a 'short' position of 30 112 contracts on SIMEX on 24 February; in fact it was long 21 928 contracts after ignoring the trades crossed with account '88888'.

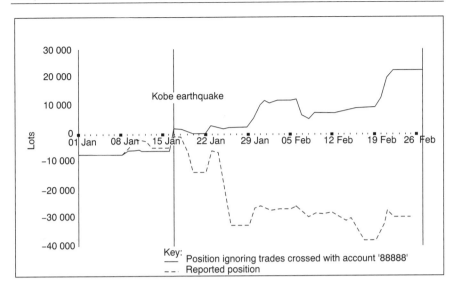

Figure 10.3 Graph to show the Nikkei Position of Account '92000'. Reproduced by permission from the Report of the Board of Banking Supervision Inquiry into the Circumstances of the Collapse of Barings.

LESSONS FROM LEESON

Numerous reports have come out over the last three years with recommendations on best practices in risk management. The most influential was the G-30 report released in July 1993, entitled 'Derivatives: Practices and Principles' which presented clear and practical guidelines that firms can use to set up and evaluate their risk management and control practices. They were embodied in 20 recommendations which have become a benchmark for the derivative industry (see Appendix 4 for guidelines on market risk and Appendix 5 for credit risk — both of which are relevant to the Barings collapse). In the US, the General Accounting Office's 'Financial Derivatives Study' released in May 1994 is also an important document. In July 1994, the Basle Committee for Banking Supervision and the International Organization of Securities Commissions (IOSCO) published risk management guidelines, which banks and securities houses should use for their derivative operations. All these reports emphasize the importance of oversight by boards of directors and senior managers; a risk management process that involves continuous measuring, monitoring and controlling of risk; accurate and reliable management information systems; timely management reporting; and thorough audit and control procedures.

Barings violated almost every recommendation. Because its management singularly failed to institute a proper managerial, financial and operational control system, the firm did not catch on, in time, to what Leeson was up to. Since the foundations for effective controls were weak, it is not surprising that the firm's flimsy system of checks and balances failed at a number of operational and management levels and in more than one location. The lessons from the Barings collapse can be divided into five main headings and are discussed below.

Segregation of Front and Back-office Duties

The management of Barings broke a cardinal rule of any trading operation — they effectively let Leeson settle his own trades by putting him in charge of both the dealing desk and the back office. This is tantamount to allowing the person who works a cash till to bank the day's takings without an independent third party checking whether the amount banked at the end of the day reconciled with the till receipts.

The back-office records, confirms and settles trades transacted by the front office; reconciles them with details sent by the bank's counterparties and assesses the accuracy of prices used for its internal valuations. It also accepts/releases securities and payments for trades. Some back offices also provide the regulatory reports and management accounting. In a nutshell, the back office provides the necessary checks to prevent unauthorized trading and to minimize the potential for fraud and embezzlement. Since Leeson was in charge of the back office, he had the final say on payments, ingoing and outgoing confirmations and contracts, reconciliation statements, accounting entries and position reports. He was perfectly placed to relay false information back to London.

Abusing his position as head of the back office, Leeson suppressed information on account '88888'. This account was set up in July 1992 — it was designated an error account in the Barings Futures Singapore (BFS) system but as a Barings London client account in SIMEX's system. But Barings London did not know of its existence since Leeson had asked a systems consultant, Dr Edmund Wong, to remove error account '88888' from the daily reports which BFS sent electronically to London. This state of affairs existed from on or around 8 July 1992 to the collapse of Barings on 26 February 1995. (Information on account '88888' was however still contained in the margin file sent to London.)

Error accounts are set up to accommodate trades that cannot be reconciled immediately. A compliance officer investigates the trade, records them on the firm's books and analyses how it affects the firm's market risk and profit and loss. Reports of error accounts are normally sent to senior officers of the firm.

The Federal Reserve Board's Trading Manual of 1994 insists that good internal controls means segregation of front and back-office duties. Banks must ensure,

> Separation of duties and supervision to insure that persons executing transactions are not involved in approving the accounting methodology or entries. Further, persons executing transactions should not have authority to sign incoming or outgoing confirmations or contracts, reconcile records, clear transactions, or control the disbursement of margin payments.

Barings' management compounded their initial mistake of not segregating Leeson's duties by ignoring warnings that prolonging the status quo would be dangerous. An internal auditor's report in August 1994 concluded that his dual responsibility for both the front and back offices was 'an excessive concentration of powers'. The report warned that there was 'a significant general risk that the controls could be overridden by the general manager (Mr Nick Leeson). He is the key manager in the front and the back office and can thus initiate transactions on the group's behalf and then ensure that they are settled and recorded according to his own instructions.'

The audit team recommended that Leeson be relieved of four duties: supervision of the back-office team, cheque-signing, signing-off SIMEX reconciliations and bank reconciliations. Leeson never gave up any of these duties even though Simon Jones, regional operations manager South Asia and chief operating officer of Barings Securities Singapore, had told the internal audit team that Leeson will 'with immediate effect cease to perform the[se] functions.' No warning lights went on in London when the report noted 'the general manager likes to be involved in the back office and does not regard it as an undue burden'. No one asked why Leeson liked being in charge of the back office since traders generally regard the back office as a tedious if necessary evil and want to have as little to do with it as possible. Also, the audit was prompted precisely because Leeson had reported $30 million profits in the first seven months of 1994, about a third of the whole group's first-half year revenues. The aim of the audit was to 'seek answers to some of the questions raised by such exceptional results: Have the rules been broken to make these profits? Have exceptional risks been taken?'

The report concluded that Barings Futures Singapore (BFS) was not taking on undue levels of market risks because most of its activity centred on arbitraging the small price differences that often arose between the Nikkei 225 contract traded on SIMEX and that traded on the OSE. This is also what senior management in London thought Leeson was doing — right to the bitter end.

Lack of Senior Management Involvement

Therein lies the crux of the Barings' collapse — senior management's lackadaisical attitude to its derivative operations in Singapore. Every major report on managing derivative risks has stressed the need for senior management to understand the risks of the business; to help articulate the firm's risk appetite and draft strategies and control procedures needed to achieve these objectives.

The first recommendation of the G-30 is on the role of senior management.

> Dealers and end-users should use derivatives in a manner consistent with the overall risk management and capital policies approved by their boards of directors. These policies should be reviewed as business and market circumstances change. Policies governing derivatives use should be clearly defined, including the purposes for which these transactions are to be undertaken. Senior management should approve procedures and controls to implement these policies, and management at all levels should enforce them.

The Basle Committee, in its July document, was even more detailed about its expectations of senior management's oversight.

Before engaging in derivative activities, management should ensure that all appropriate approvals are obtained and that adequate operational procedures and risk control systems are in place. Proposals to undertake derivative activities should include, as applicable:

- a description of the relevant financial products, markets and business strategies;
- the resources required to establish sound and effective risk management systems and to attract and retain professionals with specific expertise in derivatives transactions;
- an analysis of the reasonableness of the proposed activities in relation to the institution's overall financial condition and capital levels;
- an analysis of the risks that may arise from the activities;
- the procedures the bank will use to measure, monitor and control risks.

Senior managers at Barings can be found wanting in all these areas. For example, while they were happy to enjoy the fruits of the success of the Singapore branch, they were not so keen on providing adequate resources to ensure a sound risk management system for a unit that alone ostensibly accounted for one-fifth of its 1993 profits and almost half of its 1994 profits. The senior management's response to the internal auditor's report for a suitably experienced person to run Singapore's back office was:

We have considered making a similar appointment in Singapore, but are not convinced that there is enough work for a full-time treasury and risk manager even if the role incorporated some compliance duties. If Singapore's business changes substantially, we will reconsider this decision but, for the moment at least, the arrangements Simon has suggested look satisfactory.

In reality, none of Simon (Jones)' suggestions were ever carried out and no senior managers in London checked on whether key internal audit recommendations on the Singapore back office had been followed up.

Barings' senior management had a very superficial knowledge of derivatives and did not want to probe too deeply into an area that was bringing in the profits. Arbitraging the price differences between two futures contracts is a low-risk strategy. How could it then generate such high profits if the central axiom of modern finance theory is low risk-low return, high risk-high return? And if such a low-risk and relatively simple arbitrage could yield so much profits, why were Barings' better-capitalized rivals (all with much larger proprietary trading teams) not pursuing the same strategy?

The profitability of the business was marvelled at by all senior managers, but never analysed or properly assessed at management committee meetings. Senior managers did not even know the breakdown of Leeson's reported profits. They erroneously assumed that most of the switching profit came from Nikkei 225 arbitrage, which actually only generated profits of £4.6 million (US$7.36 million) for 1994, compared with £23.4 million (US$37.5 million) for JGB arbitrage. No wonder

Peter Baring, ex-chairman of Barings, told the BoBS that he found the earnings 'pleasantly surprising' since he did not even know the breakdown. Andrew Tuckey, ex-deputy chairman, when asked whether there had ever been any discussion about the long term sustainability of the business, told the same investigation, 'Yes... in very general terms. We seemed to be making money out of this business and if we can do it, can't somebody else do it? How can we protect our position?...' Senior management naively accepted that this business was a goldmine with little risk.

Of Ron Baker (head of the financial products group) and Mary Walz (global head of equity financial products), two of Barings' most senior derivatives staff and Leeson's bosses, the BoBS report concluded,

> Neither were familiar with the operations of the SIMEX floor. Both claim that they thought that the significant and large profits were possible from a competitive advantage that BFS had arising out of its good inter-office communications and its large client order flow. As the exchanges were open and competitive markets, this suggests a lack of understanding of the nature of the business and the risks (including compliance risks) inherent in combining agency and proprietary trading.

Given the huge amounts of cash that Barings had to borrow to meet the margin demands of SIMEX, senior managers were negligent in their duties when they did not press Leeson for more details of his positions or/and the credit department for client details. Members of the Asset and Liability Committee (ALCO), which monitored the bank's market risk, expressed concern at the size of the position, but took comfort in the thought that the firm's exposure to directional moves in the Nikkei was negligible since they were arbitrage (and hedged) positions. This same misplaced belief led management to ignore market concerns about Barings' large positions, even when queries came from high-level and reputable sources, including a query on 27 January 1995 from the Bank for International Settlements in Basle. ALCO itself appears to have paid lip service to its concerns about Leeson's position build-up. Members agreed on meetings on 26 and 27 January 1995 that Leeson should be instructed not to increase his Nikkei positions. Yet reports to ALCO showed an increase of 4200 lots for the period 7–17 February; the minutes of ALCO meetings do not contain an explanation of what, if any, action was taken in respect of these apparent breaches of ALCO's instructions.

The bank was haemorrhaging cash and still London took no steps to investigate Singapore's requests for funds — partly because senior management assumed that a proportion of these funds represented advances to clients. Even then the complacency is still baffling. BFS had only one third-party client of its own — Banque Nationale de Paris in Tokyo. The rest were clients of the London and Tokyo offices. Either London or Tokyo's existing customers had suddenly become very active or Leeson had recently gone out and won some very lucrative accounts or Tokyo and London had new supersalesmen who had brought new clients with them. Yet no enquiries were made on this front, which displays a blasé attitude about a potentially important source of revenue. In most firms, senior managers would be over-the-moon if a floor trader (Leeson) or their sales team had managed to secure so many active clients in such a short space of time, and eager to find out how they had done it. Senior managers should also have probed the credit department about the credit risk implications of such huge cash advances, especially when market rumours about client difficulties surfaced. (The credit risk of client margins will be discussed more fully under 'poor control'.)

Adequate Capital

The Basle Committee's risk management guidelines state clearly that an 'institution should ensure that its capital position is sufficiently strong to support all derivative risks on a fully consolidated basis and that adequate capital is maintained in all groups engaging in these activities'.

There are two aspects to this issue — an institution must have sufficient capital to withstand the impact of adverse market moves on its outstanding positions as well as enough money to keep these positions going. Barings management thought that Leeson's positions were market neutral and were thus quite happy to fund margin requirements till the contracts expired. In the end, these collateral calls from SIMEX and OSE proved too much to bear (as was pointed out earlier, they were larger than Barings' capital base) and the 200-year old institution was forced to call in the receivers. It was funding risk that seriously wounded Barings but the terminal shot came from the discovery that the enormous positions were unhedged.

Funding risk also nearly sank Metallgesellschaft, a German industrial company, in 1993. (This case is discussed in detail in Chapter 5.) In that year alone, Metallgesellschaft's US subsidiary paid out $900 million in margins for its crude oil hedges on NYMEX. When the American subsidiary asked for a cash infusion to meet further margin obligations, the parent refused and closed out the NYMEX contracts at a loss. The latter only survived because a consortium of German banks quickly put together a rescue package of $2 billion.

Both the Barings and Metallgesellschaft stories highlight the need for institutions to pay more attention to the interim funding needs of hedged and semi-hedged positions. But the parallel ends here. Barings' senior managers continued to fund Leeson's activities because they thought they were paying margins on hedged positions (as well as those of their clients) whereas they were actually losing money on outright bets on the Tokyo stock market. Metallgesellschaft, on the other hand, refused to grant any more interim finance because they thought they were losing money on contracts which were infact *bona fide* hedges for the company's long-term energy obligations. Both incidents illustrate the need for senior managers to be more knowledgeable about hedged positions, because the issues facing them are complex in many cases. If a hedge programme requires interim financing because the forward curve for crude oil has changed shape mid-way, should funding not be granted since the 'losses' are due to the hedge misbehaving temporarily? Or should funding be cut off anyway because there is no guarantee that the hedge will return to its normal behaviour for the rest of the hedging programme's life?

And if a hedged trading position involves two exchange-traded legs, then interim financing may be required on only one leg (different exchanges have varying margin requirements so there may not be a complete offsetting of margins between long and short positions); but certainly not on both legs of the transaction, as it was in the case of Leeson.

As it turned out, Barings had significant market risk from its naked positions so even if it had managed to borrow enough money to cover its margin costs till the contracts expired, it would have been unable to withstand the substantial losses it would suffer on expiry. Agents appointed by Barings' administrators closed out the contracts at losses totalling £869 million (US$1.4 billion), so Barings' inability to meet its margin obligations at the end of February just hastened its demise. Its fate had been sealed at the end of January when Leeson had an unauthorized Nikkei exposure of about 30 000 contracts. Japan's 'Big Four' stockbrokers which together have equity capital of $18.5 billion rarely hold more than net long 12 000 contracts; Barings had a capital base of about US$615 million.

It was pointed out in Chapter 9 that banks do not currently have to set aside capital to cover market risks. Banks and securities houses in countries of the European Union will need to do so from January 1996 and American, Swiss and Japanese banks from the end of 1997. If the European Capital Adequacy Directive (CAD) had been in force in 1995, Barings would have had to set aside at least risk capital of US$560 million just to cover the market risk arising from Leeson's Nikkei 225 contracts — this assumes of course that Leeson had not hidden the true nature of his trades from London. (CAD requires banks to set aside 8% of the notional value of equity contracts to cover general risk.) The market risk capital for the interest rate contracts is more difficult to derive because it depends on the duration and assumed changes in yields. The capital charge would have come mostly from long-term Japanese government bonds since they made up 98% of Leeson's interest rate futures contracts. If they had a duration of 7 and a 70 bp change in yield is assumed, then the capital for the interest rate positions would have been US$960.4 million ($7.00\% \times 0.7\% \times \$19.6$ billion). The capital for the short-term Euroyen contracts is US$700 000 ($0.2\% \times \$350$ million). The total market risk capital for both positions would have been US$1.520 billion since CAD does not allow for any correlation offsets between major asset classes.

Under the April 1995 BIS market risk proposals, banks are allowed to use their internal models or a building block approach to work out how much capital they have to set aside. Using the building block approach set out by the BIS, Barings would have had to set aside US$700 million for its Nikkei 225 positions (8% for general risk and 2% for specific risk). The amount required for interest rate positions depended on the maturity, coupon and assumed change in yields. If the 7–10 year bonds had coupons of more than 3%, then Barings had to set aside US$738 million ($5.80\% \times 0.65\% \times$ US$19.6 billion); with coupons of less than 3%, then US$1.02 billion ($8.75\% \times 0.6\% \times$ US$19.6 billion). The Euroyen contracts demanded minimal capital of US$700 000 ($0.2\% \times \$350$ million). So the minimum market risk capital for these two well-publicized positions would have been US$1 438.7 million ($700 m + $738 m + $0.7 m).

The CAD and BIS building block capital numbers give an indication of the capital requirements of Leeson's positions. It is clear that Barings did not have the capital base to support the futures activities of Leeson, let alone the market risks resulting from his option sales as well as the other trading activities in which the bank was involved. The estimated capital charges show that Leeson was completely out of control. His futures positions would have required Barings to set aside funds twice their entire capital base.

Admittedly, these capital charges are based on Leeson's unauthorized futures positions. But his reported positions were roughly half those of his unauthorized ones, so that still means that Barings management had to set aside about $750 million to cover Leeson's switching trades. This figure is roughly equal to Barings' capital base. No financial institution in the world, however well-capitalized, will think it prudent management to set aside so much of its money to cover one man's positions, however much of a star trader he is.

Capital based on internal models depends on the value at risk numbers generated by Barings. As explained in Chapter 9, value at risk measures the outstanding market risks of a firm, thus giving senior management an idea of their potential trading losses if market conditions turned sour. Since Barings has not released any internally-generated VAR figures and the mechanics of its VAR system unknown, it is impossible to try to work out a market risk capital charge under an internal model.

It is doubtful whether Barings would have been allowed by the Bank of England to use its internal models for market risk capital calculations. In its April 1995 supplement, the Basle Committee set out six pre-conditions for regulatory approval. They are:

- certain general criteria concerning the adequacy of the risk management system;
- qualitative standards for internal oversight of the use of models, notably by management;
- guidelines for specifying an appropriate set of market risk factors;
- quantitative standards setting out the use of common minimum statistical parameters for measuring risk;
- validation procedures for external oversight of the use of the models; rules for banks which use a mixture of models and the standardized approach.
  Barings' risk management and control system was so fundamentally flawed that it would have fallen short on all counts.

Poor Control Procedures

In many trading houses, not only is there a separation of operational duties between the front and back office (absent in Barings), but there is also a unit independent of both to provide an additional layer of checks-and-balances. The BIS recommends,

> Segregation of operational duties, exposure reporting and risk monitoring from the business unit is critical to proper internal control. Proper internal control should be provided over the entry of transactions into the database, transaction numbering, date time notation and the confirmation and settlement procedures. The operations department, or another unit or entity independent of the business unit, should be responsible for ensuring proper reconciliation of front and back office databases on a regular basis. This includes the verification of position data, profit and loss figures and transaction-by-transaction details.

Funding

Barings' control procedures were sloppy. Nowhere is this point better illustrated than in the way it funded BFS (or more accurately Leeson's unauthorized positions). Barings did not require Leeson to distinguish between variation margin needed to cover proprietary and customer trades; neither did it have a system to reconcile the funds Leeson requested to his reported positions and/or that of its client positions. (Had the London office, used the Standard Portfolio Analysis of Risk (SPAN) margining programme to calculate margins it would have realized that the amount of money requested by Leeson was significantly more than that required by SIMEX's margining rules.) London simply, automatically, remitted to Leeson the sum of money he requested, despite misgivings about the accuracy of his data. For example, senior staff in London's settlement and treasury functions were uncomfortable with the way Leeson broke down his US dollar funding requests.

The fact that no one even asked Leeson to justify his requests is all the more astounding given the size of his demands. At the end of December 1994, the cumulative funding of BFS by Barings London and Tokyo stood at £221 million (US$354 million). In the first two months of 1995, this figure increased by £521 million (US$835 million) to £742 million (US$1.2 billion). The BoBS inquiry team notes,

> We described... how [Tony] Railton [Futures and option settlements senior clerk] discovered in February 1995 that the breakdown of the total US Dollar request was meaningless, and that the BFS clerk knew the total funding requirement for that day and made up the individual figures in the breakdown to add up to the required total.

From November 1994, BFS usually requested a round sum number split equally between US dollars for client accounts and proprietary positions. The BoBS team notes,

> Tony Hawes [group treasurer] confirmed that he identified this feature of the requests: 'That was one of the main reasons why during February 1995 I paid two visits to Singapore.' If the US dollar requests had been in relation to genuine positions taken by clients and house [Barings itself], on any one day we consider it unlikely for the margin requests for these two sets of positions to be identical; as for having the requests split

50:50 most days, this is in our view is beyond all possibility. Tony Hawes appears to agree with this view. He told us that: 'It was just one of the factors that made me distrust this information.... It was quite too much of a coincidence.... Throughout I put it down to poor book-keeping and sloppy treasury management in Barings Futures [BFS].

David Hughes [Treasury Department manager] also told us that the 50:50 split: 'was a cause for concern... we said, this cannot be right'. He explained that: 'I do not think we could have house positions and client positions running totally in tandem.' [Brenda] Granger [manager, futures and options settlements] confirmed that she would have spoken to Hughes about the split. She added: 'We would joke about Singapore, "Why don't we send somebody's mother [anyone] out there to run the department since Nick is so busy now?".'

Staff in London could not reconcile funds remitted to Singapore to both proprietary in-house and individual client positions. But no remedial action was taken. Their cavalier attitude to reconciliation is illustrated by Figure 10.4 which shows total funds remitted to Singapore ostensibly to pay customer margins.

The solid line in Figure 10.4 shows the total funds sent to BFS by Barings Securities London (BSL) — the entity to which all customer trades of London were booked. The broken line shows the amount of money funded by Barings Securities Group Treasury in London (BSGT), this funding was known in the firm as the 'top-up' balance. The Group Treasury advanced this money, on behalf of clients, because it was not always possible for clients to transfer money to Barings in time to meet SIMEX intra-day margin calls. (The bank was expected to recover from clients these advances as quickly as possible.) Figure 10.4 shows that BSGT had to advance consistently a substantial portion of the funds earmarked for margins for client positions. The graph shows that from 1 January to 24 February 1995,

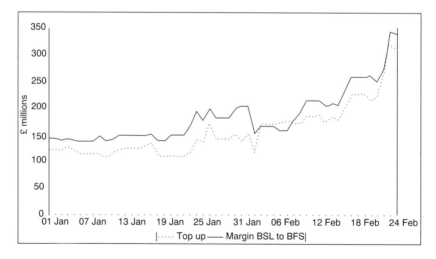

Figure 10.4 Top-up Funding from BSGT to BSL and Margin Balances from BFS from 1 January 1995. Reproduced by permission from the Report of the Board of Banking Supervision Inquiry into the Circumstances of the Collapse of Barings.

the proportion of genuine client moneys which were transferred to BFS fell as a proportion of the total funding. Indeed on 21 February 1995, BSGT had to advance all the client margins of some £275 million (US$440 million). On 24 February, only £31 million (US$50 million) of the £337 million (US$540 million) sent to Singapore to cover client positions had been recovered from individual clients (i.e. the difference between the solid and broken lines). Barings control did not reconcile the 'top-up' payments to individual client balances — if it did it would have discovered that it was sending out far too much money just to cover the margin calls of clients. (Leeson of course used these excessive payments to meet the margin calls of his unauthorized trades in account '88888'.)

Credit Risk

The credit risk implication of the client advances represented by the 'top-up' balances was significant if the total funds remitted to Singapore was to meet genuine client-margin calls. Yet the credit department did not question why Barings was lending over £300 million to its clients to trade on SIMEX, and collecting only £31 million in return. It did not seem to have any idea of who these clients were, yet Barings' financial losses would have been significant if some of these clients defaulted.

The Credit Committee under George Maclean insists that it was Baring's policy to finance client margins until they could be collected. But no limit per client or on the total 'top-up' funds was set. Indeed clients who were advanced money this way appear not to have undergone any credit approval process. When asked by the BoBS inquiry team why there were no limits, Maclean replied,

> As long as they could collect overnight, yes.... No we would not have allowed that in the bank (Baring Brothers & Co), but this is how it had worked for years and we were told to keep the business going. You had to allow them to do that. We certainly would not do that in the bank (Baring Brothers & Co.).... Our assumption was that they were very, very small amounts and very widespread amongst some good clients of long standing of Barings Securities. It was not something that we thought about. It did not seem to me to be a major issue.

The credit aspects of the 'top-up' balance were never formally considered by the Credit Committee although they could see the growth of these advances as recorded on the balance sheets. Plainly put, the credit risk controls of Barings Securities were shambolic. Those of its parent and sister companies may have been slightly better; but with the various subsidiaries working so closely together, it did not take long for the ill-effects of Barings Securities' lack of credit risk controls to infect the others. If Barings' Credit Committee had applied to Barings Securities' clients the same assessment of credit worthiness as it did to Baring Brothers & Co.'s customers, it might have found out some of these clients were fictitious. It would have been forced to reconcile the client numbers and those of the 'top-up' balance and any consequent inability to do so would have forced a better understanding of the latter. In this way, they may have learned of Leeson's scam.

It is almost inconceivable that Barings never considered the credit implications of the 'top-up' balance, since this money, to all intents and purposes, represented loans to clients (even if they were one-day loans, assuming that customers paid up immediately). Perhaps the credit personnel did not even realize that there was credit risk attached to the 'top-up balances' because they were inexperienced. The poor quality of the credit function was recognized by Ian Hopkins, director and head of group treasury and risk of Barings Investment Bank who wrote to his chief executive, Peter Norris, on the 4th November, 1994. He notes, 'Our efforts on credit are more form than substance. Deidre [O'Donaghue, head of Barings Securities' credit unit in London] and her group, although very energetic and well-intentioned, struggle due to inexperience.'[1]

Market Risk

Since Leeson controlled the back office and because Barings had no independent unit checking the accuracy of his reports, the market risk reports generated by Barings' risk management unit and passed on to ALCO were inaccurate. Leeson's futures positions showed no market risk because trades were supposedly offset by opposite transactions on another exchange. Peter Baring and Baring shareholders have learnt too painfully the meaning of 'garbage-in, garbage-out' because a system is only as good as the data it receives.

One way of measuring market risk is using the value at risk concept. Baring was supposed to have a VAR system but it returned nil market risk because it relied solely on the data provided by Leeson. The unauthorized trades which Leeson managed to hide from his bosses had enormous market risk. JP Morgan's Risk-Metric system is the only publicly available VAR system (all other systems are proprietary to the banks that have developed them). RiskMetrics' value at risk calculations for Leeson's activities would have shown that on 23 February 1995, Barings faced potential *daily* losses of up to £121 million ($195 million) on the Nikkei 225 position and £33 million ($53 million) on the JGB bond futures exposure, on 19 out of 20 trading days. (These numbers are calculated on a one-day time horizon, using 95% confidence.) Using RiskMetrics' assumptions about the correlations of the Japanese stock and bond markets, the daily value at risk for both positions was up to £126 million ($203 million) on 19 out of 20 trading days. In contrast, JP Morgan's daily value at risk for all its trading activities averaged $15 million in 1994 and ranged from approximately $10 million to $26 million.[2] JP Morgan is a triple-A rated bank with a capital base of $9600 million, almost 15 times larger than Barings'. Yet its maximum daily value at risk for 1994 was only $26 million, almost eight times smaller than Barings.

No Limits

Barings did not impose any gross position limits on Leeson's proprietary trading activities because it felt that there was little market risk attached to arbitrage trades since at the close of business, the position had to be flat. But the Barings collapse has shown that placing gross position limits on each side of an arbitrage book is perhaps not such a bad idea after all. While it is true that an arbitrage book has little price (directional) risk, it has basis and settlement risk. The former arises because prices in two markets do not always move in tandem and the latter because different markets have different settlement systems, creating liquidity and funding risk.

A detailed structure of limits is one of the primary components of sound risk control. The limit system should be consistent with the firm's overall risk management and measurement process, its risk appetite, its corporate objectives and its financial strength. It should be monitored regularly by staff independent of the trading unit and from records not under the dealer's control. It should also be reviewed at least once a year with procedures in place for changing limits when the need arises between scheduled reviews. The institution should also have a process of approving limit excesses if a trader seeks permission to go above his limit and disciplinary steps for ones who repeatedly exceed their limits. The seriousness of limit exceptions depends on how large and how often they occur as well as the conservativeness of the limits.

There are various methods of calculating trading limits — they can be based on notional value, current market/net present value, potential exposure, maximum exposure and even exposure under worst-case scenarios. These limits can be placed on gross or net positions or both. Limits on gross positions restrict the size of a long or short position in a given instrument, while net limits recognize the netting effect of long and short positions. Global limits should be set for each major type of risk — interest rates, currencies, equities and commodities, and these limits be integrated as fully as possible into the institution-wide limits on those risks as they arise in all other activities of the firm. If possible, the limit system should provide the capability to allocate limits down to the individual business units. Firms which do not set their limits on a worst-case basis should stress-test these limits to see the size of their potential losses if all limits were fully utilized. This affords a management awareness of potential worst-case losses under the firm's limit system.

For most firms there is an absolute limit for each risk class, which is further broken down into sub-limits for currencies or countries. For houses with significant option positions, there will be limits for option curvature as well as volatility. Interest rate books have limits on different maturity bands (to deal with curve risk) as well as spreads between different types of interest rate instruments (see Chapter 5 for details on spread and curve risks). The maturity gap limits of the interest rate book often take into account the curve risks between long-dated and short-dated currency and equity contracts. Maturity gap limits range from absolute amounts for each maturity band to weighted limits; but all should specify the maximum maturity of a specific instrument.

The hypothetical holding period of these limits could be overnight, weekly and monthly. In addition many large houses have 'stop-loss' limits which establish the maximum allowable losses of trading positions. Once these limits are reached, the position must be liquidated. Typically stop-loss limits are retrospective, and cover cumulative losses for a day, week or month.

Lack of Supervision

Theoretically Leeson had many supervisors; in reality none exercised any real control over him. Barings operated a 'matrix' management system, where managers who are based overseas report to local administrators and to a product head (usually based at head office or the regional headquarters). Leeson's Singapore supervisors were James Bax, regional manager South Asia and a director of BFS, and Simon Jones, regional operations manager South Asia, also a director of BFS and chief operating officer of Barings Securities Singapore. Jones and the heads of the support functions in Singapore also had reporting lines to the group-wide support functions in London. Yet both Bax and Jones told the BoBS inquiry that they did not feel operationally responsible for Leeson. Bax felt Leeson reported directly to Baker or Walz on trading matters and to settlements/treasury in London for back-office matters. Jones felt his role in BFS was limited only to administrative matters and concentrated on the securities side of Barings' activities in South Asia.

Leeson's reporting lines for product profitability are not clear cut since his 'supervisors' have disputed who was directly responsible for him from 1 January 1994. His ultimate boss was Ron Baker, head of the financial products group. But who had day-to-day control over him? Mary Walz, global head of equity financial products, insists that she thought Fernando Gueler, head of equity derivatives proprietary trading in Tokyo was in charge of Leeson's intra-day activities since the latter's switching activities were booked in Tokyo. However, Gueler insists that in October 1994, Baker told him that Leeson would report to London and not Tokyo. He thus assumed that Walz would be in charge of Leeson. Walz herself still disputes this claim. Tapes of telephone conversations show that Leeson spoke frequently to both Gueler and Walz. (The bottom line however is that Gueler reported to Walz.)

Two important incidents vividly illustrate the cavalier attitude Barings had towards supervising Leeson. The first involved two letters to BFS from SIMEX. In a letter dated 11 January, 1995; SIMEX senior vice-president for audit and compliance Yu Chuan Soo, complained about a margin shortfall of about US$116 million in account '88888' and that Barings had appeared to break SIMEX rule 822 by previously financing the margin requirements of this account, (which appeared in SIMEX's system as a customer account). SIMEX also noted that the initial margin requirement of this account was in excess of US$342 million. BFS was asked to provide a written explanation of the margin difference on account '88888' and of its inability to account for the problem in the absence of Leeson.

No warning bells went off in Singapore. There were no attempts to establish the real identity of the customer and why he was having difficulties in meeting margin payments or why he had such huge position; or the credit risk Barings faced if this customer defaulted on the margins that Barings had paid on its behalf. A copy of the letter was not sent to operational heads in London. Simon Jones did not press

Leeson for an explanation; indeed he dealt with the matter by allowing Leeson to draft Barings' response to SIMEX.

The second incident did come to the attention of London but again was dealt with unsatisfactorily, perhaps because Barings personnel themselves were unsure about what really happened. At the beginning of February 1995, Coopers & Lybrand brought to the attention of London and Simon Jones the fact that £50 million (US$83 million) apparently due from Spear, Leeds & Kellogg, a US investment group, had not been received. No one is sure how this £50 million receivable came about. One version of events is that BFS, through Leeson, had traded or broked an over-the-counter deal between Spear, Leeds & Kellogg, and BNP, Tokyo. The transaction involved 200 ¥50 000 call options, resulting in a premium of ¥7.778 billion (£50 million). The second version was that an 'operational error' had occurred; i.e. a payment had been made to a wrong third party in December 1994.

Both versions had very serious control implications for Barings. If Leeson had sold or broked an OTC option, then he had engaged in an unauthorized activity. Yet he was not admonished for doing so; nor is there any record of Barings management taking any steps to ensure that it did not happen again. If the SLK receivable was an operational error, Barings had to tighten up its back-office procedures.

Senior management realized the serious consequences of the matter. The BoBS report notes,

> The appreciation by certain members of management that there were very unsatisfactory features relating to this transaction is, we consider, illustrated by the fact that [Geoffrey] Broadhurst [group finance director] (at the request of [Peter] Norris [chief executive officer], who himself been so requested by Bax) asked Coopers & Lybrand London that no reference to this transaction be made in the auditors' management letter for BFS. We consider that it was inappropriate for Broadhurst, Norris or Bax to have caused such a request to be made, which was done with a view to attempting to avoid potential problems with the regulators of BFS in Singapore.

CUT AND PASTE...

The contents of this box are extracted from the Board of Banking Supervision Inquiry into the Circumstances of the Collapse of Barings. The extracts detail how Leeson conned his superiors and auditors about the authenticity of the Spear, Leeds & Kellogg deal and the £50 million receivable.

5.56 *Jones said that Leeson told him BFS incorrectly processed the option with BNP and on 3 December 1994 the funds relating to the premium on the options sold were paid away. Leeson is then said to have gone to Jones and Bax on 1 February 1995 with a handwritten note*

Continued on page 246

_ Continued from page 245 _

explaining the transaction and to say that he had done a pair of transactions for which he had not obtained authorization and that he needed their help to satisfy the auditors. According to Jones, believing that the transaction was genuine, it was agreed that retrospective approval should be obtained from Ron Baker and that monies would be collected from SLK.

5.57 Subsequently, a fax dated 2 February 1995 addressed from Ron Baker to Bax and Leeson was purportedly received by BFS stating: 'As Head of the Financial Products Group I confirm my knowledge and approval of the Nikkei OTC option deal with Spear, Leeds & Kellogg.' [signed, allegedly]
'Ron'.

5.58 Ron Baker informed us that he is absolutely certain that these documents, both the memorandum and fax cover sheet that accompanied it, are false. Ron Baker's secretary has stated that she has no record of these documents being typed or faxed by her.

5.59 A fax dated 1 February 1995 purportedly received by BFS from Mr Richard Hogan, managing director of SLK, confirmed an outstanding balance of ¥7.778 billion due from SLK to BFS and that the amount would be paid by 2 February 1995. In the left hand corner of this is reference to the name input into the sending fax machine as 'Nick and Lisa'. We have spoken with representatives of SLK who informed us that SLK was unaware of any OTC option transaction or receivable at 31 December 1994 and that no fax confirmation of such balances originated from SLK.

5.60 Finally, a fax of receipts and payments made on 2 February 1995 was described as being received by BFS which showed certain movements in the BFS Citibank account including a receipt of ¥7.778 billion and a payment of ¥7.778 billion. We were informed by Jones that this Citibank document was altered so as to disguise the fact that the receipt and payment were in fact transfers to another BFS account. The receipt was purported to represent repayment of the amount receivable from SLK.

5.64 We have been told by [Tony] Gamby [settlements director] and others that materials suggesting that the letter from SLK and Citibank documents were fabricated were found in Leeson's desk when opened on 26 February 1995, as described in paragraph 1.65.

1.65 At some stage over that weekend the Barings team working in the office of BFS forced open a drawer in Leeson's desk. Railton told us: 'There was a stack of paper. There were holes in some. You could see how

_ Continued on page 247 _

Continued from page 246

he had produced [the] confirmation of the SLK deal, I believe, and also I think a bank statement as well.' Granger told us she was there and: 'He [Bax] opened the folder and there was this fraudulent document'. Gamby also said that in Leeson's drawer: 'We found some cut and paste material for the SLK transaction. There was this SLK letter with a scissor cut around the signature . . . we also found a cut and paste of a Citibank statement.'

Conclusion

Many of the guidelines issued by regulators and the derivative industry itself dwell on the fact that managing derivative risks can be difficult because derivatives repackage basic risks into complex combinations which may not be clearly seen or understood. Thus the need for sound and comprehensive risk management systems to ensure the financial stability of firms which deal in derivatives.

But the Nikkei 225 and JGB futures contracts that Leeson was trading were the simplest of derivative instruments. They were also the most transparent — since they were listed contracts, Leeson was required to pay (or receive) daily margins and so needed funds from London. In January and February 1995 alone, he asked for US$835 million. His could not hide his position build-up on the OSE because the exchange publishes weekly numbers. All his rivals could see his enormous positions, and many assumed that the exposure was hedged because such naked positions were out of all proportion to the firm's capital base or even those of other players.

His senior managers also assumed Leeson's positions were hedged. But unlike outsiders who *had* to assume that these positions were neutralised, Barings' management did not. They could have done something about it — they could have probed Leeson, they could have tried to obtain more information from their internal information systems, and most of all they could have heeded the warning signals available in late 1994 and throughout January and February of 1995.

But although Barings fate was only sealed in the final weeks of February, the seeds of its destruction were sown when senior management entered new businesses without ensuring adequate support and control systems. The collapse of Britain's oldest merchant bank was an extreme example of operations risk, i.e. the risk that deficiencies in information systems or internal controls result in unexpected loss. Will it happen again? Certainly, if senior managers of firms continue to disregard rules and recommendations which have been drawn up to ensure prudent risk-taking.

SUMMARY

Rogue traders, like Nick Leeson, can always wreak havoc but their destructiveness can be contained by a well-designed and thorough risk management and control system. The collapse of Barings was the result of a total lack of control.

Simple but cardinal rules on how a trading operation should be run were broken. Leeson was allowed to be gamekeeper cum poacher. No position limits were imposed on him. The bank did not differentiate between margin for client accounts and proprietary trading and could not reconcile client debits with total positions.

The London office was unclear about Leeson's real activities — they thought he was arbitraging the price differences between Nikkei 225 contracts on the Osaka Stock Exchange and the Singapore International Monetary Exchange. Instead he was position-taking, via both futures and selling options. They ignored auditors' warnings about the dangers of Leeson's dual role, and remitted to Singapore in one month a sum larger than the bank's capital to meet margin calls. Leeson's positions were large by any standards — the value at risk of his positions alone, calculated JP Morgan's RiskMetric system shows that on 28 February 1995, Barings faced potential *daily* losses of up to £126 million ($203 million). These calculations are based on a 95% confidence interval. In contrast, JP Morgan's daily value at risk for all its trading activities averaged $15 million in 1994. JP Morgan is a triple-A rated bank with a capital base of $9.6 billion. Barings, on the other hand had a capital base one-tenth that of Morgan.

The seeds of Barings' destruction were sown when the bank entered a new business area without ensuring adequate control and support systems.

REFERENCES

1. Report of the Banking Supervision Inquiry into the Circumstances of the Collapse of Baring's, ordered by the House of Commons (1995) July, HMSO, London.
2. JP Morgan & Co. Inc. (1994) Annual Report.

Appendix 1

Extract from Robert C. Merton's Article in *The Journal of Applied Corporate Finance,* Winter 1992, Volume 4 Number 4

REAL EFFICIENCY GAINS: THE CASE OF STOCK INDEX FUTURES AND OPTIONS

In general, innovations in financial products and services can improve economic performance in three basic ways:

- by meeting investor or issuer demands to 'complete the markets' with new securities or products that offer expanded opportunities for risk-sharing, risk-pooling, hedging and intertemporal or spatial transfers of resources.
- by lowering transaction costs on increasing liquidity; and
- by reducing 'agency costs' that arise from either 'information asymmetries' between trading parties or principals' incomplete monitoring of their agents' performance.

All three of these driving forces behind financial innovation are consistent with its working to improve economic efficiency.[1-3]

Consider the case of exchange-traded futures and options contracts on stock indexes such as the Standard & Poor's 500 or the Nikkei. As noted at the outset of the paper, one of the major functions of capital markets is to provide a way of managing economic uncertainty and controlling risk. The main role of futures and options within the financial system is the risk management function. Index options and futures provide investors a low-cost means of controlling general market risk.

All risk management activities can be represented as combinations of three basic methods of managing risk. The idea that all such activities can be decomposed into three 'dimensions of risk management' is developed in my article with Zvi Bodie (1991), 'A Framework for the Economic Analysis of Deposit Insurance and Other Guarantees' (unpublished manuscript).

Reducing Risk by Selling the Source of It

In general, reducing a portfolio's risk by moving from risky assets to a riskless asset can be accomplished either in the spot cash market or in a futures or forward market. Futures and swaps usually allow such broad risk adjustments to be effected at lower cost than with cash market alternatives. For example, the alternative to using derivative securities on an index is to transact simultaneously in many individual stocks (say, 500 stocks as in the case of the S&P 500).

Reducing Risk by Diversification

Diversification consists of simultaneously pooling and subdividing risks. While it does not eliminate risk in the aggregate, it redistributes it to reduce the risk faced by each individual. Broad diversification across large numbers of different securities has the drawback that adjustments in risk exposure can require a large number of relatively small transactions in the various securities. Moreover, bounds on the subdivision of the units of individual securities limit the number of securities that can be held for a given level of wealth. The use of basket cash-market securities and futures contracts on stock and bond-market indexes both reduces the cost and increases the speed with which diversification strategies can be executed. They also permit broader diversification by allowing arbitrarily small ownership of the individual components of the various indexes.

Reducing Risk by Buying Insurance against Losses

Insurance permits the owner of an asset to retain the economic benefits of ownership, while eliminating the uncertainty of possible losses. Of course, this retention of the 'upside' while removing the 'downside' of asset ownership is not free. The fee or premium paid for insurance substitutes a sure loss for the possibility of a larger loss.

In general, the owner of any asset can eliminate the downside risk of loss and retain the upside benefit of ownership by the purchase of a put option. During the term of the put, its owner has the right to sell the underlying asset at a fixed (exercise) price. Thus, any losses on the asset are truncated at this level.

Furthermore, owning an asset and insuring its value against loss by purchasing a put option is economically equivalent to purchasing a call option on the asset. The functional and value identity is that a call option combined with holding of the riskless asset is equivalent to holding the asset together with a put option on the asset. (See Merton, *Continuous Time Finance*, (Blackwell) pp 277–278, for a formal derivation of this put/call parity theorem.) In this sense, an option, whether a put or a call, is a fundamental security that serves the central risk management function of insurance. (The classic portfolio-selection theory of Harry Markowitz and James Tobin holds that the investor should control his risk exposure first by forming a well-diversified portfolio of all the risky assets and then, if necessary to adjust the risk further, by allocating his total wealth between his risky portfolio and the riskless asset. Hence, their theory covers the first two dimensions of risk management. It does not however, explicitly take account of the opportunity structure provided by insurance.) In particular, options on aggregate portfolios of securities (such as index options) are a far more efficient means of insuring an investor's asset holdings than a portfolio of options on each of the individual assets. Beyond simply the additional costs of multiple transactions, there is a fundamental difference in both the pattern of returns and the cost of an option on a portfolio of assets and a portfolio of options on those assets.[4,5]

Note that the reference to 'insurance' here is to a class of contracts that performs a common function, as distinguished from the class of institutions called 'insurance' companies. The insurance function is often served by a variety of institutions that are not classified as insurance companies. The traded-options exchanges just mentioned are a prime example. Thus, the prime potential competitor to an insurance company offering investors default insurance on municipal bonds may not be another insurance company but instead an options exchange that can create a market for put options on those bonds. The put options serve the same down-side protection function for the investors as the insurance company product. This example also illustrates the difference between the institutional and functional approaches as applied to corporate competitive strategy analysis. Insurance companies, on the other hand, often provide products that do not serve an insurance function. For example, insurance companies in the US offer money-market accounts, equity mutual funds, and guaranteed investment contracts, none of which performs an insurance function.

In sum, index futures and options increase economic efficiency in at least two of the three ways cited earlier: they serve to 'complete the markets' by providing investors with a previously unavailable means of limiting their exposure to broad market declines — one that substantially reduces the transaction costs of quickly rebalancing a large portfolio. Furthermore, by allowing investors to avoid trading in individual stocks, index derivative securities may also address the potential 'market impact' problem arising from information 'asymmetries'.

The problem, in this case, is as follows: an investor may be buying or selling a stock simply to adjust his risk exposure or to reflect his revised assessment of expected returns on the general stock market. But, he may instead be motivated by explicit private information about the company such as an unannounced earnings report or a litigation decision. The possibility of being 'picked-off' by information-advantaged traders should make otherwise uninformed counterparties 'rationally' reluctant to trade. This reluctance in turn manifests itself in larger bid/ask spreads. The increased spread is a deadweight loss to the investor who does not have information about the individual stock. The structural opportunities to trade in market aggregates provided by index futures and options resolves this 'market impact' problem because such investors can adjust their broad asset-class allocations without having to trade in individual stocks.[6]

FINANCIAL SPIRAL EFFECT

As the case of index options and futures is meant to suggest, the dramatic changes over the past two decades are consistent with development toward a more efficient financial market and intermediation system. Indeed, such changes can be seen as part of a financial innovation 'spiral' that proceeds as follows: the proliferation of new trading markets in standardized securities such as futures makes possible the creation of new custom-designed financial products that improve 'market completeness.' Next, volume in the new markets further expands as the producers themselves — typically, financial intermediaries — trade simply to hedge their own exposures. Such increased volume in turn reduces marginal transaction costs and thereby makes possible further implementation of new products and trading strategies — which in turn leads to still more volume. Success of these trading markets then encourages investment in creating additional markets, and so on it goes, spiralling toward the theoretically limiting case of zero marginal transaction costs and dynamically complete markets.

As one example, consider the Eurodollar futures market that provides organized trading in standardized LIBOR deposits at dates in the future. The opportunity to trade in this futures market provides financial intermediaries with a more efficient way of hedging custom-contracted interest-rate swaps based on a floating rate linked to LIBOR. A LIBOR-based swap rather than a US Treasury rate-based swap is better suited to the needs of many intermediaries' customers because their cash-market borrowing rate is typically linked to LIBOR and not Treasury rates. During the last few years, basic swaps have changed from being 'one-off' customized transactions to standardized contracts traded in organized markets. Market trading of such 'pure vanilla' swaps expanded the opportunity for intermediaries to hedge, thereby allowing them to create customized swaps and related financial products more efficiently.

More generally, standardized traded-securities markets are used by financial services firms to execute dynamic trading strategies designed to replicate the payoffs to more complex securities — securities that some of them help design and origi-nate. The synthesizing of custom financial contracts and securities is for financial services what the assembly-line production process is for the manufacturing sector. Options, futures, and other exchange-traded securities are the raw 'inputs' applied in prescribed combinations over time to create portfolios that hedge the various customer liabilities of financial intermediaries.

REFERENCES

1. Black, F. and Scholes, M. (1986) 'From theory to new financial product', *Journal of Finance*, **41**, July, 645–655.
2. Benston, G. and Smith, C. Jr. (1976) 'A transaction cost approach to the theory of financial intermediation', *Journal of Finance*, **31**, May, 215–231.
3. Ross, S. (1989) 'Institutional markets, financial marketing and financial inno-vation', *Journal of Finance*, **44**, July, 541–556.
4. Merton, R. C., Scholes, M. and Gladstein, M. (1978) 'The returns and risks of alternative call option portfolio investment strategies', *Journal of Business*, **51**, April.
5. Merton, R. C., Scholes, M. and Gladstein, M. (1982) 'The returns and risks of alternative' put option portfolio investment strategies', *Journal of Business*, **55**, January, 1–55.
6. Gammill, J. and Perold, A. (1989) 'The changing character of stock market liquidity', *Journal of Portfolio Management*, **13**, Spring, 13–17.

Appendix 2

Extract from The Commodity Futures Trading Commission Filing of Administrative Proceedings against BT Securities Corporation, A Subsidiary of Bankers Trust Company, in Connection with the Sale of Derivative Products

PROVISION OF INACCURATE VALUATIONS TO GIBSON

11. BT Securities' representatives made material misrepresentations and omissions in the offer and sale of derivatives to Gibson Greetings. During the period from October 1992 to March 1994, BT Securities' representatives misled Gibson about the value of the company's derivatives positions by providing Gibson with values

that significantly understated the magnitude of Gibson's losses. As a result, Gibson remained unaware of the actual extent of its losses from derivatives transactions and continued to purchase derivatives from BT Securities. In addition, the valuations provided by BT Securities' representatives caused Gibson to make material understatements of the company's unrealized losses from derivative transactions in the notes to its 1992 and 1993 financial statements.

12. In a conversation on February 23, 1994 taped by an internal BT Securities taping system, a BT Securities managing director discussed the 'differential' between the computer model value of Gibson's positions and the valuation provided to Gibson:

> I think that we should use this [a downward market price movement] as an opportunity. We should just call [the Gibson contact], and maybe chip away at the differential a little more. I mean we told him $8.1 million when the real number was 14. So now if the real number is 16, we'll tell him that it is 11.
>
> You know, just slowly chip away at the differential between what it really is and what we're telling him. Later the same day, the managing director stated, in response to a question about whether he intended to provide Gibson with values for its positions that day:
>
> 'I want to. And the reason is that — the problem is that we are too far away between what he thinks it is and what reality is. And you know, if this continues on and on like this, we're going to have to start unwinding. And I don't think that we want to be in a position of unwinding something that's worth, I'm exaggerating, but worth $20 million and he thinks that its $11 [million]. You know, we gotta try and close that gap. And I think that on days where there's a big move, it's an opportunity to close the gap. . . .
>
> [I]f the market hadn't changed at all, or was just kind of dottering around within a couple of ticks, then you know, there's nothing that we can really say. He is going to keep thinking that it is around $8.1 [million], when it is really $14 [million]. . . . You know, which is what it was yesterday. But when there's a big move, you know, if the market backs up like this, and he is down another 1.3, we can tell him he is down another 2. And vice-versa. If the market really rallies like crazy, and he's made back a couple of million dollars, you can say you have only made back a half a million.'

13. On two occasions when Gibson sought valuations for the specific purpose of preparing its financial statements, representatives of BT Securities provided Gibson with valuations that differed by more than 50% from the value generated by the computer model value and recorded on Bankers Trust's books. In early February 1993, Gibson asked representatives of BT Securities for the value of its derivatives as of December 31, 1992 and stated that the information would be used in preparing Gibson's 1992 year-end financial statements. As of December 31, 1992, Bankers Trust's books reflected a negative value of $2 129 209 for Gibson's derivatives positions. BT Securities, however, provided Gibson with a 'mark-to-market' value for the derivatives positions of a negative $1 025 000, a difference of $1 104 209, or 52%.

14. The value that BT Securities provided to Gibson as of December 31, 1992 related to the ratio swap, and the periodic floor.

15. The next fiscal year, in a letter dated December 31, 1993, Gibson asked representatives of BT Securities to provide Gibson with the value of Gibson's derivatives as of that date to use in preparing Gibson's 1993 year-end financial statements. As of December 31, 1993 Bankers Trust's books reflected a negative value of $7 470 886 for Gibson's derivatives positions. Representatives of BT Securities, however, provided Gibson with a 'mark-to-market' value for the derivatives positions of a negative $2 900 000, a difference of $4 570 886, or 61%.

16. The value that BT Securities provided to Gibson as of December 31, 1993 related to spread lock 1 and wedding band 3.

17. On October 1, 1992, BT Securities and Gibson entered into the ratio swap. BT Securities represented to Gibson that the ratio swap had a negative value of $975 000. In fact, as of December 31, 1992, Bankers Trust's computer models showed that the ratio swap had a negative value to Gibson of $2 003 929.

18. By mid-February 1993, according to Bankers Trust's computer models the value of the ratio swap had improved to a negative value of $138 000 to Gibson. However, BT Securities failed to inform Gibson of the improvement in the value of the ratio swap at the time BT Securities presented proposals for restructuring the ratio swap. Unaware of this information, Gibson entered into a Treasury-linked swap on February 19, 1993 as a means of reducing the risk on the ratio swap.

19. In return for entering into the Treasury-linked swap, the maturity of the ratio swap was shortened from five years to four years. On February 19, 1993, the day Gibson entered into the Treasury-linked swap, Bankers Trust's books and computer models indicated that the fifth year of the ratio swap had a negative value to Gibson of $851 700. At the time, BT Securities' representatives knew that Gibson would incur a loss of $2.1 million, composed of an unrealized loss and transactional charges, built into the structure of the Treasury-linked swap. BT Securities' representatives also knew that Gibson was unaware that it would incur the unrealized loss.

20. On August 4, 1993, Gibson agreed to enter into the time swap. As part of the transaction, Gibson agreed to terminate the periodic floor entered into on October 30, 1992 and amend the knock-out call entered on June 10, 1993. BT Securities' representatives had proposed that Gibson enter into the transactions to preserve an opportunity for 'substantial' gain. BT Securities' representatives knew that, as a result of these transactions, Gibson would sustain approximately $1.4 million in unrealized losses built into the structure of the time swap, but failed to disclose that information to Gibson. The cost of entering into the time swap was almost equal to Gibson's maximum possible profit on the knock-out call.

21. Approximately one week later, as the yield on the 30-year US Treasury security continued to decline, BT Securities' representatives proposed that Gibson again amend the knock-out call, this time in exchange for adjusting the leverage factor in the time swap. On August 12, 1993, Gibson accepted the proposal and entered into an amendment of the knock-out call and increased the leverage factor in the time

swap. By entering into these transactions, Gibson unknowingly sustained unrealized losses of approximately $89 000.

22. Several weeks later, BT Securities' representatives proposed that Gibson enter into yet another amendment to the knock-out call, in exchange for restructuring the time swap. A BT Securities' representative told Gibson that the time swap 'continues to look pretty good'. In fact, at that time, the time swap held a substantial negative value to Gibson.

23. Gibson agreed to purchase the amendment to the knock-out call on August 26, 1993 by entering into another amendment to the time swap. By entering into these transactions, Gibson unknowingly incurred unrealized losses and transactional charges of approximately $578 000. The next day Gibson agreed to terminate the knock-out call and was paid $475 000 by Bankers Trust. In the amendments to the knock-out call, Gibson unknowingly incurred unrealized losses of $3 million built into the structure of the time swap. In comparison, the maximum possible payout of the barrier option never exceeded $2.3 million.

24. On January 11, 1993 and May 6, 1993, BT Securities and Gibson entered into spread lock 1 and 2, respectively. In September 1993, BT Securities recommended that Gibson amend each spread lock to reduce the amount of Gibson's payment to Bankers Trust on the swaps. On September 22, 1993, BT Securities and Gibson amended and restructured spread locks 1 and 2 by entering into wedding band 3. On the same day, Bankers Trust's books showed a positive value for Gibson of the amendments to the spread locks of approximately $380 000 and a negative value for Gibson of wedding band 3 of approximately $1.4 million. Thus, by entering into these transactions Gibson unknowingly incurred an unrealized loss and transactional charges of approximately $1 020 000.

25. On January 14, 1994, BT Securities and Gibson terminated spread lock 1 and 2 and the time swap, and entered into the LIBOR-linked payout swap and wedding band 6. On January 13, BT Securities' representatives misled Gibson by stating that Gibson would not go 'further in the hole' by entering these new positions when, in fact, Gibson immediately incurred an additional unrealized loss of approximately $4 954 000.

26. On February 23, 1994, BT Securities' representatives told Gibson that the value of Gibson's derivatives portfolio was negative $8.1 million when, in fact, the value that Bankers Trust carried on Bankers Trust's books on that date was negative $15.45 million.

27. On February 25, 1994, BT Securities' representatives told Gibson that the value of Gibson's derivatives portfolio was negative $13.8 million when, in fact, the value that Bankers Trust carried on Bankers Trust's books on that date was negative $16.25 million.

Source: CFTC.

Appendix 3

G-30 Global Derivatives Study Group: Practices and Principles

WORKING PAPER OF THE VALUATION AND MARKET RISK MANAGEMENT SUBCOMMITTEE

The recommendations of this Working paper of the Valuation and Market Risk Management Subcommittee focus primarily on derivatives, although many of the approaches are applicable to other financial instruments. Dealers and end-users undertake derivatives transactions for a number of purposes related to derivatives dealing, proprietary trading, risk management, funding and investing.

Section I presents the challenges participants face in valuing derivatives transactions or portfolios, measuring their market risk, and handling other related risks. It assesses and discusses current and planned market practices, drawing on the results of the Survey of Industry Practice. Section II sets forth principles of good management practice with respect to valuation and the management of market risk.

I. MANAGEMENT CHALLENGES

Valuing Derivatives Portfolios

The challenge of market risk management begins with proper valuation of derivatives portfolio. It is essential for market participants to apply appropriate methodologies in valuing their derivatives portfolios. Incorrect valuation leads not only to inaccurate income recognition, but also to inaccurate hedging. For instance, incorrect valuation of an option can lead to an incorrect measure of its price sensitivity (i.e. delta) and consequently an inadequate hedge. Similarly, other risk components of the option also might be improperly estimated.

Derivatives participants overwhelmingly recognize this need for correct valuation and mark their portfolios to market for management purposes even if they use a different valuation method for external reporting. Of the dealers responding to the Survey, 85% indicate that, for risk management purposes, they mark their derivatives portfolio to market as opposed to other valuation techniques, such as lower-of-cost-or-market or accruals accounting. Of the dealers that currently do not mark-to-market, the majority have plans to begin marking-to-market in the future. Dealers that the Survey classifies as 'large' or 'global, full range' tend to mark-to-market to a greater extent than dealers with a more limited scope of activity.

The Survey results suggest that 36% of responding dealers mark-to-mid-market, less specific adjustments, while 46% mark-to-mid-market without adjustments; the remainder use a bid/offer method. Examination by category of dealers reveals that of those with global, full range derivatives activities, almost 79% either do, or plan to, value at mid-market, less adjustments (although they may take credit reserves in other parts of their income statements). Sixty percent of large dealers indicate that they use adjustments currently, while 21% of smaller dealers claim the same.

Many dealers do not run perfectly matched derivatives portfolios. For those dealers, rebalancing and rehedging their portfolios with market moves and the passage of time requires the ability to value portfolios frequently, even intraday in the case of some option portfolios. Seventy-seven percent of responding dealers indicate that they value their portfolios on a daily basis. A higher percentage of large and global dealers mark daily, compared with smaller or purely domestic dealers. Among end-users that use derivatives for position taking, 54% value their positions daily and 38% monthly. When this group is broken down by geographic regions, all North American and UK respondents mark daily. Continental European end-users mark monthly, and Japanese and Australian firms vary in their frequency of marks.

Understanding and controlling market risk require quantification of the profit and loss impact of market movements. The first step, described below, is to isolate the profit and loss effect of taking market risk from other activities such as credit-risk taking and origination. The second step, also described below, is to break down the profit and loss derived from market risk, taking into account its component parts. It is common for traders at large dealers to define components that correspond to the individual risk measures used for market risk measurement. However, few dealers identify individual sources of revenue.

Measuring Market Risk

While valuation examines past movements in the value of a derivatives portfolio and the performance of risk components, measuring market risk examines similar issues with respect to the future. It helps answer questions as to what may happen and whether too much risk is being taken relative to the limits established. Risk managers within the derivatives industry are developing various ways to quantify market risks. The Survey suggests that, when measuring market risk, 43% of dealers quantify the maximum loss for an arbitrary specified scenario, while 30% responded that they employ a value at risk measurement. About 50% of large dealers employ a value at risk measurement.

Measuring market risk under all but the simplest method raises certain technical challenges. First dealers, must establish a measure of risk that can be applied to a wide variety of derivatives. This is especially relevant for large and more diverse dealers, which must aggregate and assess risks across a wide array of derivatives and markets. Second, dealers must make assumptions about underlying volatility and correlations for both instruments and markets. In addition, they must address issues such as the appropriate time horizon to use in determining historical or implied volatility and correlations and whether this data suitably predicts future levels.

Dealers using a methodology that captures risk across instruments and markets find that significant operational challenges of systems capability and compatibility emerge. For instance, to attain an accurate assessment of market risk on a total portfolio basis, dealers should make the risk measurement systems of an interest rate swap portfolio compatible with the systems of an interest rate options portfolio. For large and more diverse dealers, this issue increases in importance and requires even greater integration of systems across different derivatives.

These practical challenges are made somewhat easier by the strong consensus regarding the choice of basic risk measures. A large majority of dealers consider absolute price or rate change (delta), convexity (gamma), volatility (vega), time decay (theta), basis or correlation, and discount rate (rho) in their risk analysis. Three-quarters of the responding dealers examine these parameters across the term structure.

Another challenge involves quantifying and preparing for the consequences of abnormal market conditions when the assumptions that are valid under normal markets no longer apply. The Survey indicates that 61% of all dealers — 80% of large dealers — address this challenge through some kind of stress simulation of their portfolios.

Other Challenges

Reduced liquidity creates significant challenges for risk measurement and management. For illiquid positions, estimating mid-market value and appropriate adjustments or bid/offer levels can be difficult. Of the dealer respondents, 89% indicate that they consider market liquidity implicitly in risk limits or consider it on a case-by-case basis.

Every derivative portfolio has implicit cash investment or funding requirements arising from mismatches of future cash flows, and from credit arrangements that may produce cash or collateral receipts or payments. For example, if a firm involved in an interest-rate swap pays LIBOR quarterly but receives fixed interest rate payments semi-annually, it will need to fund the mismatch of cashflows. The magnitude and direction of net cash positions fluctuate with changes in markets and portfolio activity. Estimates must be made concerning the correct rates at which these expected future cash positions will be funded or invested. Among responding dealers, half indicate that they estimate the future cash investing or funding needs from their portfolios. Large dealers and global, full range dealers tend to pay more attention to this risk than do smaller and domestic dealers.

The challenges described in this section must be analysed thoroughly before appropriate procedures and systems are implemented. Ensuring that the procedures and systems are appropriate is in itself a major challenge. A common solution is to develop an independent risk management function. In practice, over 90% of the responding dealers across all categories either have, or plan to have in the next 18 months, an independent risk management function to implement and oversee valuation and risk management techniques.

II. HOW TO MEET THE CHALLENGES

Marking-to-Market

Recommendation 2: Marking-to-Market

Dealers should mark their derivatives positions to market, on at least a daily basis, for risk management purposes.

A valuation methodology for derivatives portfolios should meet two key criteria: first, it should reflect the current value of the portfolio cashflows to be managed, and second, it should provide information about market risk and appropriate hedging actions. Marking-to-market is a valuation technique that meets both criteria. Other valuation methods such as lower-of-cost-or-market and accrual accounting are not appropriate since they do not provide the information needed for risk management.

Dealers should mark their derivatives portfolio to market at least daily. This is because marking-to-market provides risk managers with critical information concerning both past performances of hedges and current risks. Intraday or even real-time valuation can be of great assistance especially to option risk managers, and often justifies the expense and complexity of the tools necessary to carry out the process.

Market Valuation Methods

Recommendation 3: Market Valuation Methods

Derivatives portfolios of dealers should be valued based on mid-market levels less specific adjustments, or on appropriate bid or offer levels. Mid-market valuation adjustments should allow for expected future costs such as unearned credit spread, close-out costs, investing and funding costs, and administrative costs.

Mid-market valuation is a marking practice that values a derivatives portfolio at the middle of the current (the average of bid and offer prices) less specific adjustments. In bid/offer marking, the portfolio is marked to the bid or offer side of the market. Marking to mid-market less adjustments specifically defines and quantifies adjustments that are implicitly assumed in the bid/offer method.

Once mid-market rates or prices have been determined, future cash flows are generated based on implied forward curves and prices. These cash flows are then discounted back using a zero coupon curve which is generated from the mid-market interest rate curve. The net present value of the cash flows represents the mid-market value of the portfolio. Similar calculations are made under the bid/offer method.

Even in a perfectly matched portfolio, mid-market valuation does not reflect the true value of a portfolio. Although a matched portfolio has no market risk, the failure of one counterparty to perform its contractual obligations can result in a loss. Furthermore, even a matched portfolio must be managed from an administrative and operational standpoint. Therefore, two adjustments have to be made, reflecting expected future credit costs and administrative costs. As the assumption of a matched portfolio is dropped and more complex portfolios are examined, two additional adjustments should be made: one for close-out costs and another for borrowing and investing costs. These four adjustments are explained in detail below.

Unearned Credit Spread Adjustment. Unearned credit spread represents amounts set aside to cover expected credit losses and provide a return on credit exposure. Expected credit losses should be based upon expected exposure to counterparties, taking into account netting arrangements; expected default experience for the credit rating of the counterparties; and overall diversification of the portfolio. Unearned credit spread should be adjusted dynamically to reflect changes in the factors listed above, i.e. in effect, marked to market. Participants using a more static measure of unearned credit spread may include in that measure an allowance for probable credit losses. Unearned credit spread can be calculated on a transaction basis, on a portfolio basis, or across all activities with a given client.

Close-out Costs Adjustments. This adjustment represents the costs that would be incurred if all unmatched positions were closed out or hedged. The risks to be closed out should include not only absolute price risk but all other components of market risk. There are a number of approaches to adjusting for close-out costs. They range from a simple transaction-by-transaction bid/offer adjustment to a single aggregate adjustment for a portfolio taking into account offsetting risks. Intermediate approaches take into account offsets within certain maturity or market sectors but may arbitrarily limit the offsets between them.

A recommended approach is to assume that close-out costs of a given portfolio are roughly proportional to price risk. In the case of an individual position, this represents the bid/offer that a dealer quotes based on the dealer's view of its value at risk (see measuring market risk below). In a large portfolio that is liquid as to its market risk, one could instead use a measure of value at risk based on a one-day time horizon and one standard deviation adverse-rate move (incorporating correlations of volatilities of variables). If the positions and hedges available are less liquid, it is appropriate to increase the time horizon.

Investing and Funding Costs Adjustment. All but perfectly matched derivatives portfolios have future cash surpluses or deficits embedded in them — at some point in the future, the book will be required to invest or borrow cash as a result of cash flow mismatches. Many models implicitly assume that future cash positions are lent or funded at LIBOR flat.

This simplifying assumption can lead to significant inaccuracy in the valuation of portfolios with large actual or implied cash flows mismatches. Each firm must adjust the value of its book to reflect its access to and cost of funds (investing/funding rate) in various markets and currencies. Adjustments to mid-market for cost of funding should be dynamic, reflecting changes in the magnitude of expected investing/funding requirements and in each firm's cost of funds.

Administrative Costs Adjustment. Administrative and operating costs must be protected for the life of the existing portfolio. This would include, for example, systems costs, operational costs, and allocated costs of other functions affecting the derivatives activity.

Those adjustments should be determined using consistent and objective methodologies, reviewed independently from the dealing function.

The Survey shows no set industry standard concerning which adjustments to use, if any; however, many large dealers employ the adjustments listed above, notably those for credit and administrative costs.

Profit and Loss Component Analysis

Recommendation 4: Identifying Revenue Sources

Dealers should measure the components of revenue regularly and in sufficient detail to understand the sources of risk.

Measuring the components of profit helps participants to understand the profitability of various activities over time relative to the risks undertaken, as well as to gain insight into the performance of hedges. Components of revenue generally include:

- Origination Revenue — The component of revenue that is generated by valuing new transactions at mid-market after deducting appropriate adjustments, or at the bid or offer value if that method is used.

- Credit Spread revenue, if applicable — The change in unearned credit spread over that period.

- Other Trading Revenue — The profit and loss resulting from changes in the portfolio value as a result of market changes and the passage of time. It is useful, though complex, to split this among component risk measures used by traders (e.g. delta, gamma, vega, thetas, basis or correlation, and rho).

Measuring Market Risk

Recommendation 5: Measuring Market Risk

Dealers should use a consistent measure to calculate daily the market risk of their derivatives positions and compare it to market risk limits.

- Market risk is best measured as 'value at risk' using probability analysis based upon a common confidence interval (e.g. two standard deviations) and time horizon (e.g. a one-day exposure).

- Components of market risk that should be considered across the term structure include: absolute price or rate change (delta); convexity (gamma); volatility (vega); time decay (theta); basis or correlation; and discount rate (rho).

As a general principle, decisions on derivatives should be based on an objective assessment of risk and risk capital, not on arbitrary limits for asset classes, transaction maturities, or notional amounts.

The methodology of assessing risk and implementation of risk management functions and risk controls should be as consistent across various risk types as possible. Preferably, all market risks across derivatives should be reduced to a single common denominator called 'value at risk'. This facilitates aggregation and makes comparison and risk control easier.

Value at Risk. Value at risk is the expected loss from an adverse market movement with a specified probability over a period of time. For example, participants can determine with 97.5% probability (corresponding to calculations using about two standard deviations) that any adverse change in portfolio value over one day will not exceed a calculated amount. Conversely, the probability of an adverse change in excess of the calculated amount is 2.5%. Value at risk should encompass changes in all major market risk components and can be calculated to a common confidence interval and time horizon.

Elements of Market Risk. Calculations of value at risk should consider:

- *Absolute Price (Delta) Risk.* The change in the value of the portfolio due to changes in the prices of the underlying instruments.

- *Convexity (Gamma) Risk.* The change in the delta arising from changes in the prices of the underlying instruments. Hedging gamma risk requires dynamic adjustments as prices move.

- *Volatility (Vega) Risk.* The change in the value of the portfolio arising from changes in the implied volatility of the underlying instrument.

- *Time Decay (Theta) Risk.* The change in the value of the portfolio arising from the passage of time.

- *Basis or Correlation Risk.* The change in the value of the portfolio arising from changes in correlated variables. Correlated variables include those within the same maturity band as well as those across the maturity spectrum.

- *Discount Rate (Rho) Risk.* The change in value of the portfolio arising from changes in the interest rates used to discount future cashflows.

Each of these risk components should be analysed across the term structure. For instance, the net sensitivity of the portfolio value to changes in implied volatility is useful from an aggregated standpoint; however, analysis of volatility sensitivities across maturities is important in managing risk. In addition to value at risk based on each of these static risk measures, complex options portfolios require an additional, more dynamic approach. This recognizes that risk measures recorded at a particular market level or point in time provide only a partial picture of risk. The revaluation of the portfolio in multiple scenarios is recommended to identify vulnerability to specific market levels of underlying markets and volatility at a particular date.

Standard Deviation and Confidence Interval. Making assumptions as to likely rate moves and therefore risk scenarios is a somewhat arbitrary process, but consistency across activities is important. Using two or three standard deviations to assess value at risk corresponds approximately to the expectation that assessed risk will be exceeded only one trading day out of 40 or one out of 500, respectively. Of those dealers that use a value at risk measure, 64% indicate they use 95% confidence intervals (1.65 standard deviations) for their calculations.

For forward-based portfolios, the relationship between value at risk and the number of standard deviations is linear. Thus a dealer with a $20 million position limit measured to two standard deviations is taking the same risk as one with a $30-million limit measured to three standard deviations. Therefore, for such a dealer, the choice of confidence interval is of no great significance.

For option-based portfolios, however, the relationship between value at risk and the number of standard deviations is non-linear. In the case of portfolios dominated by a single option position, higher confidence intervals for market variables will give rise to the most extreme portfolio value changes. In the case of a more diverse options portfolio, the largest exposure to loss may occur at some quite modest move in the underlying market. Therefore, the choice of confidence interval or intervals to be used should be left to management in the light of the particular characteristics of its option portfolio.

Assumptions concerning the appropriate distribution to best describe future price movement of the underlying instrument are also important. Such distributions could be normal, log normal, mean reverting, or historical. The choice can affect both pricing and risk measurement.

Time Horizon. What time period should be used when assessing value at risk? Some dealers use a variable time horizon based on liquidity, but this practice makes sensible comparisons across businesses difficult. To aggregate risk and assess aggregate risks in a meaningful way, risk measurements must be comparable across activities and products. This implies that consistent assumptions such as time horizon must be employed. One day is recommended, corresponding to the recommendation for daily marking to market.

Market Risk Limits. Once a method of risk measurement is in place, market risk limits must be chosen; this is primarily based on judgement. The risk component of risk/reward analysis has been well defined for a number of standard deviations. But the question of how much value should be at risk remains. The answer depends on such issues as: management tolerance for low-probability, extreme losses versus higher-probability, modest losses; capital resources; market liquidity; expected profitability; trader experience; and business strategy.

Stress Testing

Recommendation 6: Stress Simulations
Dealers should regularly perform simulations to determine how their portfolios would perform under stress conditions.

Simulations of improbable market environments are important in risk analysis because many assumptions that are valid for normal markets may no longer hold true in abnormal markets. Since confidence intervals by definition do not encompass all unlikely scenarios, contingency plans for such occasions can best be developed through such simulations. Testing the extremes, or tails, of probability distributions is especially important for option-based derivatives, because portfolio values will not change in a linear fashion and, depending on the structure of the portfolio, may move by large amounts in the tails.

These simulations should reflect both historical events and potential future events and include not only large and non-standard directional market moves but also periods of prolonged market inactivity. The tests should consider the effect of price changes on the mid-market value of the portfolio, as well as changes in the assumptions about the adjustments to mid-market, such as the impact on close-out costs of decreased liquidity in times of market stress. The results of stress tests should be evaluated and contingency plans developed accordingly.

According to the Survey of Industry Practice, most large dealers conduct some kind of stress tests on their portfolios and more plan to do so in the future. Practice among smaller dealers is, for the most part, not to conduct such tests. Most smaller dealers, however, do recognize the importance of stress tests and plan to run some in the future.

Handling Market Liquidity Risk. Liquidity of a product or an entire market can be reduced substantially as a result of some market event or change in market psychology, or the actions of the individual participants. If for whatever reason, liquidity in a product or market is reduced or increased substantially, changes in the underlying assumptions about close-out costs may be needed. Similarly, assumptions about close-out costs and market access depend upon the firm's market presence. Size of positions should be tracked relative to the total size of the market. When position sizes grow substantially as a percentage of the daily market turnover or size of the market, previous assumptions about close-out costs may need to be changed. If close-out costs are measured on value at risk, such changes can be effected by lengthening the time horizon to the number of days necessary to neutralize a position without significantly moving the market.

The liquidity of risk provisions should be monitored and aggregated on a firmwide basis. This would provide an answer to questions such as: How long would it take to halve the aggregate market risk of the firm? Just as it may be appropriate for a firm to invest in illiquid assets such as real estate and term lending, so it may be appropriate to enter into some illiquid derivatives transactions. Prudence dictates, however, that a firm should be cognizant of its mix of liquid and illiquid risk positions.

Projecting Cash Investing and Funding Requirements

Recommendation 7: Investing and Funding Forecasts

Dealers should periodically forecast the cash investing and funding requirements arising from their derivatives portfolios.

The frequency and precision of forecasts should be determined by the size and nature of mismatches. A detailed forecast should determine surpluses and funding needs by currency over time. It also should examine the potential impact of contractual unwind provisions or other credit provisions that produce cash or collateral receipts or payments.

Independent Market Risk Management

Recommendation 8: Market Risk Management

Dealers should have a market risk management function, with clear independence and authority, to ensure that the following responsibilities are carried out:

- The development of risk limit and policies and the monitoring of transactions and positions for adherence to these policies (see Recommendation 5).

- The design of stress scenarios to measure the impact of market conditions, however improbable, that might cause market gaps, volatility swings, or disruptions of major relationships, or might reduce liquidity in the face of unfavourable market linkages, concentrated market making, or credit exhaustion (see Recommendation 6).

- The design of revenue reports quantifying the contribution of various risk components, and of market risk measures such as value at risk (see Recommendations 4 and 5).

- The monitoring of variance between actual volatility of portfolio value and that predicted by the measure of market risk.

- The review and approval of pricing models and valuation systems used by front-and back-office personnel, and the development of reconciliation procedures if different systems are used.

The growth of activities in derivatives and other financial instruments has led many firms to establish market (and credit) risk management functions to assist senior management in establishing consistent policies and procedures applicable to various activities. The market risk management function typically is headed by a board level or near board level executive.

The market risk management function acts as a catalyst for the development of sound market risk management systems, models, and procedures. Its review of trading performance occurs typically in the context of answering a question such as: Are results consistent with those suggested by the analysis of value at risk? The risk management function is rarely involved in actual risk-taking decisions.

According to the Survey, a large majority of dealers already have such a function in place and, of those that do not, over 50% plan to establish one in the near future.

Practices by End-users

Recommendation 9: Practices by End-users

As appropriate to the nature, size, and complexity of their derivatives activities, end-users should adopt the same valuation and market risk management practices that are recommended for dealers. Specifically, they should consider: regularly marking-to-market their derivatives transactions for risk management purposes; periodically forecasting the cash investing and funding requirements arising from their derivatives transactions; and establishing a clearly independent and authoritative function to design and assure adherence to prudent risk limits.

From an end-user's perspective, derivatives are customer-specific transactions often designed to offset precisely the market risk of corresponding business positions. While many end-users do not expect significant change in the combined value of their derivatives positions and underlying positions, others do. End-users are encouraged to implement performance assessment and control procedures that are appropriate for their derivative activities.

III. CONCLUSION

The implementation of individual recommendations by a participant should not be based solely on its nature (dealer versus end-user) but should be decided and adjusted in the context of the participant's volume of derivatives activity, the complexity of transactions, and the commensurate commitment of human capital and systems resources to support the activity.

Whatever the nature of the participant, however, the importance of accurate and frequent valuation of derivatives portfolios and the implications on proper risk management should be emphasised. Mark-to-market valuation reflects true portfolio value which inturn implies proper hedging techniques. More frequent marking practices produce more up-to-date risk-measurement information and therefore enable precise risk management practices. Daily marking-to-market is essential for dealers. As indicated from Survey results, most dealers recognize the importance of daily marks, while fewer end-users practice daily marks.

For participants using mid-market valuation, the determination of an accurate portfolio value requires adjustments. Derivatives participants vary in their extent of usage of adjustments to mid-market. More progress and uniformity in this practice should occur over time.

Practice and methods of risk management of derivatives portfolios have evolved and are still doing so. Risk measures such as value at risk are replacing more rudimentary risk measurements such as those based on notional amounts, as more participants recognize the benefits of their accuracy. Similarly, dealers are also examining non-standard market moves to determine how their portfolios would perform under stress conditions. These simulations, which enhance the understanding of the risks of managing derivatives portfolios, should be encouraged. Another important risk management tool that should become more broadly and frequently used is the forecasting of cash investment and funding requirements.

Market risk management functions that establish and monitor valuation and risk management procedures are now common among dealers. Many of those without one are planning to set up such a function in the near future.

The recommendations of this Global Derivatives Study provide guidelines for techniques in valuing and managing risk in derivatives portfolios. They do not make judgements concerning the amount of risk which should be taken or the amount of capital to be allocated. These issues should be dealt with by senior management and should be based on individual objectives and circumstances.

Reproduced with the permission of the G-30.

Appendix 4

G-30 Global Derivatives Study Group: Practices and Principles

EXTRACTS FROM A WORKING PAPER OF THE CREDIT RISK MEASUREMENT AND MANAGEMENT SUBCOMMITTEE

Credit risk is the risk that a loss will be incurred if a counterparty defaults on a derivatives contract. The loss due to a default is the cost of replacing the contract, less any recovery. The replacement cost represents the present value, at the time of default, of the expected future net cashflows. It is important to emphasize that a credit loss will only occur if the counterparty defaults and the derivatives contract has a positive mark-to-market value to the nondefaulting party. Both conditions have to be satisfied simultaneously for a loss to be incurred.

While the measurement of exposures resulting from derivatives transactions is more complicated than the exposure measurement of many traditional banking products, the principles that govern the assumption and management of credit risk remain the same. Credit exposure management should be procedurally consistent across an organization and, where appropriate, should be fully integrated. Specifically, the evaluation of the credit exposures for derivatives transactions should be made comparable with that of exposures for on-balance-sheet activities. This consistency allows for the integration of derivatives with other on-balance-sheet activities in the credit allocation and review process.

In this Working Paper, the Credit Risk Measurement and Management Subcommittee provides an overview of how credit risk can be measured and monitored. The first half focuses on the measurement of credit risk. It discusses the credit components of exposure on a derivatives contract and presents concepts of current and potential exposure. The following section addresses the calculation of credit exposure on a portfolio of derivatives transactions. Next, the paper discusses the expected credit loss measurements, which are measurements useful for calculating risk-adjusted returns on capital and for allocating capital.

The second half of this working paper addresses the management of credit risk. Practices that are helpful in assessing, monitoring, and limiting credit risk are discussed. In this context, the paper analyses how internal controls, documentation provisions, and credit support arrangements can be used to control credit risk.

I. CREDIT RISK MEASUREMENT

Credit Exposure on a Derivatives Transaction

Recommendation 10: Measuring Credit Exposure

Dealers and end-users should measure credit exposure on derivatives in two ways:

- current exposure, which is the replacement cost of derivatives transactions, that is their market value;
- potential exposure, which is an estimate of the future replacement cost of derivatives transactions. It should be calculated using probability analysis based upon broad confidence intervals (e.g. two standard deviations) over the remaining terms of the transactions.

Credit risk fluctuates over time with the variables that determine the value of the underlying contract. In assessing credit risk, one needs to ask two questions. First, if a counterparty was to default today, what would it cost to replace the derivatives transaction (i.e. what is the current exposure)? Second, if a counterparty defaults at some point in the future, what is a reasonable estimate of the potential replacement cost (i.e.what is the potential exposure)?

The first question is highly straightforward, as it simply asks for the current mark-to-market price of the underlying contract. This price can be positive or negative. As an example, consider a $100 million, five-year swap executed at the prevailing market condition in which one party pays a fixed rate of 6.0% and the other party pays a floating rate of LIBOR. The mark-to-market value of such a swap (i.e. its current replacement cost) is zero at the time the swap is executed;

however, as time passes and interest rates move, the mark-to-market value of the swap will also move. Suppose that in six months, the prevailing swap rate for a 4.5-year swap is 5.5%. If the counterparty paying the fixed rate of 6.0% defaults, the nondefaulting counterparty receiving the fixed rate (and paying the floating rate) will be forced to replace it with a 5.5% swap and will thereby suffer a replacement cost equal to 0.5% per annum for the remaining 4.5 years plus whatever net unpaid swap payment has accrued.

The second question is more difficult to answer in that it asks for an assessment of what the replacement cost could be in the future if the variables that determine the value of the underlying contract were to move adversely. Returning to the swap example, the value for the $100 million, five-year swap could attain a significant positive or negative value over the life of the swap. The extent to which the value of the swap could become positive is the potential exposure.

Dealers use Monte Carlo or historical simulation studies, option valuation models, and other statistical techniques to assess potential exposure. The analysis generally involves modelling the volatility of the underlying variables (such as interest rates, exchange rates, equity prices, or commodity prices) and the effect of movements of these variables on the value of the derivatives contract. These techniques are often used to generate two measures of potential exposure: expected exposure; and maximum or 'worst case' exposure.

Expected exposure at any point during the life of the swap is the mean of all possible probability-weighted replacement costs, where the replacement cost in any outcome is equal to the mark-to-market present value if positive and zero if negative. Loosely speaking, expected exposure is the best estimate of the present value of the positive exposure that is likely to materialize. As such, expected exposure is an important measure in derivatives dealers' capital-allocation and pricing decisions.

The maximum potential exposure is calculated as an estimate of 'worst case' exposure at any point in time. These calculations are based on adverse movements in the underlying variables that are extreme enough that they are unlikely to be exceeded. For example, if two standard deviations in a one-tail test are used to calculate maximum potential exposure, there is statistically only a 2.5% chance the actual exposure will be greater than the calculated maximum exposure. This 'worst case' exposure is important in assessing the maximum amount that could possibly be at risk to a given counterparty. As such, it is important in the dealer's credit-allocation decisions.

The expected and maximum potential exposure profiles for an interest rate swap executed at current market levels is shown in Figure A.1. The 'hump-back' profile is due to the offsetting effects the passage of time has on the magnitude of the potential movement in the underlying variables, and the number of cashflows that need to be replaced if a default should occur. The first effect of the passage of time on potential exposure is that it increases the probability that the underlying variable will drift substantially away from its initial value. This 'diffusion effect'

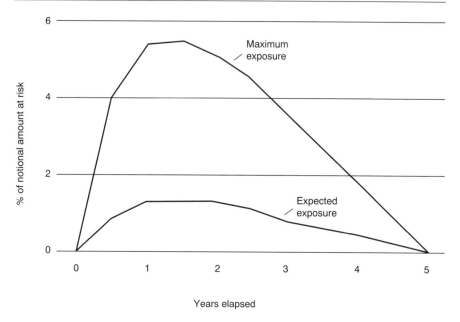

Figure A.1   Credit Exposure of Interest-rate Swap.

is determined by the volatility of the underlying variable and its other stochastic properties. The second effect of the passage of time, called the 'amortization effect', is the reduction in the number of years of cash flows that need to be replaced. The offsetting influences of the diffusion effect and the amortization effect create the concave shape in Figure A.1 as the passage of time increases the potential for large per annum replacement costs, but reduces the number of years of cashflows that need to be replaced.

Figure A.1 can be deduced by looking at the present value of the replacement cost if a default occurs immediately after the swap is executed and immediately prior to its maturity. If a default occurs immediately after the swap is executed, five years of cashflows will need to be replaced but it is unlikely that the swap rate will have moved very far from its initial level in such a brief period. Consequently, the expected and maximum potential exposures are low because the diffusion effect is low. At the other extreme, if a default occurs just prior to the swap's last payment date, the swap could be substantially different from its initial level, but because only one semi-annual cash flow will need to be replaced, the expected and maximum potential exposures are low. The peak exposure (top of the 'hump') occurs at an intermediate point during the swap's life when sufficient time has passed for the per annum replacement cost to be high, and sufficient time still remains for the impact of a high per annum replacement cost to be meaningful. The potential exposure profile depends on the cashflow pattern of the underlying asset class and on the type of the derivatives transaction. Standard interest rate swaps and other derivatives with periodic payments and no final exchange of principal tend to have the hump-backed shape depicted in Figure A.1. Interest rate swaps that are deep 'in-the-money' will have potential exposure profiles with much less pronounced 'humps' or which can be monotically downward sloping. If the derivatives transaction calls for a final exchange of principal, as currency swaps do, the potential exposure profile tends to be upward sloping as in Figure A.2. The final exchange of principal increases the importance of the diffusion effect and reduces the amount by which the currency swap amortizes, thereby creating the upward slope of the exposure profile.

The exposure profile of purchased options tends to be greater than the credit risk for comparable swaps. Options do not generally have periodic payments but are characterized by an upfront payment of the option premium and a final option payoff payment. Accordingly, the amortization effect is limited to the time decay of the option price and is outweighed by the diffusion effect. That is, the longer the time period, the greater the scope for movements in the underlying variable, which can generate a large exposure on the option payoff. Moreover, in contrast to swaps, purchased options with the premium paid upfront initially create an immediate mark-to-market exposure equal to the option premium. If the option seller defaults immediately, the option buyer must pay another option premium to replace the option even if there has been no movement in the underlying variables (see Figure A.2).

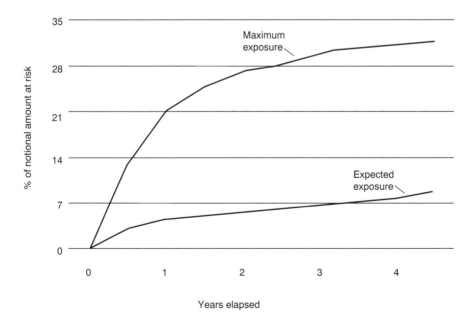

Figure A.2 Credit Exposure of Cross-currency Swap.

Finally, and again in contrast to swaps, credit risk is always asymmetric for options. The counterparty purchasing the option always has some exposure to the counterparty selling the option, regardless of how far the underlying variables move.

The calculation of expected and maximum exposure profiles, such as those in Figures A.1 and A.2, provides management with an important tool to assess how credit risk can evolve over the life of the transaction. In Figure A.1, the maximum exposure profile peaks at about 6.0% of notional amount after two years and declines steadily thereafter. This is known as the 'peak maximum exposure.' Similarly, the peak expected exposure is the highpoint of the expected exposure profile, or 1.5% of notional amount, and occurs after one year.

Another useful summary measurement of potential exposure profiles is based on the average of the potential exposures over the life of the contract. Returning again to Figure A.1, the maximum exposure profile starts at zero and rises rapidly to about 6.0% during the first year and declines steadily to zero over the final four years. The average of these exposures over the life of the contract is 3.25%, known as the 'average maximum exposure.' The average of the expected exposure profile is calculated in an identical fashion and is 0.9%.

As Figures A.1 and A.2 demonstrate, the maximum ('worst case') exposures on derivatives transactions are typically equal to a relatively small fraction of the notional amount of the contract; expected exposures are much smaller than maximum exposures. This is important to keep in mind when discussing the aggregate notional amount of the derivatives business. Aggregating derivatives transactions by notional amounts indicates the volume and growth of the business, but it provides virtually no information on the underlying credit risk in the system.

The analysis of potential exposure profiles enables management to evaluate credit exposures on derivatives transactions on a comparable basis with credit exposures for on-balance-sheet transactions, such as loans. Many institutions use measures such as the peak of the maximum, or expected exposure profiles, or the average of the maximum exposure profiles for aggregating and comparing credit exposure on derivatives transactions with on-balance-sheet transactions for a given counterparty.

The Survey of Industry Practice reveals that approximately two-thirds of dealers use internally developed methods to assess credit risk that are based on maximum exposure calculations using historical volatilities. Of this group, the majority of dealers assign counterparty exposures to individual transactions that are based on tables calculated for a variety of generic transactions (e.g. interest rate swaps, currency swaps, etc.). In the future, most dealers intend to refine this method by calculating the exposure of the individual transactions rather than relying on generic tables. Only 22% of dealers surveyed use the original exposure method (OEM), which is a static model of credit risk, and only 12% of dealers surveyed intend to use the OEM in the future.

The Survey asked dealers to indicate the initial exposure that would be assigned to a variety of derivatives transactions with varying maturities. The results reveal that most dealers differentiate sharply by the type of transaction and the maturity of the transaction. For instance, the average dealer assigns an initial exposure of about 22% of notional amount for a three-year currency swap and about 5% of notional amount for a three-year interest rate swap. This differentiation according to the type of transaction would be expected by the analysis presented above of Figures A.1 and Figure A.2.

The practices of end-users differ from those of dealers. A majority of the end-users indicate that they use some method based on notional amount to measure the exposure of an individual transaction. Twenty-six percent of end-users measure exposure according to the notional amount alone. An additional 39% of end-users measure the exposure as a percent of notional amount, but differentiate by type and maturity of transaction. (This is similar to OEM.) Fourteen percent of end-users measure exposure on a mark-to-market basis.

Credit Exposure on a Portfolio of Derivatives Transactions

The discussion thus far has focused on calculating the credit exposure for a single transaction. It becomes more complicated, but extremely important, to obtain an accurate assessment of the total credit exposure on a portfolio of transactions with the same counterparty.

Recommendation 11: Aggregating Credit Exposures

Credit exposures on derivatives, and all other credit exposures to a counterparty, should be aggregated taking into consideration enforceable netting arrangements. Credit exposures should be calculated regularly and compared to credit limits.

In calculating the current replacement costs for a portfolio of transactions with a counterparty, it is important to know whether netting applies (and is enforceable). If netting applies, the current credit exposure is simply the sum of the positive and negative mark-to-market values of the transactions in the portfolio. If netting does not apply, only the positive mark-to-market transactions should be added in calculating current exposure because the positive mark-to-market positions could not be offset against negative mark-to-market positions in the event of default.

It is more difficult to calculate measures of the potential exposure for a portfolio of transactions. The simplest method is again to simply add the measure of potential exposure of each transaction in the portfolio. Unfortunately, this procedure will in most cases dramatically overstate the potential exposure because it does not take into account transactions in the portfolio with offsetting exposures, or with peak potential exposures that occur at different times.

Consider a counterparty with which two interest rate swaps have been executed. The swaps are identical in all respects except that in one swap the counterparty is receiving the fixed rate and in the other swap the counterparty is paying the fixed rate. Obviously there is no net exposure. Suppose we correctly calculate the total maximum exposure as $5 million for each transaction. If we add the exposures, the total maximum on the portfolio would be $10 million. This is clearly an overstatement. If the counterparty was to default, only one of the swaps would result in a loss because both swaps could not have a positive mark-to-market value at the same time. The proper exposure in this portfolio is $5 million if netting does not apply and is zero if netting does apply.

Another shortcoming of adding the maximum exposures on a transaction-by-transaction basis in a portfolio relates to the timing of the default if one was to occur. Consider a portfolio in which there is a purchased interest rate cap and a long-term swap. Assume that the last rate setting on the cap has taken place and that a final cap payment of $5 million is due in two months. The credit risk on the cap is $5 million. Assume that the swap was executed recently and the swap currently has a zero mark-to-market value and a peak maximum exposure of $6 million which will occur in two years (according to the hump-backed schedule discussed earlier). If we add the peak maximum exposures, the peak maximum exposure on the portfolio is $11 million.

This is clearly an overstatement. The peak maximum exposure on the cap occurs in two months and the peak maximum exposure on the swap occurs in two years. It is not appropriate to add the peak exposures of transactions that occur at different dates. In this situation, we should calculate the maximum exposure on the swap that could occur in two months. If that peak exposure is $2 million, we should conclude that the peak maximum exposure on the portfolio is $7 million, not $11 million.

The potential exposure of a portfolio of transactions with a given counterparty can be analysed more thoroughly by simulation analysis. This requires sophisticated mathematical modelling and systems capability. In this approach, a statistical model generates multiple scenarios and investigates the stochastic properties of the derivatives portfolio. At each point in time under a given scenario, the mark-to-market value of each transaction in the portfolio is computed and the present value of the replacement cost of the entire portfolio is calculated, taking account of netting provisions where applicable.

This process is repeated for a large number of scenarios to generate a probability distribution of the present value of the replacement cost of the portfolio at each point in time. This information can be used to calculate the expected and maximum exposure profiles for the portfolio over its life span. The main advantage of this portfolio-level simulation is that it directly measures complex portfolio effects and thereby provides a much more accurate measure of expected and maximum potential exposure to a counterparty than would be obtained by aggregating exposures on individual transactions or by making an (educated) guess.

Market participants who do not have and cannot justify having the necessary simulation and statistical systems to perform such potential exposure calculations should use tables of factors developed under the same principles. They should also make sure that the factors used to differentiate appropriately by type of transactions are adjusted periodically to reflect changes in market conditions and the passage of time.

It is extremely important to recognize that, much like current exposure, potential exposure is constantly changing due to the passage of time and movements in the underlying variables (i.e. amortization and diffusion effects). Accordingly, calculations of potential maximum and expected exposures should be reviewed and updated to reflect these factors. Firms that aggregate potential exposures without quantifying portfolio effects through simulation analysis will generally overstate their counterparty exposure. Therefore, they do not need to perform calculations as frequently as firms that use simulation analysis to measure portfolio exposure more precisely. In any event, the frequency of calculation should be increased when credit limits are approached or exceeded.

Because it is relatively simple to calculate current exposures, and relatively more difficult to calculate potential exposure, several institutions update the current exposure on a daily basis but allow for potential exposure as a constant 'add-on' to the current exposure. This 'add-on' factor remains constant for the life of the transaction. This practice generally will result in a material overstatement of credit risk. This inaccuracy ignores the dynamic relationship between current and potential exposure and may be avoided by periodically updating the potential exposure calculations.

The Survey indicates that for dealers, the methods of aggregating derivatives exposures with a counterparty vary widely. Approximately one-third of dealers surveyed aggregated exposures with a counterparty by summing the exposures as initially calculated, while two-thirds of the dealers update aggregate exposures based, at a minimum, on the change in current exposure. Aggregation practices vary widely with respect to aggregating exposures on a net or gross basis. The diversity of practice probably reflects varying degrees of comfort regarding enforceability of netting in various jurisdictions. Thirty-four percent of dealers surveyed calculate aggregate exposures for credit line utilization purposes on both a net and gross basis. Fifty-one percent of dealers surveyed calculate credit limit utilization solely on a gross basis, while only 5% calculate it solely on a net basis. It is also worth noting that the systems most dealers use to aggregate credit exposures are not able to automatically take into account the specific terms and conditions in the legal documentation pertaining to netting provisions. In the future, over three-quarters of dealers surveyed plan to develop such systems.

For purposes of credit limit utilization, there is wide diversity in how end-users aggregate credit exposures to a single counterparty. Specifically, approximately 28% use a net basis, 35% use a gross basis, 15% use both bases, and 22% have no formal credit limits. As expected, the responses to this question are extremely sensitive to the home country of the end-users. In the United States, where netting is widely accepted and legally enforceable, 57% of all respondents use a net basis and 61% intend to do so. In contrast, only 11% of end-users in the United Kingdom use a net basis and 56% use a gross basis.

The discussion on current and potential exposure emphasized that credit risk is a dynamic concept that changes with the passage of time and with movements in the underlying variables. The Survey showed that three-quarters of all dealers monitor counterparty exposures on an intraday or overnight basis and 87% of the dealers can review derivatives exposures as needed between reporting intervals. Moreover, 95% of dealers surveyed have information on credit exposures and credit line availability for new derivatives transactions in the dealing room, with an even split between paper-based systems and on-line computer systems. However, it is important to note that, while most dealers regularly update and monitor measurements of current exposure, only 23% of dealers surveyed review the factors that influence potential exposure as frequently as quarterly. Forty-four percent of those surveyed report that they review potential exposure only on an *ad hoc* basis.

Sixty-one percent of end-users surveyed report that they measure the counterparty exposure of all derivatives products on an ongoing basis over the life of the transaction. Moreover, 75% of all respondents plan to follow this procedure. A majority of end-users report that they monitor their derivatives exposures to counterparties on a monthly basis or quarterly basis. Forty-two percent monitor exposures monthly and 26% do so quarterly. Sixty-nine percent of end-users surveyed have the capacity to review derivatives counterparty exposure as needed during intervals between reporting periods.

Most end-users update their exposure calculations to reflect the passage of time over the life of the transaction. Specifically, two-thirds of end-users measure overall risk to a counterparty based on the remaining maturity rather than the original maturity of the transactions. Three-quarters of all respondents plan to adopt the practice.

The Survey results indicate that many dealers recognize the importance of aggregating the measurement and integrating the analyses of exposure from derivatives transactions with exposures from more traditional on-balance-sheet banking products. Almost half of the dealers surveyed currently aggregate exposures from derivatives and non-derivatives activities across all products and all business lines; 73% of those surveyed intend to do so in the future. Approximately one-third of the dealers have credit systems for derivatives that are fully integrated with on-balance credit systems and almost three-quarters of the dealers plan to have such fully integrated systems.

The Probability of Default and Expected Loss Measurements

The measurement of credit exposure to a counterparty focuses on the loss that would occur if the counterparty defaulted, but does not address the probability that a default will occur. To calculate the expected loss or expected worst case loss on derivatives transactions, it is necessary to weight the credit exposure calculations discussed above by the probability of default. Probability-weighted exposure calculations enable the institution to estimate expected default-induced losses. Accordingly, such calculations are useful for measuring return on risk-adjusted capital and for comparing exposures across counterparties.

There are a variety of methods used to calculate loss or expected maximum loss. The simplest approach is to multiply the expected or maximum exposure by specified probability of default factors. An alternative, and more complex, approach is to run simulation analyses that incorporate a probability of default function. Once again, the degree of sophistication and complexity that is appropriate for measuring expected loss depends on the size and nature of the derivatives portfolio.

Participants use a variety of approaches to estimate the probability that a given counterparty will default. Most dealers, but few end-users, have an independent credit department that provides in-depth credit analyses of the counterparty. This credit research is often augmented by an analysis of credit spreads, bond ratings, and by empirical evidence on actual defaults over a long period in order to estimate the probability of default. In this regard, Standard & Poor's and Moody's have carried out extensive studies of defaulting institutions which are frequently used in assessing the probability of default.

The probability of default is generally deemed to be a function of credit ratings and of the maturity of the transaction. These relationships show up strongly in empirical evidence and are borne out in market credit spreads. Specifically, higher-rated companies tend to issue bonds with tighter credit spreads than lower-rated companies, and tend to default less; credit spreads tend to increase with the maturity of the bond, and the incidence of default tends to increase similarly.

II. CREDIT RISK MANAGEMENT

The first half of this Working Paper focused on measuring credit risk. It now addresses policies and procedures that can be taken to manage counterparty credit risk. These policies and procedures can be broken down into: internal controls to ensure that credit risk is assessed before entering into a transaction with a counterparty, and that credit risk is monitored over the life of the transaction; documentation provisions to control credit risk and to ensure transaction enforceability; and credit enhancement structures to further reduce or limit the credit exposure of dealing with a particular counterparty. The standard practices used to control counterparty credit risk in each of these areas are discussed below.

Internal Controls

Recommendation 12: Independent Credit Risk Management
Dealers and end-users should have a credit risk management function with clear independence and authority, and with analytical capabilities in derivatives, responsible for:

- approving credit exposure measurement standards;
- setting credit limits and monitoring their use;
- reviewing credits and concentrations of credit risk;
- reviewing and monitoring risk reduction arrangements.

The most effective method for minimizing credit risk relating to over-the-counter derivatives transactions is to establish appropriate internal guidelines and practices to assess and manage credit risk. The internal controls should be applied prior to the execution of a transaction and during all stages of the transaction's life. For derivatives dealers, the establishment of credit lines and the monitoring of credit exposures should be done by an independent credit analysis group, rather than by people directly involved in the execution of the transaction (e.g. marketing or trading personnel). End-users also should follow comparable procedures. Separation of responsibility is intended to prevent conflicts of interest and to ensure that the assessment of credit exposure is done objectively.

Before Executing Transactions

An independent credit group should conduct an internal credit review prior to engaging in transactions with a counterparty and should guide the use of documentation and credit support tools. Specifically, credit guidelines should be employed to ensure that only potential counterparties that meet the appropriate credit worthiness criteria, with or without any relevant credit support, become actual counterparties. Measures typically employed include: determining an acceptable credit rating (external, such as Moody's or Standard & Poor's, or internal), developing a thorough understanding of the industries and the performance within such industries of potential counterparties, and reviewing the financial history and prospects of potential counterparties.

Dealers may also consider the potential for correlation between market levels and the credit quality of their counterparties. If an end-user is using derivatives to hedge a business exposure, the dealers' exposure to an end-user will occur when the end-user's business operating results improve. In other cases, however, the opposite may be true: an extreme example would be the purchase of an over-the-counter put option on the common stock of the seller of the option. The exposure to the seller will be greatest when the credit quality of the seller is at its worst. Credit levels should be established which generally reflect the maximum potential exposure to a counterparty that is authorized by management. Dealers should set documentation and credit support strategies for different levels of counterparty exposures and maturities of transactions.

Almost 90% of end-users rely on credit ratings as the primary factor to approve counterparties. Of those that rely on credit ratings, 60% require uniform minimum credit ratings for all counterparties; a substantial number (approximately 30%) of respondents also impose minimum ratings that vary according to the types of transactions, their maturities, and the country in which the counterparty is domiciled. As a general rule, the counterparties are approved by either the treasurer or the chief financial officer of private sector corporations; in public sector entities and financial institutions, the counterparty approval also is often provided by the board of directors or a risk committee.

As discussed above, the potential exposure of a specific transaction depends on the transaction and the underlying instrument (e.g. interest rates, currencies, equities or commodities.) Before executing a new transaction with a counterparty, it is necessary to quantify the incremental risk that the transaction adds to the portfolio of transactions with that counterparty. There may be a natural offset to a proposed transaction within the existing portfolio of transactions, or a natural offset may be created.

Participants should also review exit strategies and liquidity implications prior to executing a transaction. Exit strategies that can be used to manage counterparty credit exposure include the outright termination of a transaction, the assignment of the transaction to another counterparty, and entering into an offsetting transaction with the counterparty to lock in the current credit exposure. Each of these exit strategies has different liquidity implications. For example, it may be difficult to assign or terminate a transaction with a troubled counterparty if the rest of the market is also trying to reduce their exposure to that counterparty. Liquidity can also be a factor in turbulent or thin markets. Finally, unusually complex transaction structures will have a limited number of potential assignees.

Parties should, whenever possible, execute a master agreement prior to entering into a transaction. This practice is designed to avoid potentially costly mistakes by ensuring that both parties fully understand the terms of the transaction prior to its execution. If time does permit, parties should at least agree on all essential elements of the agreement first, particularly credit and tax matters. When transactions are executed, a dealer confirmation specifying the essential terms of the transactions should be sent out to the counterparty as soon as possible after the transaction and should be promptly signed and returned by the counterparty. When transactions are executed without a master agreement in place, strenuous efforts should be made to negotiate and execute the master agreement as soon as possible. In this regard, management should ensure that the backlog of deals lacking complete documentation is monitored. A report on ageing, showing how long each transaction has been in place without a master agreement, should be prepared regularly and reviewed by management.

Monitoring the Counterparty Transaction Over Time

The credit risk exposure measurements and methodology discussed in previous sections of this report need to be applied on an ongoing basis. Current and potential exposures change with both the passage of time and movements in the underlying variables and therefore need to be checked periodically. The frequency with which credit exposures are monitored depends on the size of the derivatives portfolio and nature of the derivatives activity. Derivative dealers should monitor current credit exposure on a daily or weekly basis depending on the size of the portfolios and the type and volatility of the underlying transactions. The frequency should be increased as limits are approached or exceeded. Measurements of potential exposure should be made as frequently as possible or as appropriate for the nature of the activity.

End-users should also periodically review their own credit exposures to counterparties. The frequency depends on the size of the portfolio, the number of counterparties, and the extent to which credit exposures can be material.

In addition to monitoring the current and potential exposures of derivatives transactions, it is extremely important to monitor the credit worthiness of the counterparty and its compliance with any documentary financial standards. This practice enables dealers and end-users to take full advantage of any risk management tools available to them.

Credit risk exposure should be managed in relation to specified credit limits. Most institutions have a credit department that reviews the creditworthiness of its counterparties on an ongoing basis and increases and decreases the credit limits for these counterparties as appropriate. Systems should be in place to identify exposures to counterparties that are approaching or exceeding their credit limits. When these warning signs are triggered, policies aimed at bringing existing exposures within their credit limits and preventing exposures from increasing further should be implemented. For instance, such policies should include the following: no new transactions with that counterparty should be executed that increase exposures; active efforts should be made to assign or reverse existing transactions or to execute new transactions that reduce total credit exposure; and negotiations relating to collateral or other credit enhancements should be initiated.

Credit losses can occur. Accordingly, it is important that derivative dealers appropriately reflect their credit exposures when measuring the results of their derivatives activity. Credit risk of derivatives transactions should be treated in the same manner as credit risk of on-balance-sheet transactions. There are two components of credit risk which should be recognized: the unearned credit spread or general credit allowance which will be earned over time as compensation for being exposed to credit risk and an amount, if appropriate, to cover probable credit losses. The magnitude of these adjustments should be based on a prudent estimate of the credit losses the portfolio could experience, and can be related to the overall credit reserve of the dealer.

Factors that should influence the credit allowance include the creditworthiness of the counterparties, the magnitude of the potential exposure on the underlying transactions, netting arrangements, collateral arrangements, and the maturity of the underlying transactions. As stressed in this Working Paper, credit risk is a dynamic concept that changes with the passage of time and movements in the underlying variables. The credit adjustment to the value of the derivatives portfolios should be based on procedures that reflect this dynamic nature and that provide for an increase or reduction in credit adjustments as the credit risk parameters in the portfolio change.

The Survey asked dealers how they calculate unearned credit spread. Almost half say they currently use a transaction-by-transaction approach. In contrast, only 18% follow a counterparty-by-counterparty approach at the present time, but 33% intend to do so in the future. Provisions for unearned credit spreads typically are taken into earnings over time. The most common approach is on a straight-line basis over the life of the transaction(s). Only 16% reported that the credit spread earned over time is made as a function of the counterparty exposure.

The Survey indicated that dealers are adopting a conservative approach with respect to providing for probable credit losses. Approximately two-thirds of the dealers surveyed currently allow for probable credit losses in addition to unearned credit spread. Specifically, 39% of the dealers surveyed have a general allowance (reserve) and about 25% have an allowance (reserve) for specific probable losses. In the future, approximately 80% of those surveyed intend to have reserves with about half of them opting for general reserves and about half planning for reserves against probable losses.

Recommendation 14: Credit Enhancement

Dealers and end-users should assess both the benefits and costs of credit enhancement and related risk-reduction arrangements. Where it is proposed that credit downgrades would trigger early termination or collateral requirements, participants should carefully consider their own capacity and that of their counterparties to meet the potentially substantial funding needs that might result.

Collateral arrangements are negotiated by the counterparties to address the concerns of both parties. As such, collateral arrangements differ according to the conditions under which collateral must be provided, the amount of upfront collateral required (if any), and the frequency with which collateral calculations are made. Specifically, some collateral arrangements are structured so that the obligation of a counterparty to post collateral is triggered by an event such as a credit downgrade or a material adverse change in financial condition whereby the other party has 'reasonable grounds for insecurity,' or a specified threshold level of exposure has been reached. It should be noted that trigger provisions based on credit downgrade or other adverse changes have the potential to create sudden and sizeable liquidity requirements. Derivative dealers and end-users should carefully consider their capacity and the capacity of their counterparty to meet such potential liquidity requirements when they negotiate such provisions.

To enhance the enforceability of collateral arrangements, a security agreement addendum may be attached to the customer master agreement. The agreements generally are customized. If all trades made between the two counterparties within a particular product group — that is, all cities, branches, subsidiaries, or affiliates — are netted, then the collateral agreement would reflect this and thus avoid sending collateral to one location while receiving collateral from another. Similarly, cross-product netting agreements may be considered in the collateral agreement.

An alternative to collateral arrangements is periodic cash settlement of the underlying positions. In this structure, two counterparties agree to periodically send cash to cover any negative mark-to-market position that exists. The counterparty with the positive mark-to-market position takes actual ownership of the cash and the terms of the transaction are reset at market rates to have a zero mark-to-market value. These arrangements also often permit the early termination of the derivatives contract on a predetermined cash settlement date if either party so desires.

The Survey indicates that the most common forms of credit enhancement accepted by dealers are cash, government securities, and third-party guarantees or letters of credit. Most dealers report collateral arrangements whereby the amount of collateral is adjusted up or down over the life of the derivative according to the level of current exposure. While most dealers will accept the credit enhancement arrangement discussed above from end-users, 48% of dealers surveyed do not provide credit enhancement of any form to counterparties.

Collateral arrangements represent a small portion of gross credit exposure. Most dealers report that less than 5% of their gross credit exposure to counterparties is collateralized; similarly, less than 5% of their counterparties' gross exposure to the dealers is reported to be collateralized.

With respect to end-users, the Survey reported that 42% of end-users accept third party guarantees, 22% accept cash collateral, and 22% accept government securities as collateral. In the future, end-users plan to increase their acceptance of cash and securities collateral. Thirty-nine percent of respondents do not accept any forms of credit enhancement, presumably preferring to deal with relatively strong counterparties. End-users that accept credit enhancement tend to require it from counterparties on a case-by-case basis rather than refer to a minimum acceptable credit rating.

The majority (60%) of end-users surveyed are not prepared to provide any form of credit enhancement in derivatives transactions. About 20% of respondents provide cash as collateral and 20% provide securities as collateral. The responses to this question are remarkably uniform across countries and types of end-user.

Reproduced with the permission of the G-30.

Appendix 5

Standard and Poor's Criteria for Securities Receiving an 'R' Rating

The 'r' symbol is attached for some of the following types of securities:

- Interest-only and principal-only mortgage securities, because of their extreme variability caused by mortgage payments.
- Mortgage residuals, if the issue contains elements of risk associated with either Interest Onlys (IOs) and Principal Onlys (POs). (Most mortgage residuals would not be included, because they predominantly are short-term issues with fixed payment expectations.)
- Structured notes whose interest payments are derived from a swap that could terminate at any time. While the total return of a terminating swap could be positive, it may not be what the investor was expecting.
- Debt or preferred stock whose terms provide for the automatic conversion to common stock, because the buyer could be better or worse off with the common stock at the end of the set period. However, conventional convertible debt will not be highlighted with a symbol, because it only converts if it benefits the investor.
- Debt issued by a corporation or government whose principal is dependent upon the performance of an index that could either rise or fall, such as debt repayment tied to the stock market or currency exchange rates. However, an obligation that can only benefit the investor, and cannot reduce expected repayment, will not be assigned an 'r'.

- Leveraged inverse floaters that do not move parallel to an index, but expand and contract relative to the index, depending upon the terms, will receive an 'r' because of the additional risk.

- Obligations with interest rates linked to non-interest related indices, such as the price performance of a basket of stocks.

- Obligations with fixed interest rates, if the rate has been reduced in anticipation of gains from a third-party noncredit related source. For instance, some bonds are sold at rates well below market rates, because there is an expectation of additional returns from a third-party source, such as tax credits, a pledge of a percentage of the company's revenues, or the positive performance of some index. Bonds with provisions like those would receive an 'r', because the instrument passes additional risk of earning a market rate of return to the investor.

Source: Standard & Poor's Structured Finance Group.

Glossary

Accrual Notes. A floating rate note that accrues interest daily at the rate of LIBOR plus a spread. However for every day that LIBOR is above a prespecified strike rate, or outside a prespecified range, the notes accrue no interest.

Add-on. The credit risk capital that banks are required to set aside to cover the changes in the potential value of a derivative transaction. Part of the 1988 Basle Capital Accord.

American-style Option. An option which may be exercised at any time during its life up to and including its expiration date. Because the buyer has this luxury, American-style options are more expensive than European-style options. Semi-American-style options are those which can be exercised on a limited number of dates before expiry.

Arbitrage. A riskless trading strategy designed to profit from the price differences of two similar instruments which are traded in different markets. The trader simultaneously buys the cheaper instrument and sells the more expensive substitute.

At-the-money. An option whose exercise price, i.e. strike, is equal to the prevailing forward price of the underlying asset.

Average rate/price Option. Also known as the Asian option. It is an option that pays the difference between the average rate/price of the underlying asset during the option's life, compared with a predetermined strike rate. This is unlike American-style or European-style options which pay the difference between the price of the underlying asset on exercise/expiry date and the predetermined strike rate. Since the volatility of an average rate/price is lower than the volatility of a single rate/price, Asian options are cheaper than European and American-style options. This cheapness is one of the main reasons for their popularity.

Backwardation. A situation where the forward price of an asset, often a commodity, is lower than the spot price. For all assets, the forward price is a function of spot and the cost of carry; with commodities there is the added cost of storage and insurance. When assets can easily be borrowed or lent, the forward price never strays too far from the carry-cost basis. If the forward price is higher than the carry-cost basis, arbitrageurs will buy the spot and sell the forward; and if the former is lower, they will sell short in the spot market and buy forward and capture the mispricing on settlement date, if not before. Because commodities have inconvenient storage and delivery terms, and cannot be borrowed, it is difficult to arbitrage the carrying-cost basis as conveniently as it is financial assets. Consequently when the forward price is lower than the spot, it can remain that way for a long time because commodity markets are essentially one-way markets. The forward contracts can never get expensive relative to cash because if they did, market participants will just buy the physical asset and sell the future. But they can get extremely cheap relative to cash because you cannot short the physical and buy the future.

Barrier Option. An option that ceases to exist or is activated once the underlying asset reaches a predetermined level. Those that are cancelled are more commonly known as knock-out options, of which there are two main sub-categories — up-and-out and down-and-out options. Those that are come alive are known as knock-ins; again there are two main types — up-and-in and down-and-in options.

With an up-and-out, the option is cancelled if the underlying asset rises above a certain point and with a down-and-out, if the underlying asset falls below a predetermined point. The up-and-in or down-and-in option, on the other hand, will have no value at maturity unless the underlying asset rises, or falls, in the interim above the predetermined price, at which point it becomes a standard European-style put or call option. These extinguishing or activating features make barrier options cheaper than ordinary options.

Basis Point (bp). One one-hundredth of one percentage point, most often used in quotation of spreads between interest rates or to describe changes in yields on securities or coupons on swaps.

Basis Risk. The risk that arises when a hedge and the instrument being hedged are imperfectly matched; since their prices may not move in tandem there is a possibility of losses arising. For example hedging a portfolio of 75 American stocks, some of which are not constituents of the S&P 100 index, with futures on that index will incur basis risk because the price movements of the 75 stocks will not be perfectly reflected in price changes of the S&P 100 future.

Basle Capital Accord. A 1988 accord which established a common credit risk measurement system and minimum capital standards to protect against credit risk. In line with the accord, which came into full effect in 1992, banks' risk-weighted on- and off-balance-sheet positions should be covered by at least 8% capital. This Accord has been implemented not only in the Group of Ten countries, G-10, but in most countries in the world where banking business is significant.

Basle Committee on Banking Supervision. A committee established in 1975 by the central bank governors of the G-10 countries. It consists of senior representatives of banking supervisory authorities and central banks from Belgium, Canada, France, Germany, Italy, Japan, Luxembourg, Netherlands, Sweden, Switzerland, the United Kingdom and the United States. It established the 1988 capital accord for credit risk and in 1995 was in the process of finalizing a supplement to the accord for market risk capital.

Bid/ask Spread. The difference between the buying (bid) price and the selling (offer/ask) price for any instrument.

Black-Scholes Model. The most widely-used option pricing model which was developed by Fischer Black and Myron Scholes in 1973. The theoretical value of an option is calculated from five inputs — underlying asset price, strike price, interest rates, time to expiry and, volatility.

The model assumes that the underlying asset's returns are normally distributed (i.e. have lognormal prices), that there are no transaction costs, that volatility and interest rates remain constant throughout the life of the option.

Break-even Point. The price of the underlying asset at which an option buyer makes no profit or loss.

Bond Index Swaps. A swap in which one counterparty pays the return of a bond market in exchange for receiving a money market rate, or vice versa. Counterparties may also swap the returns of two bond markets. The two most common indexes used to measure bond market returns are the JP Morgan government bond index and the Salomon Brothers world government bond index.

Building-block Approach. A method of measuring price risk which breaks it down into risk specific to a security/issuer and general market risk.

Butterfly Spread. An option strategy designed to profit from stable or decreasing volatility, with limited risk and limited profit potential. A butterfly call spread involves trades in four call options, all with the same expiry date. The buyer of a butterfly spread buys one call at the lowest strike rate, selling two calls with an intermediate strike price, and buying the fourth call with the highest strike price. A butterfly put spread involves put options.

CFTC. The Commodity Futures Trading Commission (CFTC) is the US federal government agency which regulates commodity futures trading.

Cap. A contract whereby the seller agrees to pay the buyer the difference between a reference rate and an agreed strike rate once the reference rate exceeds the strike. Commonly the reference rate is three- or six-month LIBOR. A cap is therefore a strip of interest-rate call options which protects the buyer from interest rate rises but simultaneously allows him to enjoy rate reductions.

Call Option. An option giving the buyer the right but not the obligation to buy an underlying asset at a predetermined price.

Cash Market. The underlying or spot market, as opposed to a futures or options market.

Collar. A collar is created by simultaneously buying a call (put) and selling a put (call) option, or a cap and floor in the case of interest rate options. The premium earned from selling one option reduces the cost of buying the other option and the amount saved depends on the strike rate of the two options. If the premium raised by the sale exactly matches the cost of the purchase, then it is a zero cost collar.

Collateralized Mortgage Obligation. An asset-backed security which in this case is backed by an underlying pool of mortgages. Such securities offer their investors a higher return than normal fixed-rate bonds but buyers suffer prepayment risk if mortgage holders redeem their mortgages early. Different types of CMOs include Planned Amortization Classes (PACS), Interest Onlys (IOs), Principal Onlys (POs), and Z-bonds.

Commodity Swap. A swap in which one leg is pegged to a fixed price, and the other to the floating price, of a commodity. If the floating-rate price of the commodity is higher than the fixed price, the difference is paid by the floating payer, and vice versa. Commodities that have been swapped include oil, natural gas, precious and base metals and some agricultural products such as wheat.

Compound Option. An option on an option, allowing the buyer to sell (or purchase) an option on an underlying asset at a fixed price within a set time frame. The upfront premium is less than for a normal European-style option but if the option is exercised, the overall cost will be greater than buying a straightforward option.

Condor Spread. An option strategy which has limited risk but limited profit potential. It involves four options with four different strike prices. A buyer of a call condor spread buys one call at the lowest strike, sells another two calls at the second strike and third strike, and buys the final call at a fourth strike.

Confidence Interval. An estimate of the probability that a price observation will fall within or outside a range which is itself defined by standard deviation (SD) intervals. One SD will encompass 68% of the price observations; two SD test 95% of the observations and three SDs 99% of the price observations (see normal distribution and standard deviation).

Constant Maturity Treasury (CMT) Linked FRN. A floating rate note whose interest payments are linked to the yield of US constant maturity treasuries (CMT), an interest rate benchmark. The US Federal Reserve publishes a series of indexes of one-, two-, three-, five-, seven- and ten-year US Treasuries based on the average yield of Treasuries of similar maturities but adjusted to a constant maturity.

Contango. A situation where the forward/futures price of an asset is higher than the spot; the differential explained by the net cost of carry (for financial assets) plus the cost of storage and insurance (for commodities). It is the opposite of backwardation.

Convertible Bond. A bond issued by a company that must be exchanged for a set number of the company's shares at a predetermined price. Because the bond embeds a call option on the company's equity, convertibles carry much lower rates of interest than traditional debt and are therefore a cheap way for companies to raise debt. The problem for existing shareholders is that conversion dilutes the company's outstanding shares.

Convexity. The price-yield relationship of a fixed-income instrument cannot be represented by a straight line but one that is slightly curved. This is why fixed-rate bonds and swaps have convexity which is technically defined as the difference in the rate of the price change of a fixed-income instrument from that implied by its duration, for a given move in interest rates. Fixed-rate bonds and swaps are positively convex: their price increases at a faster rate than they decrease than that suggested by their duration. This means they are more sensitive to yield changes when interest rates are declining and less sensitive when rates are advancing. The higher the bond's duration, the more its convexity. Bonds or swaps with embedded call options, e.g. CMOs, have negative convexity: when rates fall their price increase is slower relative to the interest rate move. Convexity effectively describes the same attribute as gamma or curvature of options.

Correlation. Correlation is a measure of the extent to which two variables move together. It is a statistical measure of the relationship between two variables and is normally expressed as a coefficient between $+1$ and -1. The former means variables are perfectly correlated (in that they move in the same direction to the same degree) and the latter means that they are perfectly negatively correlated (in that they move in opposite directions to the same degree). A correlation of zero means that there is no relationship between the two variables.

Corridor Swap. An interest-rate swap which has embedded digital options on one leg. The party that has sold these embedded options, normally the floating-rate receiver, will receive less coupon income every time LIBOR falls outside a pre-agreed range. For taking on this risk, the floating rate receiver (fixed-rate payer) pays a below-market fixed-rate on the fixed leg of the swap.

Cost of Carry. The interest rate expense on money borrowed to finance buying an asset. If the cost of financing is lower than the interest received, the asset has positive carry; if it is higher, the asset has negative carry.

Credit Risk. The risk that a counterparty to a transaction will not live up to its financial obligations. Derivative credit risk is different from loan credit risk because the amount at risk is dynamic and reflects changing prices and volatilities of the underlying asset.

Currency Swap. A transaction where two parties exchange initial principal amounts of two currencies at the spot exchange rate. During the life of the swap, they exchange fixed (or floating) interest payments in their swapped currencies. At maturity, the principal amount is reswapped at an exchange rate that was agreed at the start of the swap.

Curve Risk. The risk that arises from non-parallel shifts of the yield curve; i.e. long-term rates and short-term rates responding differently to interest rate movements. Sometimes the long-end moves more than the short-end, sometimes not at all, causing the yield curve to change shape. Curve risk arises whenever an instrument of one maturity is used to hedge a related instrument on the same underlying asset but with a different maturity. It is a subset of basis risk.

Curvature. A term used mainly in conjunction with options and is also known as gamma or convexity. It describes the curved price profile of an option and measures the change in the delta of the option is response to a change in the price of the underlying asset (see gamma).

Deep Discount Bonds. Generally refers to fixed-income securities which are trading at prices well below par value because their fixed coupons are way below current market rates. In the 1990s though, deep discount floating-rate notes emerged because their floating-rate coupons were also well below prevailing floating interest rates.

Delta. A measure of the rate of change in option's price for a given move in the price of the underlying. It is derived by dividing the change in the option's price by the change in the price of the underlying asset.

An at-the-money option has a delta of 50%, an out-of-the-money less than 50% and an in-the-money more than 50%. Changes in delta are non-linear giving rise to the curvature of an option.

Delta-hedging. A method option sellers use to hedge the price risk of their options, by taking a position in the underlying asset(s) in proportion to the option's delta. For example, a seller of a $1 million call option with a delta of 50% will buy $500 000 of the underlying asset. Such a hedge will leave him delta-neutral with no exposure to changes in the price of the underlying, but only if these price changes are infinitesimally small.

Derivative. A contract whose value depends on the prices (and the volatilities) of an underlying asset but which does not require any investment of principal in the asset. The main types of derivatives are forward-based and option-based instruments (see futures, forwards, forward-rate agreements, swaps and options).

Differential Swap. A swap with one of the payment rates/returns denominated in a currency different from that of the other leg and from the notional principal of the swap.

Digital Option. A digital or binary option pays out a fixed amount if the underlying reaches a predetermined level (the strike price). The option's payout does not depend on the price of the underlying asset on expiry date unlike conventional options.

DV01. The dollar value of a basis point which is simply the change in the present value of a bond/swap/portfolio of bonds and swaps, given a one basis point change (upward/downward) in interest rates (see duration).

Duration. Duration is a measure of a security's maturity which takes into account all coupon payments of the security. Specifically it is the weighted average life of the present value of all future cashflows of a security. For a given maturity, the higher the coupon, the shorter the duration of the security. Duration measures the sensitivity of a security to changes in the overall level of interest rates; so the higher the duration, the more sensitive the security is to interest rate changes (see also convexity).

Dynamic Replication. Also known as synthetic option or replicating the pay-out of an option. This involves buying or selling the underlying asset or futures contracts in proportion to movements in the theoretical option's delta. Essentially it is delta-hedging with nothing to hedge. Those trying to replicate a long option position lay themselves open to increases in market volatility. Conversely they benefit if volatility declines.

Embedded Option. An option that is an integral part of a debt instrument thus affecting the latter's redemption value.

Equity Swap. A swap where one counterparty pays the total or price return of an equity index, a basket of stocks or a single stock; and the other party pays a floating-interest rate. Sometimes both legs involve the payment (exchange) of the total or price returns of different equity indices.

European Style Option. An option which the buyer can only exercise on expiry date.

Exercise Price. Also known as the strike price. It is the fixed price at which an option buyer has the right to buy an asset, in the case of a call; and sell an asset, in the case of a put.

Exotic Option. Any option with an unusual or complicated pay-off. Examples are average rate, digital, lookback and barrier options.

Extension Risk. The risk that a security will have a longer maturity than originally anticipated because the underlying mortgages have not been prepaid according to predicted prepayment rates. A risk normally associated with CMOs when interest rates rise.

Fat Tails. See kurtosis and tails.

Financial Accounting Standards Board. The American professional body primarily responsible for determining financial reporting standards in the United States.

Floor. A contract whereby the seller pays the buyer the difference between a reference rate and predetermined strike rate should the reference rate fall below the strike rate. The reference rate is often a short-term floating rate like six-month LIBOR. A floor is effectively a series of interest rate put options.

Forwards. An over-the-counter future (see future).

Forward Curve. An interest rate curve derived point to point from the traditional yield curve and represents the changes in the yield curve shape that are discounted in the current interest rate environment.

Forward Rate Agreement. A contract which allows the buyer or seller to fix in advance the interest rate for a single specified period. It is an interest rate forward contract written on a notional amount, with the difference between the contract rate and the prevailing rate, cash settled on expiry. A swap is a strip of FRAs.

Future. An exchange-traded contract between a buyer and a seller to exchange a standard quantity of a given instrument, at an agreed price, on a given date. Contracts are highly standardized and the buyer and seller need only agree the price and number of contracts traded. A future is an exchange-traded forward; after a trade is cleared, the exchange's clearing house is the counterparty to the trade, so the credit risk of a future is the credit worthiness of the clearing house. Both a future and a forward differ from an option in that the two parties to a future/forward transaction are obliged to go ahead with the deal whether prices are in their favour or not.

Most futures contracts expire on a quarterly basis. Contracts specify either physical delivery of the underlying instrument or cash settlement at expiry.

G-30. Group of 30. A private think-tank based in Washington DC, consisting of bankers, regulators and academics. Their two most important pieces of work so far have been the development of a plan for faster, standardized clearance and settlement for securities transactions and a report on derivatives which presented a clear, practical set of best practices for derivative risk management.

Gamma. A measure of the rate of change in the delta of an option for a one unit price move of the underlying asset. It is also known as the curvature of an option. Gamma is thus the sensitivity of an option's delta to small changes in the price of the underlying and indicates how quickly an option becomes unhedged when the underlying price changes. An at-the-money option expiring soon has the highest gamma. Gamma decreases as the price of the underlying moves further away from the strike price. When a trader is long options, he has positive gamma and when he is short options, he has negative gamma.

General Risk. The risk from a general market movement arising from, for example, a change in interest rates or official foreign exchange policy.

Hedge Funds. Originally investment funds which had to hedge their investment risks by simultaneously buying and selling securities. The more accurate term for them now is leveraged funds. They are pools of aggressively-managed money which maximize returns for their investors by actively speculating in any market which takes their fancy. They maximize the funds at their disposal by leverage — by borrowing against their capital and by using derivatives.

Hedge Ratio. The proportion of the underlying asset needed to delta hedge an option (see delta).

Holding Period. The length of time that a financial institution is assumed to hold a given financial instrument for the purpose of calculating price volatility.

Index Amortizing Rate (IAR) Swap. An interest rate swap with a notional principal that amortizes off the back of movements in a reference index, such as LIBOR. The notional principal amortizes as LIBOR falls and remains constant if LIBOR increases or stays at the same level. Since the interest payments paid or earned by a counterparty in a swap are based on the notional principal of the transaction, the interest payments earned by the fixed-rate receiver fall as LIBOR decreases. The fixed rate receiver enjoys a rate higher than prevailing market rates as compensation for the possibility of receiving less interest in the future.

Interest Rate Swap. A contract in which two counterparties exchange net future cashflows. The most common interest rate swap is the fixed-floating swap, where one counterparty pays a fixed rate and the other pays a floating rate. There is no exchange of principal — the interest rate payments are based on a notional amount.

In-the-money. Describes an option whose strike price is more advantageous than the current market price of the underlying so that there is a net financial benefit to be derived from exercising the option immediately. A call option is in-the-money if the price of the underlying asset is above the strike price and a put option is in-the-money if the price of the underlying asset is below the exercise price.

Intrinsic Value. The net benefit to be derived from exercising an option immediately; i.e. the amount by which an option is in-the-money.

Kurtosis. A measure of how fast the tails of a probability distribution approach zero, evaluated relative to a normal distribution. The observed price distribution of financial assets tend to be clustered around the mean and to have a wider dispersion of extreme events — called outliers — than normal distribution would predict. These outliers are also called fat tails. Going hand-in-hand with fat tails is a higher peak around the mean. The condition of fat tails and higher peak is known as leptokurtosis. The fatter the tails, the greater the chance a variable will reach an extreme value.

Leverage. To the layman, leverage is equal to gearing - the ratio of borrowed money to a firm's or an individual's assets/cash in hand. In finance, leverage describes the multiplied effect on profit (or loss) or the value of a position from a small change in prices. It can also be used to describe the ratio between the amount an investor deposits as an upfront payment and the notional amount of exposure he gains. Say a stock is trading at $100 and an option on the stock worth $10. The option gives the investor ten times leverage.

A more obvious leverage appeared in the early 1990s. This is the explicit leverage factor or multiplier embedded in the payout formula of a security/swap which magnifies the profit/loss impact of a 1% change in the cash value of the underlying instrument/asset by the numerical size of the multiplier. The leverage afforded by the multiplier is constant throughout the transaction.

Leveraged Floating Rate Note. Built into the payout formula of this floater is a multiplier which magnifies changes in interest rates.

LIBOR. London Interbank Offered Rate. The rate at which banks offer to lend funds in the international interbank market.

Liquid Yield Option Note (LYON). A zero coupon convertible, callable by the issuer and puttable by the investor.

Liquidity Risk. There are two types of liquidity risk. Market liquidity risk arises when a large transaction in particular instrument has a significant effect on its price, making it difficult for a participant to hedge or layoff its positions at reasonable cost. Funding liquidity risk is defined as the inability to meet cashflow obligations as they become due.

Long. The act of buying or enjoying the economic impact of owning an asset, security or instrument. A person who is long wants prices to rise.

Lookback Option. An option which gives the buyer the right to exercise the option at the lowest price (in the case of a call) or the highest price (in the case of a put) reached by the underlying asset within the lookback period. The lookback period often coincides with the life of the option.

Margin. The amount of money, or collateral, that a market participant will be required to lodge with the clearing house of an exchange before it is allowed to trade. This is known as the initial margin and is payable on all contracts whether the participant is going long or short. The amount depends on how much the clearing house considers prudent to set aside to protect against a dramatic move in the underlying market. Each day, the clearing house also pays or receives variation margin, which is the difference between the original contractual price and the daily closing price.

Margin Call. A demand from the clearing house of an exchange or broker carrying a customer's position for more cash or collateral to guarantee performance on a contract.

Mark-to-Market. The process of revaluing an instrument or a portfolio of instruments on the basis of its prevailing market price or liquidation value. Since there is little liquidity in complex derivatives, marking them to market is more accurately described as marking-to-model since such complex derivatives are priced according to proprietary in-house models; consequently the prices received from different houses can vary substantially.

Market Risk. The risks brought about by changes in market conditions. The components of market risks are price (delta), curvature (gamma), volatility (vega), time decay (theta), basis (correlation), spread and discount rate (rho) risk.

Mean Reversion. The name given to the process in which interest rates and volatility appear to return to a long-run average.

Mortgage Swap. An interest rate swap that replicates the economics of owning mortgage-backed securities; i.e. the investor pays floating and receives a fixed rate that is higher than prevailing fixed rates available on conventional interest rate instruments. The principal amount of a mortgage swap amortizes according to how much of the underlying pool of mortgages are prepaid. But unlike MBS, the underlying pool of mortgages for a mortgage swap is a set of mortgage pass-throughs, so the investor is spared pool-specific prepayment risk.

Net Present Value. A method for assessing the worth of future coupon payments by looking at the present value of those future cashflows by discounting them at current interest rates.

Normal Distribution (Lognormal Distribution). A statistical term which describes the behaviour of variables which move randomly. Because the prices of financial assets are supposed to move randomly, they are assumed to be normally distributed. But since their prices can rise indefinitely but not fall below zero, their behaviour is described by a form of cumulative distribution called lognormal distribution. Both sorts of distribution are captured by a bell-shaped curve which can be completely described by its average (mean) and its standard deviation (how widely the observed the returns on financial assets are around the mean).

Generally, approximately two out of three outcomes (68%) will occur within one standard deviation of the mean, 19 out of 20 outcomes (95%) within two standard deviations of the mean, and 369 out of 370 (99.7%) will occur within three standard deviations of the mean.

Notional Amount/Principal/Value. The nominal or hypothetical value used to calculate a derivative instrument's cashflow payments. For FRAs, interest rate swaps, and options, the value is purely notional because no exchange of principal ever takes place.

Option. A contract which gives the buyer the right, but not the obligation, to buy or sell an underlying asset at a certain price (the exercise, or strike price) on or before an agreed date in the future (the expiry date).

For this right, the purchaser pays a premium to the seller. The seller (writer) of an option has a duty to buy or sell at that price, should the purchaser exercise his right. A call option confers to the buyer the right to buy and a put option the right to sell.

Operational Risk. The risk of unexpected losses arising from deficiencies in management information, support and control systems.

Out-of-the-money. Describes an option whose strike price is above the forward price of the underlying asset in the case of a call, or below, in the case of a put. An out-of-the-money option has no intrinsic value.

Over-the-counter (OTC) Market. Describes the trading of financial instruments that takes place off organized exchanges, usually over the telephone or on computer screens. Generally, the parties must negotiate all the details of every transaction and so each deal can be customized to one party's desires.

Payoff/Payout Profile. The graph of a derivative's or a structural note's value at expiry date over a range of underlying prices.

Plain Vanilla Instruments. A standard bond, swap or option with no hidden/embedded complexities.

Prepayment Risk. The risk that arises when payment of principal is made before the scheduled or expected date. Associated mainly with mortgage-backed securities and index-amortizing swaps.

Premium. The price of an option that the buyer pays the seller.

Price Risk. The exposure resulting from a change in the price of an underlying asset or instrument (see delta).

Portfolio Insurance. Another name for dynamic replication, it was a strategy developed by Hayne Leland in the late 1970s as a way of limiting losses on an equity portfolio. He realized that limiting the losses on a portfolio was similar to buying a put option on the entire portfolio but because put options were not widely available then, the strategy synthetically reproduced the payout of a put option by dynamic replication. As long as markets move continuously, transaction costs are minimal and volatility relatively stable, option returns are easily replicated. The strategy was discredited in the 1987 stock market crash when markets gapped and no buyers could be found for the underlying assets or futures contracts.

Put Option. The right but not the obligation to sell the underlying asset.

Quanto Option. An option (also known as guaranteed exchange rate option) on an asset denominated in a currency different from that of the asset. The exchange rate at which the purchaser converts the currency is fixed when he buys the option. These options are popular with investors who want exposure to foreign assets without the currency risk.

Repurchase (Repo) Agreement. To buy (sell) a security while at the same time agreeing to sell (buy) it back at a predetermined price at a fixed date in the future. The price at which the reverse transaction takes place sets the interest rate over the period (the repo rate). The security buyer effectively lends the seller money for the period of the repo agreement, and the terms of the agreement are structured to compensate him for this. The buyers often receive a better return than that available on equivalent money-market instruments; while sellers, particularly financial institutions, are able to get sub-LIBOR funding.

Reset Date. The date at which a swap, floating rate note or a structured note's periodic coupon payment terms are re-established.

Reverse (Inverse) Floater. A floating-rate note in which coupon resets are inversely proportional to the level of interest rates, usually LIBOR. As LIBOR rises, the floating-rate coupon falls and as LIBOR falls, the coupon increases. It is called a reverse (inverse) floater because a conventional floater has coupon payments that rise as LIBOR increases and fall when LIBOR declines.

Rollover Risk. The risk that arises from a mispricing of a futures contracts at the time an old position is closed and a new one opened.

Rocket Scientists. A term to describe the creators of complex derivatives or new bond structures with embedded derivatives.

Short. The act of selling an asset, security or instrument not really owned, or the economic impact of doing so. It is the opposite to going long. Market participants who go short want prices to decline.

Specific Risk. The risk that the price of a given instrument will move out of line with similar instruments, due principally to factors related to its issuer.

Spread Risk. The risk that arises because the yield differential (spread) between two interest rate instruments is not constant, varying according to demand and supply factors, and credit concerns.

Standard Deviation. The quantification of uncertainty is a principal objective of statistics. The most familiar measure of uncertainty is standard deviation — which measures the dispersion of values (in the case of financial assets — their returns) around the average. It is represented by the formula:

$$\sigma = \text{square root} \left(\frac{1}{n} \sum_{i=1}^{n} [x_i - \mu]^2 \right)$$

where σ = standard deviation
n = number of observations
μ = mean of observations
x_i = value of each observation
Σ = summation sign

(see confidence intervals and normal distribution).

Straddle. A volatility-trading strategy involving two options. A straddle buyer expects volatility of the underlying asset to increase while a straddle seller hopes for the opposite. A straddle consists of a put option and a call option, with the same strike price and same expiry date. The buyer benefits if the underlying asset moves either way. However, because he has paid two premiums, the market movements either way must be large enough for him to make a lot of money on one option to offset the wasted premium on the option that expires worthless. Large market moves imply an upturn in volatility. A straddle seller on the other hand expects volatility to decrease and hopes the underlying asset does not move. He assumes unlimited risk for limited gain. Straddles are primarily trading instruments.

Strangle. This is also a volatility-trading strategy and is similar to a straddle, except that the put and call option have strike prices equally out-of-the-money. This trading position costs less than the straddle because both options are out-of-the-money, but the buyer requires the underlying market to move even more dramatically than he does under a straddle before he makes any money. Sellers of strangles make money if the underlying asset keeps in the range between two strike prices, but lose if the price moves outside the break-even range (the strike prices plus the premium received).

Strike Price. An option's exercise price.

Structured Note. A fixed-income or floating-rate security that contains embedded options. If the investor sells the options, he receives a higher coupon as compensation; if he buys the options, he earns a lower coupon income as payment for the options he has bought.

Structured Product. A financial instrument designed to meet the needs of one or a small number of investors. They are often a combination of the basic building blocks of derivatives — swaps, forwards and options — packaged together to produce a particular payout profile.

Swap Curve. A yield curve showing the relationship of the fixed-interest-rate leg of swaps of various maturities.

Swap Spread. The interest rate difference between a swap and a government security of similar maturity.

Systemic Risk. The risk associated with segments of the financial system breaking down due to its (their) inability to cope with large quantities of market, credit or settlement risks.

Tails. The ends of a probability distribution where the chances of an observation are small (see kurtosis).

Theta (Time Decay). This measures the effect on an option's price of a one-day decrease in the time to expiration. Because the life of an option can only decrease, the term 'time decay' is used to describe how the theoretical value of an option erodes with the passage of time.

Time Value. One of the components of the value of an option, the other being its intrinsic value. Since an out-of-the-money option has no intrinsic value, it only has time value.

Transaction Costs. All the costs of executing a financial transaction including explicit costs such as brokerage commissions, margin interest and indirect costs such as the bid/ask spread.

Ultra Vires. A transaction performed without any legal authority, or beyond the scope of powers of the entity that entered into it.

Value-at-risk. A measure of the aggregate market risk facing a firm. It is the amount of money a firm could lose or make due to price changes in the underlying markets. Since firms are more worried about potential losses rather than gains, VAR has become synonymous with the maximum losses over a certain time period and for a selected level of confidence. An institution with a daily VAR number of $10 million at 95% confidence interval means that the firm could lose up to $10 million on 19 out of 20 trading days, and more than $10 million on one day out of 20.

Vega. A measure of the rate of change in an option's price caused by changes in volatility. When volatility of the underlying asset increases, so does the option price and vice versa. This relationship is independent of the price levels of the underlying asset. Volatility risk is more associated with long-dated options because there is more time for the volatility of the underlying asset to work in the option buyer's favour or against the option seller.

Anyone who buys options is long vega and wants volatility to increase. It follows that anyone who sells options is short vega and hopes that volatility will decline.

Volatility. A measure of the price fluctuation of an asset. Volatility is measured in terms of standard deviations, and the norm is to express the volatility of an asset as a one standard deviation price change, in percent, over a one-year period. So if an asset had a volatility of 15%, that meant that the asset's price would be expected to fluctuate within a range 15% higher or lower than the forward price. Because it is one annualized standard deviation, this price change would be observed for two-thirds of the days in a year. The higher the volatility, the higher the expected price range and the more expensive the option (since the chances of the option becoming profitable are higher).

It is an important variable in the pricing of an option yet the only input not decided by other markets or dictated by the buyer. The strike price and life of the option are decided by the buyer or the standardized contracts on an exchange; the current price is set in the cash market while carrying costs are determined by the relevant yield curves. Volatility is the only input on which the seller of the option has to make an educated guess.

Volatility Smile and Skew. Volatility smile describes the situation where out-of-the-money options trade at a higher implied volatility than at-the-money options. The reason there is a smile is because option pricing models for most part assume a normal distribution of the returns of financial assets. But because this is not completely true, i.e. because option buyers and sellers realize that the possibility of more frequent extraordinary moves in the underlying asset is higher than that suggested by normal distribution, out-of-the-money options are more valuable than theoretical pricing models dictate. Option buyers are prepared to pay more for an out-of-the-money option, relative to an at-the-money option, because they realize that extreme moves can happen more frequently than normal distribution suggests.

But the volatility smile is not symmetrical which it would be if both out-of-the-money calls and puts traded at the same higher implied volatility. In fact, out-of-the-money puts trade at a higher implied volatility than out-of-the-money calls, giving rise to a volatility skew. This phenomenon is largely due to demand and supply.

Volatility Trading. Because volatility can be considered an asset class by itself, it can be traded like any other financial asset. The most common way of buying or selling volatility is to buy or sell an option, hedging out the price risk of the option so that the trader is left only with the volatility risk with the underlying.

Other methods of buying or selling volatility are to buy or sell combinations of options, the most usual being to buy or sell straddles and strangles.

Yield. The interest rate that will make the present value of the cashflows from an investment equal to the price (or cost) of the investment. Also called the internal rate of return.

Yield Curve. A curve or graph showing the relationship between the yields of fixed income instruments of a given type against their maturities. Such curves normally start from six months and stretch out to at least ten years.

Zero Cost Option. An option strategy which requires the selling of one option to completely offset the cost of buying another option (see collar).

Zero-Coupon Bonds. Bonds which pay no interest during their life but only one interest payment which is at maturity. The bonds are sold at deep discounts from par and the investor's entire return is realized at maturity.

Index